ECHOS PAST
Links To The Mayflower

Front Cover:

    The photo of the Mayflower is self-explanatory. The photo of what was left of the Myrtle and Chauncey Ingraham's homestead was taken in 1986. The illustrator placed the actual homestead site into the landscape just behind the house. By looking closely to the left of the grove of trees one can see the same homestead as pictured in the foreground.

    On page 124 is a photo of the original homestead, about 1918 painted by the author, Willard Ingraham.

Back Cover:

    This photo is a 60th wedding anniversary celebration (1953) for Myrtle and Chauncey Ingraham. All of their sons and daughters in the photo with them grew up in the homestead pictured on the front cover.

ECHOS PAST
LINKS TO THE MAYFLOWER

AUTHOR: WILLARD INGRAHAM

ILLUSTRATOR: LOUISE INGRAHAM

PUBLISHER:
BIZY ENTERPRIES, INC
MESA, ARIZONA

ECHOS PAST
LINKS TO THE MAYFLOWER

Published by:
Bizy Enterprises, Inc.
9115 East Baseline Rd.
C-102 PMB 141
Mesa, Arizona 85209
WWW.Mindseyevision.com

Copyright 2007
Published: November 2007
ISBN, first print edition 0-9722621-6-4

DEDICATIONS

I am dedicating ECHOS PAST, Links To The Mayflower to my grandparents, Chauncey and Myrtle Cowles Ingraham and Gunder and Laura Bah Johnson. Both of these grandparents built on homesteads in North Dakota during those early years of the 1900s.

I am also dedicating this book to my parents, Lyle and Gena Johnson Ingraham. They were North Dakota farmers that survived the great depression of 1929, the hardships of the draught and dust storms, and the grasshopper influx of those years that destroyed much of the vegetation. They persevered through all of those years raising a family. In the early 1940s, they moved with our family to the great state of Washington State. This move framed the life style of each of their children.

I give thanks beyond words to my wife, Louise for the many hours she dedicated to formatting my text to manuscript form, the hours and hours it took to insert photos and the illustrations that she designed and placed.

I also give gratitude and thanks to our daughter, Mary Ann Hicks for all of her great suggestions that she freely gave to me then set about publishing the works through Mary Ann and Joe Hick's corporation, Bizy Enterprises Inc.

I am grateful for the family input in my brothers, Ray and Norman and sister, Lorraine's chapters.

This book is a living text of the lives of all my family who I love very much.

By: Willard Ingraham

TABLE OF CONTENTS

ABOUT THE AUTHOR

(Willard Ingraham) As I grew up on a farm in the hills of North Dakota there were many times as a boy that I would find myself looking out over the prairie land and wondering what life had in store for me. As I progressed through grade school it became very apparent to me that one must learn many things in order to enjoy the beauty around us that God gives to us each day. We take for granted things like the sun to warm us and provide light that nurtures everything from the beautiful flowers, trees and fields containing various growths. To heighten this beauty God provided the music of the air with beautiful song birds, countless types of flowers, small animals, bugs and wonderful multicolor butterflies buzzing around.

My test was in naming the various flowers and other miracles around me. These were all wonders that God created and what was the purpose? It soon became apparent to me that there would be only one way to learn about all these marvelous things. My answer was apparent; the one way to learn was to get as many books as I could on different subjects and study them. Knowing would fill my mind and satisfy my curiosity.

I discovered a treasure of information at school where in the corner of our little one room schoolhouse there was a shelf of twenty books called, "The Encyclopedia Of Knowledge". I would hurriedly finish my written lessons in study periods and then lose myself in those encyclopedias; sometimes even while the teacher was teaching other grades in the same room I poured over those books. It did not bother me with the noise around me from other students to be able to concentrate because it was my time to learn about all the new things in life and the outside world that was a mystery to me.

As the years went by I continued to read every book that I could get my hands on. Just when I began to think I had learned about all the necessary things of life to get me by I would discover how little I really did know. I knew then that one must always study because more new things were happening each day to make the knowledge of yesterday obsolete. I realized that the knowledge of the present and future must also be taken into account in order to keep ones-self updated about all of things around us.

Then World War II came along; this gave me another view point about life. I was inducted into the Armored Infantry and completed my basic training in Fort Knox, Kentucky then continued my training in tent city in the Arizona desert. Here again I learned the importance of studying for along with basic army life there was much we had to learn about plane identification and the enemy we would be facing.

After our training was completed we were taken to England to wait for the unknown assignment we knew was coming. The big day, "D Day Landing" finally came then in two months we were thrust into France and in the combat Zone. We thrust through France, Belgium, Luxemburg and Germany to the finish of the war.

I served almost three years in the 526 Armored Infantry Battalion with two years on the front lines. This was a time that I realized that we do not walk alone in this world but must satisfy our spiritual part of our body as well as our physical being. I felt the protective hand of our Lord, Jesus Christ over me many times. I carried my bible in my breast pocket at all times. When I tried to study the bible it was still very confusing to me. My spirit told me that the book of God was very real and important to me but the light of knowledge did not come through to me at that time.

After the war, I returned home and married my lovely wife, Louise. We raised two daughters in the church; thinking we were doing our duty because now again came important things to do in education. Going to college was a must to make a good living for my family. The importance of continued study, the importance of scheduled study periods and study habits all became a must in order to wade through the necessary material each day to keep up with the technical world I had entered in my chosen job vocation.

I worked for the Benton PUD for nineteen years and the Cowlitz PUD at Longview, Wa. almost twelve years advancing to head the Meter Department. Here I was responsible for installations and testing of meters, installing telemetering, trend metering, reclosure and all automatic control systems in the sub stations that furnished power to the various areas.

All was going well with me for I studied hard and continually to maintain the expertise that was required to keep up with this fast changing field of work. Although I had all this and we did attend church there was still something missing. It was in 1972 I had a personal experience with our Lord, Jesus Christ. I asked the Lord to show me if there was more to life than just the daily routine.

Believe me I learned very quickly that one does not ask the Lord for something lightly. My life began to change and he gave me the most exhilarating peace of heart that any one could experience. For several weeks, I knew I had experienced a piece of heaven.

The Holy Spirit within me began to open up scriptures that before had no meaning and now became an important faction of my life. It was then that I could not put the bible down. I just had to find out what this great book had to say; as now it had seemed the scriptures were speaking personally to me. I studied the bible at every spare moment I could find.

I had always experienced very good health all my life but the Lord was soon to show me that we should not take our health for granted but enjoy it as a blessing of God. I came home from work one Friday night with a small headache thinking it was the flu. Saturday and Sunday, I still experienced a headache that aspirin would not cure. Monday morning my wife was able to get an appointment with the doctor for 3:00 PM that day. I had slept very little all week end so at this point I almost did not care after fighting this blazing headache that would not go away. My neck had swollen up, I had lost my voice and I was so weak I could hardly walk across the room.

The doctor diagnosed my problem as acute thyroiditus. He gave me medicine to control the pain but the lump on the left side of my neck remained. It was about the size of a golf ball. The doctor told me he must operate to remove it.

My wife and I had arranged a tour to the Holy Land so I asked the doctor if it would be all right to go on the trip. Finally, he said OK but I would then have to have the operation as soon as I returned.

We went on the three-week tour and the first night into Jerusalem, I could not find my pills so of coarse I did not take them. The next day we visited the place where Jesus ascended into heaven on Mt Olives and I had another personal experience with the Lord. It was then that I knew my problem as gone and healing had taken place. From then on, I never took another pill and when I got home, visited the doctor, and told him I was healed he was in disbelief. He examined me and just shook his head saying, "you had it when you left but you now are as healthy as can be."

I have not been sick since that problem in 1976. The Lord allowed me to retire from my career job of thirty years and take on new priorities. With this the Lord soon changed all those priorities around to make a different life style; only now it always included the Lord and he opened new and wonderful doors to me.

The Lord had opened the door to travel for me and my wife. We took groups of travelers around the world. Our specialty was the Mid East. Included in our many tours we conducted seven successful tours through the Holy Lands with the Lord having control all the way.

Again, it became very important to me to continue studying. I set up my study habit of reading the bible first thing in the mornings. It was in 1979 and 1980 that I studied two years to become a Bethel Bible teacher. During 1981 and 1982, I taught the Bethel Bible series of the new and Old

Testament at the Kennewick Methodist Church covering the stories of the bible. In 1983, I studied the Kerygma which is the prophecies of the bible. In 1984 and 1985 I taught Kerygma of the bible at Kennewick Methodist Church.

I had found that all through our lives we must never stop our learning process through study. We must always include our spiritual growth along with our physical growth I WILL CONCLUDE WITH St. Paul's quote to the Romans in Romans, Chapter 3: 21-26. "But now the righteousness of God apart from the law is revealed, being witnessed by the law and the prophets. Even the righteousness of God that is through faith in Jesus Christ comes to all and on all who believe; for there is no difference. For all have sinned and fall short of the glory of God; being justified freely by his grace through the redemption that is in Christ Jesus whom God set forth to be a propitiation by his blood through faith to demonstrate his righteousness; because in his forbearance God had passed over the sins that were previously committed to demonstrate at the present time his righteousness that he might be just and the justifier of the one who has faith in Jesus.

Below: Willard Ingraham, author
        Louise Ingraham, illustrator

INTRODUCTION

Many years ago when I (Willard Ingraham) was a young boy growing up in North Dakota my parents Lyle and Gena took us all to visit our grandparents Chauncey and Myrtle Ingraham. They lived on their homestead farm North of Woodworth, North Dakota.

My brothers Ray, Norman and my sister Lorraine and I had a lot of interesting things to investigate there. There was a big pond that was fed by a spring that kept clean clear water running the year around. East of the pond was the cave that grandpa Chauncey had dug and they had lived in when they first started their homestead. The cave when I saw it was just a sunken spot in the side of a small hill. It was fun running up and down the caved in walls of what had been once the cave that they lived in.

When we went to the house Grandma would talk to us about our relatives that came from across the ocean from England on a ship called the Mayflower back in the year 1620. There were 102 passengers aboard this ship and they included John Alden and Priscilla Mullens who later married.

Priscilla's parents were William and Alice Mullins; the Alden families extended to the Eddy families then down to the Ingraham families. Also on this ship was Captain Myles Standish who had a family that extended down through the Sampson families then on to the Ingrahams.

Grandma said all of these families were ancestors of ours. I have documented records of this. To hear Grandma tell about these families it sounded mystical and interesting.

Then Grandpa would tell everyone about the hardships they had incurred to get this comfortable home they now lived in. About that time Grandma would say it was now time to eat. Looking over the table with all the wonderful smells from all of that food on that table and observing all the beautiful dishes with knifes, forks and spoons placed ever so carefully around the table is a memory I still have.

After lunch and the dishes were all washed and put away everyone gathered in the living room. If we were lucky we got Grandma to play that fascinating big pump organ with Grandpa and Dad joining her playing good old time foot stomping fiddle music. After that the day was gone and we had to go home.

Many years later when I was studying genealogy Grandma sent me the documents about the Alden and the Standish families. Receiving these I really became interested in pursuing family history to fill in the blanks with information.

A person must be like a detective to work on genealogy because so many things can send you down the wrong trail; like finding a name like John in every generation and find that you are trailing the wrong John.

I worked five years to document our ancestors to the Mayflower and I am now a member of the Mayflower Society so anyone that can cut their relationship into mine will find the same relationship to our ancestors from the Mayflower.

Many of the stories I have written in this book would be lost if I had not written about them. Everything in the stories that I know of these times were either passed on from other persons now gone or too old to remember these events.

I have written this book to show the reader the transition in genealogy from family to family by identifying the generations descending from the Mayflower to the present generation in 2007.

Through research and documentation, the information in this book was gathered and written as factual although I recognize that occasionally records can be misleading. I have endeavored to write truthfully and with clarity but take no responsibility for any errors that may appear except any errors in editing.

Note: my material is from public records, documents allowable for printing, history and information gathered from personal visits to sites, my own records and photos I took.

CHAPTER I
MAYFLOWER SAILS TO NEW WORLD IN 1620

I will take you on a journey through this book that will show a direct relationship to the Ingrahams of the 21st century from five people who sailed on the Mayflower as part of the original 102 passengers. These ancestors sailed to America to raise their families in freedom of religion, speech and a new way of life regardless of all the hardships and unknowns ahead of them.

This group was the original group who settled at Plymouth, Massachusetts and became known as pilgrims of the Plymouth colony in 1620. The five people were William Mullins, his wife Alice and daughter Priscilla and John Alden and Captain Myles Standish. Now follow me as I take you step by step and show you how all of this happened through all the generations to the Ingrahams.

In the days of the reformation in England, 1550 – 1607 under King Henry VIII there was much strife, hunger and hardships because of the dictatorial ruling of the king. His proclamation against freedom of religion caused many hardships and dissention among the general population of England.

With the new world in America opening up and encouraged by the King many people were willing to uproot their present living to take a chance on a new frontier in America to raise their families and look forward to the freedom of worshipping their God in the way of their own beliefs. The king of England wishing to completely control the church took over the organization of the Roman Catholic Church by appointing the archbishop and maintaining it as the established church of England. Under this government no other church was permitted, no minister other than Episcopal could perform a marriage ceremony. During the sixteenth century and the early seventeenth century we find the established church of England ruling with an iron hand refusing to permit any

1

difference of opinion. This brought about many protests and around the year 1600 there were many demands arising for reform.

This brought about two schools of thought. The Separatists, who demanded complete separation from the Church of England. This group developed the Congregational Church. This later became the church of the Pilgrims that was brought to America and with a settlement at Plymouth Rock, Massachusetts. The other group, the Puritans, wanted to reform the church from within and later immigrated to America to form the Massachusetts Bay Colony that settled in Salem, Massachusetts. This group became the group that was involved in the witchcraft group in Salem, Massachusetts.

Less than half of the Mayflower passengers were separatists. All were welcomed to join the company to sail to America on the Mayflower to start a new way of life for their self's. All were welcomed regardless of religious believes.

Pastor John Robinson was the spiritual leader as well as the Pilgrim leader while in England and Holland. He had a strong spiritual and breath of vision that was hard to parallel. Along with other pilgrims he was connected with the great Leyden University of Holland. He was first known as a teacher then as a lecturer and finally as one of the most famous of that group. He laid down the principle that the human conscience is of too subtle a nature to be circumscribed. He taught the only measure of a man's religion is his direct relation to God. He coined the word "Independent" and governed this little group on the basis of equal rights and equal duties, all for the common good. His people were intensely devoted to him.

He personally guided them during their lives in England and Holland and prompted there going to America. He sent them on their way with a letter containing a plan for setting up a new government. This letter is too long to render here but every American should be familiar with it. The Mayflower compact, the first American state paper, was the outcome although he never set foot upon American soil. His mind first conceived and expressed the principles of Americanism and saw to it that it was put into effect.

There were seventy Pilgrims selected to go on the Mayflower to America because of their strong health and the ones who would most likely survive the hard conditions of life that it would take to start a new life in a new land. The largest part of the group stayed back with Pastor John Robinson.

Photo below: Captain Myles Standish served in the British Army in the Netherlands at the time the Pilgrims were at Leiden in the Netherlands. It was at this time that the Captain got acquainted with this group of people. He did not join the group but apparently agreed with their philosophy of life because when the Mayflower sailed out of South Hampton, England to America in 1620 we find Captain Myles Standish on that ship.

The Pilgrims lived at Leiden, a city located a short distance south of Amsterdam, Netherlands. The ship Speedwell with Captain Reynolds at its helm picked the Pilgrim group up at Leiden with the destination to Southampton, England where he then joined Captain

3

Christopher Jones of the Mayflower. They loaded their ships and both ships were to sail to America together.

Below are the ports the two ships sailed from. When the two ships got underway out of the Port Southampton they sailed a good distance when the ship Speedwell sprung a leak so both ships returned to Portsmouth, England for repairs.

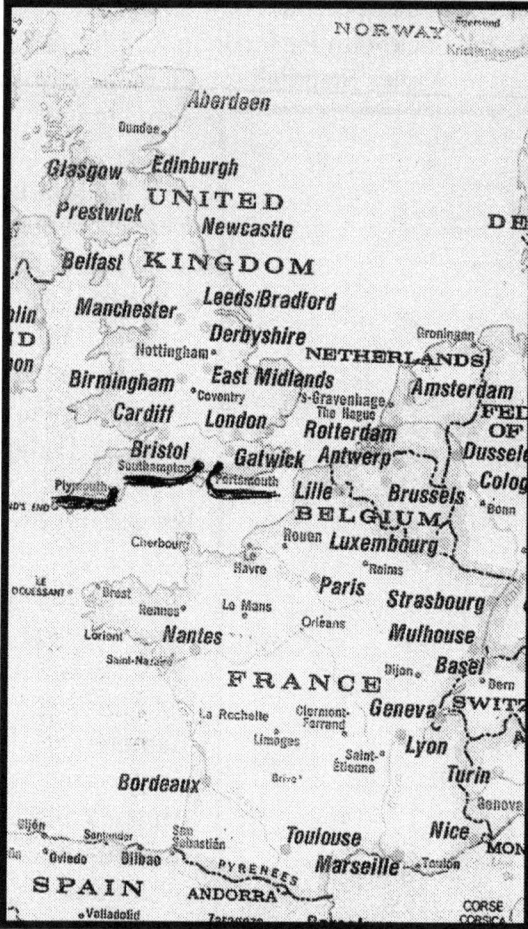

Having spent the previous few days during the repair time in town eating and drinking with friends and relatives some relatives were left behind in England. William Bradford left a son. Stephen Hopkins of London brought the largest family, a wife and four children including one later born at sea named Oceanus.

4

MAYFLOWER SAILS TO NEW WORLD IN 1620

Below is a photo of the two ships: Mayflower and in

back is the Speedwell. Back on their way again, the Speedwell had problems and the two ships returned to Plymouth, England for repairs. After the repairs, the ships sailed off on September 6, 1620 from Plymouth, England but did not sail very far. The Speedwell developed problems again. This time the passengers on the Speedwell that wanted to go to the new land of America were transferred to the Mayflower while on the high seas and the Speedwell returned to England sailing alone. The Mayflower with its overload of 102 passengers continued on to America on their own as a lone ship.

Everyone mourned a servant William Butten who died on board during the voyage. Another person, a profane sailor infamous for his angry threats to throw seasick passengers over board to the sorrow of no one he suddenly took sick and died. A third death almost happened when John Howaland was thrown over board in a fierce mid-Atlantic storm but the strong youth grabbed onto the ship and was fished out with a boat hook.

It was a long and stormy voyage. Captain Christopher Jones must have been an excellent Master to having brought them through this voyage. How happy they must have been when the cry "Land Ho" was shouted and the ship dropped anchor at the end of Cape Cod.

Below is Mayflower at sea. The passengers of the Mayflower after six weeks sailing on the rough waters of the Atlantic Ocean were sick, weary and some of them died coming over. Those that survived rejoiced for finally finding a suitable site for their settlement. Land had not come too soon as most of the remaining passengers were sick or dying of poor nutrition. It was a burden on the well to care for the sick and to go ashore to gather wood and food and still fight the cold and starving conditions after this long grueling trip.

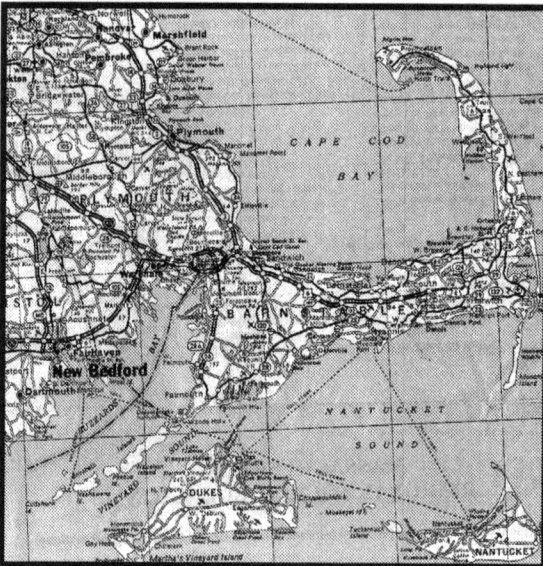

At left is Cape Cod and the landing area. It was November 11, 1620 when the Mayflower first reached the harbor.

Below is the Mayflower and the small boat (shallop) that they

brought with them stored in prefabricated sections on the Mayflower's lower deck. The shallop was to be for rowing or sailed along the coast and up rivers. Soon after the ship anchored sixteen men rowed off in the shallop to explore the land and to see if it was right for them to build their settlement. Upon looking at the surrounding area the site was soon deemed a likely spot as they had found a tall hill suitable to erect a fort, a brook with clear fresh drinking water for them by clearing an area of trees. This left a perfect site for building their settlement of buildings for new homes.

The site was named New Plymouth. The site for homes was far from ideal, the harbor was uncomfortably shallow and soil was fairly depleted from early growths of corn by the Indians. The colonists were also nervous that the Indians who had first cleared the land and cultivated corn might return and want their land back.

Soon after anchoring the Mayflower the news started to circulate around the ship about the death of William Bradford's wife, Dorothy, having fallen overboard and drowned while the Shallop party was on its mission. One of the men on that Shallop was William Bradford.

The mood on the ship was also solemn because of the very cold weather, which had hampered attempts to hunt and fish for food and vegetation to eat and store. The Pilgrims had hoped to store whatever they found beyond the immediate need to eat for survival during the winter. The remaining passengers began hauling their tools and furniture and other belongings by boat to the shore which was a mile and half away. They began to construct a makeshift shelter for storage. It was arduous work and it was forbidden on the Sabbath to work so they all worked to do as much as they could on each day of the week.

The week went like this; on Monday the women began the task of collecting and washing all of the clothes. The children and the dogs were exercising their legs on the sand and some of the men were mapping out building lots. Lots measuring eighty feet by forty nine feet was staked out while still others were mulling over what form of government should be put in place in the colony.

Some men had threatened mutiny after learning that the ship was not headed anywhere near Virginia for which the company had chartered the Mayflower. Some men asked to turn back and others vowed they would not follow the government that was to be set up on shore. The grumblers though turned cheerful after the signing of a compact that bound the passengers into a civic body called the Mayflower Compact

It was after the Mayflower had anchored that Captain Miles Standish led a team of men, armed with swords and muskets along the seashore. They encountered some Indians who fled from them. The men found an Indian grave that they

covered with soil and after they stumbled onto a rich cache of
Indian corn. The Pilgrims filled their pockets and vowed to
repay the Indians.

The first male English child born on American soil
came when Susanah White gave birth to a son aboard the
anchored Mayflower. She named her son Peregrine.

Complete Genealogical List of "Mayflower" Passengers

Prepared and reprinted through the courtesy of
George Ernest Bowman, editor of "The Mayflower Descendant"

The 50 passengers from whom descent can be proved:

John Alden	Dr. Samuel Fuller
Isaac Allerton	Stephen Hopkins
wife Mary	2d wife, Elizabeth
daughter Mary	son Gyles (by 1st wife)
daughter Remember	daughter Constance (by 1st
John Billington	wife)
wife Eleanor	John Howland
son Francis	Richard More
William Bradford	William Mullins
William Brewster	wife Alice
wife Mary	daughter Priscilla
son Love	Degory Priest
Peter Brown	Thomas Rogers
James Chilton	son Joseph
wife ————	Henry Samson
daughter Mary	George Soule
Francis Cooke	Myles Standish
son John	John Tilley, and wife ————
Edward Doty	daughter Elizabeth
Francis Eaton	Richard Warren
wife Sarah	William White
son Samuel	wife Susanna
Edward Fuller	son Resolved
wife ————	son Peregrine
son Samuel	Edward Winslow

The 54 passengers from whom we cannot prove descent:

Bartholomew Allerton	Edmund Margeson
John Allerton	Christopher Martin
John Billington	wife ————
Dorothy Bradford	Desire Minter
(1st wife of William)	Ellen More
Wrestling Brewster	Jasper More
Richard Britteridge	(a boy) More
William Butten	Joseph Mullins
Robert Carter	Solomon Prower
John Carver	John Rigdale
Katherine Carver	wife Alice
(wife of John)	Rose Standish
Maid servant of the Carvers	(1st wife of Myles)
Richard Clarke	Elias Story
Humility Cooper	Edward Thomson
John Crakston	Edward Tilley
son John	wife Ann
———— Ely	Thomas Tinker
Thomas English	wife ————
Moses Fletcher	son ————
Richard Gardiner	William Trevore
John Goodman	John Turner
William Holbeck	son ————
John Hooke	son ————
Damaris Hopkins	Roger Wilder
Oceanus Hopkins	Thomas Williams
John Langmore	Elizabeth Winslow
William Latham	(1st wife of Edward)
Edward Leister	Gilbert Winslow

CHAPTER II
CAPTAIN MYLES STANDISH, THE PROTECTOR

On April 15, 1621 the Pilgrims all gathered to watch the Mayflower ship that had brought them to America now sail away. As the group assembled on the hill there came a puff of smoke from the side of the ship. The roar from the sea had hardly ceased when the report of the cannon from the platform on the hill in the clearing returned its salvo. These were the signal guns of departure, the union Jack on the ship was run up and down three times while the shrill note of the boatswain's whistle came feebly ashore. The sails of the ship then fluttered down from the yards filling the masts with their whiteness as the ship sailed out of sight.

The colonists sank reverently to their knees while Elder Brewster prayed for the safety of the departing ship. He also asked that God would not forget them here in the wilderness. This was the day of renunciation and reconfirmation to a noble purpose. Having lost so many of them and weakened by the terrible suffering that first winter the Pilgrims stood proud as men and women of moral courage in their unanimous choice to remain steadfast and complete the work of establishing civil and religious liberty in a new land. This handful of men, women and children faced famine, the wilderness, pestilence and Indian foes as they turned to grapple with the unknown.

The first year the Plymouth colony suffered such drastic hardships that by the end of the first year they had lost half of their people from sickness and from living on meager rations as well as suffering from the cold winter and living in crowded quarters the first winter in the hull of the ship in life defying conditions. It was a miracle alone that any of them had survived.

In the fall after the first harvest William Bradford declared a day of Thanksgiving and invited their Indian friends to join them. They had made treaties with the Indians that were never broken and it enabled them to all live in peace and help each other.

The background for the first thanksgiving is found in Bradford's history. In that fall of 1621, the first fall in the new world, they gathered in the small harvest they had and fixed up their houses and dwellings against the winter that was coming. All had now recovered in health and strength and there was adequate food for all.

Some Pilgrims were thus employed in affairs abroad, and others were experienced in fishing about for cod, bass and other fish of which they took extra to store. Every family had their portion. All summer there was no want and now they had began storing food as the winter approached. This place had not provided when they had first come but later as winter passed and warmer degrees the land provided. Besides water fowl there was a great store of wild turkeys of which they took many and venison etc. Besides they also had about a peck of meal a week to a person and now since harvest they had Indian corn in that pro portion. And it was thus they found the lord to be with them in all their ways and to bless their out-goings and in-comings for which they let his holy name have the praise forever and to all posterity.

The original account of the first Thanksgiving is in a letter dated Dec. 21, 1621 to George Morton in England. It was printed in "Mourt's Relation," London 1622. Here is the story: *"We set last spring some twenty acres of Indian corn and sowed some six acres of barley and peas according in the manner of the Indians. We manured our ground with herrings which we have in great abundance and take it with great ease at our doors. Our corn did prove well and God be praised, we had a good increase of Indian corn. Our barley did indifferent good but our peas not worth the gathering. We feared they were too late sown. They came up very well and blossomed but the sun parched them in blossom. Our harvest being gotten in our governor set four men on fowling that so we might after a special manner rejoice together after we had gathered in the fruits of our labors. They four in one day killed as many fowl as with a little help besides served the company for almost a week at which time amongst other recreations we exercised our arms. Many of the Indians coming amongst us and amongst the rest their great king, Massasoit, with some ninety men whom for three days we entertained and feasted. They went out and killed five deer which they brought into the plantation and bestowed on our governor and upon the captain and others. Although it be not always so plentiful as it was this time with us yet by the goodness of God we are so far from want that we often wish you partakers of our plenty. We found the Indians very faithful in their covenant of peace with us' very loving and ready to pleasure us. Some of us have been fifty miles into the country by land with them. There is now great peace amongst the Indians, themselves, which was not formerly. Neither would have been but for us and we for our parts walk as peaceably and safely in the woods here as in the highways of England. I never in my life remember a more seasonable year than we have here enjoyed. If we have but one kine, horses and sheep, I make no question but men might live as contented here as in any part of the world. The country wanteth only industrious men to employ for it would grieve your hearts to see so many miles together by rivers uninhabited and withal to consider those parts of the world wherein you live to be even greatly burdened with abundance of people. You might on our behalf give God thanks who hath dealt so favorably with us."*

In spite of their numbers having been cut in half by sickness and death they found reasons for thankfulness. They had gained their foothold on the edge of an inhospitable continent but at what price! They were well recovered in health and strength. They were making the best of a hard life in the wilderness. They had proved that they could sustain themselves in the new free land. They were assured of the success of their purpose of establishing freedom. They had made firm friends with the Indians who had been so kind to them. They lifted their thanks to the almighty for his gifts and abundant food, courage and hope.

Just as told in the letter back to England it was for three days that the Pilgrims and their Indian guests gorged themselves on venison, roast duck, goose and turkey as well as clams and other shell fish, succulent eels, corn bread, hasting pudding, leeks and water cress and other sallet herbs with wild plum and dried berries as dessert. All was washed down with wine made of the wild grape.

If the Pilgrims had not found the native corn to eat and to use for seed for the next year the colony probably would not have survived the second year. The Indians also introduced to the Pilgrims something new called pop-corn and how it was used as food. The gathering of the Pilgrims and the Indians was more like a big family reunion with a barbecued picnic. The feasting involved the preparation of unusually large quantities of food.

Of the Pilgrims only four of their married women had survived the great sickness and only five of the teen age girls, three of these being the sole survivors of their respective families. They must have worked very hard trying to fill a hundred and forty demanding hungry people for three days. These women have never been given enough credit for the task that was asked of them to do in such trying times.

For entertainment they showed their skills and strength running, jumping, wrestling etc. The Indians were amazed to see the white mans games that were much like their own. The Indians performed their dances and struck up their singing. Captain Myles Standish put his little army of fourteen men through their military review. They followed with feats of marksmanship with muskets performing against bows and arrows in the spirit of good sportsmanship. The Indians left for their homes with a warm feeling for their white friends.

The successful festival was over when only a few days after this the ship Fortune came into the harbor. It was the first ship to arrive after the Mayflower had landed. The Fortune brought them thirty-five colonists, only one woman. Only five of the colonists were of their own group. The others were mostly adventurers and paupers thrown upon the charity of the Pilgrims.

According to Bradford's records, **"they came empty handed and poorly clothed and equipped for the approaching winter. They were lusty young men, many of them wild enough who little considered whether or about what they wanted. But there was not so much as biscuit or cake or any other victuals for them, neither had they any bedding but some surry things they had in their cabin. Not pot nor pan to dress any meat in and not over many clothes. The plantation was glad of this addition of strength but could have wished that many of them had been of better condition and all of them better furnished with provisions. It was excessive imprudence if not downright crueltry in those who sent this ship thus miserably to furnish her with provisions and some of the promised supplies to the colony but instead thirty-five more mouths to feed; even leaving the ship itself to be victualed from the scant stores of the colony for the return voyage. It is a wonder that the colony was not ruined by this ship and grim starvation now threatened their annihilation."**

Bradford writes, **"they dispose of these late comers into the several families as best they could, took an exact account of all provisions in store and proportioned the same to the number of persons and found it would not hold out above six months at half allowance and hardly that and they could not well give less this winter time till fish came in again. So they were presently put to half allowance one as well as another which began to be hard but they born it patiently under hope of supply.**

After a month the Fortune returned to England. We are forced to spare her some of our provisions to carry

back home which threatened a famine among us unless we have timely supply"

This timely supply never came and they could only tighten their belts. From the first they had been repeatedly promised provisions from England but the much needed and hoped for relief never came. Instead the Pilgrims many times supplied unexpected arrivals and distressed mariners and at times in large numbers from their slender store.

The new arrivals that came busied themselves by making such additions to the seven existing houses where they were quartered as the increased numbers required. The houses were very small; barely large enough for the families who despite cold and hunger and sickness had built them.

The Pilgrims believed that the chief purpose in this life was the preparation for the eternal life to come and was guided only by enlightened conscience. For this there must be freedom from unnecessary restraint that was tyranny and freedom of the soul of thought a larger measure of freedom of life. These have been the sources of our national fortunes. Today we behold all around us the vast achievements of free men and women working together from choice in industry, rectitude, happiness and leadership.

After the Pilgrims had blazed a trail in a decade the larger groups settled in Boston. They found the Pilgrim colony well organized and governed according to democratic principles and so through the later colonies the ideals of the Pilgrims have prevailed through out our country.

The story of the Pilgrims belongs to the heroic age of America. Of all the nations of the world no other nation can boast of such an exalted origin. No other nation can adorn its earliest annuals with such a story as true as it is beautiful; as authentic as it is sublime. Why did they come? Hear their own words ring down the ages, **"For the glory of God and advancement of the Christian faith and honor of our king and country."**

CAPTIAN MYLES STANDISH, THE PROTECTOR

Their history reads like a work of the imagination rather than a recital of events in the prosaic world. There is a certain poetic quality about it that makes its simple annals very fascinating. The sublime faith of the people, their patience under adversity, their charity toward those who differed with them and their ready forgiveness of those who wronged or injured them had been purified by the fires of persecution. Their gentleness had made them great. The beauty and the poetry of New England have come in great part from those who landed on Plymouth Rock. They have taught the world a larger tolerance, gentler manners and purer law.

We have learned from them the grand possibilities that wait for men of faith unto the lord. In the varied tapestry that pictures our national life the richest spots are those where gleam the golden threads of conscience, courage and faith set in the web by that little land. There is no loftier statelier presence in human history than the Pilgrims of Plymouth. Of all the colonies the Pilgrims established the only system in which the people actually governed themselves. It gave new impulse and direction with hope to the struggling masses of humanity and made it evident that men determined to be free can somehow find a way.

The Pilgrims were a diverse people. They consisted of members representing all the different classes of English life outside the circle of noble families bound together by a common religious faith regardless of differences of education, culture or social standing. Their situation forced upon them a disregard of social distinction from which came the soundest and most characteristic ideals of our nation today. Their condition was equal, they stood together in their common manhood undistinguished save only by these differences which intellect, character, culture of their higher nature and promotion of their supreme welfare. As the germ and nucleus of an independent political state this little ban included as many elements and guarantees of strength of safety and of growth as lay within the whole resources of human nature. Their belief was that church and state were made for man and not man for them. The culture and development of the individual for the immortal life were the superior and controlling objects raising man to the very threshold of heaven. The message that the Pilgrims bring to humanity is greater than any since the time of the apostles. The great obligation is on us, now to act with the same devotion to principle, the same fidelity to duty so may our nation stand forever as the mighty guardian of human liberty of God like justice of Christ like brotherhood. The conceptions and ideals that dominated the lives of the Pilgrims have profoundly influenced the lives of the best part of ten to fourteen subsequent generations in this hemisphere. They still exhibit today, under social and bounding and apparently inexhaustible vitality. They held the fruitful conception of unlimited progress as the law of human institutions both civil and religious. This means the progressive discovery and application of truth to the conduct of human life.

This doctrine to follow was instilled in them by their leader in Holland, Pastor John Robinson. The recent advance of science has made it familiar to all thinking people but for the Pilgrims in their day to accept it and preach it discloses and extraordinary and indistinguishable love of freedom. The fruits and issues of their pioneering are the most prodigious in all history. It was the duty of the strong to help the weak. They had no theory of social structure that was not perfectly consistent with the facts concerning the extreme diversity of human capacities and powers. They established a community and a government solidly founded on love of freedom and belief in progress on civil liberty and religious toleration on industrial cooperation on individual honesty, evenhanded justice and real equality before the laws on peace and good will, supported by protected force.

With long suffering, devotion and sober resolution they illustrated for the first time in history the practices of a genuine democracy. Therefore they are to be forever remembered with love and honor by the vast republic that has inherited their ideals.

Captain Myles Standish is the first generation descendant from the Mayflower that will show in genealogy recorders the following families of the Standish and Sampsons that will lead to the Ingraham families that are a direct relationship to Captain Myles Standish who came to America on the ship, Mayflower in 1620 A.D.

Information about Myles Standish is as follows:

Born about 1584 at Ellenbane by Sulby, Isle Of Man. At left is a map that shows the Isle of Man in the Irish Sea. Myles married Rose who died in 1621. He then married Barbara in about 1623 and she died on October 3, 1656 at Duxbury, Mass.

The parents of Myles Standish were John Standish and Catharina Lace Standish. Myles was in the military service for England and sent to the Netherlands where he became acquainted with some of the pilgrims who were living there.

He was not one of them as far as their religious convictions were concerned but was sympathetic to their cause. He never joined their church in Leiden, Holland or in New England.

He was much respected because of his military background and became very important to the Pilgrims in relation to their problems with the Indians in the New World. He learned to speak the Indian language that was very helpful in negotiations.

Upon landing in Plymouth, Myles Standish was given twice the amount of land that others were given, indicating that he was considered a very important man in their settlement. He organized the colony militarily and commanded the fort that they built for their protection.

Myles Standish also had a very kind nature. He was one of the few people that were not ill the first difficult winter of 1620 – 1621 and it is recorded that he took care of many of the sick.

Pilgrim Hall that is still located in Plymouth contains the sword of Myles Standish as well as his bible and his razor. There is also a large monument to his memory at Duxbury, Mass.

Looking back at Myles and Barbara's life we know they moved their family from Plymouth across the bay to Duxbury in 1630. Their home site there is still preserved as well as the burial place of Myles, his daughter and daughter-in-law.

There is an interesting story regarding Myles Standish surrounding the legacy to which he felt he was entitled to an inheritance in England. There is a Pilgrims document center located in Leiden that Myles Standish had been reported wounded at a battle at Ostend, Holland and died at St. Catherines Hospital, Leiden on the list of November, 1601. Therefore if the executors of his grandfather's estate had tried to locate him they may have encountered that report.

After Captain Myles Standish was wounded and served another year in the army he heard of his fathers death. He then returned back to the Isle of Man to find his younger brother William had accepted the inheritance of Standish properties thinking that Captain Myles Standish had died of wounds in the army. In finding out about this; it made the captain very angry and he left the Isle of Man to take up the problem later because at this time he was also wanting to go to the new land called America and could settle this later.

It seems that Captain Myles Standish was always of the opinion that he was entitled to a legacy from his great grandfather and in his own will of 1655 he gave lands for which he thought he was the rightful heir to his son, Alexander. He mentioned such land in several areas of England as well as the Isle of Man. There were Standish descendants residing in all of these areas.

Genealogists interested in English backgrounds have methodically dug up land records from the early 1500s trying to fasten together the various families but unfortunately each family contained many Williams, Johns and Thomas so it is a tedious job. I shall leave that to the experts and accept the theory that Captain Myles Standish was entitled to an inheritance that he never received.

At any rate Captain Myles Standish's father, John, did have substantial land holdings on the Isle Of Man. Ordinarily it would have been left to the oldest son. That son John died young. The next son was Myles and the younger son called William. It seems that William inherited all of the land.

The land was still in the name of the grandfather in 1607 at which time both he and his son John who was Myles father were dead so the land at that time should have passed to Captain Myles Standish. However he was serving in the army at that time and was probably located in the Netherlands. At any rate the younger brother William took over the grandfather's lands and by the time Captain Myles Standish died the land had been in William's possession for many years. Twenty-one years was the maximum length of time that a person had to claim an inheritance without paying for it.

Perhaps Myles did not have enough money to buy the property known as Ellenbane when he was in England and left the land in his own will to his son Alexander to figure it all out.

Myles Standish was born on the Isle Of Man in 1584 and died at Duxbury, Mass. on Oct. 3, 1656.

Myles Standish's wife rose had died on the Mayflower the first winter on Jan. 29, 1621. Myles married Barbara in 1623 and she died at Duxbury, Mass. after Oct. 6, 1659. Barbara had come over in 1623 on the ship Anne.

As to the division of the new land in 1623, Captain Myles Standish received 2 acres and Mrs. Standish received one acre. This proves he had married Barbara by this time. In the 1627 division of cattle Captain Standish is listed with wife Barbara and children Charles, Alexander and John.

Myles Standish is listed as Captain Standish in the 1643 list of Duxbury men 16-60 able to bear arms. This implies he was born after Aug. 1583. His son Alexander is also in the same list. The will of Captain Myles Standish Sr. of Duxburrow dated March 7, 1655-56 proved May 4, 1657 mentions daughter Lora Standish as deceased and Mary Standish, my daughterinlaw deceased. Son Josias Standish upon his marriage had sons Alexander, Myles, Josias and Charles Standish and Marcye Robinson as well as servant John Irish Jr. The inventory of Elizabeth Hopkins dated Oct. 6, 1659 mentions a small matter in Mrs. Standishes hand. This is the last known reference to Barbara.

The following lists the records of the generation linked to Myles Standish:

Myles Standish family: the Isle of Man

Thurston De Standish Great Great Grandfather
Ralph Standish Great Grandfather
Hugh Standish Grandfather
John Standish and Catharina Lace were parents of:
John Standish
Myles Standish born about 1584 D Oct. 3, 1656

CAPTIAN MYLES STANDISH, THE PROTECTOR

William Standish

1st Generation

Capt. Myles Standish M. Barbara Standish 1623
Parents of:
Charles Standish b 1624
Alexander Standish B 1626- Plymouth, Mass.
John Standish Jr. B. 1627 Plymouth, Mass.
Lora Standish B. 1627 Plymouth, Mass
Miles Standish B. 1629 Plymouth, Mass
Josiah Standish B. 1633 Plymouth, Mass.
Charles Standish B. 1634, Plymouth, Mass.

**NOTE: ALL BOLDED NAMES follow the
genealogy link from Myles Standish down to my family link
with the Ingrahams. Follow the bolded text beginning on
this page and the following pages in this chapter.**
Barbara Standish arrived on the ship Anne in 1623
from England and she was the mother of all Myles children.

2nd Generation

Alexander Standish B. 1626, Plymouth, Mass; d July
6, 1702 at Duxbury, Mass.
His parents, Captain Myles and Barbara Standish
He married Sarah Alden; B about 1630; D before June
13, 1688. Sarah Alden was the daughter of Pilgrims John and
Priscilla Mullins Alden.
Alexander M 1688 Disire Holmes; they had two sons
and one daughter.
Children of **Alexander and Sarah Alden**
Lora Standish M. Abraham Sampson
Lydia Standish M. Isaac Sampson

Elizabeth Standish M. Samuel Delano
Mercey Standish M. 1684 Caleb Sampson
Myles Standish M. 1702 Experience ShermanSarah B
1666 M. 1694 Benjamin Soule
    Ebenezer B 1672 M 1697 Hannah Sturtevant
    David Standish died before Feb. 14, 1689

The following children of Alexander Standish and
Desire Holmes:
    Desire B. May 5, 1689 M 1715 Nathan Weston
    Thomas B. Jan 29, 1690 M. 1717 Mary Carver
    Ichabod B. June 10, 1693 M. 1719 Phebe Ring

Alexander gave power of attorney to Robert Orchard in
1687 to claim his right to this property per insert. There was a
great deal of intermarriage of cousins in those days and it is
suspected that the first wife of Myles Standish who came on
the Mayflower with Myles may have been a cousin whose
name was also Standish. Barbara, Myles second wife may also
have been a cousin.
    The name Standish in parts of England is very early and
as many other names of that period began with "DE" and was
called Destandish there were also many varied spellings of the
name that also makes that early research very difficult.
    Myles Standish's father, John, died about 1602 and his
grandfather also named John died about 1603. Both were
clerks in the parish of Kirk Andreas appointed by the king.

3rd Generation

Lydia Standish B. April 30, 1734, Duxbury, Mass.
Her parents Alexander Standish and Sarah Alden
She married Oct. 26, 1686 to Isaac Sampson who was b
1661 and d 1726 and was a son of Abraham and (Nash)
Sampson
    Children of **Isaac Sampson and Lydia Standish**:

Isaac Sampson B. April 18, 1688
Jonathan Sampson B. Feb. 9, 1690
Josiah Sampson B. June 5, 1692 D Mar. 29, 1730
Lydia Sampson B. April 22, 1694
Ephraim Sampson B. May 8, 1698 M. Abigail Horrel
Peleg Sampson B. Nov. 12, 1700
Priscella Sampson B. Nov. 12, 1700
Barnabas Sampson B. Feb. 12, 1704
On 28th, Sept. 1726 Isaac Sampson was appointed
administrator of the estate of his father Isaac Sampson of
Plymouth.

On 20 March, 1733/4 Jona Sampson of Plympton,
Husbandman, quitclaimed to Ephraim Sampson of Plympton,
Cordwainer, his right in estate of Josiah Sampson, late of
Plympton on the same day, Isaac Sampson of Plympton,
Husbandman, made a similar quit claim as did Peleg Sampson
of Plympton, Narler, and Lydia Sampson Jr. of Plympton and
Priscilla Fuller, widow of Plympton and Barnabas Sampson of
Plympton, Cordwainer. On the same day abt. 30 April, 1734
Lydia Sampson of Plympton widow also quit claimed her
share. No Plymouth Co. Pr for Lydia Sampson or daughter
Lydia Sampson.

4th Generation

Ephraim Sampson B. Plymouth May 8, 1698, D.
Middleboro April 11, 1787. He m. Plympton, Nov.. 15, 1728
Abigail Horrell Born May 11, 1708 D. Middleboro Mar. 29,
1777; parents Humphery Harrel and Elizabeth Smith. Ephraim
Sampsons parents were Isaac Sampson and Lydia Standish
Children of **Ephraim and Abigail Sampson**
Abigail Sampson b Oct. 25, 1729
Elizabeth Sampson b Mar. 29, 1732
Lusanna Sampson b. Nov. 7, 1734
Eunice Sampson b. May 15, 1737, m. Nathan Eddy

Sarah Sampson b. Jan. 31, 1742
Mary Sampson b. April 10, 1745
Priscilla Sampson b. April 10, 1745
No other personal information on Ephraim

5th Generation
Nathan Eddy B. Sept. 8, 1733, Middleboro, Mass. d.
Feb. 28, 1802
Pittsfield, VT Parents – Samuel Eddy –Lydia Alden
He married Eunice Sampson b. May 15, 1737, Plympton,
Mass. d Mar. 25, 1802 Pittsfield, Vt. Her parents – Ephraim
Sampson and Abigail Horrell
Children of **Nathan and Eunice Sampson** b Middleboro
Ephraim Eddy b. Dec. 21, 1759
Lydia Eddy b. Sept. 16, 1762
Hannah Eddy b. Feb. 1, 1766
Nathaniel Eddy b. July 6, 1768
Nathan Eddy b. April 21, 1771
Isaac Eddy B- June 24, 1774
Zachariah Eddy-B-Nov. 18, 1778
As Eunice Sampson was the granddaughter of Isaac and
Lydia (Standish) Sampson and since Lydia Standish was the
daughter of Alexander and Sarah (Alden) Standish and
granddaughter of Myles and Barbara Standish all Eddys that
can trace their descendents to Nathan and Eunice (Sampson)
Eddy are eligible to the Mayflower Society membership
through both Nathan and Eunice.

CAPTIAN MYLES STANDISH, THE PROTECTOR

ALDEN CONNECTION TO STANDISH

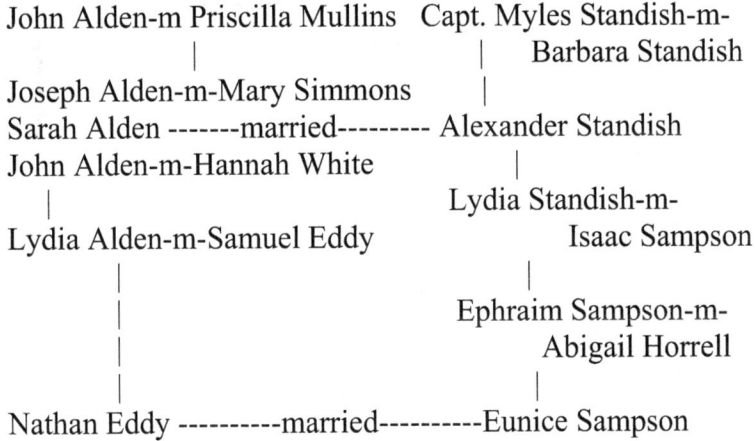

```
John Alden-m Priscilla Mullins   Capt. Myles Standish-m-
              |                          |      Barbara Standish
Joseph Alden-m-Mary Simmons        |
Sarah Alden -------married--------- Alexander Standish
John Alden-m-Hannah White          |
     |                          Lydia Standish-m-
Lydia Alden-m-Samuel Eddy            Isaac Sampson
     |                               |
     |                          Ephraim Sampson-m-
     |                               Abigail Horrell
     |                               |
Nathan Eddy ----------married----------Eunice Sampson
```

The above genealogy lines show how the Alden and Standish families came together and later will show how they extended on to the Ingraham families.

The ship Fortune landed 1621.

Those Who Came on the "Fortune," the "Anne" and the "Little James"

FORTUNE

John Adams
William Basset
William Beale
Edward Bumpus
Jonathan Brewster
Clement Briggs
John Cannon
William Conner
Robert Cushman
Thomas Cushman
Stephen Dean
Philip De le Noye
Thomas Flavell
Widow Ford

Robert Hicks
William Hilton
Bennet Morgan
Thomas Morton
Austin Nicolas
William Palmer
William Pit
Thomas Prince
Moses Simonson
Hugh Statie
James Steward
William Tench
John Winslow
William Wright

ANNE and LITTLE JAMES   1623

Anthony Annable
Jane Annable
Sarah Annable
Hannah Annable
Edward Bangs
Robert Bartlett
Fear Brewster
Patience Brewster
Mary Buckett
Edward Burcher
Mrs. Burcher
Thomas Clarke
Christopher Conant
Hester Cooke
Cuthbert Cuthbertson
  wife and four children

Experience Mitchell
George Morton
Patience Morton
Nathaniel Morton
John Morton
Sarah Morton
Ephraim Morton
George Morton, Jr.
Thomas Morton, Jr.
Ellen Newton
John Oldham
Francis Palmer
Christian Penn
Joshua Pratt
James Rand
Robert Ratcliffe and wife

Anthony Dix
John Faunce
Goodwife Flavell
Edmund Flood
Bridget Fuller
Timothy Hatherly
William Heard
Margaret Hicks
  three children
Mrs. William Hilton
William Hilton, Jr.
Edward Holeman
John Jenney
  wife and three children
Robert Long

Nicholas Snow
Alice Southworth
Francis Sprague
  wife and child
Barbara Standish
Thomas Tilden
Stephen Tracey and wife
Sarah Tracey
Ralph Wallen and wife
Elizabeth Warren
Mary Warren
Ann Warren
Sarah Warren
Elizabeth Warren
Abigail Warren

Our First National Thanksgiving

The Salem Mercury (Massachusetts), 1789 volume 111, number 158, front page

By the President of the United States of America, A Proclamation

WHEREAS it is the duty of all nations to acknowledge the Providence of Almighty GOD, to obey his will, to be grateful for his benefits, and humbly to implore his protection and favor; And whereas both Houses of Congress have, by their joint committee, requested me to recommend to the people of the United States, a Day of Public Thanksgiving and prayer, to be observed by acknowledging with grateful hearts the many and signal favors of Almighty GOD, especially by affording them an opportunity peaceably to establish a form of government for their safety and happiness.

NOW, THEREFORE, I do recommend and assign Thursday, the twenty-sixth day of November next, to be devoted by the people of these states, to the service of that great and glorious Being, who is the beneficent Author of all the good that was, that is, or that will be: That we may then all unite in rendering unto him our sincere and humble thanks for his kind care and protection of the people of this country previous to their becoming a nation; for the signal and manifold mercies, and the favourable interpositions of his providence in the course and conclusion of the late war; for the great degree of tranquility, union and plenty, which we have since enjoyed; for the peaceable and rational manner in which we have been enabled to establish Constitutions of Government for our safety and happiness, and particularly the national one now lately instituted; for the civil and religious Liberty with which we are blessed; and the means we have of acquiring and diffusing useful knowledge; and in general, for all the great and various favours which he hath been pleased to confer upon us.

AND ALSO, that we may then unite in most humbly offering our prayers and supplications to the great Lord and Ruler of Nations, and beseech him to pardon our national and other transgressions, to enable us all, whether in publick or private stations, to perform our several and relative duties properly and punctually; to render our national government a blessing to all the people, by constantly being a government of wise, just and constitutional laws, discreetly and faithfully executed and obeyed; to protect and guide all sovereigns and nations (especially such as have shewn kindness unto us) and to bless them with good government, peace and concord; to promote the knowledge and practice of true religion and virtue, and the increase of science among them and us; and generally, to grant unto all mankind such a degree of temporal prosperity as he alone knows to be best.

GIVEN under my Hand, at the city of New York, the third day of October, in the Year of our Lord one thousand seven hundred and eighty-nine.

G. WASHINGTON

CHAPTER III
JOHN ALDEN THE BUILDER

We have now traveled from the Mayflower down through the Capt. Myles Standish genealogical family lines through the Sampson family lines and end up with the Eddy family and the Sampson family coming together by the marriage of Nathan Eddy to Eunice Sampson.
We are now going to go back to John Alden and Priscilla Mullins at the Mayflower and take the Alden families down through several Eddy families and end up at the Nathan Eddy and Eunice Sampson marriage thus joining the Alden family and Capt. Myles Standish to the Mayflower and to all the following families down to the Ingraham families ending at the present time.

The ship, Speedwell was scheduled to travel to America at the same time as the Mayflower. The first time the two ships sailed a great distance out to sea the Speedwell developed problems requiring both ships to go back to England. After the speedwell was repaired both ships set sail again on their long journey.

The two ships had not sailed out to sea a great distance when the Speedwell developed problems again. At that time it was decided that the Speedwell was not sea worthy to sail on what would be a long and perilous voyage. The Speedwell again turned around and sailed back to England on her own.

The Mayflower continued on the voyage with other problems that appeared later but they were be able to repair them temporarily. It was enough to get them through 66 days and over some very rough storms at sea and finally end up at Cape Cod in the Massachusetts Bay in America.

John Alden was about 21 years old in 1620. He was a tall blue eyed blonde; very strong and of Scandinavian decent and was the tallest man in the colony. He was hired as a cooper at South Hampton, England just before the voyage of the Mayflower. The British Parliament required that a ship carrying beer should have a cooper aboard to replace barrel stock. John was also a cabinetmaker and a surveyor.

After the ship, Speedwell had to turn around and return back to England the Mayflower went on alone as they continued on their way the storms began to rage tossing the Mayflower around like a cork in the water.

About half way across Captain Jones listening to the grunts and the groans of the Mayflower detected there was something not right about the sounds that he was hearing from the Mayflower.

Captain Jones was talking to William Brewster at the time and commented that he hoped his fears of what might be happening would not be so. He then said that he must go down to the lower deck to confirm his fears. William Brewster asked if he could go with him. Permission was granted. When they got to the lower deck, the Captain checked the large beam running across the ship and exclaimed his fears were correct and that they had no tools large enough to repair the cracked beam. There was no other choice but to go back to England because if they hit another storm the ship would break like a nut and there would be no survivors.

William Brewster who was the spiritual leader of the group said that he did not believe that God would bring the group all together and drop them off in the middle of the ocean. God would certainly bring them on to complete the journey.

Captain Jones said that they must turn around and go back but William Brewster asked Captain Jones if he would follow him as there was something he wanted to show him. They went down to the bottom hold where many boxes and crates were stored on the ship.

William Brewster continued to move boxes until he finally located a crate he was looking for. He asked the Captain to come and look; as the captain looked with amazement he asked William Brewster, "what is that?"

Brewster said that it was his printing press that he used for making books and it had a large screw jack contained in it's make up. Captain Jones told him, "let's get busy and repair this ship."

I am sure that John Alden helped in the repair with the skills he had as a carpenter. With the repair successfully made, they sailed through storms to end up at Cape Cod Bay, New England. It was here that they anchored in the New World.

The Mayflower had left England on September 6, 1620 with 102 passengers stuffed in that small ship and due to the continuous raging Atlantic storms; the passengers spent most of the time in the cramped lower deck for better than two months with dim lights from candles and a small fire to cook their meals.

Captain Christopher Jones said that sailing along the coast of New England looking for a good place to land was necessary because of the stormy weather. He came close to wrecking the Mayflower before he found the quiet waters off Cape Cod Bay and anchored here away from the lashing waves of the Atlantic Ocean. His original plans were to drop his passengers off and immediately return to England but now he realized that the passengers could not survive if left in the rigid cold weather with no way to protect themselves without shelter built first before leaving the ship.

The coastline was too rough with shallow waters with rocks for the Mayflower to enter too close to shore so the ship had to anchor out in the bay and send the shallop in to investigate the best place to build their village. Several excursions sent out to find the ideal place along the inside of the bay from where they had anchored.

The shoreline covered about eighty miles of shoreline for them to inspect and to determine the best harbor and location to build their village. The area to consider also had to have a good fresh water supply and areas that would give them good soil to grow their food supplies for their survival in the new land. The location called Plymouth was the place they selected to build their village.

Several hardship excursions during this very cold weather were dispatched to explore and to determine their final decision. On one of these trips led by William Bradford they were out several days and on their return to the Mayflower William Bradford was told while he was gone on their expedition that his beautiful wife fell overboard the Mayflower and drown before the crew could rescue her. They had left a two-year-old son, John, back in England before sailing away to the New World.

While still living on the Mayflower it was noted the growing signs of rebellion by the Pilgrim leaders. They knew that they needed to take some action immediately in order to get the rule of order back to having a responsible group of people. Elder Brewster, William Bradford and Jon Carver came up with a plan to stop a social chaos from happening. Together they drafted a document called the Mayflower Compact that they had agreed upon; every male passenger on the ship signed the document. Below is a photo of the signing.

From left to right Captain Miles Standish, Elder Brewster, Governor Carver, Edward Winslow, and William Bradford gathered round a table in the cabin of the *Mayflower* at the signing of the Mayflower Compact.

The pilgrims total being was based in the presence of God so it is no surprise that they would include in their constitution, "in the presence of God," in writing the Mayflower Compact. Our leaders in writing the constitution of the United States borrowed the thought of the Mayflower Compact, "In the Presence of God and the freedom of each and everyone in faith and the government of the people, for the people and by the people to enforce our freedoms."

Below is a copy of the Mayflower Compact.

The Mayflower Compact

In the name of God Amen. We whose names are under-writen, the loyall subjects of our dread soveraigne Lord King James, by the grace of God, of Great Britaine, France, & Ireland, king, defender of the faith, etc. Having undertaken, for the glorie of God, and advancemente of the Christian faith and honour of our king & countrie, a voyage to plant the first colonie in the Northerne parts of Virginia, doe by these presents solemnly & mutualy in the presence of God, and one of another, covenant & combine ourselves togeather into a civill body politick, for our better ordering & preservation & furtherance of the ends aforesaid; and by vertue hereof to enacte, constitute, and frame such just & equall lawes, ordinances, acts, constitutions, & offices, from time to time, as shall be thought most meete and convenient for the generall good of the Colonie: unto which we promise all due submission and obedience. In witnes whereof we have hereunder subscribed our names at Cap-Codd the .11. of November, in the year of the raigne of our soveraigne Lord King James of England, France, & Ireland, the eighteenth, and of Scotland the fiftie fourth. Ano:dom. 1620.

John Carver	Samuel Fuller	Edward Tilley
William Bradford	Christopher Martin	John Tilley
Edward Winslow	William Mullins	Francis Cooke
William Brewster	William White	Thomas Rogers
Isaac Allerton	Richard Warren	Thomas Tinker
Myles Standish	John Howland	John Rigdale
John Alden	Stephen Hopkins	Edward Fuller
John Turner	Degory Priest	Richard Clark
Francis Eaton	Thomas Williams	Richard Gardiner
James Chilton	Gilbert Winslow	John Allerton
John Crackston	Edmund Margeson	Thomas English
John Billington	Peter Brown	Edward Dotey
Moses Fletcher	Richard Britteridge	Edward Leister
John Goodman	George Soule	

Some men had threatened mutiny after learning that the ship was not headed anywhere near Virginia for which the company had chartered the Mayflower. Some men asked to turn back and others vowed they would not follow the government that was to be set up on shore. The grumblers though turned cheerful after the signing of a compact that bound the passengers into a civic body.

Writing the compact prevented having mutiny for the Pilgrims arriving in a land far from any government. They realized they had a problem with governing because less than half had any religious affiliation and came from different walks of life that were bound to cause differences of opinions. There was no one they could appeal to and knowing this they would be dependent upon themselves for government controls.

Over a month before making a permanent landing, they had written the Mayflower compact though this instrument was simple and brief it was comprehensive and fundamental. It was the foundation of all the democratic institutions of America and was the basis of our republic. The obligation and duties of the citizens to the state were definitely expressed. Duty was their very life and the signing of the compact has been called one of the most important acts known to history. It is certainly the most notable contribution that has ever made to the civic thought of the world. Former charters of freedom, notably the Magna Carta and the English Bill Of Rights were basically efforts to wring concessions from monarchs who were acknowledged to be the source of power. The compact for the first time assumed the power to vest in the people. It was most fortunate that King James refused them a charter though it was a great disappointment to the Pilgrims at the time. They then were forced to stand on themselves and discovered the power that comes from within and so doing they established popular constitutional liberty. It was while the Mayflower lay in Provincetown harbor that the Pilgrims had made numerous trips in the shallop seeking the right location and it had been on December 26, 1620 that the Mayflower had come into Plymouth Harbor. It was here, as the story goes that the Pilgrims stepped off the boat onto Plymouth Rock and onto shore into Plymouth. The Mayflower remained here through the winter and served as their home until houses were built.

I should remind the reader that the original destination of the Mayflower was the northern part of Virginia but instead they ended up at Cape Cod and later at Plymouth Harbor. History must surely have been changed by this event. There they found a very good harbor and much of the upland cleared and in former years planted with corn by the Indians before the pestilence had destroyed them and so depopulated the region leaving it for the Pilgrims to take over peaceably.

In this area was found several running brooks of fresh water and bubbling springs with the best water they had ever drank. The Pilgrim group was made up of eighteen married couples, sixteen men, unmarried or had wives that did not come with them; twenty eight of both sexes under 21 years, nineteen laborers and three hand servants. Each of the eighteen couples became the nucleus for the family unit by dividing among them all the other people, 18 buildings and a large common house and a platform on the hill for defense was built.

During the first winter at Plymouth, it was a mammoth program for the Pilgrims to undertake during the dead of winter and immediately following their long and tiresome voyage.

The bad food and crowded quarters on the ship coupled with terrible exposure they had suffered on their exploring expeditions resulted in the outbreak of their greatest sickness of both scurvy and pneumonia often progressing into quick consumption. The sicknesses got so bad and the fatalities so many that sometimes only six or seven persons remained able to bury the dead, feed, and care for the sick.

They also had to get wood for the fires, haul the water from the springs and care for those who were too sick to get out of bed. To the very end, each person kept valid the solemn and sacred bond that united him or her. The validity of which they made in great consciousness and by virtue of which all were straightly tied to care for the others welfare. The devotion with which they preformed the most menial tasks for one another during these terrible times is simply beyond all praise.

As spring came, the deaths dropped and convalescence set in. Fifty-two had died and fifty-two remained. Four households had been completely obliterated and the others felt lucky to escape entirely. Above is a memorial for the dead.

The building program was revised and instead of eighteen dwellings to be built now, they estimated that seven buildings would be sufficient. The food was improved through hunting and fishing. The fact that the colony had no cattle greatly handicapped them. It was a problem that would be over come in the future.

The crew of the Mayflower was getting restless to go. They had lost many of the crew due to sickness. Captain Jones lost his carpenter, the master gunner, the boatswain, the cook, three of the quartermasters and many of the foremast men. When the sick Pilgrims began to get well all of their gear was set ashore from the Mayflower. The man that was even the toughest sea-rower was glad to leave this place because they thought it was bad luck.

The Mayflower crew that remained happily prepared to leave. They collected heavy rocks from the shore and loaded the ship for ballast because when the Pilgrims and all their possessions were unloaded the ship was riding too high in the water for safe sailing.

Captain Jones realized that the families he brought here onto the savage infested shore had little hope of survival. All the time they had been here there were hostile Indians demonstrating hostility in the woods but staying at a safe distance.

Captain Jones used his best efforts to persuade the pilgrims to leave America with him. Surely, he thought that ordinary prudence would call for their returning to a place of security. Some of the people bravely and persistently declined the offer to leave. It was even more amazing to Captain Jones that he could not find one of them who had become faint-hearted and ready to give up.

Two years later in 1623, two ships landed in Plymouth Harbor. Some passengers that were on the Anne and Little James were Barbara Standish who would become the wife of Captain Miles Standish and become the mother of all of his children. Other passengers were Alice Carpenter Southworth with her two sons. She was a widow who would soon to be the wife of Governor William Bradford. Soon Governor Bradford's son, John would join their family. At that time John, Governor William Bradford's, now four year old son was still living in England.

HISTORY OF PLYMOUTH ROCK
Plymouth Rock while small in stature this modest

landmark is a symbol of strength and determination of New Englands earliest colonists. Some have called it America's doorstep. Above is a photo of Plymouth Rock. To the right is a photo of myself (Willard), Arnold and Lucille Steffens when we visited the site in 1994. Historians say that the Pilgrims stepped on the rock after they rowed ashore from the Mayflower on Dec. 21, 1620. The rock lay unnoticed for 121 years when an elderly Plymouthean, Thomas Faunce identified it in 1741 as the landing place of the Pilgrims. In 1775, the rock split as it was

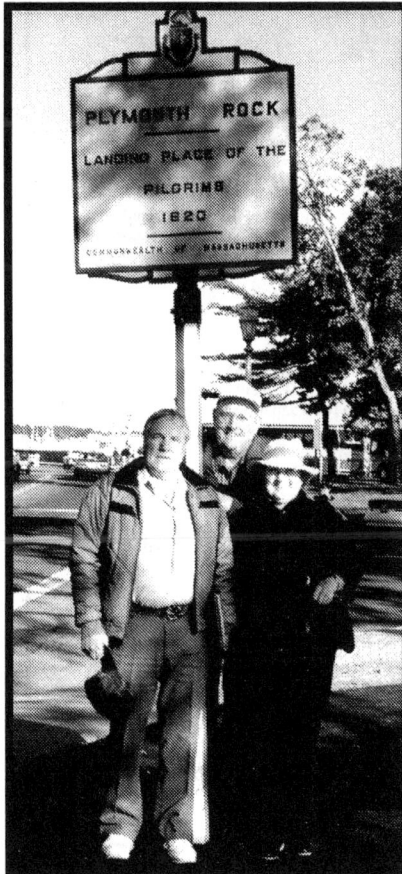

raised from its bed by oxen. The upper part was hauled to the town square and the remainder left on the waterfront.

Below is a photo of the monument for Plymouth Rock. Taken 1994

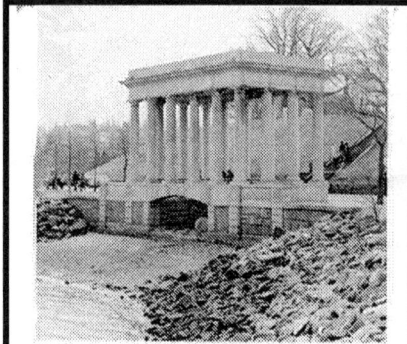

Plymouth Rock – America's Doorstep

While small in stature, this modest landmark is a symbol of the strength and determination of New England's earliest colonists. Some have called it "*America's Doorstep.*"

Plymouth Rock languished in obscurity until 1741, when a 95-year-old elder of the Plymouth church identified it as "the rock" on which the first group of Pilgrims landed.

In 1774, the patriots of Plymouth recognized the symbolic value of Forefathers Rock and attempted to move it to Town Square to sit next to the Liberty Pole. As a yoke of oxen raised the Rock, it split in two, foretelling the division of the colonies from England. Only the upper portion of the Rock left the waterfront.

By the 1830's the romance of the Pilgrim story had captured the fancy of Americans, and the Town Square piece of Plymouth Rock attracted both tourists and souvenir hunters. In 1834 the town fathers moved that piece of the Rock to Pilgrim Hall Museum, inside an iron fence.

By 1859 the Pilgrim Society had acquired the waterfront site in which the lower part of Plymouth Rock was embedded. Following the Civil War, the Society hired designer Hammatt Billings to erect a protective canopy over Plymouth Rock.

In 1880, the Pilgrim Society, finding itself the owner of both pieces of Plymouth Rock, cemented them together at the waterfront site. As part of the tercentenary celebration of 1920-1921, the old Italiante canopy was replaced with a new Greek Classical canopy, which continues to protect the landmark.

By the 1830s, the Pilgrim story had captured the attraction of tourists and souvenir hunters. The rock stayed in the town square then in 1834 the town fathers moved that piece of rock to Pilgrim Hall Museum inside an iron fence on Court St. The first section remained in its water front bed.

By 1859, the Pilgrim Society had acquired the water front site in which the lower part of Plymouth Rock was embedded. Following the Civil War the Society hired a designer, Hammatt Billings, to erect a protective granite canopy over Plymouth Rock. In 1880 the Pilgrim Society finding itself the owner of both pieces of Plymouth Rock; the part which had rested on the Pilgrim Hall lawn was returned to the waterfront and the two parts were cemented together at the water front site.

In 1921 as part of the tercentenary observance the old Italiante canopy was replaced with a new Greek classical granite portico over the historic site by the National Society of the Colonial Dames Of America that continues to protect the historical site to the present time.

I am sure John Alden was in great demand in building the Plymouth Colony because John Alden had received skilled training when he lived in England to become a surveyor, carpenter and furniture maker. All of these skills were in great demand in building their colony. The houses were all laid out in a row with a street running by all of these houses with each house on about a half of an acre. Each house was placed about a hundred feet apart leaving each family with enough ground to fence each place with a fence about three foot high making it possible to have some goats and chickens on each place and still leave plenty of ground for a garden that could grow enough vegetables to more than supply each family. The house about 39 ft. by 10 ½ ft was placed in the middle of their plot and placed near the street. The houses varied in size according to the size of their family. Some houses had a single bedroom, some two bedrooms and some with second stories.

The front room and kitchen were combined into one with a big fireplace on one side of the room in the center of that wall for good heat dissipation. The fireplace was built with an opening of about three foot high and about

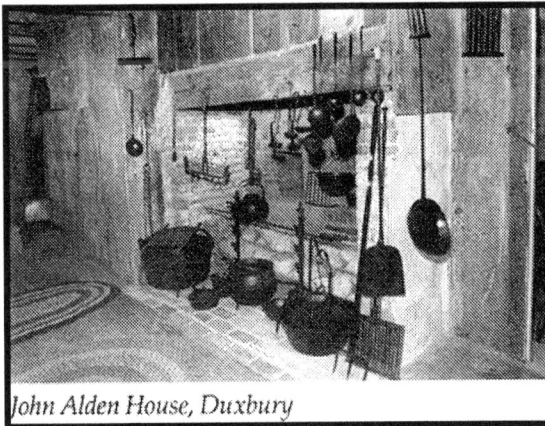

John Alden House, Duxbury

four foot wide with hooks built in the upper side to hang their large pots in the fire for cooking their meals. If they did have an upper story they would have a hole in the ceiling with a control register in it to control the heat going upstairs. John was also a skilled furniture maker. He made chairs, cabinets and tables out of the wooden wine barrels that the Mayflower brought over with the Pilgrims to this new land. John must have been very busy making enough furniture to fill all of those houses.

NOTE INSERT FROM AUTHOR: In September, 1994 when I (Willard) and Louise Ingraham and Arnold and Lucille Steffens traveled to Plymouth, Massachussetts we visited many of the Interesting places in that area. In the Plymouth Harbor was parked Mayflower 11 that we immediately went to and toured all the holds of the ship. Our photo is above.

At the time we were there many local residences of the area was sitting, standing and talking to all new comers in the dialect of the 1620s. When we asked a question other than the days of the 1620s they would quickly tell us that the only news they knew was the days of the present time of 1620. They would tell us that the time of what you speak has not come yet so how could we report on such a thing. All the residents on the ship were dressed in clothes of the 1620s. Above is Captain Christophor Jones and he was dressed as a captain of those days. The women had their very long

dresses on and some ladies were working on a spinning wheel and others patching cloths.

At left is photo of one of the men at work. It was a very interesting tour of the ship.

As we stepped off the Mayflower ship we noticed a small opening like enclosure that housed the Plymouth Rock that supposedly was the rock that all the Pilgrims stepped out of the shallop onto and onto the land of America. The housing for the Plymouth Rock was called Plymouth Rock Portico.

To the right we had a last photo taken with the Mayflower II in the background.

We then went up the hill a short distance from Plymouth to visit the Plimouth plantation that is a village built like the buildings that were built in 1620. The village was laid out the same with people living there in the same way and conditions of the 1620s.

In the village, the women were inside cooking by the fireplaces with the pots hanging above the fire. The men were chipping wood and sharpening their axes as well as other projects.

FOLLOWING IS A GALLERY OF PLIMOUTH

Below is photo of the entrance to the village

Arnold and Lucille Steffens with Louise are posing at the entrance of the village in (photo taken 1994)

Willard below with view of Plimouth

Explore Another World in Time

In 1620, America's most famous immigrants -- the Pilgrims -- set foot on the land which would be their new home. Today their lives, experiences, concerns and those of the Wampanoag Indians on whose land they settled come alive again at Plimoth Plantation. Enjoy the time of their lives aboard *Mayflower II*, in the *1627 Pilgrim Village* and at *Hobbamock's (Wampanoag Indian) Homesite*.

I was thinking as I (Willard) took the walking tour of Plimouth and snapping photos that every child studies about the Pilgrims from books in school; would it not be wonderful if they all could walk through this restored village as we are. The setting and atmosphere is as unique as what it must have been in the 1600s and to see would bring this important history alive to each child as it did for me.

45

Work in the kitchen and then the feast follows.

Left is how it was with no electri city

Left is how the meat for the feast was given to the cooks

Left: And then it was feast time.

Everyday life in the village went on as follows practicing shooting with muskets.

Life must have been hard in the 1600s. Everything was handwork. The young person above is sitting outside on a wooden bench with her work around her. She has only a needle and thread to sew the clothes they wore.

All tools were made and repaired or sharpened by hand

A vegetable garden at Plimouth. If it were not for the Indians giving the Pilgrims corn they would have starved that first winter until the season for planting came in the spring.

A last view of Plimouth; Lucille and Arnold are on the left with Louise behind.

THE HOBBAMOCK VILLAGE GALLERY

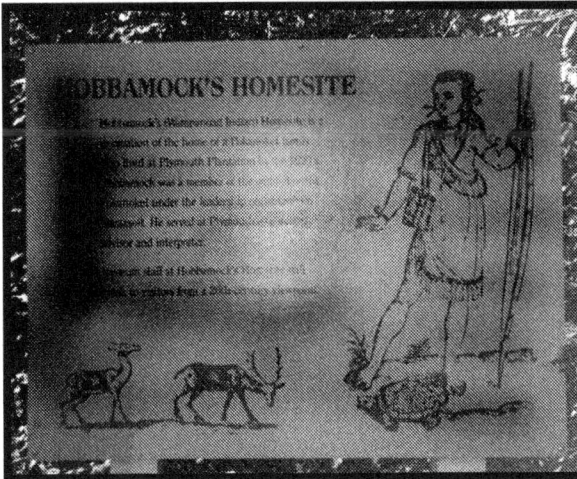

From the village we walked down to the Hobbamock home site. Hobbamock was the Bkanoket Wampanoag; a native who with his family lived adjacent to the new Plymouth colony and provided guidance and council to the Pigrims.

49

Below is how the village appears

Hobbamock was the Pokanokët Wampanoag man who, with his family, lived adjacent to New Plymouth, providing guidance and counsel to the Pilgrims regarding the ways of the land and its Native People.

Speak with the program guides, some in period, native costume, in the shade of the wetus. Learn about their culture as you watch them create a dugout canoe, cook, weave a mat or storage bag.

Below: Construction of a village hut

Left
Village
hut ready
for meeting

51

Below a fire was started for cooking

Below she has the pot on the fire and is sewing

It was an interesting walking tour of the village. Most of the settings were framed with Indian descendents at work as if it were in the 1600s.

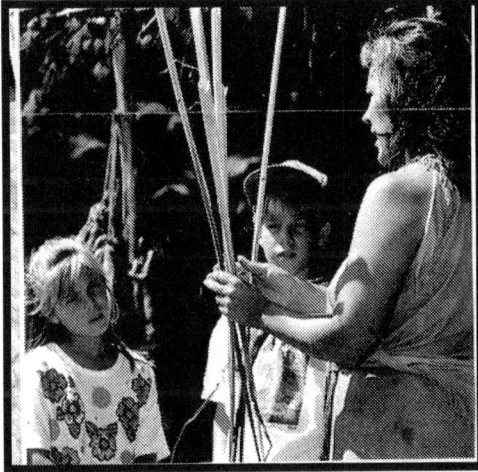

At left is an Indian
lady teaching the
visiting children
how the huts were
put together.

Willard and Louise below finishing their walking tour.

We spent a lot of time at both the Plimouth village and
visiting the Hobbamack site. We felt like we had stepped back
into time. At Plimouth they spoke the language of a Pilgrim
with all the accents. At Hobbamack all the Indians spoke
English but they also spoke their native language.

53

I can not imagine that the store below that we visited looked as well stocked in the Pilgrim's early years at this site.

From this point, we walked down into the village of Plymouth to view the monuments and statues.

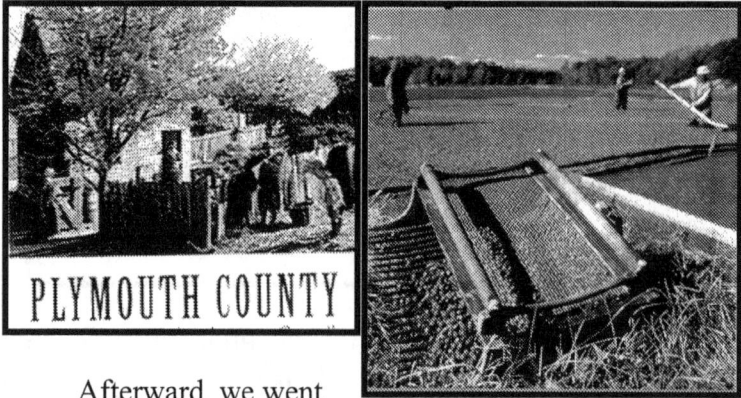

Afterward we went to see the cranberry bogs; photo is above.

We can vouch for the delicious recipe below

Cranberry Cobbler

1 pound cranberries
3/4 cup sugar
1 cup rolled oats
1/2 cup flour
1 cup brown sugar
1/2 cup butter

Preheat oven to 350 degrees. Butter a 1 1/2 quart casserole dish. Combine cranberries and sugar in saucepan and cook over medium-low heat, stirring, until cranberry skins have stopped "popping" (about 10-15 minutes). Pour into casserole. In a separate bowl, combine the oats, flour and brown sugar. Cut in the butter until mixture is crumbly. Pour on top of cranberries. Bake 45 minutes and serve warm with vanilla ice cream.

Served with ice cream this tasty dish could easy be made with a substitute fruit from our own region

Duxbury below is a quaint small town; it did not fit the 1600 era but still there was an early 1900 era look about the store fronts.

Duxbury, Mass. was about ten miles from Plymouth. Duxbury is the town where John Alden built a house for Priscilla.

In the 1860s, many farmers that lived in the southern states in the United States had large farms and plantations that required a lot of hand work to produce the crops that were planted such as tobacco. In order to farm this land the southern farmers thought it was necessary to own black slaves to do the work. Many abuses of the black people happened during this time much to the disgust of the people that lived in the northern states. Many black people escaped the human bondage each year to the north aided by the underground railroad or called, "the Liberty Line." This loosely organized group lived along the Ohio River that was the border between the free and the slave states. These people took great risks to help shelter the blacks that ran away during the day. They guided them along an intricate and constant changing route of back roads at night to their freedom protecting them at homes called freedom stops.

It was the freedom stop in the network that was called the Underground Railroad. The angry Southerners called it a deliberate theft of their property to the northerners. Many northerners called it obedience to a higher morality.

One of the freedom stops along this network was the

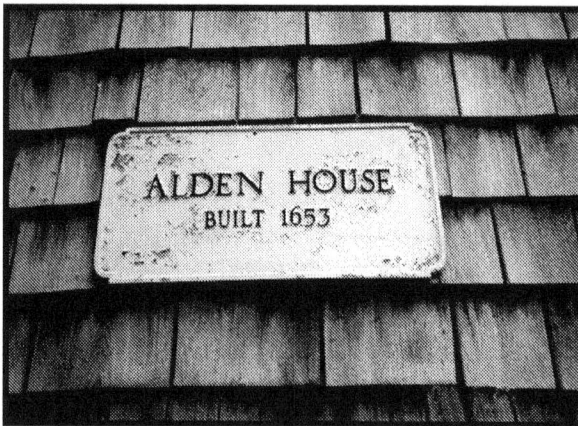

home that John Alden built for Priscilla Alden in 1653. Left is the sign that one sees on that home as the ancestors of Alden have opened the home for tours.

Our tour of this home is covered in a personal story later in this chapter.

The house looks very much like it did in the 1600s.

JOHN ALDEN BUILT THIS HOUSE IN 1653

Many times, it is said that the searchers of the fleeing black people ended up at the Alden house. The searchers would loose their trail making them suspicious but in their search of the home they always found nothing.

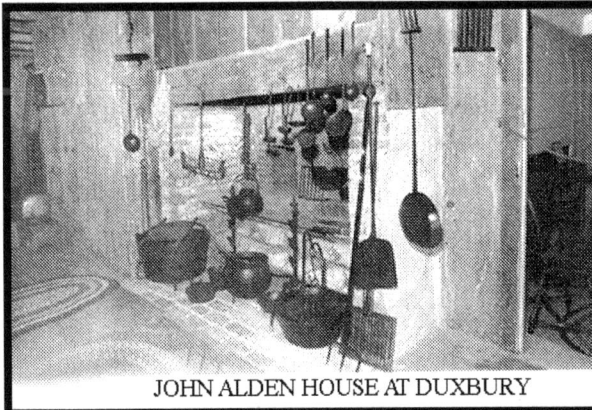

JOHN ALDEN HOUSE AT DUXBURY

The secret was in how the Aldens accomplished this without getting caught. When John Alden built this house for Priscilla in 1653 he also built a big fireplace that a big black pot hung over a fire in the fireplace. John and Priscilla had ten or eleven children so a large fireplace had been necessary.

In revealing the secret, one would have to look inside the fireplace up above and there inside this huge fireplace was bench boards that had been easily installed. They could easily sit four or five people about ten feet up inside of this chimney with the fire burning very low under the big black pot. No one thought of looking up into the inside of this fireplace.

There were three principle lines of freedom from the south converging from Cincinnati, Ohio, Madison, Wisconsin and Jefferson, Indiana. The roads were always in good running order and a week seldom passed without receiving people on these long and mysterious roads that gave many black people the freedom they were seeking.

Governor William Bradford recorded that Duxbury in 1632 had become an independent community. "For several years a few Plymouth families spent their summers there. With crops in their lands just north of the Pilgrim colony now instead of returning to the Plymouth colony for the winter they sued to become a body of themselves," wrote Bradford.

The beginning of Duxbury was the result of Plymouths increasing population now that they owned cattle they needed more land to increase their stock. Duxbury had easy access by water and was New England's first summer colony even though it was anything but a vacation resort.

It began several years before 1632 when the clamor for distribution of common lands finally brought action. The first cattle arrived in Plymouth aboard the Charity in 1624 and the need for land increased as the livestock multiplied.

John Alden and Captain Myles Standish left their plot on the high brow of Plymouths Fort Hill and broke ground across the bay close to Eagle Tree Pond. John Alden built his home and two miles away at what is now Captains Hill Capt. Myles Standish erected his house.

Among their neighbors was the aging elder Brewster now nearing seventy and his sons, Love and Wresling. Brewster's daughter Patience also came as the wife of Thomas

Prence; so did George Soule, Philip Delano, Moses Simmons, Experience Mitchill and numerous others.

In their first years at Duxbury, the original settlers had gone on Sundays to Plymouth to attend services, crossing the water in shallops whenever weather permitted. By land, the trip was a tedious ten miles either by foot or on the backs of oxen because there were no horses in the colony until 1644. There was no road and the trail was rough and often blocked by mires or made dangerous and hazardous by bridges crudely built of felled trees.

Once their new Duxbury houses were snug and the farms providing themselves the summer community sought to establish its own Sunday meeting. Large flocks of waterfowl nested in the salt marshes near Duxbuy that supported the theory that the settlement was first called Ducks Burrow as the name was often written in documents.

As a matter of record there were at least eleven spellings used by the Pilgrims until Duxbury prevailed late in the seventeenth century. No matter what derivation of its name Duxbury soon established its own identity. John Alden now had five children through his marriage to Priscilla Mullins.

Captain Standish had brought not only his growing family but also the Christian Indian, Hobbamock, who was to stay in the Standish household until his death in 1642.

In 1637, Ralph Partridge became the village's first minister and the following year America's first annual fair was held in Duxbury.

John Alden found time outside the demands of his farm and his official duties to create serrated cabinets, chests and cupboards for other prosperous colonists. At his table, he ate the Pilgrim food that his wife cooked in the fireplace. A usual breakfast included rye pudding and bread or ye Indian porridge along with pea or bean soup or a stew of pork or salt fish. A typical Duxbury dinner of Alden's time was served in the middle of the day and consisted of bean soup or pork and beans along with squash, turnips, onions or other vegetables from the garden. Supper was largely a repetition of breakfast with addition of gingerbread, cheese or pie and beer. The beer was the beverage served at all meals even to the children.

The hospitality of the Alden house, as did those of other Colony officials, often served also as a courtroom or as a place for counsels to take place.

John Alden more than once risked personal fortunes to keep the colony alive. It is difficult to imagine the fate of Plymouth and Duxbury without the contributions of Alden and friend Standish. When they joined those who assumed responsibility for the colony's indebtedness, they pledged their estates as security and when final settlement was made each had to sell three hundred acres to satisfy their English creditors.

Their lives may not have been quite as romantically interlocked as Longfellow's famous poem would indicate but romance did link the two families when John and Priscilla's daughter Sarah married Captain Standish's son Alexander.

Longevity was one more distinction that John Alden passed on to his descendants. He was in his eighty ninth year when he died in the Alden house that was built in 1653. A bold and purposeful man he was once described as stern, austere and unyielding. He was above all the true Pilgrim. In 1633 he became an assistant to the governor which position he held until his death except from 1640 to 1650 when he was deputy to the general court from Duxbury. He held many offices, treasurer of the colony for a time. He was highly respected and distinguished in both Plymouth and Duxby and John Alden was the last survivor of the signers of the Mayflower Compact.

Little is known of Priscilla except the story of her courtship with John Alden. They settled in Duxbury, Ma. and both she and John are buried in the old burying ground in Duxbury. The Alden home built in 1653 is still standing and is now used as a museum.

JOHN ALDEN THE BUILDER

GHOSTS AND MORE GHOSTS
By: Louise Ingraham, Sept. 29, 1994

THE FOUR OF US, WILLARD AND LOUISE INGRAHAM, LUCILLE AND ARNOLD STEFFENS PLANNED ANOTHER DAY OF RESEARCHING THE PAST; ESPECIALLY WILLARD IN HIS QUEST FOR THE LIVES OF HIS ANCESTORS. WILLARD WAS DRIVING THE CAR AND ARNOLD WAS THE CO-PILOT; THE DESTINATION WAS THE JOHN ALDEN HOUSE IN DUXBURY, MA. IT TOOK A LITTLE WHILE TO FIND THE RIGHT DRIVEWAY BUT FIND IT WE DID. THE HOUSE LOOKED OH SO VACANT AND ONLY ONE CAR WAS PARKED OUT FRONT.

WILLARD APPROACHED THE HOUSE WITH HIS BEST SMILE AND INTRODUCED HIMSELF AS A DESCENDENT OF THE ALDEN FAMILY. THE DIRECTOR, A YOUNG MOTHER WITH A 5-MONTH-OLD BABY WILLINGLY AGREED TO TAKE US ON A TOUR THRU THE HOUSE. THE OLD HOUSE HAD ONCE BEEN MOVED FROM ITS ORIGINAL SITE BY JOHN ALDEN AND THEN ADDED ON FOR MORE SPACE.

THE DIRECTOR, AS I WILL RELATE TO, AS OUR HOST WAS VERY KNOWLEDGEABLE ABOUT THE ALDEN FAMILY. SHE WAS A DESCENDANT OF THF WAMPANOAG INDIANS. THE HOST WITH HER FIVE-MONTH-OLD LITTLE GIRL IN HER ARMS TOOK US THRU THE HOUSE EXPLAINING HISTORY AND OBJECTS TO US ROOM BY ROOM.

AN INTERESTING THING ABOUT THIS HOUSE WAS THAT IN THE CENTER OF THE HOUSE THERE WERE NO DOORS TO OTHER ROOMS. IN THE CENTER OF THE HOUSE, THERE WAS A VERY IARGE CHIMNEY AREA AND DIFFERENT ROOMS SURROUNDED IT. AS YOU WALKED AROUND THE CENTER FIREPLACE, EACH ROOM HAD ITS OWN FIREPLACE WITH THE

CENTER FIREPLACE BECOMING A PART OF THAT
ROOM. IT WAS AS IF EACH ROOM HAD AN
INDIVIDUAL FIREPLACE BUT ALL CONNECTED WITH
THE SAME CHIMNEY.

IN THE KITCHEN AREA THE HOST TOLD US
THERE WAS SPACE UP IN THE CHIMNEY WHERE
NORTHERNS COULD AND DID HIDE BLACKS FROM
THE SOUTH THAT WERE ESCAPING TO FREEDOM
FROM SLAVERY TO THE NORTH. FROM TIME TO
TIME, THE ENFORCEMENT OFFICERS WOULD COME
LOOKING FOR THEM DURING THESE CIVIL WAR
TIMES BUT NOT ONCE DID THEY LOOK UP INTO THE
SPACES ABOVE THE CHIMNEY WHERE THE BLACK
PEOPLE HID FROM VIEW.

JOHN ALDEN HAD HIS OWN OFFICE AND FROM
THERE SETTLED DISPUTES AMONG NEIGHBORS,
MARRIED THE YOUNG SWEETHEARTS, EVEN
MARRIED THREE OF HIS OWN DAUGHTERS. HERE HE
ALSO OFFICIATED OVER THE DEAD.   IN FACT
THERE WAS A ROOM NEXT TO JOHN ALDEN'S OFFICE
CALLED THE BORNING ROOM. IT WAS A BIRTHING
ROOM BUT ALSO A ROOM WHERE ONE NOT ONLY
CAME INTO THE WORLD BUT ALSO WENT OUT OF
THIS WORLD.

JOHN ALDEN AT AGE 89 YEARS DIED IN THE
BORNING ROOM WHERE IN ALL CASES OF DEATH A
24 HOUR VIGIL WAS MADE OVER THE BODY. THE
PURPOSE WAS TO MAKE SURE THE PERSON WAS
DEAD. THEY WERE NOT BURIED UNTIL THE DEAD
BEGAN TO SMELL. AT THIS TIME THE BODY WAS
MOVED INTO JOHN ALDEN'S OFFICE AND FROM
HERE SERVICES WERE HELD AND THEN THE BODY
WAS TAKEN TO THE GRAVE SITE.

THE HOUSE HELD MANY INTERESTING
ARTICLES, THE BED WAS HAND MADE WITH ROPE
STRETCHED TO HOLD THE HAND MADE

JOHN ALDEN THE BUILDER

MATTRESSES.   THE ROPE WOULD EVENTUALLY
LOOSEN AS THE BED WAS SLEPT ON AND AN UNIQUE
WOODEN VISE WAS USED TO TWIST THE ROPE TIGHT
SO ONE SLEEPING WOULD NOT FALL TO THE FLOOR.
ALSO THE BED HELD TWO MATTRESSES. ONE WAS
FILLED WITH STRAW FOR A LIGHT AND AIRY
SUMMER MATTRESS AND ONE WAS FILLED WITH
FEATHERS FOR THE COLD MASS. WINTERS. THE
MATTRESSES WERE SIMPLEY EXCHANGED ONE ON
TOP OF THE OTHER DEPENDING ON THE SEASON.
     WE SAW SHOES FOR THE OXEN MADE FROM A
SQUARE OF WOOD AND METAL STRAPS TO ATTACH
THE WOOD SQUARES TO THE OXEN HOOFS. THESE
WERE USED FOR OXEN IN THE MARSHY AREAS TO
KEEP THEM FROM BEING STUCK IN THE MUD.
ON THE SECOND FLOOR WE COULD SEE WHERE THE
HOUSE HAD LITTERLY BEEN SAWED THRU ON THE
FLOOR.   THE HOST SAID AFTER JOHN ALDEN DIED
ANCESTORS LIVED IN THE HOUSE UNTIL 1956. AT
ONE TIME, THE HOUSE BELONGED TO MARY (POLLY)
ALDEN, WIDOW OF JOHN ALDEN II. BEFORE MARY
DIED, SHE WILLED THE HOME TO HER SONS, ONE
HALF TO HENRY AND ONE HALF TO JOHN.
     THE TROUBLE CAME AFTER MARY (POLLYS)
DEATH WHEN THE BROTHERS WERE IN A DISPUTE
AND DID NOT WANT TO SHARE THE HOUSE. THEY
SETTLED THE PROBLEM IN THE FOLLOWING WAY.
SINCE THEY LIVED IN THE SAME HOUSE UNDER THE
SAME ROOF, THEY SAWED THE FLOOR AS A MARKER
AND EACH BROTHER AND HIS FAMILY COULD NOT
STEP OVER THE CRACKS INTO THE OTHER
BROTHER'S HOUSE.
     THE MOTHER OF HENRY AND JOHN ALDEN
WAS MARY; BETTER REFERRED TO AS AUNT POLLY
AS SHE WAS CALLED BY ALL WHO KNEW HER AT
THAT TIME. WE SAW AUNT POLLY'S ROOM ON THE

SECOND FLOOR AND SAW HER PICTURE IN AN OLD
TIN TYPE PHOTO. SHE APPEARED IN HER PICTURE AS
A VERY STERN LADY WITHOUT A SMILE. THE HOST
SAID MAYBE AUNT POLLY LOOKED SO STERN
BECAUSE IT TOOK AT LEAST 5 MINUTES TO POSE
FOR A TIN TYPE PICTURE AS WAS TAKEN IN THOSE
DAYS.

　　　IT WAS WRITTEN IN THE BOOK "THE ALDEN
FAMILY IN THE ALDEN HOUSE" BY DOROTHY
WENTWORTH THAT AUNT POLLY'S NAME WAS
MARY WINSOR ALDEN, THE WIFE OF JOHN ALDEN
2ND.

　　　JOHN LEFT THE HOUSE TO HIS BELOVED WIFE
MARY (AUNT POLLY).   JOHN'S AFFECTION AND
RESPECT FOR HIS WIFE SHOWS SOMETHING OF HER
CHARACTER AS WRITTEN BY DOROTHY
WENTWORTH WHEN SHE SAID, "THERE ARE OTHER
WAYS OF KNOWING HER. SHE WAS AUNT POLLY TO
FRIENDS AND NEIGHBORS AS WELL AS TO FAMILY.
AUNT POLLY AS THEY REFERRED TO HER ON HER
90TH BIRTHDAY WAS A SPRIGHTLY LOVABLE OLD
LADY; LAME BUT IN GOOD HEALTH. AUNT POLLY
DIED IN LATE MARCH 1882 WHEN SHE SUCCOMBED
TO PNEUMONIA. SHE WAS 93 YEARS OLD."

　　　THEN MY NEXT QUESTION TO THE HOST WAS,
"ARE THERE GHOSTS IN THE HOUSE?"

　　　"OH YES, SHE SAID, SEVERAL TIMES THE
GHOSTS HAVE LOCKED THE OUTSIDE SCREEN
DOORS SO I COULD NOT GET IN." THE HOST TOLD ME
THAT SHE HAD NEVER SEEN THE GHOSTS BUT
CERTAINLY FELT THEIR PRESENTS MANY TIMES
AND HEARD THEM OFTEN. THE HOST HAD AN
OFFICE IN THE BACK CORNER OF THE HOUSE AND
ACCORDING TO HER SHE WANTED TO STAY ON THE
GOOD SIDE OF THE GHOSTS SO EACH NIGHT BEFORE
SHE LEFT FOR HER OWN HOME SHE SAID SHE

ALWAYS SAID GOOD NIGHT TO THEM AND TOLD THEM TO HAVE A GOOD NIGHT.

JUST THEN THE CARETAKER CAME IN FROM OUT SIDE AND HE CHIMED IN, "YES, INDEED THERE ARE GHOST. I HAVE HEARD THEM AND SEEN THEM. THEY ARE DARK FIGURES AND THEY DO NOT FRIGHTEN ME. AUNT POLLY'S GHOST IS IN HER UPSTAIRS BEDROOM AND IT GIVES ME THE SHIVERS. AUNT POLLY HAD EMBROIDERED SAMPLER SHE HAD DONE IN THE DRAWER IN HER ROOM WITH SYMBOLS I DO NOT UNDERSTAND. THE ROOM WHERE AUNT POLLY SLEPT IS CREEPY."

THE HOST AGREED; THE CARETAKER TOLD US THAT HE STAYS OUT OF AUNT POLLY'S ROOM AWAY FROM THAT LADY BECAUSE HE DOES NOT TRUST HER.

THE HOST TOLD US THAT SHE LIVES ON THE OTHER SIDE OF TOWN IN A HOUSE BUILT IN 1840 AND IT IS WAS DEFINITELY HAUNTED ALSO. IN THIS CASE SHE TOLD US THAT SHE DOES NOT RECOGNIZE THE GHOST BUT SHE ASSURED US THAT HE APPEARS IN A TRENCH COAT AND BLACK TOP HAT. SHE TOLD US THAT SHE HAS SEEN HIM NUMEROUS TIMES.

THERE YOU HAVE IT; THE GHOSTLY SPIRITS OF DUXBURY ARE REAL TO SOME FOLKS. THIS IS ONLY A FEW OF THE STORIES THAT FREQUENT THE CONVERSATIONS OF THOSE WHO ARE WILLING TO LISTEN. A TALE YOU SAY; ONLY TO THOSE DISBELIEVERS! WOULD YOU BE WILLING TO VISIT FOR A FULL NIGHT IN ONE OF THOSE DARK HISTORIC HOMES WITH THE GHOSTS OF SOME OF OUR GONE BUT NOT FORGOTTEN ANCESTORS?

After leaving the John Alden house of 1653, we went looking for Myles Standish's monument reservation. I had heard that there was a statue of Myles Standish overlooking the bay. I assumed it would be a small statue no larger than the size of a man but to my big surprise when we arrived there, we saw a Myles Standish monument one hundred sixteen feet tall and a large statue of Captain Myles Standish standing on the top of this monument facing the bay. It was a tribute to the Pilgrim's military leader.

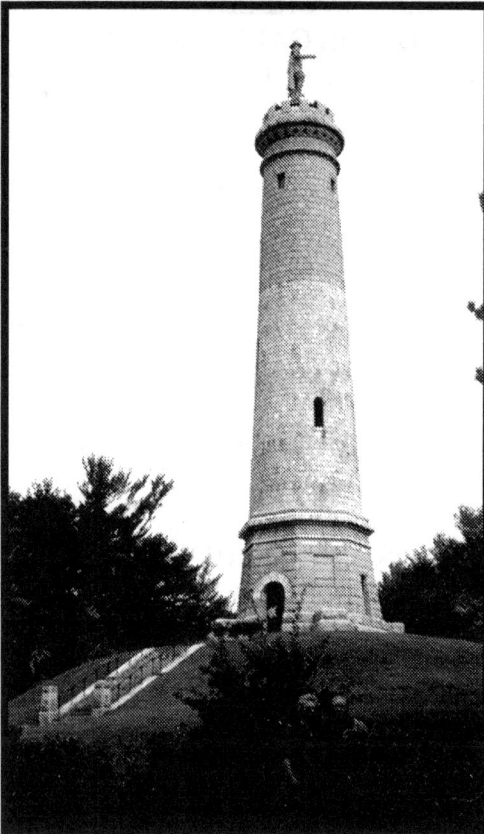

The photo I had taken of the monument is on the left. Louise and I (Willard) are standing in the shadows of this great monument.

Below an artists sketch of Capt. Myles Standish

From there we went on a hunt for the old burial grounds; our search was successful. After finding the grave stones it was easy to find Captain Myles Standish's grave because in the center of the grave yard we located a stone fence about two foot tall. It was built in a square and on the wall of each side was mounted a cannon pointing out so that all directions were covered. Then inside was his marked grave.

Also inside this square were gravestones of Captain

Myles Standish's daughter Lora Standish and a gravestone indicating his daughter-in-law, Mary Quincley Standish.

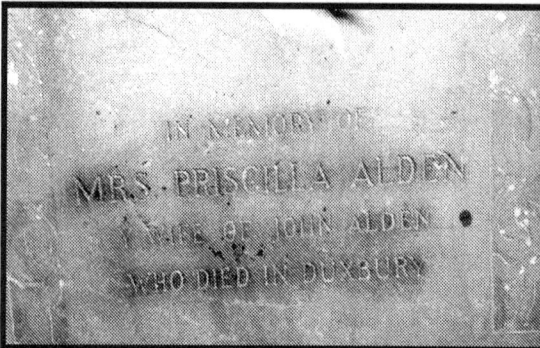

Photo left: By continuing our hunt, we found the grave markings of John and Priscilla Alden.

Later I was talking to a lady in a store in Plymouth about the grave markers of the Alden's and she told me that the bodies may not exactly be located where those markers are because the markers were installed there years later. There were other gravestones of Alden's there so I assume it is the area where the Alden's presently had been buried.

By this time it was getting late in the day so we made our way to the Days Inn in Middleboro, Ma. We made our home there for three days while doing all this investigating.

Following our stay there, we had reservations at a Days Inn in Boston. It was only a short drive into Boston but lots of traffic to contend with. Our hotel was situated across the river from Cambridge University. It was early in the day when we checked in at the hotel and after asking questions, we were told that the train stop going into Boston was only a short distance away. We decided to explore and took the city bus to the train station. The train took us right into the center of Boston where we could find a tour of the area. It was from there that we obtained tickets to ride the Blue Trolly Lines thru the inner Boston area.

These tickets on the Blue Trolley Lines were important as they gave us transportation to all the historical sites and we could get on and off all day within the city. The four of us, Louise and I (Willard) and Arnold and Lucille Steffens each bought tickets with 19 stops to get on and off as we pleased. It was perfect as we could get off, when we were ready to go on the trolley was only minutes apart, and we could easily catch the next one.

The first event was Paul Reveres famous midnight ride to alert the Minute Men that the English were coming during the Revolutionary War, April 18, 1775. Paul Revere first went to the old North Church and alerted everyone by a predetermined signal from the church tower; one if by land and two if by sea. We saw Paul Reveres home and statue of him and his horse at the old church tower. After that, we took the Blue Trolley and followed the Freedom Trail thru Boston getting off and on the trolley to view events.

After riding and viewing events for a couple of hours we decided to go get something to eat like their famous Boston Beans. We found a quaint restaurant and it was packed with customers but we were able to get a table and it was not long our food was served. I was so impressed with the taste of their beans that I will include the recipe here:

BOSTON BAKED BEANS
    2 lbs dry beans
    1 lb. salt pork
    8 tabl. Brown sugar
    2/3 cup molasses
    2 teasp. dry mustard
    4 teasp. salt
    ½ teasp. Ground black pepper
    1 medium sized onion chopped

Soak the beans overnight. In the morning parboil them for 10 minutes with a teaspoon of baking soda. Then run cold water through the beans in a colander or strainer. Dice the rind of salt pork into inch squares cut in half. Put half in the bottom of a 2 quart bean pot with the whole onion. Put the beans in the pot. Add the rest of the pork on top of the beans and mix other ingredients with hot water then pour over the beans. Bake in a 300 degree oven for six hours; adding a little water as necessary to keep the beans nice and moist.

      It was a wonderful day of sight seeing and with evening approaching, we found ourselves too exhausted to reverse our steps using train and bus so it was a treat to catch a taxi and ride in comfort back to our hotel.

      In the Cambridge, area of Boston is the home where poet Henry Wadsworth Longfellow lived. This home also served as George Washington's Revolutionary War headquarters.

      The next day was Sunday and we decided it was a perfect time to leave the city with only Sunday traffic and go north to Vermont. We followed the Apache trail into the world of fall colors. Talk about the majestic fall shades; we saw them all in the landscape. Even the stacks of pumpkins piled up at roadside stands were a beautiful sight.

We stayed all night in New Hampshire then traveled east to the Atlantic coast. As we drove north up the East Coast we stopped at a restaurant where they had shrimp; all you could eat for seven dollars and ninety- five cents. Arnold and I really had our fill of shrimp.

After Rockport we continued north up the East Coast to Portland, Me. The first thing we did was to drive eight miles out to Portland's Head Light Station where poet Henry Wadsworth Longfellow used to walk and got many inspirations for some of his poems like, "The Light House." He also wrote the "Courtship Of Myles Standish."

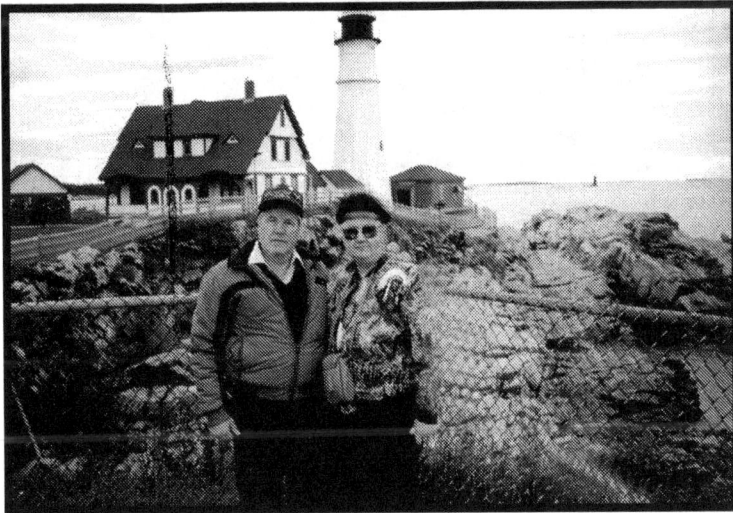

We posed above for a picture before leaving to drive back to Portland, Me.
Our journey was coming to an end but we had one more stop for the day

We were fortunate to be able to tour the Wadsworth Longfellow home. This was the boyhood home of Maine's famous poet, Henry Wadsworth Longfellow. The home had been built in 1785 by Henry's grandfather, General Peleg Wadsworth.

This family home is a true Maine landmark. Anne Longfellow Pierce, Henry's sister and the last resident of the house, bequeathed it to the Maine Historical Society in 1901.

The Wadsworth-Longfellow Home, Portland, Maine. Beautifully restored and preserved, this is the boyhood home of Maine's famous poet, Henry Wadsworth Longfellow. Built in 1785 by Henry's grandfather, General Peleg Wadsworth, this family home is a true Maine Landmark. It was bequeathed to the Maine Historical Society in 1901 by Anne Longfellow Pierce, Henry's sister and last resident of the house. The public can view the beautiful rooms, gardens and atmosphere which bring one back to another time...a wonderful part of our Maine adventure!

Henry Wadsworth Longfellow's genealogy line goes back to John and Priscilla Alden.

All the furnishings in the home had been preserved so we were fortunate to have this opportunity to view it all.

This was a great portrait of the famous poet.

HENRY WADSWORTH LONGFELLOW
(1807-1882 BY: CHARLES COLE, 1844

    We have all read Longfellow's poems in school and I
for one loved his style.

    The furnishings in the home were all of the era of the
Longfellow family. The deep wines were evident of the
favored colors of that period in time. There were many rooms
in the house; some for the worker that were employed.

We cannot leave this period of time without one last look at another family portrait of Henry Longfellow's sister.

Sister of Henry Wadsworth Longfellow
1830 portrait

Anne Longfellow Pierce
(1810-1901HENRY (1810-1901)

It was Louise's birthday and we celebrated the day by having dinner on one of the ships in the harbor. It was named Dimillo's floating restaurant. We all indulged in one of the famous Maine lobster meals.

The next morning we flew back to Kennewick, Wa. and home but not without wonderful memories. Especially, for me, were those memories that I could link with my own generation genealogy to the Standish and the Alden families.

ALDEN 1ST GENERATION
JOHN ALDEN AND PRISCILLA MULLINS FAMILY

We know very little about John Alden prior to the sailing of the Mayflower. Evidently, he wanted it that way because no positive information tying him to documented records can be found. We know that in the year 1620 he was a young man of about 21 years old. He was a tall blue eyed blonde who was very strong and of Scandinavian decent. He was the tallest man in the Colony. He was hired in South Hampton, England by Captain Christopher Jones of the Mayflower as part of his crew as a cooper. We also know that he received his skills as a carpenter, cabinetmaker and as a surveyor in England.

The in depth relationship from a genealogical point of view can be found in the index in the back of the book. John Alden was born they believe in England 1598 and died in Duxbury, Ma., Sept. 12, 1687-Married 1621. He was buried in the old burying grounds at Duxbury, Ma.

He married Priscilla Mullins-B-1602 in England. Priscilla died at Duxbury, Ma. and was buried in the old burying grounds at Duxbury, Ma.

William and Alice Mullins were born in England and came over on the Mayflower with Priscilla and her brother Joseph Mullins. There were two more children of William and Alice who were William and Sarah that stayed in England but went to Duxbury, Ma. at a later time.

The sadness of this is William and Alice Mullins with their son Joseph died the first winter at Plymouth, Ma. of the sickness that half of the passenger that came over on the Mayflower died with; mostly pneumonia.

Little is recorded of Priscilla Mullins except the famous poem written about her by Henry Wadsworth Longfellow about the courtship of Myles Standish when Captain Myles Standish lost his wife Rose he sent John Alden to the Mullin's house to ask William Mullins if he could come to court

Priscilla. When John asked William Mullins his reply was you must ask Priscilla. When she was called and John delivered the message Priscilla looked at John and said, "why don't you ask for yourself John?"

John's face got red and he left to go back to Capt. Myles Standish and deliver Priscilla's answer. Needless to say soon after that **JOHN ALDEN** and **PRISCILLA MULLINS** were married.

They had ten or eleven children; ten known Elizabeth, John, **JOSEPH**, Sarah, Jonathan, Ruth, Rebecca, Mary, Priscilla and David. Their first four children were born at Plymouth, Ma. The rest were born at Duxbury, Ma.

2ND GENERATION

From his father, John Alden, Joseph Alden obtained a parcel of land at Bridgewater, Ma. which he farmed and lived on for the rest of his life. He was one of the sons that probably helped his father, John Alden build his house for Priscilla in 1653 in Duxbury, Ma. Joseph was also a surveyor that probably accomplished all the surveying jobs around Bridgewater, Ma. Joseph was also a soldier in Capt. Myles Standish's fighting guard unit.

JOSEPH ALDEN and **MARY SIMMONS** had seven children, Sarah, Isaac, Joseph, Mercy, Hopestill, Elizabeth and **JOHN**, all born at Bridgewater, Ma.

3RD GENERATION

This **JOHN ALDEN** who was the grandson of John of the Mayflower inherited his father Joseph's homestead in West Bridgewater but he conveyed this to Isaac Johnson and moved to Middleboro, Ma. in 1700. One of his sons lived there for 102 years. His will remains on record and names his wife and 10 children. It gave to son John the homestead "to be used by his wife during her lifetime and other land to sons. The daughters received money. Thankful and Hannah received 50 pounds less than their equal portion. They already received so much of my estate."

The wife Hannah died before the completion of the estate and David Alden was appointed guardian for his brothers, John (14 years old) and also Ebenezer and Noah both minor age. John's will also specify the reserving of 20 acres to be used for a burying place perpetually for the family.

All of **JOHN ALDEN** and his wife **HANNAH WHITE'S** children were born at Middleboro, Ma. John Alden and Hannah White had thirteen children. The children were, Thankful, David, Priscilla, Hannah, **LYDIA**, Mary, Abigail, Joseph, John, Ebenezer, Samuel, Nathan and Noah.

NOTE: All bold typed names are direct descendents to the Ingrahams

CHAPTER IV

THE EDDYS

The Eddy homestead ties in with the earliest days of Massachusetts for it is on land bought from the Indians in 1661 by Samuel Eddy the Pilgrim that landed in Plymouth in 1630. The land has been held by Eddy progeny ever since.

The oldest of Samuel's four sons, John, moved to Martha's Vineyard from Plymouth and remained there. The next two Zachariah and Caleb moved to Swansea, Mass. after a few years in Middleboro. The youngest, Obadiah, remained in Middleboro to live and pass on the land to his descendants. As the first Eddy to remain in Middleboro he is

---

THE EDDY HOMESTEAD

Eddyville, Middleboro, Massachusetts

In 1962, descendants of the Eddy Pilgrims of 1630, and other Pioneer Eddys of the 1600's organized the Eddy Homestead Association to preserve this graceful, historic house and use it to display valuable family mementos that have been discovered over the years. Unlike many similar houses, which were originally the abodes of the wealthy aristocracy, the Eddy Homestead represents gracious country living of Zachariah Eddy, a country lawyer of fine character and practice. The house has been attractively restored since 1962, with many interesting exhibits now on display.

"There's a story that goes with it!" — is certainly true of the Eddy Homestead. It comes from the Eddy Genealogies that tell of family lore of 400 years ago. And Eddys helped make early history in five nearby towns in eastern Massachusetts, and thereafter in many parts of the U.S.A. Family mementos go back almost 400 years, each with its contribution of history or mystery that ties in with America's own history and growth. The story is there — for a fascinating hour or two, or for years of study.

AMERICA'S MOST HISTORIC EDDY HOME
WHERE GENEALOGY ADDS LIFE TO HISTORY

Built in 1803

honored by the memorial boulder and plaque on the green in front of the homestead that was erected in 1934.

The property passed from Obadiah through his son, Samuel and grandson, Zachariah to his great grandson, Joshua who distinguished himself as a captain in the Revolutionary War. The house of Joshua's

grandfather, Samuel, built in 1721 formerly stood where the homestead now stands. It was moved across the street to the south in 1803 to the present location. It was greatly enlarged many years later by Caleb Francis Eddy and is in good condition today. It is one of the oldest houses in town.

Capt. Joshua erected the homestead building in 1803 for his son, Zachariah who had been living in Bridgewater,

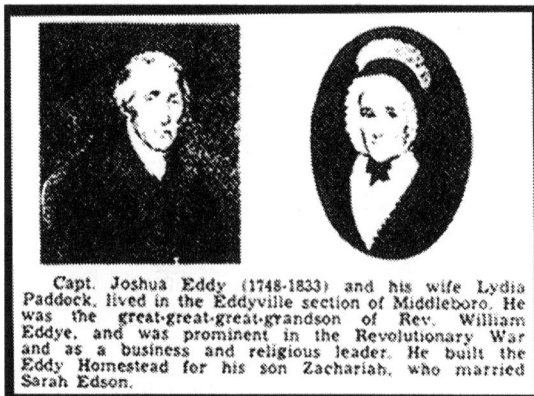

Capt. Joshua Eddy (1748-1833) and his wife Lydia Paddock, lived in the Eddyville section of Middleboro. He was the great-great-great-grandson of Rev. William Eddye, and was prominent in the Revolutionary War and as a business and religious leader. He built the Eddy Homestead for his son Zachariah, who married Sarah Edson.

Mass. He was then studying to become a lawyer. On

Zachariah's death in 1860 the property went to his daughter, Charlotte Eddy Pratt. She died in 1904 and left it to General Samuel Breek, the son of her sister, Sarah Amelia.
On the General's death in 1918 the place went to his son, Dr. Samuel Breek who lived and practiced in the Boston area and had already used it during the summers since 1904. After the doctor's death in 1926 some members of his family continued to live there.

THE EDDY COAT OF ARMS

Family tradition says that the Eddy Coat of Arms was inherited from Sir David Edie, who fought in the Crusades or Holy Wars in Jerusalem in the eleventh century. However the Reverend William Eddye (c 1560-1616) of Cranbrook, Kent, England is the earliest known Eddy ancestor. He was Vicar of Sr. Dunstan's Church there from 1591 till his death and much is known about him from the 80 pages that he wrote in the old Church Register while vicar. Thus Cranbrook has become a shrine for pilgrimages by his Eddy descendants in modem times. Rev. William's sons, Pilgrims John and Samuel,

arrived in Plymouth on October 29, 1630 on the ship
Handmaid. Two of William's daughter, Abigail and Anna also
came over in 1632 or so and married into the Benjamin and
Wines families.

ZACHARIA EDDY AND HIS LAW OFFICE
From the "Middleboro Gazette" October 13, 1922

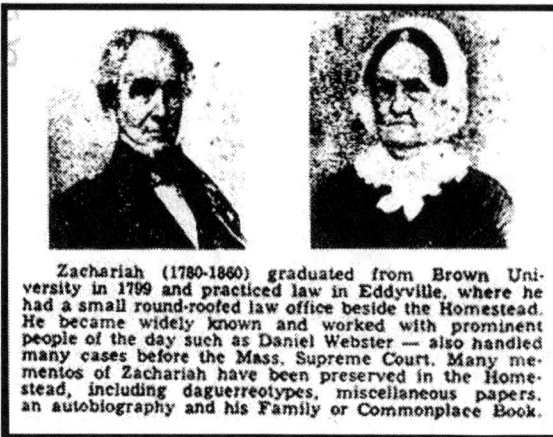

Zachariah (1780-1860) graduated from Brown University in 1799 and practiced law in Eddyville, where he had a small round-roofed law office beside the Homestead. He became widely known and worked with prominent people of the day such as Daniel Webster — also handled many cases before the Mass. Supreme Court. Many mementos of Zachariah have been preserved in the Homestead, including daguerreotypes, miscellaneous papers, an autobiography and his Family or Commonplace Book.

Zachariah Eddy, one of the most prominent lawyers in southeastern Massachusetts was born in 1780. He was graduated from Brown University in 1799 with the second honors of his class and taught school before he commenced the study of law in the office of Joshua Thomas, one of the leading lawyers in Plymouth. He was admitted to the Plymouth bar in 1806 and as a counselor in 1810. Such were his talents that soon after his admission as counselor he was acknowledged the leader of the bar in southeastern Massachusetts and in the intricacies of special pleading he had no equal in the state. He was a personal friend of Daniel Webster and often associated with him in different cases. The late Chief Justice Shaw said that he was on of the ablest lawyers in the state. Among his personal friends were John Quincy Adams, Judge Hubbard, Timoth G. Coffin, William Baylies, Marcus Morton and other prominent men. Something of the extent of his practice may be inferred from the fact that more than three hundred cases that he argued in the Supreme Court are given in the Mass. reports. At the height of his career he was offered a place in the Supreme Court of Massachusetts but declined. He died Feb. 14, 1860. Among the list of students who studied law in his office was the late Everett Robinson. Mr. Eddy's home and law office were in Eddyville. His residence, on the northerly side of the green at Eddyville is now the property of Dr. Samuel Breck one of his descendants and is known as "Pilgrim Farm". The law office still stands as he left it just north of the Homestead on Plympton Road (I 922).

Following is an article written by the author's wife, Louise Ingraham, after they had visited the Eddy home:

GHOST OF EDDY HOUSE

By: Louise Ingraham written Sept. 28, 1994

It was a pleasant afternoon when we arrived at the Eddy house in Middleboro, Mass. only to find the house was closed to visitors for the day. Willard, my husband, was researching ancestral lines to the Mayflower and had traced a linage to the Eddy family. My sister, Lucille and brother-in-law, Arnold Steffens were also interested in the Plymouth ancestors therefore we were all delighted when the caretaker offered to open for a tour of the old house. Zacharia Eddy, the owner of the house, had lived there until he died at the age of 79 in 1835. The caretaker lived in the carriage house near by and he related incidents when strange footsteps and noises came from the attic. He said even sometimes the ghost was known to tap a shoulder or brush the face. Yet the caretaker never saw the ghost. Others had ghostly experiences also as related by the caretaker.

One time when the care taker was in the hospital and his wife was alone, according the care taker, "lots of antics

took place that although not frightening were disturbing to my wife."

The caretaker and his wife having lived several years in the remodeled carriage house on the property say they frequently heard strange footsteps and noises in the attic at night. One night the caretaker's grandson, Justin, age 7 stayed over night with grandpa and grandma. This was soon after the caretaker had moved into the carriage house. During the night Justin became frightened and ask grandpa and grandma if he could sleep in their room.

Grandpa and grandma had also heard the noises in the attic and grandpa investigated finding nothing but allowed Justin to stay the rest of the night in their room. The next morning Justin was still frightened and neither grandparent could get out of him what it was that he had seen except that the occurrence had indeed frightened him. A few days later grandpa took Justin through the Eddy house and asked Justin if the ghost looked like any of the pictures on the wall. Justin pointed to the picture of Zacharia Eddy and said that was who he had seen.

Now this is the story of the Eddy house ghost who is said still today to rustle around and walks in the attic of the old carriage house. The caretaker will vouch to this and so the story of the Eddy house ghost lives on.

EDDY CEMETERIES
AS RELATED TO MIDDLEBORO

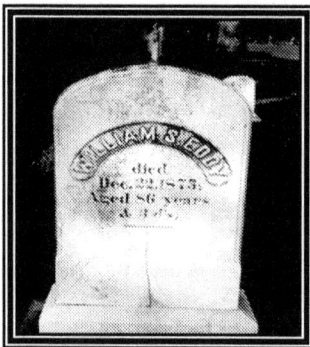

Swansea Cemetery

Perhaps the best known cemetery to all Eddys is the Swansea Cemetery in Swansea, Mass., for there is the burying place of Samuel Eddy, the Pilgrim, his wife, Elizabeth Savery, and several of their children.

On March 19, 1696 Zachariah, son of Samuel and Elizabeth deeded to their son, Zachariah Jr., 20 acres of land but excluded the following: "excepting and reserving the burying place on the premises which is to lie and remain as a burying place for and to families of the said Eddys and for such of the neighbors as the said Eddys shall admit forever." This exception was carried down by deed for three generations and the right of ownership established.

Left pretty much ignored over the years that intervened, it was "rediscovered" and confirmed as the burial place of Samuel and Elizabeth by Ruth Story Devereaux Eddy, Eddy family genealogist in the late 1920s. Through careful research and much personal effort by many, the "Burying Place" was restored. The tangled weeds and scrub, accumulated over the years of neglect were cleared out and the headstones were raised and numbered. The area was surveyed and the lot lines established with the Swansea Dye Works.

Still rustic in nature, as well it should be, the cemetery is maintained by the Eddy Family Association through a fund that was established in the 1930s and is still receiving contributions. Despite the ravages of nature over the years and the loss of many area trees, "Old Monarch" the gnarled oak, still stands at the crest of the knoll constantly guarding the resting place of our ancestors.

THE OLD SMALLPOX CEMETERY

At the comer of Brook and Soule streets, near the Plympton line and about 5 minutes from the homestead is the Old Smallpox Cemetery which was established in 1777-1778 for the burial of those who succumbed to this disease during the terrible epidemic of that period for it was thought unsafe to bury them in the other cemeteries. There are only 9 headstones in this small burying place but there are IO names inscribed on the markers for the two Eddys are buried in the same grave.

Below is Willard searching through the Small Pox cemetery for names.

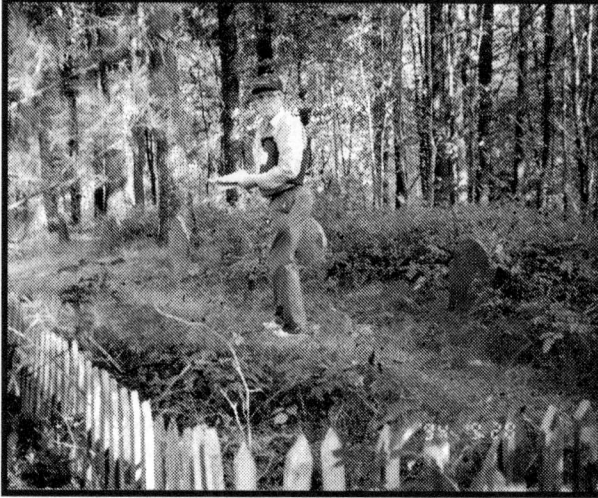

Lieutenant Zachariah Eddy, father of Joshua, died of the disease on December 6, 1777 in the 65th year of his life. His epitaph is as follows:

A husband kind and good, a parent dear to all obliging and to all sincere True to his God
The orphans friend and guide
He lived beloved and lamented died

Inscribed below this is the name of the son of Lieutenant Zachariah and Mercy Eddy, Zachariah Jr., who died of smallpox at the age of 25 while serving in the Revolutionary War at Mt. Independence.

The cemetery across from the Dean farm is easily passed by for the area is now completely surrounded by houses. However the cemetery itself is untouched. A little picket fence surrounds it, wild blueberries wind around the edges and each year an American flag is placed there by "those who remember."

CHURCH ON THE GREEN

Religion was the nucleus for survival for our forefathers and their families. It was basically for freedom of religion that they came to America and it was because of this new-found freedom that they endured the hardships of the New World and constantly gave thanks to the Lord in their every word and deed. It is no wonder, therefore, that the majority of the records of that period, those that are still evident today, are all highlighted in one way or another by praise and thanksgiving.

The "Church on the Green" above was organized December 26, 1694 as "The First Church Of Christ In Middleboro." Only thirty-one parishes in the state of Mass. are older than this first parish in Middleboro, now called the First Congregational Church.

Its organizers were the sons of the Pilgrim settlers, none of whom were transferred from the parent church at Plymouth. Eight were original members of the "Twenty-six Men's Purchase" (the first purchase of land from the Indians) and all were living at the time of the town's incorporation in 1669. Among this original group of organizers was Pilgrim Samuel Eddy.

The first church was built in 1680 by the town and sat about a mile east of the present structure on Plymouth Street. It was an enclosed building having no windows and only rough wooden benches and served its worshippers for twenty years. In 1701 it was sold at auction for 5 pounds and 2 shillings. The second church building, erected in 1700, was directly across the street from the present "Church on the Green." It served as the parish for over forty years. This church as "thirty-six feet by thirty and sixteen stud." It had two ridge poles and four gable ends. In 1745 the roof was taken off and a pitched roof put on, the same year that the third meeting house was build on the "Upper Green." The parish had separated into two meeting; one held by the "old lights" of which Captain Joshua was a member and the other by "new lights" of which his wife, Lydia was a member. The "old lights" broke up in 1754 soon after the old building was sold.

CEMETERY AT THE GREEN

Left is photo: This beautiful burying ground, the final resting place of many of our ancestors including Captain Joshua and Lydia Eddy was established as the "Parish Burying Ground," on March 3 0, 1717 when about two acres were purchased from James Soule by approximately 60 people including Obadiah Eddy. Although Nemasket Hill Cemetery across from where the last parish house was located (on Plymouth Street) is the oldest cemetery in Middleboro the land having been purchased from the Indians in 166 1, many prominent persons from the early days of Middleboro are buried in the "Green Cemetery" as many call it.

General Samuel Breck, in the early 1900s was the leader in the movement to incorporate the cemetery. Those interested had been working for this purpose for some time as there were several trust funds available. At a meeting in 1909 it was voted to incorporate to buy additional land for all present lots were in use and to adopt bylaws for the corporation. Once this was done, General Breck compiled a two-part book listing all persons buried in the "Cemetery at the Green" with pertinent data on each one. Since then, another two-part book has been printed which lists deaths prior to 1850 after 1850 and locations of each lot. These books are available at the Middleboro Public Library.

Situated on a gently sloping knoll in one part and the flats in another this cemetery which was only about ten minutes from the Zachariah Eddy homestead, is a spot of peaceful solitude. Time spent wandering among the old headstones points out the solemnity given to the deceased. Yet the dry humor of the epitaphs shows the openness and love for the departed. It is well worth your time to visit this cemetery, especially if you have ancestors there.

Samuel Eddy:

Samuel's home was near that of his father in Eddyville in the house now known as the Clark house. He was admitted to the church June 12, 1735. Lydia also was a member. In 1745 Samuel's name was on a list of those who agreed to build a new meeting house. In 1746 he was appointed executor to the estate of John Alden since both executors named by John in his will, namely wife, Hannah, and son, David, were dead.

Samuel also died before he made his report and his eldest son Nathan was appointed in his place. The probate records contain an inventory of the possessions of Samuel

showing the value. Samuel's brother Zachariah was appointed
to administer his estate. When he filed his account the estate
was valued at l-245; the house and the most westerly part of the
land where the house stands was worth l-145 and the easterly
part that is separated by a cart way was valued at l-100.
Note: the letter before the numbers represents value at English
lbs.

Some fifty years later a person who knew him well said
of him that he was among the best hopes of the church that he
had joined at an early age. We find his name in every important
connection and especially in the tumulus times.

On September 28, 1994 Louise and I (Willard Ingraham) with Arnold and Lucille Steffens stopped at the Eddy homestead near Middleboro, Mass. I talked to the caretakers and they graciously allowed us to tour the homestead after they learned I am a direct descendent of the Eddys that lived there.

The following pictures add clarity and understanding of Eddyville and the Eddys that lived there.

The Eddy House below

Above is how the Eddy house looked in 1994 when we toured it.

Louise and I (Willard Ingraham) in front of Eddy house.

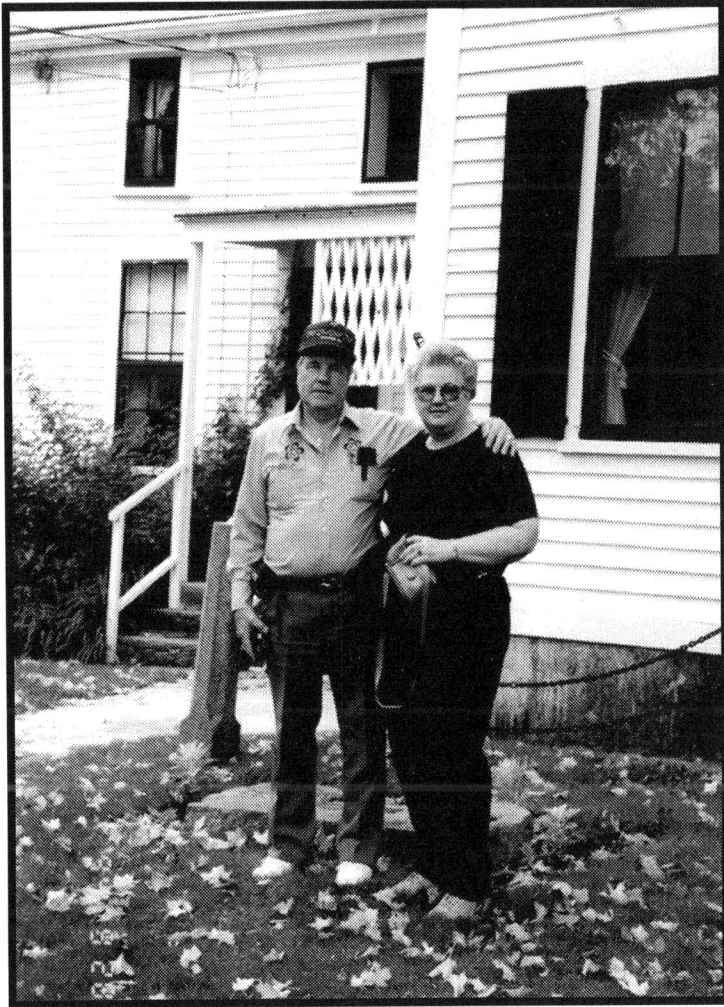

It was in the fall when we visited this homestead. The fall leaves were everywhere and it added to the atmosphere of a historical site.

Above is a photo of the homestead in 1982

Above Zachariah Eddy and headstone, Zachariah and Sarah Eddy

Map below shows Middleboro, Mass. with arrow. Also
note that
Plympton,
South
Duxbury and
Plymouth are
all on the
same map.

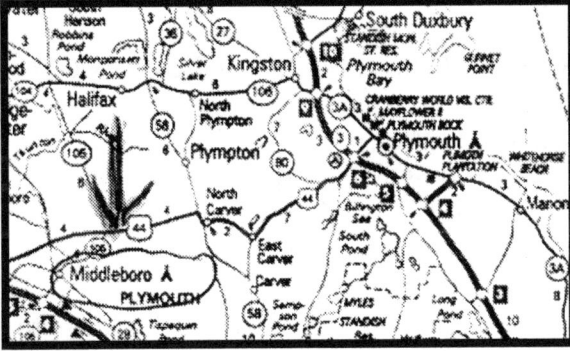

4TH GENERATION

SAMUEL EDDY-B- 1710-Middleboro,Married Lydia Alden-
D-Nov.3,1746-age36-Middleboro,Mass. Parents-Samuel Eddy-
Melatiah Pratt
Lydia Alden-B-Dec.18,1710-D-Mar. 1,1803 -age 92 years
Parents-John Alden and Hannah White
Children all born-Middleboro,Mass. Of SAMUEL EDDY and
LYDIA ALDEN
NATHAN EDDY-B-Sept.8,1733
Joshua Eddy B-Mar.6,1734-d.y.-
Susannah Eddy-B-Nov.22,1736-D-July29,1817-Not M.
Mary Eddy-B-May 9,1740-D.y-
Samuel Eddy-B-Jan12,1742
Seth Eddy-B-Feb. II, 1 744 d.y-
    After Samuel's death and 36 years old Lydia married
April 27,1792 to John Fuller-B-Mar.20,1692. He was the son
of John and Mercy (Nelson)Fuller.
    All Eddys that can trace their descendents back to
Samuel and Lydia(Alden)Eddy are eligible for membership to
the Mayflower Society.

5TH GENERATION

NATHAN EDDY-B-Sept.8,1733-Middleboro,Ma-D-Feb.28,1804-Pittsfield,Vt.
Parents-Samuel Eddy-Lydia Alden
He married EUNICE SAMPSON-B-May,l5,1737-Plympton,Ma.-D-Mar.25,1802-Pittsfield,Vt.
Her parents-Ephraim Sampson and Abigail Horrell

Children of Nathan Eddy and Eunice Sampson-B-Middleboro
Ephraim Eddy-B-Dee.21,1759
Lydia Eddy-B-Sept. 16,1762
Hannah Eddy-B-Feb.1,1766
Nathaniel Eddy-B-July 6,1768
Nathan Eddy-B-April 2l,1771
ISAAC EDDY-B-June 24,1774-M-Betsy McCary- Aug. 12,1796
Zachariah Eddy-B-Nov.18,1778

As Eunice Sampson was the granddaughter of Isaac and Lydia (Standish) Sampson and and since Lydia Standish was the daughter of Alexander and Sarah (Alden) Standish and granddaughter of Myles and Barbara Standish; all Eddys who can trace their descendents to Nathan and Eunice (Sampson)Eddy are eligible to the Mayflower Society through both Nathan and Eunice.

6th GENERATION

ISAAC EDDY

Soon after his birth Isaac's parents went to Vermont and finally settle in Woodstock. After his marriage he moved to Pittsfield, Vt. He became a leading citizen of that place. He was a justice of the peace and also served several terms in the Vermont assembly. In 1802 he was in the clothier business, then a merchant, but his position as scribe in the little church in

Pittsfield that had been formed in 1803 with sixteen members soon developed. He was forty-four years of age when he was licensed to preach. He then moved to Locke,N.Y. in 1824. He settled in Jamestown, N.Y. He was known as "good father Eddy" in the town. In his church at Jarnestown,N.Y. a tablet has been placed to his memory.

Isaac Eddy-B-Middleboro, Mass, June 24,1774-D- June 26,1833-at Jarnestown, N.Y. Parents were Nathan Eddy and Eunice Sampson. He married Aug.12,1796, Woodstock, Vt. to Betsy McCary. She was born Sept. 7, 1772 at Lyme, Conn.-d-Feb.16,1863

Children born Woodstock, Vt.

Children of **ISAAC EDDY** and **BETSY(MCCARY)EDDY**

Elizabeth Eddy-B-June 5,1797

EUNICE EDDY-B-Dec.29,1799-m.Alvah Brown

Isaac Eddy-B-Nov.29,1801

William McCary Eddy-B-Sept.16,1803

Nathaniel Eddy-B-Nov.29,1805

Elmina Eddy-B-Aug.10, 1807

Safford Eddy-B-April 15,1810

Hiram Eddy-B-Mar. 17,1813

Zecheriah Eddy-B-Dec. 19,1815(he changed his name to Zachary)

7TH GENERATION

Eunice Eddy: She married Alvah Brown, Mar. 8, -1821, Locke, N. Y., D. Dec. 29,1860, Parents – Daniel Brown and Steadman Brown

Children of **ALVAH BROWN and EUNICE EDDY**

Epharaim Eddy Brown-b-Jan.20,1822 -Groton, N.Y.

Russell Meary Brown b., June 13, 1823, Locke N. Y.

Amos King Brown, b., July 9,1825, Locke, N.Y.

Williarn Eddy Brown b., Feb. 22,1828

Albert Alfonzo Brown b., Dec. 25, 183 0, Ellicot, N.Y.

Safford Zachary Brown b., Oct. 1, 1833, Kiantone, N.Y.

MARY ELIZABETH BROWN-b-Aug.14, 1836-Kiantone,
N.Y.
Charles Henry Brown-b-June 27, 1839
     Alvah Brown was bom at Rensselaerville, N.Y. He was
a farmer. Daniel Brown and Steadman Brown are Alvah
Browns parents. Alvah and Eunice son, Charles Henry, born
1839, m. Mary Louise Hunn, Oct. 14, 1869, born- m
Oct.19,1851. They had a son Cory Don Williams Brown, b.
Sept. 28, 1874, married June 17,1896, Gertrude Heloise
Pressnell, b. Feb. 7,1877.
Gertrude and Cory Don Wn Brown children:
Donald Cory Don Brown b., June 24, 1899
Leonard Frank Brown b., Feb. 17, 1902
Bonnie Benjamin Brown, b., Feb. 18, 1911
Doris Gertrude Brown b., June 15, 1913

EDDY ANCESTRY OF MYRTLE COWLES INGRAHAM

1. Rev. Wm. EddyVicar of the church of St. Dunstan of the town of Crambrook of the county of Kent, England. He was educated at the Trinity College in Cambridge where he was graduated with a Bacheler of Arts in 1583. He is buried in the church yard where he served for 26 years. Two of his sons came to America on the ship "Handmaid" and landed in Plymouth in 1630. The two sons were Samuel and John Eddy.

2. Samuel Eddy-M-Elizabeth Savory

3. Obadiah Eddy-M-Bennet Ellis

4. Samuel Eddy-M-Melatiah Pratt

5. Samuel Eddy-M-Lydia Alden

6. Nathan Eddy-M-Eunice Sampson-descendent of Myles Standish

7. Isaac Eddy-M-Betsy McCary

8. Eunice Eddy-M-Alvah Brown

9. Mary Elizabeth Brown-M-Demarcus LeRoy Cowles

10. Myrtle Cowles-M-Chauncey Ingraham

MARY ELIZABETH BROWN was born on Aug. 14, 1837 in the town of Kiantone, Chuataugua County, New York in 1857. She moved with her parents **ALVAH BROWN** and **EUNICE EDDY** to Lee County, Ill. on April 6, 1857.

His father Rev. Remember Joshua Cowles was born in Elmira, New York. His wife Sybil Might was born in Chester County, Massachusetts. At the age of 12 she moved to Byron Genessee County, New York where she married R.J. Cowles at the age of 16. Left is photo of Mary Elizabeth and Demarcus Leroy Cowles. Their first home was in Mightville and later Sugar Grove, Pennsylvania. He was a Baptist minister, school teacher and singer. She was a mother of 13 children and raised Rachel Cowan, a granddaughter when her mother died of typhoid fever. Rachel's daughter Florence Norton lives in Minneapolis, Mn.

101

This is the lineage as far back as 1615 in England.
1. John Cowles-B-1615-D-1662 (came to Mass. 1635
2. John Cowles-B-1645-D-1711
3. Jonathan Cowles-B-1670-D-1756
4. John Cowles-B-1700-D-1745
5. Capt. John Cowles-B-1737-D-1811
6. Corp. John Cowles-B-1757-D-1830
7. Remember John Cowles-B-1796-D-1874
8. Demarcus LeRoy Cowles-B-1834-D-1925

DEMARCUS LEROY COWLES (one of Rev. R.J.
Cowles 13 children) was born in the parsonage in Sugar Grove,
Penn. on Oct. 5, 1834. He worked three years as an apprentice
to the carpenter trade and two years of the Big Woods, a
shingle maker. In the spring of 1857 he married Miss **MARY
ELIZABETH BROWN** at Dixon, Ill. He learned of the
opportunities of Minnesota and moved to Manterville, Dodge
County, Mn. And they settle on a farm about the middle of
April of the same year. They had 5 children (3 boys and 2
girls).
Ardellie Cowles married Wm. Kellogg
Eddy Jerome Cowles married Cora Vandenhyde
Fred Jay Cowles married Louesa Orcutt
Willis Eugene Cowles married Elsie Peck
Myrtle June Cowles married Chancey Ingraham
In the year of 1900 Demarcus retired from his farm and
moved to West Concord, Mn. His wife Mary Elizabeth passed
away June 29, 1909. On July 1920 Demarcus moved to
Sowtell, Ca. and died there March 30, 1925. He was buried in
West Concord Cemetery, Mn.
It was early in 1864 that Demarcus L. Cowles had enlisted
in Co.K-2D-Calvary, Mn. It was from exposure and lack of
proper treatment that he was placed in the hospital and was
given an honorable discharge and sent home on the ground of
physical disability.

It was on December 30, 1873 in Dodge County, Milton Township seven miles north of Mantorville, Mn. In a two story farm house (pictured below) that Myrtle June Cowles was born. She was the fifth child of five children born in that house; two girls and three boys. They were the children of Demarcus LeRoy Cowles and Mary Elizabeth Brown.

Looking back at the reason Demarcus moved his family in 1857 to Minnesota it was for opportunities that he had heard was good there. Their farm was north of Mantorville, Mn and all five of their children grew up on this farm. It was during early times when Indians still roved in bands through the county.

Much of the information I will be writing about came from Myrtle June Cowles who was my (Willard Ingraham's) grandmother. The first memories that Myrtle could recall was when she was four years old. It was her first Christmas tree in her school house. That Christmas she received her first doll. The doll was tied in a little rocking chair with blue ribbons on it. She said she just loved that doll and rocking chair, "they were so pretty."

The same year that Myrtle was four years old there was much sadness for her because her Aunt Thankful Cowles passed away. Her aunt was lying in a coffin which left quite an impression on such a young girl who had loved her Aunt Thankful so much. Myrtle said, **"Oh, how I missed her."**

In the 1880s at Mantorville, Dodge County Minnesota there was only four months of school in the winter for the older children and only three months in the summer for the smaller children.

Below is a photo of Myrtle at age 3 years.

Myrtle said that the summer when she was six years old the teacher had a picnic the last day of school. She told her story, **"we had to travel by horse and buggy for fifteen miles to get there. My parents took my brother Willis and I both to this pot luck dinner. Other schools also participated at this once a year- get together.**

For entertainment they had different children get up front of the people there and speak their poems and jingles that they had prepared in advance. To this day I remember when it was my turn I got up to speak my piece and as I stood there I was so scared that our school Supt. who was one quarter Indian and so nice. He sat right behind me.

I still remember the piece that I spoke, it went like this:

Don't send me to school this afternoon
 I'd rather stay here and play
Too bad to leave my dolly so soon
And study hard every day

The Supt. Told me afterwards that he thought that was the best piece spoken that day and that made me feel so good when he told me that even though I was shaking with fear."

Myrtle goes on to say, "on December 4th when I was eight years old my Grandma Brown passed away. She was 84 years old. She was also Eunice Eddy Brown and the year would have been 1882.

That was the same winter my Pa bought me my first pair of overshoes and my new red leggings. I was so delighted to have these nice warm clothes. From that time on I started to go to school winters and summers. The winters in Minnesota were awful cold with very deep snow.

The spring after my 10th birthday the Dr. told my Pa to take Willis, my brother, to another climate for he was sickly. The Dr. thought that California would be a better place for Willis to live because of his bad health.

Note: Left is a photo taken years later of Willis and Elsie Cowles in California.

Myrtle continues her story: On our way west we stopped off at Flandrew, South Dakota where my sister

Ardille who had married William Kellog lived. In a few days Willis began to feel better so my folks decided to stay there for a while. My Pa, Demarcus Cowles, was a logger and a carpenter so he obtained a tree claim there in South Dakota and began to work it.

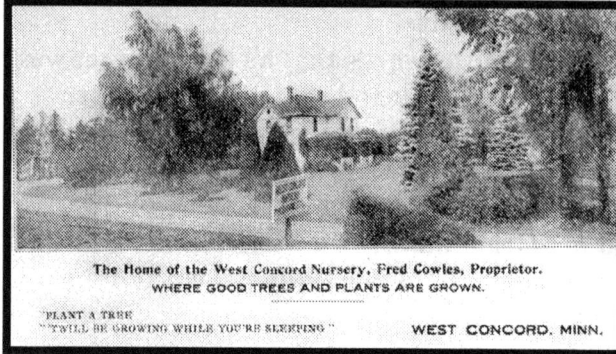

The Home of the West Concord Nursery, Fred Cowles, Proprietor.
WHERE GOOD TREES AND PLANTS ARE GROWN.

'PLANT A TREE
"TWILL BE GROWING WHILE YOU'RE SLEEPING "   WEST CONCORD. MINN.

Left is a photo of a tree planting farm owned by Mrytles brother Fred Cowles.

Mrytle goes on with her story; The first summer we lived there Pa was hired to build a big skating rink in the town four miles from our home. Everything was going well for everybody and Pa sent word back to Mantorville for my brother Fred to bring the household furniture. The following summer Pa built a house and barn on his tree claim.

That fall we went to Brookings, South Dakota to visit my cousins. We crowded five of us in a two seat buggy pulled by two horses. On our trip back home we stopped in Tracy Minnesota to spend the night in the hotel but wouldn't you know it that the next morning when we woke up it was so cold and snowing so much that Pa decided to put Ma, (Mary Elizabeth) Willis and I on the train to Kasson, Minnesota and Pa and Fred would drive the horse and buggy home when they would get a break in the weather.

When our train arrived in Kasson, Minnesota we were lucky to find a neighbor of ours (Art Mutchler) had come to town for a barrel of apples. Our neighbor came in a wagon pulled by a team of horses with a wood rack on the wagon. He let us ride in the wood rack standing up leaning on the barrel of apples all the way home.

Below is a photo of Mr. and Mrs. Ed Cowles; Ed is a brother of Myrtle Cowles.

1943

Mr. and Mrs. E. J. Cowles
West Concord, Minnesota
60th Wedding Anniversary
September 20, 1883 - 1943

Open House, September 19th
2:00 to 5:00   7:00 to 9:00

My brother, Ed Cowles was still living at home place back at Mantorville, Minnesota. He was living on the home place while the rest of the family was in South Dakota. The following spring Ed moved his family to South Dakota on Myrtle's father's tree claims where later Ed bought the tree claim from his father."

Myrtles story goes on, "In 1892 we celebrated my Ma and Pa's 35th wedding anniversary with a surprise party. We were now living back in our home in Mantorville, Minnesota. My brother, Ed, came from the tree claim in South Dakota.

I was 19 years old then and I asked Ma to sew a dress for me. I went into the kitchen and made a big fruit cake, a layer cake and some cookies then I hid them so no one

would get into them until we needed them for the party.
When my brother, Ed, came it was so cold he froze his
cheeks and they cracked open. That evening the neighbors
brought a pretty hanging lamp and a rocking chair then
hid them in the front room. When all the people arrived
they opened up the parlor doors and presented the gifts to
Ma and Pa.

Ma began to worry what she would feed the people at
the party but I told Ma don't worry I have baked a lot of
stuff for this party. It was a nice party and I'll always
remember it.

I went to school with a young man that I was seeing and
would get together every once in a while to the point we
became very fond of each other.

Note below is an important family photo of the Cowles
and includes Chauncey Ingraham.

They are as follows: Back row left to right is Ardille
and husband Wm Kellogg, Eddie Cowles, Cora
Vanderhyde and Willis Cowles. Center left is Mother
Mary Elizabeth, Demarcus Cowles and Fred Cowles.
These make up Mrytle Cowles family. In the front row is
Myrtle and Chauncey Ingraham.

Sept. 1892 I went to visit my Aunt Mary Brown who was a dress maker. I stayed and worked for her for four months but my mind kept going back to this young man that I wanted to be with. Finally I made up my mind that I was going to marry this young man on Jan. 9th. I left Aunt Mary's and went to Dodge Center, Mn. That is located a few miles from Mantorville, Mn where I met my one and only Chauncey Ingraham and his sister Mary."

That same evening of Jan. 9, 1893 **CHAUNCEY LEE INGRAHAM** and **MYRTLE JUNE COWLES** married. WE have followed the genealogy line from the Aldens and the Standish families and now I will be talking about the Ingraham families. First I will take you back to the earlier Ingraham families to Chauncey Ingraham and go on from there.

We find that David F. Ingraham was born, we think, in Shoemaker, N.Y., Dec. 3, 1824 to parents Clyde and Chloe Ingraham. David died in Mantorville, Mn., Dec. 15, 1881 and was buried in the Evergreen Cemetery, Mantorville, Mn. He married Sophia, born 1823 in Wales, Great Britian. David and Sophia were married in 1845. We are not sure how many

children they had. We do know that they had two children in Ohio, George D and Charles H. Ingraham. George was born Dec. 11, 1846. Charles was born 1849. The family then moved to Mantorville, Mn. in 1857. More children were born in Mantorville, Mn.

Above is Emma Amanda George D. Ingraham brother of Charles H. Ingraham. George D. Ingraham grew up in Mantorville, Mn. and married Emma Amanda Calhoun on Dec. 16, 1868. They had two girls, Bertha and Grace. Emma died

May 16, 1906 and is buried at Evergreen Cemetery at
Mantorville, Mn.

George D. Ingraham was inducted into the Army Feb. 6,
1864 and assigned to B Sixth Regiment. He was discharged
May 18, 1865 and went on to become a railroad engineer.
After 1910, in California, he married Margaret Skinner. On
May 26, 1925 he died at the National Soldiers Home, Sawtelle,
Ca. and was buried at the National Cemetery at Sawtelle, Ca.

Charles H. Ingraham also grew up in Mantorville, Mn. and
in 1870 at the age of 21 he married Edna L. Strong.

Left is Edna Strong's photo.

Edna was born in 1852 and was married at the age of 18 to Charles. They are my great grandparents. From that union two children were born. Chauncey Lee Ingraham, my grandfather and Mary Ingraham. Chauncey Lee Ingraham was born Oct. 28, 1868 in Dodge County a few miles North of Mantorville, Minnesota in a log house. It was located near the old Casner Place, a short distance from where Myrtle June Cowles lived.

Photo below in later years: is left to right: Pearl Leeper,

half sister to Chauncey Ingraham and Mary a sister of Chauncey next is Myrtle and Chauncey Ingraham and on the right is Lyle Ingraham

The photo at left is of Edna Strong with Chauncey and Mary Ingraham when they were little. Chauncey's sister, Mary was born April 18, 1872 at Mantorville, Mn. She lived for years at Mantorville, Mn. In later years she moved to California and lived to the age of 86. She never married and was buried at Rose Hill Memorial Park, Whittier, Ca.

It is my understanding that about 1876 Charles H. Ingraham left his family leaving his wife Edna with two small children. Chauncey would have been about eight years old at that time. From that time on life became tough for Chauncey because in 1879 his mother, Edna, died.

Chauncey was 11 years old and his sister 7 years old. Some of the family took his sister but Chauncey was old enough to work at 11 years old so he was sold as a slave. At that time by law it was legal because he was an orphan. I certainly would have loved to talk to him about those years. I do know that he learned how to defend for himself at a young age because I know of some of those times when he grew up.

Chauncey was a small man; about five foot six inches tall but what he lacked in size he made up in speed. He was strong and well built and fast as lightening as some 200 lb. men found out. He would never give up and landed some of his opponents in the hospital. He never went looking for trouble but some men miscalculated him because of his small size and it was soon known that he was not one to tangle with.

Getting back to Chauncey's mother; she died at Mantorville, Mn. and was buried at St. Charles or Winona, Mn. a close distance from Mantorville, Mn. She was only 27 years old at the time of her death.

Years later it was discovered where Charles H. Ingraham had gone. My grandpa, Chauncey, heard he was farming near Michigan, North Dakota (above is a photo of that town). This was years later but Chauncey was still mad as hops for his father, Charles, to have left them when he was so young and caused so much hardship to all of them afterwards.

Chauncey made a remark to someone once that if he did go see his father he would have it out with him for leaving them. He was quickly told by the person that also knew his father Charles that he didn't think that would be a good idea because Charles was also some one who knew how to take care of himself. Chauncey did go to see his father sometime later but not much was found out about that visit.

This is what happened to Charles H. Ingraham when he left his family in Minnesota. He went to Michigan, North Dakota and there met Lucretia June Shipton.

June's photo is at left.

Charles had another family with her. There were seven children, two boys and five girls. They were Charles Eugene, Jessie Evelyn, Nellie Pearl, Lucy Blanche, George Robert, Ella May and Ethel Ingraham.

One of the boys grew up to be a good violinist and the other boy became a school professor and ended up in Seattle. There is speculation that he was the one that started the Ingraham University in Seattle.

One of the girls, Ella M, Ingraham, married Fred Wright who was a cousin of the Wright Brothers, Orville and Wilbur who built the first airplane that made a successful flight on Dec. 17, 1903 at Kill Devil Hills near Kitty Hawk, N.C.

Below is a photo op the Wright Brothers were in with their famous flight.

Celebrating a century of flight

Ella and Fred Wright had six children. They were George Montman, Edith Pearl, Clarence, Fred Leon, Lee and Glendon Wright. All of the family was born in Michigan, North Dakota and ended up at Auburn, Washington.

Our family, (Louise and I (Willard Ingraham) spent numerous times visiting George and Clarence Wright and families in Auburn, Washington over the years. In fact one of our trips was overnight at the George Wright's home before we went to the opening of the World's Fair in Seattle. George also came to Prosser to visit Lyle and Gena Ingraham and families.

I am inserting a nice photo of Fred and Ella (Ingraham) Wright. Ella is a half sister to Chauncey Ingraham.

Below is a photo of the Wrights: Left to right; Glenn, Leon, George, Clarence and Lee with parents Ella and Fred.

.Charles H. Ingraham again left this family and Claude Ingraham, Chauncey's son, talked to a man who said there was a Charles Ingraham in Arkansas who had a family there.

Now you know a little more about the previous Ingrahams and I will take you back to Chauncey and Myrtle Ingraham to find out what happened to them. From here on as the author, (Willard Ingraham) I know most all of the people I will be writing about.

My grandmother, Myrtle Ingraham has more to say about her life beginning two days after CHAUNCEY and MYRTLE got married. Myrtle goes on with her story, "**on Jan. 11, 1893 we took the train to Minneapolis, Mn. where Chauncey had a job. We lived with his cousin until March then moved into our own apartment on Lindale Ave. That summer I** took care of his aunt Martha who had fallen and broken her hip. Then I went to Kasson, Mn. to visit with my parents. After my visit I returned to Chauncey.

Chauncey changed jobs and was driving a paint wagon. We moved to 6th and Girage Ave. We lived there for 2 years. The doctor told Chauncey he should quit his paint job so on June 1895 we decided to move to where my folks lived at Mantorville, Mn.

June 25, 1895 Lee was born in the same house that I was born. We stayed with my folks until Sept. that summer I had canned a lot of fruit. Chauncey worked for a neighbor until we moved onto a farm across the road from my parents. We lived there until 1896 then moved to Frank VanHorn's farm near Pine Island, Mn.

On Jan. 30, 1897 Lyle Jay was born. That August Chauncey was taken sick with typhoid fever. I nursed him night and day for one and a half weeks then I came down with typhoid fever. My mother took the two children, Lee and Lyle and cared for them until I gained my health again. That fall we didn't know who we owed or how much; it was awful hard for us then.

On August 27, 1898 Ralph was born. In the spring of 1899 we moved near my folks and rented the Ollen Place then in the fall of 1901 we moved on the Sy Britts Dairy Farm. On Jan. 29, 1902 Edna was born. We nearly lost her with pneumonia. She didn't walk until she was 1 ½ years old. In 1903 Chauncey and Ett Newman went to North Dakota and staked a claim in Gerber township about 5 miles northeast of Woodworth, North Dakota in Stutsman County."

CHAPTER VI: 9TH GENERATION
INGRAHAM'S NORTH DAKOTA HOMESTEAD

After Chauncey Ingraham got back to his home near Mantorville, Mn. from his trip in North Dakota where he staked his claim near Gerber County, Woodworth, North Dakota there was much now to do to get ready for his move. Also to complicate the move on Sept. 5, 1903 Esther Sophia was born.

Below is part of the family L to R: Lee, Ralph and Lyle Ingraham at Mantorville, Mn.

By the first of Dec. 1903 Chauncey got his 3 horses, two cows, furniture and family all together. Baby Esther was now two months old and ready to go after getting everything loaded onto the train and on the way. Somewhere along the way traveling through Minnesota the horses in the stock car on the train got scared and began to protest their ride by fighting their caged existence. One good horse got trampled so the train was stopped and the horse unloaded somewhere in Minnesota and shot because the horse was injured too badly to leave it go on living.

When they arrived in Medina, North Dakota everything

The Homestead Act

What was the Homestead Act?

The Homestead Act of 1862 has been called one the most important pieces of Legislation in the history of the United States. Signed into law in 1862 by Abraham Lincoln after the secession of southern states, this Act turned over vast amounts of the public domain to private citizens. 270 millions acres, or 10% of the area of the United States was claimed and settled under this act.

A homesteader had only to be the head of a household and at least 21 years of age to claim a 160 acre parcel of land. Settlers from all walks of life including newly arrived immigrants, farmers without land of their own from the East, single women and former slaves came to meet the challenge of "proving up" and keeping this "free land". Each homesteader had to live on the land, build a home, make improvements and farm for 5 years before they were eligible to "prove up". A total filing fee of $18 was the only money required, but sacrifice and hard work exacted a different price from the hopeful settlers.

The Filing Process

People interested in Homesteading first had to file their intentions at the nearest Land Office. A brief check for previous ownership claims was made for the plot of land in question, usually described by its survey coordinates. The prospective homesteader paid a filing fee of $10 to claim the land temporarily, as well as a $2 commission to the land agent.

With application and receipt in hand, the homesteader then returned to the land to begin the process of building a home and farming the land, both requirements for "proving" up at the end of five years. When all requirements had been completed and the homesteader was ready the take legal possession, the homesteader found two neighbors or friends willing to vouch for the truth of his or her statements about the land's improvements and sign the "proof" document.

After successful completion of this final form and payment of a $6 fee, the homesteader received the patent for the land, signed with the name of the current President of the United States. This paper was often proudly displayed on a cabin wall and represented the culmination of hard work and determination.

The Homestead Act remained in effect until it was repealed in 1976, with provisions for homesteading in Alaska until 1986. Alaska was one of the last places in the country where homesteading remained a viable option into the latter part of the 1900s. The Taylor Grazing Act of 1934 substantially decreased the amount of land available to homesteaders in the West. Because much of the prime land had been homesteaded decades earlier, successful Homestead claims dropped sharply after this time.

that belonged to Chauncey and Myrtle was taken off the train and moved to the Marston ranch that was near the railroad station. They were still over 20 miles from their staked claim. Arrangements were made so that on Dec. 5, 1903 they arrived at their staked out claim. They had no buildings, no place to put their belongings and they had with them 5 small children.

If any one knows North Dakota in December they would know that with no house it was a catastrophe to happen. This did not phaze Chauncey; he immediately grabbed his shovel and proceeded to dig a cave into the side of a small knoll on his claim. To make matters even worse he only had fifteen dollars left in his pocket. He dug this cave back into the hill and built a block sod front to the cave with an opening for the door. He made a boxcar roof over the front side with a hole in the ceiling to stick the stove pipe through. He ended up with about a 10 x 12 ft. room.

This was their first home on their 160 acre staked out land claim that they now owned according to the homestead act laws as stated on the preceding page.

Myrtle said, **"my cave home had a half window and a door on the front side of the cave. It had a dirt floor that would get so hard that I could sweep it like a wood floor. The grass would grow and hang down about three foot on the walls making the walls green. It was so warm inside the cave that we had to later install a vent in the roof so the steam would then pour out of the ventilator like smoke.**

In the winter the snow would pile up and drift against the door. When that happened I would pull the door open swinging it to the inside then I would shovel the snow into a tub until I could crawl out to shovel the rest of the snow away.

I never put lignite coal into the stove after 2 o'clock in the afternoon because the lignite coal would cause deadly gas fumes to form when burning. One night Lyle woke up and complained of being sick. Soon Ralph woke up and felt sick. I immediately wondered if it was gas from the stove. I remember thinking that we must not go to sleep.

After a while as I lay there thinking about the boys, I too began to feel funny. I immediately got up and tried to get to the door and falling over the table I finally made a lunge for the door and jerked it open. The wind had switched direction and had filled the house with fumes.

I was left alone with the children because Chauncey worked 12 miles away and only came home every two weeks.

The claim had a spring running into a pond about two hundred feet across that Indians traveling through were very familiar with. One day I was in the cave. It was located just above the pond. A band of Indians stopped at the pond to water their horses. Soon they came up to the cave. I was alone with the five children and no one lived for miles from there. I was afraid but made up my mind as I went out the door leaving the children inside that I was not going to show that I was afraid of them. When I was outside standing in front of them as they sat mounted on their horses they indicated to me by putting their hand to their mouth that they were hungry.

I shook my head that I understood what they were telling me. As I shook my head I lifted my hand to tell them to stay put and I would get something to eat for them. I went back into the cave shutting the door as I went to make some sandwiches for them. As I brought the food out they acted pleased and continued to sit on their horses which pleased me. They all left with no problems.

In that day there were many stories going around where there was bands of rogue Indians traveling around and killing the settlers.

The next fall we made another dug out only larger and this one had a wood floor in it. At Thanksgiving while we were moving into it Chauncey's horse that he was riding slipped and fell breaking Chauncey's leg which landed him in bed for the rest of the winter. John Standfield helped us with the chores all winter. In the spring Dave Gerber hired

**Chauncey to herd 500 head of cattle. In the fall Lee, Lyle
and Ralph took over the herd while Chauncey went
thrashing and was gone for a month. Lee was eleven years
old, then Lyle was 9 and Ralph was 8."**

In those days children were used to working at that age.
In the fall in North Dakota the weather is cold and the boys
were herding the 500 head of cattle barefooted. Times were
tough at that time for the Chauncey Ingraham family. The
boy's feet were so cold that when a cow produced a cow paddy
the boys would race to see who could get to that warm cow
paddy first to warm their feet. Sounds crude huh? But when
your feet are freezing and cold you use methods on hand. By
using the paddy to warm their feet it accomplished two things.
It immediately warmed their feet and also coated their feet to
protect their feet from the extreme cold weather.

Chauncey had so impressed the boys the importance of
keeping the cattle from straying that Lyle was afraid of the
cattle straying and then getting punishment from his father for
allowing the cattle to get away.

On one night he found himself half a mile from home
when he woke up. Lyle, my father, told me (Willard) that was
about the only time he remembers sleep walking. The night
was a dark night also and when he woke up it was a shock how
he found himself out there. It took him a while to get his
bearings for his location so he could walk home.

Nov. 24, 1907 Floyd was born. It had been four years
since Myrtle had seen her parents and she was getting real
lonesome to see them so Demarcus and Mary Elizabeth Cowles
came to visit. Myrtle said, **"It was so nice to see them again."**

The soil on Chauncey Ingraham's claim was nice black
soil that was rich for growing most anything that was planted.
Most of North Dakota is flat land but his 160 acres of land was
gentle rolling hills that all had to be broken up and plowed with
horses. This took time before it was all worked up and planted
into growing crops like wheat, oats and other grains.

He also had milk cows so there were some acres that were fenced and left for pasture.

Myrtle said, **"It was the summer of 1909 that we built our big sod house. It had four rooms, 2 bedrooms, front room and kitchen with a root cellar to keep food cool."**

Below is an oil paint I (Willard) painted of how the Chauncey and Mrytle Ingraham homestead eventually looked. In the beginning though the dark circle behind the pond was where the first sod house was built.

My Grandpa Chauncey was pretty smart in the way he built the house. He dug out sod about 18" x 18" slabs and laid up all the walls by stacking all the sod slabs on each other. He built them up to about 8 foot high then he put a wood gable roof on the slabs with reinforced wood corners and also at the top of the walls, windows and doors. He must have realized how comfortable and warm it would be after living in the cave with a sod front. Warmth is very important in North Dakota where it can get 50 degrees below zero in the winter storms.

He also dug a well outside near the back wall then
piped water inside to the kitchen with a pump on the counter
and they could get all the water they wanted just by pumping it
out.

Two years later in 1911 they concreted the outside
walls of the sod walls. The next year they lath and plastered
the inside walls of the house, painted the walls and varnished
the woodwork, the doors and frames, window frames and so
forth.

I (Willard) visited the old homestead site in 1986 and
the following photo is how a distant picture looked of that land
then.

Left is a
photo of
the spring
lake as
seen in
1986.

Below is what was left of the old house in 1986

Lyle and Ralph were little dare devils always getting into trouble by their mischief ways. For instant when they brought the cattle into a corral it was rodeo time for the boys. They would jump on anything that gave them a good ride. The two year old steers, milk cows, horse or any other animal that they could catch and let them have their play time rodeo. After the fun time rodeo slowed down they would turn the milk cows into the barn where the cows would stand side by side locked in stanchions. After getting the cattle all secured they decided now was the time to play tag. They would race down the backs of the cows by crawling on them as fast as they could go then drop down between the cows to crawl under the cows as fast as they could go. The idea was the person that was tagged it would have to tag the other one to make the other one it. The problem in catching the other person was catching up to him as he popped up on the backs of the cows then down between the cows and crawling like crazy in either direction; like where did he go! It was not easy to know where!

One night it was taking the boys a long time to get the milking done so their father went to the barn to check on them. As he opened the barn door the dog ran to him and continued to bark thus aggravating Chauncey to no end. He then kicked the dog to get the dog out of his way and growled at the boys saying, "and I suppose this is your lion of the circus."
Needless to say the boys were very busy milking.

Chauncey Ingraham sometimes dealt with the discipline of his children very harshly. It showed especially with Lyle and Ralph because maybe they were always little live wires who always had something interesting going on in their lives. Chauncey also did have a quick temper that could get away from him now and then.

The discipline also happened to the girls. Aunt Edna told me once about the times she got disciplined by her father. Apparently one time Aunty Edna said they were out in the yard playing when her father told her to come to him. Thinking he was playing with her she ran away from him. That was a mistake because he always had his bull snake whip nearby. The bull snake whip was used when he drove his horses. He grabbed the whip that was maybe 15 to 20 feet long and lashed that whip around Edna; that stopped her. He recoiled the whip and lashed her again. Aunty Edna said that she knew he wanted her to cry but she made up her mind that she was not going to do that. She said that it hurt but she did not give in so he finally quit.

In those days there were no milking machines. All the cows had to be milked by hand. In fact no farms had electricity then. I might add that the cows got so used to the boys playing tag after a while they just stood at the manger eating the hay leaving the boys do their tag game.

Years later when Grandpa Chauncey and I were patching holes in a granary on Lyle Ingraham's farm in 1940 he talked to me about his temper when he was younger. He told me how sorry he was of the harsh discipline he did to his children. When he was talking to me about this I noticed tears roll down his cheeks. This surprised me but neither one of us said anything about that. He did tell me never let your temper get away from you; it will only hurt you. It was good advice that I always remembered.

Below is a cream separator.

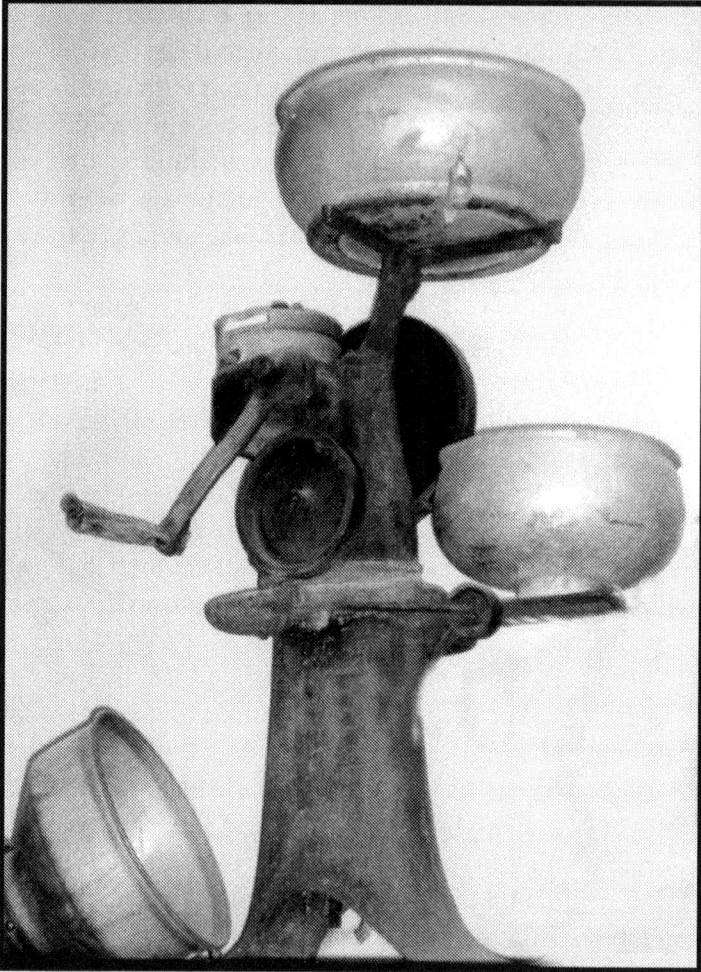

The value of having milk cows at that time was not for the milk because milk had no value except the dairy farmers that lived near big cities and delivered bottle milk to customers in large cities. Individual farmers fed the milk to the pigs they raised. Their value of the milk was for the cream. After each milking which was twice a day the milk would go to the separator that separated the milk from the cream. The way it was done was the cream separator stood about 5 foot high with a handle and two spouts coming from the bowl that held about 160 disks. The milk was poured into a big container bowl on the tope of the separator and by turning the handle the bowl would spin. With the 160 disks inside the bowl it would separate the cream from the milk with each coming out of a separate spout. The towns had companies with creamery buildings that would buy the cream that usually was delivered to them in 8 gallon cream cans like seen below.

Most farmers would survive by selling the cream and eggs; the summer crops gave them the bigger money for the year.

Lyle was always trying to harness the steers and hook them up to a wagon then drive them. Of course this was always done when his father was away from home. Lyle and Ralph wanted some other excitement so they turned two stallions loose in the barn and sat up in the rafters of the barn and watched the big fight that always happened.

Then they got the bright idea to get two cows tied by their tails together and make them see which one could pull the other. They were doing this one day when they were watching as the cows pulled each other back and forth when the hair brush on the end of their tails that the boys had tied together pulled completely off on one of the cows. Later Chauncey came out to the barn and looked around in a general inspection when he saw this one cow with her tail brush missing. He stood there and pondered the situation for a minute and said, "for cripes sake I sure didn't think it got that cold in the barn to freeze their tail off!"

Below is the town of Woodworth, N.D.

The sale of cream and eggs was the main source of income for the farmers in the Woodworth area during the early years. At one time there were six cream stations in the village.

As many as one hundred, ten gallon cream cans could be seen on the platform of the railroad station, ready to be shipped out.

The person who named Woodworth the "Cream City" is unknown. Perhaps it was the late Editor W.H. Wright.

Myrtle goes on with her own story, **"In 1913 Woodworth, N.D. was a pretty town. It had 2 banks, grocery store, dry goods store, post office, hardware store, a hotel, black smith shop, a big community hall a livery barn, a pool hall and several small stores. The pride of Woodworth was a delco system that served the whole little town with electric lights.**

**On Dec. 28, 1918 Claud was born. Below is Claud at
two years. His capers earned the nickname of Tuffy.**

**That was the summer we built our big barn above
the pond. It had a nice hay loft where that fall we held a
neighbor barn dance to celebrate our new barn. A lot of
people came from miles around. We served refreshments
and the money we made we gave it to the Red Cross."**

What my Grandmother Myrtle did not say was that
Chauncey was an old time fiddler and she accompanied him by
playing the cord organ. They played very well and were very
popular for playing for most of the dances and gatherings
around that area.

Myrtle continues her story, **"The next summer we built the granary. Now we had most all the buildings we needed. The crops had done well and our homestead had turned out very well for our family.**

It was now 1916 and our family of 9 was all at home yet but the children were growing up fast.

Photo above of family was taken 1916 from L to R: Lyle, Ralph, Edna, Floyd, Esther with Claud in front.

**All of the homesteaders on their homes around this
part of the state were now living well with their building on
their claims all approved on and grain crops all producing
very well. Chauncey and our neighbor decided to purchase
a steam engine and threshing machine to harvest a lot of
the grain in the area. They called their investment,
"Gerber and Ingraham Rig."**

Above is a photo of the threshing set up working.

A steam engine was a power that could replace horses
in pulling a lot of different machinery. It was also used to
power the threshing machine attached to the side of the steam
engine that had a power take off wheel. This allowed a twelve
inch wide belt about 100 feet long to be attached to a power
wheel on the threshing machine that powered it to separate the
grain from the straw.

The process started with cutting the grain in the field.
After the grain was cut and stacked into shocks and cured the
threshing crew would come with a team of horses pulling a hay
rack and they would collect the bundles out of the field;
bringing the load of bundles to the separator there it would be
threshed.

It was three years later that the Chauncey and Myrtle
Ingrahams' older children started marrying and the rest of the
children followed. On Jan. 7, 1919 Lyle married Gena
Johnson. Nov. 13, 1920 Ralph married Rose Wutzke. Dec. 19,
1921 Edna married Henry Anklam. Nov. 4, 1922 Lee married

133

Elien Thompson. Nov. 6, 1922 Esther married Otto Warnke.
April 1, 1927 Floyd Married Inez Milspaugh. June 10, 1937
Claude married Lorreine Nelson.

Below is a 1943 Ingraham family photo:
L to R Floyd, Ralph, Claud, Lyle, Esther, Myrtle and Chauncey

After 51 years of farming Chauncey decided the
farming was getting too hard for him so in 1935 they sold their
homestead and moved into Woodworth to take it easy for a few
years.

In April 1943 because of the war there was a demand
for shipyard workers. Claud Ingraham decided that was better
money than working where he was working for a school.
Claud was the youngest of Chauncey and Myrtles children and
the elders were now depending on Claude to watch over them.
They all decided that they would be going with Claude,
Lorreine, and children Cenra and Denel who was a baby at that
time.

Claud pulled a trailer filled with all their household
belongings and off they went headed for California. Myrtle
tells of their journey, **"On our way we stopped at Fromberg,**

Montana to visit Ralph and Rose and their family who
lived there at that time. After a short visit we again headed
for California. We arrived at Floyd and Inez and family's
home who lived near Los Angeles, California on May 7,
1943. Chauncey started work for a wealthy lady who
owned a large dairy farm. She hired Chauncey to care for
the grounds and gave us a house to live in. We liked it very
much. On her birthday she and her husband took us and
29 other couples out to supper at the Berry Place
restaurant in Los Angeles. Later that year the owners
rented the dairy farm and moved to the mountains in
California. That left Chauncey out of a job so we went to
live with Claud and his family who lived close to Los
Angeles. Claud was working in the shipyards. Chauncey
and Lorreine worked in the Tyle factory while I took care
of Cenra and Denel.
In 1944 two doctors told Claud to return to North Dakota
for his health so on Aug. 28, 1944 we packed our two wheel
trailer and started back to North Dakota. On our way back
we stopped to visit Ralph and family and then on to
Jamestown, North Dakota where Claud started work for
the schools in Jamestown, North Dakota.
        Chauncey and I went to Yakima, Washington to
visit Lee and Elein and family who were living there at that
time. After an extended visit with them we returned to
Jamestown, North Dakota to find Lorreine in the hospital.
I helped with the house work and took care of Cenra and
Denel (they were both in school by now. We moved in
upstairs in Claud's house.
        In June 1951 Chauncey and I and all of Claud's
family went to visit our daughters Esther and Otto and
family and Edna and Ted Anklam and family. Both
families lived in Chicago, Illinois. On our way we stopped
at Mantorville, Minnesota to visit relatives and friends then
proceeded to Chicago to visit Esther and Edna.

After getting back from Chicago we all started to get ready for our move. We packed up and moved to Laurel, Montana. We all lived in a house trailer with Claude's for a while until we bought our house on Woodland Ave in Laurel, Montana. Clauds stayed in the house trailer until they built their home. Claude went to work for the Burlington Northern Railroad Co.

Claud's brother, Ralph and wife Rose and four of their sons worked for Burlington Northern. Claud's wife, Lorreine, went to work for Sears in Billings, Montana, a city 18 miles from Laurel, Mt. where they all lived.

Photo below: All the Ingraham family together L to R Floyd, Claud, Lee, Edna Anklam, Myrtle and

Chauncy and Esther Warnke and Ralph and Lyle.

It was 1952 that we celebrated our 60th wedding anniversary. Many friends and relatives were there and all of our 7 children, all living at that time and their spouses helped celebrate with us. It was a very eventful day with many memories to last me for the rest of my life.

**In 1954 Chauncey took sick; the doctor said to put
him to bed and make him comfortable and for eleven weeks
I took care of him."**

On August 2, 1954 at Laurel, Montana Chauncey Lee
Ingraham passed away. He was buried at the Sunset Memorial
Gardens at Billings, Montana. Edna, Esther, Otto, daughter,
Lois and husband Dick came from Chicago. Lyle and Gena
came from Prosser, Washington and were there when
Chauncey passed away.

Myrtle continues, **"In 1954 in the fall of the year I
went to Billings, Mt. with Claud and fell down the stairs at
a music store. They took me to the hospital in an
ambulance. I was in the hospital for 6 days. It was the only
time I was ever in a hospital in all my life. When they sent
me home Claud made me stay with them after that fall at
the music store.**

**In 1958 my grandson, Walter Ingraham, was killed
at the ice house at Burlington Northern Railroad Co. He
was one of Ralph and Roses sons. He was loading ice into a
railroad car and fell from the top of the car onto the
railroad track.**

**After the funeral I went with Claud and his family
to visit Lyle and Gena who lived in Grandview,
Washington at that time then on to Yakima, Washington to
see Lee and Elien and family. After that we took a train
back home to Laurel.**

**In 1962 Edna, Claud's family and I traveled to
Washington by train. We stopped over to visit Lyle and
Gena and family who then lived in Kennewick,
Washington. We stayed a few days then went on to Lee
and Elien's place. They now lived in Tacoma, Washington.
They all went to the Worlds Fair in Seattle, Washington
but I stayed with George and Edna Wright who lived in
Auburn, Washington and had a very enjoyable visit.**

**We saw Lee and Elien's children Robert and Fern.
On the way back home we spent one night at Helena,**

Montana. The next day we went through the capital
building in Helena then on to our home in Laurel,
Montana. We all had a very nice trip.

In 1965 when I was 92 years old I wrote the story of
the Chauncey Ingraham family. In Sept. 1965 Edna and
Esther came from Chicago to visit me for a week. I enjoyed
them very much"

As a Mom and Grandma Myrtle Ingraham ended the
story of the Ingraham families with, **"God bless my children,
relation and friends, yours truly, signed Myrtie June
Ingraham."**

Grandma's birth name was Myrtle but in later years she
liked and used Myrtie as her name. By 1968 she had to be
taken to Fairhaven Nursing Home in Billings, Montana.

In 1968 my Grandmother Myrtle was 95 years old.

Lyle and Gena, Louise and I (Willard) with our daughter Carol Jean Rosson and grandson Jon Rosson drove to Billings to see her. Left: we had a five generation picture taken.

In 1973 Myrtle Ingraham celebrated her 100th birthday
at Yellowstone County Nursing Home in Billings, Montana.
She had many friends and relatives come to visit her at the

nursing home. She was by then blind and deaf but she was the woman who one could trace her family tree back to John Alden and Priscilla Mullins and her parents and Captain Myles Standish. She had seen the world from a dugout cave on the North Dakota plains in the early 1900s to the World Fair in Seattle, Washington in 1962.

Below: Myrtle June Cowles Ingraham

Her death certificate shows that she passed away February, 18, 1982 at Yellowstone County Nursing Home in Billings, Montana **at 108 years old.**

Myrtle was laid to rest next to her husband at Sunset Memorial Gardens in Billings, Montana on February 22, 1982.

We have covered the life of Chauncey and Myrtle Ingraham from their birth to their final resting place. I will now write a short history on each one of their children from the first born to the last in consecutive order.

Lee George Ingraham was born June 25, 1895 at Mantorville, Mn. in the same house and same room his mother, Myrtle, was born. He grew up on the homestead of his parents at Woodworth, N.D.

Below is Lee and Elien Ingraham

He met his wife Elien Thompson and they were married Nov. 4, 1922 at Jamestown, North Dakota. Elien was a local schoolteacher in Woodworth, N.D. After their marriage, they stayed at Woodworth, N.D. where two children were born to them, Robert and Fern Ingraham. Photo of Robert and Fern at left.

Sometime in 1919, Lee and Lyle got together and started a drey line business in Pettibone, North Dakota. Pettibone is a small town about 5 miles west of Woodworth. The drey line was a delivery service where they would haul and retrieve material from farms, etc. with horse and wagon and many other service oriented work. After a few years Lee decided to move his family to Chicago, Illinois. Some time later they moved to Indiana. In 1940 he moved his family to Prosser, Washington and from there to Yakima, Washington then to Tacoma, Washington and the last move to Gig Harbor, Washington.

On Jan. 10, 1985 Elien Ingraham died at Gig Harbor, Wa. and was laid to rest at Gig Harbor at Haven Of Rest Memorial Park. Then on Nov. 4, 1987 Lee George Ingraham passed away at Gig Harbor, Wa. and is laid to rest also at Haven Of Rest Memorial Park at Gig Harbor, Wa.

Lee and Elien's son Robert Leland Ingraham born Aug. 6, 1923 at Woodworth, N.D. went with his parents to Prosser, Wa. then Yakima, Wa. He married Shirley Johnson Oct. 25,

1947 in Yakima, Wa. They moved to Tacoma, Wa. where they had two boys, Mark David and Rick Olen Ingraham.

Robert's second marriage was to Norma Beatrice Hawker Howard. She was born Sept. 29, 1922 at Tacoma, Wa. She had three boys, Brian Douglas, Bruce Neil, Roy Warren Howard at the time of her marriage to Robert. There were now 5 boys in the Robert and Norma Ingraham family. They all lived in Gig Harbor, Wa. until on June 25, 1990 Robert Leland Ingraham passed away. He was laid to rest at the Haven Of Rest Memorial Gardens at Gig Harbor. Norma still lives in Washington near one of her sons.

Fern Elaine Ingraham was born Dec. 8, 1924 at Woodworth, N.D. She is the daughter of Lee and Elien Ingraham. She moved to Prosser, Wa. with her parents and on March 30, 1944 at Prosser, Wa. she married James Harland Goemmer. James lived in Prosser and had come from Jerome, Idaho where he had been born on Nov. 21, 1919.

The Goemmers made their home in Yakima, Wa. where they adopted two children, Robert James Goemmer was born Sept. 15, 1947, Seattle, Wa. and Carolynn Elien Goemmer was born Jan. 7, 1951 at Tacoma, Wa. The family moved to Gig Harbor, Wa. on April 9, 1994.

Jim and Fern celebrated their 50th anniversary at which Louise and I had the privilege of attending. As of 2006 Fern and Jim are still living at Gig Harbor.

Lyle Jay Ingraham the second oldest of Chauncey and Myrtle Ingraham was born Jan. 30, 1897 at Mantorville, Minnesota. I will be writing later in this book about the life of Lyle Ingraham and Gena Johnson Ingraham and their family.

Ralph Dean Ingraham was born Aug. 21, 1898 at Pine Island, Minnesota and grew up in the homestead with his parents Chauncey and Myrtle Ingraham in Woodworth, North Dakota. It was here that he married Rose Wutzke and she was born 1899. They were married on Nov. 13, 1920 at Jamestown, N.D. They had 7 boys, Harold, Harry, Leonard,

Walter, Curtis, Roy and Marvin. All were born in Woodworth except Marvin, the last boy, was born in Edgar, Montana.

Below is a photo of Ralph and Rose Ingraham seated in front with their sons; back row: l to r; Harry, Curtis, Roy and Harold. Front Row l to r is Walter, Rose, Ralph, Leonard and Marvin.

Ralph moved his family in the 1930s to Fromberg, Montana then to Edgar, Montana then to Laurel, Montana. Ralph and Rose and four of their sons went to work for Burlington Northern Railroad Co. at Laurel, Montana. Ralph and Rose lived there the rest of their lives. Ralph Dean Ingraham passed away on July 5, 1989 at St. Vincent Hospital and Health Care Center at Billings, Montana. He was laid to rest at the Sunset Memorial Gardens, Billings, Montana. He was 90 years old at his last birthday. His wife, Rose Wutzke Ingraham passed away on May 6, 1993 at Laurel, Montana. She was laid to rest at Sunset Memorial Gardens at Billings, Montana. She was 94 years old. They had celebrated their 60th wedding anniversary in 1980.

143

Harold Ingraham was born June 4, 1921 at Woodworth, N.D. He was the son of Ralph and Rose. He married Wilma Blohm. She was born May 9, 1925 at Beulah, N.D. They lived all their married life in Laurel, Mt. They had three children; all born in Billings, Mt.

Dean Ingraham was born Dec. 26, 1945

Diane Ingraham was born May 28, 1948

Donna Rose Ingraham was born June 27, 1950

Harold worked and retired from the Burlington Northern Railroad at Laurel, Mt. He passed away June 14, 1998 at Laurel, Mt.

Harry Ingraham was born Nov. 9, 1923 at Woodworth, N.D. He is a son of Ralph and Rose Ingraham. He married Mary Fox in Laurel, Mt. They had four children all born in Laurel, Mt..

Sandra Fay Ingraham was born Aug. 6, 1947

Harry Wayne Ingraham was born Feb. 20, 1948

Farren Allen Ingraham was born Feb. 20, 1957

Sarah Ingraham was born Feb. 19, 1955

Harry Ingraham married Wildred Miller, his second wife and they lived at Great Falls, Mt. Wildred was born Nov. 18, 1926 at Conrad, Mt. She had a son from her first marriage, Larry Empereur that was born June 17, 1944. Wildred passed away 2004 at Great Falls, Mt.

Harry Ingraham, the 2nd boy of Ralph and Rose Ingraham remembers as a young boy when Grandpa Chauncey would cut his hair. One day he cut it all off the top of Harry's head making him bald and leaving just a little fringe of hair around the edges. Chauncey stood back a ways and laughed and laughed then he would say, "doggoned it if that kid doesn't look just like me," Ha,ha, ha!!!

Harry tells another story on his grandfather Chauncey. It was a time when he was about 2 years old and Chauncey came in the room where Harry was standing in front of a swill pail (swill is what they called "pig food" all mixed up together with scraps from the table etc). Chauncey came in and clicked his false teeth out at Harry scaring Harry so bad he fell back into the bucket of swill. Chauncey thought that was really funny seeing Harry try to get himself out of that mess!

Harry also remembers his Grandma Myrtle very well as a very proper lady. He said that her house was always in order with a lot of doilies and nice things setting around in different places in their home. Her table was always set just perfectly with silver ware lined up in her special way etc. When they ate she kept the kids behaving; insisting on good manners. You could have second helping but you couldn't pile it on your plate all at once. She was about 5 foot 7 or 8 inches tall, a little taller than Chauncey.

Harry said that his grandfather Chauncey stood about 5 foot 6 inches tall and one time a fellow came that was about 6 foot tall; towering above Chauncey. Apparently the fellow had done or said something that Chauncey didn't like so Chauncey jumped up and grabbed the tall man by the shirt collar and shook him. Harry said Chauncey buffaloed the guy. The man backed down and the fight was over.

Leonard Roy Ingraham was born Dec. 28, 1925 at Woodworth, N.D. He is the son of Ralph and Rose Ingraham. He married Carol Kellor in 1947 at Laurel, Mt. They had one boy; Leonard Warren Ingraham born Oct. 24, 1948 at Laurel, Mt.

Leonard Roy Ingraham's second wife was Sharen Allen. They had two children. Miles John Ingraham was born April 9, 1963 at Paloalto, Ca. Meagan Rose Ingraham was born July 16, 1964 also at Paloalto, Ca.

Walter Ray Ingraham was born Aug. 4, 1924 at Woodworth, N.D. He was the son of Ralph and Rose Ingraham. He married Marijean McKinney on Sept. 21, 1947 at Laurel, Mt. They had 3 sons, Larry, Gary and Stevan all born in Laurel, Mt. Walter also worked for the Burlington Northern Railroad at Laurel, Mt. His job was loading ice in the refrigerator cars for the rail road. This young man was killed by a fall from the loading platform while icing cars in the railroad yard. The accident was witnessed by his father, Ralph and brothers who were also members of the crew that Walter was working with. Walter served as a member of the Merchant Marines in 1947 and 1948. He was killed in 1958 and is buried at Mountview Cemetery at Billings, Mt. His wife Marijean took her boys to Salt Lake City area after Walter's death.

Curtis Norman Ingraham was born July 19, 1934 at Woodworth, N.D. He is a son of Ralph and Rose Ingraham. Curtis married Paulette Cook. She was born Jan. 18, 1939 at Juliet, Mt. They married on June 7, 1958 at Laurel, Mt. They had 5 children.

> Bridget Ann Ingraham born Jan.3,1959 at Missoula,Mt.
> Mark Curtis Ingraham born June 18, 1961
> Scott Walter Ingraham born April, 1964
> Mathew Ingraham born May, 1968
> Paul Joshua Ingraham born Sept. 24, 1972

Curtis Norman Ingraham died at Idaho Falls, Idaho and was buried April 5, 1989 at Sunset Memorial Gardens, Billings, Mt.

Roy Ingraham was born Sept. 22, 1931 at Woodworth, N. D. He is a son of Ralph and Rose Ingraham. He married Pat Bender and they had 4 children.

> Kathy Ingraham was born April 27, 1955
> Rick Ingraham was born Nov. 15, 1956
> Tammy Ingraham
> Tim Ingraham

They were all born at Laurel, Mt.

Marvin Ingraham was born May 15, 1939 at Edgar, Mt. He is the son of Ralph and Rose Ingraham. He married Joanne Kreger. They had 4 girls, Paula Jane, Lisa Rosanne, Jaqueline and Nickola Ann Ingraham. All the girls were born in Laurel, Mt.

Marvin Ingraham was born May 25, 1939 at Edgar, Mt. He married Mavy Francis Odom. She was born Jan. 20, 1942 at Plentywood, Mt. Mavy's children from a previous marriage are Tom, Tammy and John Jr. Odom.

Edna Ione Ingraham was born Jan. 29, 1902 at Mantorville, Mn. She was the oldest daughter of Chauncey and Myrtle Ingraham. She married Henry Anklam on Dec. 19, 1921 at Woodworth, N.D. Henry Anklam died Jan. 27, 1923 at Woodworth, N.D. and was buried at Woodworth, N.D. Cemetery.

They had one boy; Henry Albert Anklam that was born Jan. 29, 1923 at Woodworth, N.D. Henry Albert Anklam died March 1932 at Chicago, Illinois.

Edna Ione Anklam then married Theodore Ernst Anklam on Nov. 25, 1924. Theodore was born on Sept. 18, 1891 at Woodworth, N.D. They had two children. Harriet Bernice Anklam born on Sept. 17, 1926 at Milwaukee, Wisconsin.

Harold Theodore Anklam was born on Aug. 10, 1935 at Chicago, Il.

The family portrait is at left.

Father, Theodore Ernst Anklam died Aug. 7, 1951 at Chicago, Il.

147

Edna Ione Anklam married June 5, 1970 at Chicago, Il. to Clarence Theodore Patno. Their photo is below.

Clarence Patno was born 1907 and died Sept. 25, 1977 at Chicago, Il. Edna Ione Anklam died Nov. 3, 1982 at Chicago, Il. And was buried at Merrionette Park, Il. She was 80 years old.

Esther Sophia Ingraham was born Sept. 5, 1903 at Mantorville, Mn. She was the daughter of Chauncey and Myrtle Ingraham. She married Otto George Warnke. He was born Sept. 22, 1901 at Wisconsin. They were married on Nov. 6, 1922 at Woodworth, N.D. They had 7 children, Gustave Ott, Marvin Melvin, Lois Augusta Myrtle, Deloris Jean, Arlene Phillis, Donna Joan and Carol Mar Warnke.

After Esther and Otto married at Woodworth, N.D. they moved to Eauclair, Wi. Then to Chicago, Il where they lived the rest of their lives. Esther Sofia Warnke died July 23, 1968 at Chicago, Il. She was buried at Justice, Il. at Bethania Cemetery. She was 65 years old. Otto George Warnke died June 16, 1969 at Chicago, Il. He was buried at Justice, Il., Bethania Cemetery.

The children of Otto and Esther Warnke are captured in the following family portrait: They are l to r in back Marvin Lois and Gustove. Left to right in front Deloris Jean, Otto, Donna, Esther and Arlene. The insert is Carol Mar.

Gustave Otto Warnke born April 16, 1923 at Eauclair, Wi. Married Genivieve Marie. She was born Dec. 12, 1923 at Chicago, Il. They had three children,

Charles John Warnke born Dec. 20, 1942
Sharon Lynn Warnke born Feb. 29, 1948
Lloyd George Warnke born Jan. 20, 1952.

All were born at Chicago, Ill. Gustave was a soldier in WWII. He died Oct. 19, 1963 at Chicago, Il. He was buried at Justice, Il., Bethesda Cemetery.

Genevieve Marie Warnke married again to Ron Ray. He was born June 21, 1929 at Chicago, Il.

Marvin Melvin Warnke was born May 16, 1925 at Eauclair, Wi. He married Dorthy Forester at Chicago, Il. He was a soldier in WWII and was killed in Germany. He was buried at Justice, Il, Bethesda Cemetery.

Lois Augusta Myrtle Warnke was born July 22, 1926. She married Clarence Kunstman. He was born Feb. 13, 1917. They were married March 5, 1945 at Chicago, Il. They had three children.

Marvin Melvin was born Oct. 30, 1945 at Chicago, Il.

Terrina Lee was born Oct. 15, 1951 at Chicago, Il.

Dennis Lee was born Oct. 15, 1969 (an adopted son)

Deloris Jean Ann Warnke, daughter of Otto and Esther Warnke, born June 10, 1935 at Chicago, Il. She married Robert Leroy Stamp. He was born March 28, 1934. They married Jan. 16, 1954 at Chicago, Il. They had three children, Michael Leroy, Barbara Jean Ann and Donna Gail Stamp.

Arlene Phillis Warnke was born Oct. 10, 1937 at Chicago, Il. She married Albert Alex Sawicki. He was born May 28, 1932 at Chicago, Il. They had two children, Bruce Albert born Sept. 23, 1959 at Chicago, Il. and Cherilene Esther Sawicki born March 6, 1964 at Chicago, Il.

Donna Jean Warnke was born Feb. 8, 1939 at Chicago, Il. She married Fred Schuster. He was born May 14, 1943. They married on Nov. 18, 1972.

Carol Mar Warnki was born March 24, 1947 at Chicago, Il. She married Garry Robert Hine at Chicago, Il. He was born May 18, 1947. They were married on May 21, 1966. They had two children. Garry Robert Hine Jr. was born Feb. 20, 1967 at Chicago, Il. Allan Stevan Hine was born June 20, 1970 at Chicago, Il.

Floyd Ray Ingraham was born Nov. 24, 1907 at

Woodworth, N.D. He was a son of Chauncey and Myrtle Ingraham. He married Inez Milspaugh. Inez's photo is left. She was born June 16, 1905 at Indiana. They married in 1927 at Woodworth, N.D.

They had four children.

      Orland was born Jan. 4, 1929 at Chicago, Il.

      Delmer Dean; born Sept. 11, 1934 at Mt. Pelier, N.D.

      Gordon Ray was born May 24, 1940 at Paloalto, Ca.

      Lorna Gayle born Nov.21, 1942, Paloalto, Ca.

      After Floyd and Inez married at Woodworth, N.D. they moved to Chicago, Il. They were in Chicago, Il. two or three years then moved to Mt. Pelier, N.D. They lived there five or six years then they moved to Palo Alto, Ca. where Floyd worked for a big diary farm.

Floyd Ray Ingraham was born Nov. 24, 1907 and he married his second wife, Oma on Dec. 17, 1950, California. Their photo is on the left.

Floyd Ray Ingraham died Feb. 10, 1991 at Aileene, Arkansas and was buried at Ash Down, Arkansas.

Orland Floyd Ingraham son of Floyd and Inez Ingraham was born Jan. 4, 1929. He married Evelyn Zanders. They had one child; Orland L. Ingraham.

Delmer Dean Ingraham son of Floyd and Inez Ingraham was born Sept. 11, 1934 at Mt. Pelier, N.D. He married Ruth Olive Moorehouse. She was born Feb. 2, 1935 at Corvalles, Or. They were married on June 15, 1952 at Yuma, Az. They had five children.

Deana Rae born July 25, 1953 at Cottage Grove, Or.
Michael Dean was born Sept. 1, 1955 at Arcadia, Ca.
Kathryn Jean was born Aug. 17, 1957 at Arcada, Or.
Bruce Allen was born Feb. 13, 1959 at Eureka, Ca.
Melanie Ann was born March 26, 1960 at Fortuna, Ca.

Delmer Dean Ingraham born Sept. 11, 1934 married Roberta Kenower. They had one child, Joyce Inez Ingraham; born Dec. 21, 1965

Delmer Dean Ingraham born Sept. 11, 1934 married Jeanette Severance. Jeanette had two children, Cliff Severance and Kathy Severance.

Gordon Ray Ingraham son of Floyd and Inez Ingraham was born May 24, 1940 at Garden Grove, Ca. He married Sandy Noyes and they had one child, Ricky Ray Ingraham.

Gordon Ray Ingraham was born May 24, 1940 and married Sharon Kemper. They had one child, Donny Ingraham.

Gordon Ray Ingraham born May 24, 1940 married Beverly.

Lorna Gayle Ingraham, daughter of Floyd and Inez Ingraham was born Nov. 21, 1942. She married Harry Hart Miller on Nov. 21, 1973. From Harry's previous marriage there were 2 children, Chuck Miller and Leo Miller.

Lorna Gayle Miller was born Nov. 21, 1942. She married James Donald Lindeman on Dec. 31, 1978. James had one child from a previous marriage, Jeff Lindeman.

Claude Melvin Ingraham was born Dec. 28, 1915 at Woodworth, N.D. He is a son of Chauncey and Myrtle

Ingraham. He married Lorreine Gennett Nelson. She was born
Aug. 21, 1918 at Woodworth, N.D. They were married on
June 10, 1937 at Jamestown, N.D. They had three children.
Below is photo: Claud, Lorreine, and children Cenra
and Denel.

Delton Dean
Ingraham was born
Sept. 22, 1938. He
died Feb. 3, 1939.

Cenra Jean
Ingraham was born
June 2, 1940. She
married Robert
Weatherford on June
25, 1960.

Denel Owen
Ingraham was born
April 9, 1942. He
married Judy Shay on
June 22, 1962.

All the
children were born at
Woodworth, N.D.
Claude Melvin
Ingraham and family
lived in Woodworth,
N.D. until April 1943
when he moved his
family to Los Angeles, California to work in the ship yards
there. Lorreine worked at a Tyle Company. In 1944 two
doctors told Claude it would be better for his health if he would
return back to North Dakota so they packed up and headed to
Jamestown, North Dakota where Claude got a job at the school
district in Jamestown, N.D.

In 1951 they again moved their family to Laurel,
Montana where Claude started to work for Burlington Northern

Railroad Co. On his off time he built his own new house for his family in Laurel, Mt. Lorreine went to work for Sears in Billings and apparently went to work at Nikola's in Billings, Mt. later. In 1997 Claude and Lorreine celebrated their 60th wedding anniversary. Their celebration photo is below.

They both loved to dance through the years so they joined a group of nineteen couples of the Sons of Norway dancing group where they danced in many tournaments dressed in their colorful black and white clothes with red vests. I have seen them dance with their group; it was very interesting dance maneuvers to watch all in their colorful dance attire.

Claude is now retired from Burlington Northern Railroad Co. and Lorreine has retired from her job at Nikola's. Both still live in Laurel, Mt.

Cenra Jean Ingraham was born June 2, 1940 at Woodworth, N. D. She is the daughter of Claude and Lorreine Ingraham. She married Robert Weatherford on June 2, 1960 at Laurel, Mt. They had three children.

Kimberly Ann Weatherford born on June 11, 1961 at Laurel, Mt.

Keith Robert Weatherford was born Sept. 11, 1964 at Laurel, Mt.

Kenneth Todd Weatherford was born March 29, 1975 at Laurel, Mt.

Robert and Cenra bought the skating rink at Laurel, Mt. and Cenra has managed it for years. Robert has been a truck driver for years. He drives the big 18 wheelers wherever the load takes him. They still live in Laurel, Mt.

Kimberly Ann Weatherford daughter of Robert and Cenra Weatherford was born June 11, 1961 at Laurel, Mt. She married Paul Edward Jeroma. He was born Nov. 19, 1960 at Laurel, Mt. They were married June 19, 1982 at Laurel, Mt. They had two children.

Krist Elizabeth Jeroma born Dec. 10, 1985 at Kent, Wa.

Mathew Paul Jermoma born May 11, 1993 at Kent, Wa.

Keith Robert Weatherford son of Robert and Cenra Weatherford was born at Laurel, Mt. He married Kirsten Lee. She was born Jan. 5, 1971. They had one child, Keenan Robert Weatherford born Mar. 9, 1991.

Kenneth Todd Weatherford son of Robert and Cenra Weatherford was born Mar. 29, 1975. He married Meghen Louise DeMarco at Billings, Mt. on Aug. 11, 2001.

Kenneth became a very talented roller skater and competed at the National Roller Skating Derbys.

Denel Owen Ingraham son of Claude and Lorreine Ingraham was born on April 9, 1942 at Laurel, Mt. He married Judy Shay. They had two children.

Randy Allen Ingraham was born June 7, 1963 at Bozeman, Mt.

Kerri Rae Ingraham was born Sept. 5, 1965 at Bozeman, Mt.

Denel and Judy live in Spokane, Wa. where Denel has been an insurance agent for many years.

Randy Allen Ingraham, son of Denel and Judy was born on June 7, 1963. He married Julie Bold. They have twin boys

born 27, Dec, 1992: Nathan Ingraham and Jesse Ingraham.
Randy owns a restaurant in Spokane, Wa.

      Kerri Rae Ingraham daughter of Denel and Judy
Ingraham was born Sept. 5, 1965. She married Lee McGuire.
He is an attorney at law and they live in Davenport, Wa.

      Below is a photo op of Ingraham's and cousins with last
living uncle Claud Ingraham center on July 25, 1992 at Laurel,
Montana. Back row l to r; Willard, Harold, Harry, Norman,
Ray, Roy, Marvin, Leonard; front r; l to r Lorraine Johnston,
Lorna Lindeman, Claud, Harriet Drawns and Fern Goemmer.

CHAPTER VII
THE VIKING CONNECTION

Norway is a rugged country with the Kjolen mountain range extending the full length of the country from north to south. The mountain peaks vary from 4,000 feet to 8,400 feet. The mountain slopes are steep and short; many narrow arms of the ocean extend inland between the mountain peaks. These are called Fjords. They extend 90 to 100 miles inland and are very deep.

Below is a photo of the icy beauty of Norway's Fjords

Norway lies between 50 degrees and 72 degrees north latitude. One third of Norway lies north of the Artic circle where the sun shines day and night from the latter part of May through July. For this reason Norway is called, "The land of the midnight sun,"

The last long age of ice began about 100,000 years ago and lasted 90,000 years. During this period Europe was settled from Africa by two species of man, the Neanderthal and the Cro-Magnon. The Neanderthal became extinct about 30,000 years ago but the other also known as Homo Sapiens, the thinking man who survived and reigned supreme. All people on earth belong to this species.

Above is a typical Scandinavian peninsula. The Scandinavian Peninsula was not completely covered by ice for the entire period of 90,000 years. Huge areas became dry land when glaciers shrank so animals and people could establish themselves. Wild reindeer have roamed the Norwegian mountains since the ice age. In our time the largest herd can be found on the Hardanger mountain plateau. Starting about 1800 BC the hunting people of northern Scandinavia also began using bronze for weapons, tools and ornaments.

The Bronze Age culture of the artic had links to Russia and differed from the Scandinavian bronze age farming culture further south. The first period of the Iron Age from 500 BC to the birth of Christ is termed the Celtic Iron Age in southern Scandinavia. This new metal was produced from ore that was easily found in bogs enabling most people to acquire knives, sickles, axes, arrow heads and other weapons and tools made of iron.

The beginning of the Viking period began at the end of

the 8th century and continued into mid 11th century. Scandinavia played an important part for the first time in European history. In this period Swedish, Danish and Norwegian Vikings set off on voyages to distant lands and coasts.

The Viking ship above was used to travel long distances. The ship was made for both sailing and rowing. Sixteen oars on each side and a crew of around seventy men powered this ship.

The Vikings were sea faring people who ventured out to many of the unknown areas they had no knowledge of. The Vikings were also known as Norsemen.

The term Viking can be related to the Norwegian word Vik, meaning by or love. This would suit the Vikings who often hid in bays and inlets with their ships. The term can be said to also be derived from the Germanic word Wic which means market place. Viking could have been a term used for the Scandinavian seamen who came to the trading centers lying on the southern coast of the North Sea. The Norsemen were not known to the other tribes living in Europe until 800 AD at that time the Vikings, as they were called, came to Great Britain and Ireland raiding and pillaging villages. They even captured villages in northern France.

The province of Normandy in France gets its name from the Norsemen who remained there. Like other Scandinavian people the Norsemen are tall and sturdy and usually have fair skin, blonde hair and blue eyes.

The Viking long ship is the very symbol of the Viking age; representing the climax of the Vikings technical achievements. The ship had a solid keel, flexible hull and efficient sails that enabled them to cross long stretches of open sea regardless of the weather.

Their knowledge of the use of sails probably came about through contact with the Frisian Wic merchants who dominated trade in the North Sea area in the 7th and 8th centuries. Even though the ships had relatively, low free boards they were extremely seaworthy. Because they were shallow drafted they could row up shallow rivers.

Cooking equipment tents and non perishable provisions were stored on board enabling Vikings to carry out long voyages to uninhabited wilderness areas. The ship could run ashore on sandy beaches and if necessary be drawn on log rollers from river to river and past water falls. Ships with such characteristics gave the Vikings a wide range of action. They could attack suddenly and make a quick retreat. The Vikings were extremely competent navigators. They set their course by observing the stars and by measuring the sun's meridian.

Norwegian Vikings would join forces with the Danes and both go on raiding parties into Spain and from there go farther into the Mediterranean. By the end of the 8th century the Swedish, Danish and Norwegian Vikings set off on voyages to distant lands and coasts. Their expeditions reached as far east as the Russian plains, as far south as the Mediterranean including Crete, the Black Sea and Caspian Sea and as far north as the Barents Sea and as far west as America.

Christianity was brought to Norway from England by Olay Tryggvesson. He later became Norway's king known as Olaf I. and ruled from 995 to 1000 AD. During his reign the first churches were built. Some of these Stave churches are still standing. After the reformation in Europe in the early sixteenth century the Lutheran faith was adopted and became the state religion of Norway.

Above is a Viking ship exploring the coast of Iceland. Eric, the Red discovered Greenland late in the tenth century and established a colony on the southwest coast. The last horse settlers disappeared early in the sixteenth century. Many of the Viking rulers were exiled from Norway and fled to Iceland. Eric The Red, father of Leif Erikson was one of those rulers.

Viking life among the Norsemen as depicted below whose people followed explorations to Iceland and Greenland where intelligent and progressive people.

Eric The Red lived in Iceland for several years until he killed a friend of his. He was then banned from Iceland for three years. He was exiled from Norway so he could not go back there. His next option was to go to sea sailing westward. He discovered Greenland. He encouraged others to come there to live. Some tried.

Twenty five ships set sail to go to Greenland and only fourteen ships made it to start a settlement there on the Island of Greenland. The Norseman made a settlement and named it

Erickfjord. This settlement is where Leif Erikson, the son of Eric The Red grew to adulthood.

Leif wanted to see Norway so he obtained a ship and crew and sailed directly to Norway. This was the first nonstop voyage across the Atlantic Ocean. Map is below.

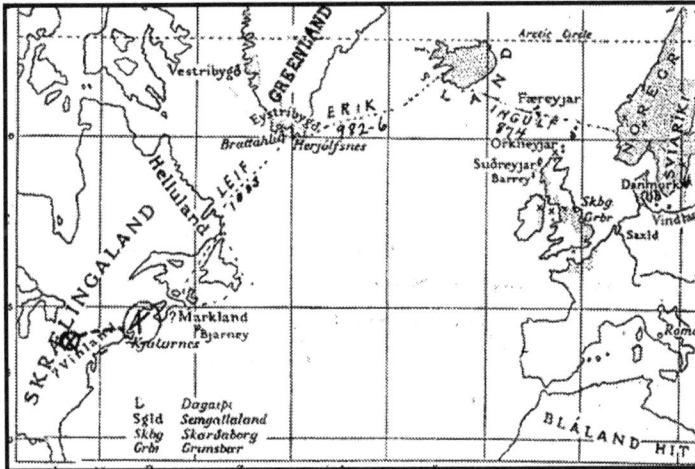

Leif Erikson became interested in a story he heard where a trader was blown off course and found a strange land. Leif Erikson secured a ship with 35 men and set sail south and west. He discovered the coasts of Labrador, Nova Scotia, the Cape Cod region and Long Island in the year 1003. He named his new find Vinland because of the abundance of fruit growing there.

After Leif Erikson discovery Thorfinn Karlsefne led 3 ships with 160 people, livestock, farming equipment and made a settlement. Possibly on the west end of Long Island. They found a lot of fish and game for food. There were a lot of trees around to use for building their shelter. The first year many Indians came to trade with them. After a time the Indians became hostile to the point in three years they had to leave their settlement and return to Greenland. Many years later no contact was made between the settlement in Greenland and

Norway. In the fourteenth century the king of Norway sent ships out to look for the Greenland settlement.

Minnesota became a territory in 1849 and new lands were opened up. The first permanent settlements of Norse immigrants were in Good Hur County in south eastern Minnesota in 1851. In 1870 there were 50,000 Norwegians in the state of Minnesota.

The Kensington Runestone is a possible record of a Viking expedition to North America in 1362. The stone was found under the roots of an aspen tree by a Minnesota farmer in 1898.

NORSE INSCRIPTIONS ON AMERICAN STONES

Collected and Deciphered by OLAF STRANDWOLD

In 1946 I purchased a twenty acre ranch in Prosser, Wash. At the southwest corner of my land joined the land that belonged to a man who was a retired school professor who dedicated his life to the study of Norse inscriptions and writings on American stones displaying the ancient Runic Calender and deciphering these writing. His name was Olaf Strandwold. In 1948 he wrote a book; photo on left.

Olaf deciphered all the runic inscriptions of these various stone writings. He also deciphered the Runic Alphabet. It is a very interesting book and I own one of these books.

The Kensington Rune stone pictured below was found in 1898 near Kensington, Douglas County, Minnesota under the roots of a tree. This stone is in Olafs Standwold's book and was deciphered by him. The message the Norsemen put on that Rune Stone in 1898 goes as follows: (We are) 8 Goths (Swedes) and 22 Norwegians on (an) exploration journey from Vinland through (or across) the west (1.E, round about the west) we had camped by (a lake with) 2 skerries one days journey north from this stone. We were (out) and fished one day. After we came home (we) found 10 (of our) men red with blood and dead.

Av (E) M (aria) save (us) from evil. (We) have 10 of (our party) by the sea to look after our ships (or ship) 14 days journey from this island (in the) year (of our lord) 1362.

One of the people Olaf Strandwold received much of his material for his book was from Magnus Bjorndal of Wee Hawken, N.J. Magnus says this of Olaf Strandwold:

"If people were less sophisticated these days this book by Mr. Strandwold would be such a sensation that it would make headlines in all the newspapers. One can imagine what would have happened if this book had instead been issued in Mr. Strandwold's younger days; say about 1898. It would then have been one of those great events which would have been later considered milestones in our history.

The last fifty years have seen the development of modern science and technology to a point where the great flood of daily impressions impinging upon human consciousness has produced a mental fatigue which dulls our minds and causes most of us to hide in a shell of sophistication. This book will therefore hardly make much of a ripple upon the sea of emotions; yet, it is historical value is very considerable.

The present book represents the results of fifteen years of intensive research and study. Mr. Strandwold is retired as superintendent of schools and lives at Prosser, Washington. He was born in Cass County, North Dakota in 1871 where his father, a graduate of Jonsberg Agricultural College in Norway became the first postmaster of a small settlement on the prairie.

In those days the people of Cass County spoke their various Scandinavian dialects more often than English. Young Strandwold therefore soon became adept in these languages and was useful as a scribe to the patrons of the post office who mostly did not master the English language. After completing the local public school and the Norwegian

Parochial Schools and doing much reading in his father's well stocked Norwegian Library he spent several terms at Concirdia College, Moorhead, Minnesota. He next attended a normal course at the University of North Dakota and transferred his credits as was then the custom to the State Department of Education for the first grade certificate. He devoted 35 years to teaching and supervising schools in North Dakota and the State of Washington and holds a life diploma and also superintendent's credential. At the completion of eight years as School Superintendent of Benton County, Washington he retired from active school work and continued to reside in that county.

The present small but comprehensive volume is the outcome of a long cherished ambition of the author to collect and preserve exact copies of runic inscriptions left in America by the Norsemen. Mr. Strandwold has not only been able to obtain photographs but also has visited most of the stone monuments. This was thought to be important as there is nothing like studying the original.

Mr. Standwold has made the original translations of all the scriptions himself; except that the Kensington Stone is by H.H. Holand and these are presented herewith as everyone knows such translations are not simple due to the many variations that occur in runic writings. The Icelandic and even the Norse grammars do not cover all the Norse Idioms and dialects. The author has followed the example of other Runologists to refer to actual Rune Stones in Scandinavia. The many references in the text will serve as help to the reader and a background for the correctness of the translation.

After visiting and studying most of these inscriptions the present writer believes that the translations in themselves are of less importance than the fact that due to their peculiarities they can be dated as belonging to the first half of the eleventh century A.D. This fact together with certain correlations with the sagas and some of the data given in the translations definitely proves that the Norsemen were here for hundreds of years before Columbus.

Some of the stones shown have been known for more than a century while others are recent discoveries; mostly grave stones. In addition the author has included pictures of noted Scandinavian Rune Stones for comparison. He has also given a short but fairly complete course in Runic Art to enable the student to begin translating for himself. This feature of the book will undoubtedly be of great value to the lay reader.

It is believed that Mr. Strandwold's most important contribution lies in the careful analysis and classification of the Runic Symbols used in the various inscriptions. In this manner a definite dating has been possible. He has also made some progress in the understanding of runic numerals. It was no easy matter to make sense of some of the translations, but Mr. Strandwold has conquered all difficulties through his perseverance and through knowledge of Old Norse.

Some of the stones are obviously grave stones and in some instances graves have been found. In 1838 the Grave Creek Tablet with human remains and a lot of trinkets was found while a Rune chamber was excavated in the mammoth mound.

In 1898 the Ellsworth (Maine) Rune stone with other important material was found at the bottom grave. No other efforts have been made to explore the ground under the grave stones and there remains a great deal to be done in digging out whatever may be buried there. Mr. Strandwold has shown the way and furnished the incentive for younger men to take up his work. One thing is certain from the work done by Mr. Strandwold, the Norsemen were here in large numbers in the eleventh century and

Leif Erikeson is entitled to a place on the first page of any American history."

Kensington Runestone

By Willard:

There remains a question from many; what is the Kensington Runestone? It is a gray colored slab of rock measuring 36 inches thick with runic writings on the face of the slab. Norse explorers wrote the writings in the 14th century in Minnesota. It is now on display at the Runestone Museum in Alexandria, Minnesota.

A farmer Olaf Ohman and his sons and neighboring farmers found this rune November 8, 1898 when they were pulling stumps in preparation for plowing. Ohman was having trouble pulling a tree stump out that was estimated later to be between 10 to 40 years old.

Finally, after uprooting the stump entwined in the roots of this aspen was a 200-pound slab of graywackli; it was the Kennsington Runestone. The roots of the tree were especially the largest root was flattened by contact with the stone and noted by several people who were there as well as by visitors at the site. The stone was found face down in the soil about six inches below ground level.

Later after finding the stone, it was sent to the University of Minnesota for scholars to examine. The stone was then sent to Chicago where several Swedish, Danish and Norwegian scholars declared it a fraud and of recent date. The stone was returned to Mr. Ohman who put it to use as a doorstop for his granary.

In 1907, a young scholor purchased the stone from Mr. Ohman and began to promote it giving speeches and writing books about the stone and Viking settlements in America and about the Holy mission of Paul Knutson who left it behind in 1948.

The stone was placed on exhibit at Smithsonian institute where the curator and director praised it as the most important archeological object found in North America.

The stone was returned to Minnesota in March 1949 and was unveiled in St. Paul in honor of States Centennial. In August, it came to a permanent home in Alexandria, Minnesota at the Runestone Museum where it is to this day.

Additional information is in the insert below

Are there other runestones in America?

There are many claims of other runestones, along with assorted relics and "mooring holes" found in areas of Minnesota, Iowa, and South Dakota, lending evidence to the idea that there were significant Norse incursions into the the continent. The relics include halberds, battle axes, spears, and boat hooks. Many of the relics have been claimed by critics to be modern items mistaken for ancient relics, although some (like the "Beardmore Relics") are known to be ancient, but are claimed to have been planted in order to fool the gullible.

The mooring holes are a different story, however. Mooring holes are holes in large boulders into which the Vikings dropped a peg, attached to the ship, to "anchor" it to the shore. Friedrich claims that more than 200 such holes have been found, from South Dakota to Michigan, and that they show that there was a significant Viking presence in North America from about 1000 to 1400. Critics argue that the holes were drilled by modern folk for blasting, but Friedrich argues, who would go to the trouble of drilling a blasting hole and then fail to blast it? Also, drilled holes are round with "V" shaped bottoms, while the mooring holes are rounded triangles with "U" shaped bottoms.

On the subject of rune stones, there is one which is worth mentioning: the "Heavener Runestone" of Oklahoma. The Heavener Runestone is a slab about 12 feet high, 10 feet wide, and 16 inches thick with runic letters spelling out the word "Gaomedat". By reversing two runes which appear to be different from the others, the inscription becomes "Glomedal", or "Glome's Valley". It could also be rendered "G. Nomedal", Nomedal being a Norwegian family name.

Several smaller runestones are claimed to have been found (Poteau, Shawnee, Tulsa, all found in the area of Heavener, Oklahoma), although none so famous (or controversial) as the Kensington or Heavener stones.

Other Comments by the author Willard Ingraham:

My parents Lyle and Gena Ingraham owned a 20 acre farm just east of Mr. and Mrs. Olaf Stranwold's farm. Louise and I owned a 20 acre farm just north of Lyle and Gena Ingraham and east of the farm owned by Olaf Strandwald's son, George and Stella Strandwold. All four properties joined at the 4 corners.

We knew the Standwold families well; they were all wonderful neighbors. As it was in most communities, the neighbors were invited to special family occasions as it was on my parent's 25th wedding anniversary on January 9, 1944. There was a signed guest list and it was my pleasure to have seen Olaf Strandwold's signature as well as his son and wife George and Mrs. Geo. Strandwold along with other family and friends that attended this monumental occasion celebrating my parent's anniversary.

Now I am going to go back to the oldest ancestors of the Ingraham line that comes down from the Vikings to Gena Johnson Ingraham who is my mother. We will now go back to Gena's grandparents who came from Norway.

Thosten Soiem was born in Telemark (Tin) Norway in October of 1830. Telmark is located in the southeastern part of Norway where the location is ideal for farmland to raise good crops because of its fertile soil and climate

Thosten Soiem married Gunhild Tangen who was born Oct. 1840. 5 children were born to Thosten and Gunhild Soiem Johnson:

Gunhild (1861-1937) M-Sen Olson (1851-1926
Olean (1863-1915) unmarried
Johan (1866-1933)-M- Carrie Olson (1860-1951)
Jacob (1869-1935)-M-Gunhild Synstedgaard
Lewis (1871-1956)-M-Kari Synstegaard

Thosten Soiem moved his family to Evansville, Minnesota in 1868. Sometime while living here Thosten changed his last name to Johnson. This was a normal practice for the Norwegians that came to America to do.

On record of the famous Minnesota winter storms:

Jan. 7-10, 1873 started as a mild day. People were active outside then the blizzard struck. There was a drastic temperature drop, 70 deaths, hundreds of cattle were lost and trains stuck for days in high drifts.

Thosten Soiem Johnson died on Jan. 6, 1873 during the great blizzard. The great blizzard of 1873 had come up

suddenly on a mild and pleasant morning. Snow commenced
falling about 10:00 AM with the wind rising and soon reached
to gale velocity. Winds filled the air so full of snow that
nothing could be seen a few feet distance and with the
temperature, rapidly falling the air soon became bitterly cold.

      Thosten was on his way to Fergus Fall, Minnesota to
have wheat ground into flour when he was caught in the
sudden snowstorm. Fergus Falls, Minnesota is about ten to
fifteen miles from Evansville, Mn. He had a loaded sledge of
wheat. He was found under the sleight a few miles above
Pomme De Terre on the prairie. He had unhitched his team of
horses and turned them loose. They were found nearby still
alive. Thosten tried to ward off the extreme fridged cold and
the biting snow from the high wind blizzard by crawling under
the sleigh but to no avail for that is where they found his body.

CHAPTER VIII
JOHNSON HOMESTEAD

After the tragic death of her husband Thosten Johnson in the terrible blizzard in 1873 later remarried. According to the records; Gunhild Tangent Soiem Johnson was born Oct. 1840 at Sygdale, Norway and was married about 1874 at Evansville, Mn. to Gunulf Soiem Johnson who was born July 14, 1840, Telmark (Tin), Norway. He was the brother of Thosten Johnson.

Above is photo of farming near Telmark, Norway

Gunulf and Gunhild had 3 children; Bertina, Theodore and Gunerious who later changed his name to Gunder. Gunder later became my grandfather.

Gunhild Tangent Soiem Johnson died Aug., 1899 in Evansville, Minnesota. Gunulf Soiem Johnson died at the age of 53 years old in Norway and was buried there.

Gunder Johnson was born Oct. 11, 1879 in Evansville, Mn. He grew up in Evansville but when he was a grown man and was ready to begin a life for himself. It was the year 1899 and he was very serious with a pretty young lady whose name was Laura Bah. Of course she was also a Norwegian. Her parents lived at Erdahl, Minnesota.

Martin Gunerius Olson changed his name to Bah when he came to the United States. Martin Gunerius Olson Bah was born Nov. 9, 1849 at Rodnes, Norway. He died Dec. 10, 1915 and was buried at Erdahl, Minnesota.

Anna Maria Thompson Aasjer was born May 18, 1857. She married Dec. 21, 1880 at Erdalhl, Mn. and died July 30, 1926. From this union there were 5 children:

Laura Bah-B-April 12, 1883-D-Mar. 3, 1965
Olga Bertina Bah-B-Mar. 10, 1886-D-June 4, 1959
Gilbert Theodore Bah-B-Now.25, 1892-Erdahl,Mn.
Thora Alfia Bah-B-Nov. 25, 1893-D-Mar. 24, 1976
Minnie Sophia Bah-B-June 3, 1896-D-Sept. 3, 1961

There is in my collection of pictures and notes that reads that Anna Marie Aasjer, (Laua Johnson's mother) is a sister to Thosten Thompson.

Thosten and Nekolinae Thompson were born in Norway and came to America settling in the Erdahl Evansville, Minnesota area.

Nekolenae had two sons; Martin and Ole Johnson from a previous marriage.

Thosten and wife Nekolenae and Melvin Thompson, their son settled in the Woodworth, N. D. area in 1909, section twelve Wadsworth Township. Thompsons always spoke Norewegian. Nekolenae was unable to speak English. Nekolenae lost her eye sight and Thosten became a victim of Parkinsons disease. Nekolenae died at the age of 83 on May 2, 1934. Thosten died at the age of 79 in 1943. Both are buried at Woodworth, N.D. at the Lunde Cemetery.

Melvin then moved to Hoodriver, Oregon and worked at a saw mill. He met Lora Rose in the 1940s, they married and moved to Lancaster, California. That is where they are both buried.

Left: is a photo of Melvin and Lora Thompson

When Laura Bah was a young girl she attended school at Erdahl and Ashby, Minnesota. After her marriage to Gunder Johnson (photo left) they farmed in Grant County near Erdahl until 1907 when they moved to a farm in Stutsman County near Woodworth in Wadsworth Township, N.D.

Gunder

Johnson's parents were Gunulf and Gunhild Tangent Johnson
of Erdahl, Mn. Laura Bah was the daughter of Martin
Gunerius Bah and Anne Marie Aasjer Bah of Ashby, Mn.
Gunder and Laura were married Nov. 10, 1899 at Erdahl,
Minnesota. After their marriage they farmed in Grant County
near Erdahl, Mn. until 1907.

I remember Grandpa Gunder telling me that in the
winter he would have to go to town several miles from home to
get groceries. In those days everything was done with horse so
he would hook up the team of horses and take off in the bob
sleigh. Most of the time there were no problems but
occasionally in the dead of winter the wolves were so hungry
they would come in close in packs to get some food like the
horses or whatever they could get to eat. One time he told me
that to survive he would have to throw a package of meat out
and let them fight over it while he would get away on his way
home.

Gunder and Laura Johnson decided in 1907 to move
from Erdahl, Minnesota. They packed up their three daughters,
Gena, Louise, and Nora. All three girls had been born at
Evansville, Mn. They all traveled by train to Melville, North
Dakota where Ole and Tille Bah met the Johnsons with horse
and wagon. All their worldly belongings were loaded into the
wagon for the twenty five mile trip to the Bahs.

They lived with Ole and Tille approximately a year
while their one room wood house was being constructed
nearby. This is the place that Gladys was born on Feb. 16,
1908.

It was on October 1907 that 160 acres of farm land was
purchased from Thomas Seaborn Jr. and Clara Seaborn for
$2500. It was located on the SE ¼ section of 10 township, 143
N of range 68.

In the meantime the family moved northwest of Bah's
about two miles. A basement was dug for the one room house
which was moved onto this site. This is where Gunder and
Laura purchased 80 acres of land from the U.S. Government,

Department Of Interior General Land Office through the enactment of the three year homestead law called a patent. This land was located on the W ½ of NW ¼ of section 14 in township 143 N of range 68.

Woodworth, North Dakota, the only city in Strong Township was incorporated Feb. 15, 1916. The land in this area is rolling and hilly with many rocks and potholes. In the late 1800s there was only prairie grass and few trees as one would expect. There have been changes in the government of Woodworth throughout the years. It began as a village then became a town. About ten years ago Woodworth was named a city.

The Delco electric plant was installed by John Hames in 1919 and operated by him for ten years. The first street lights were installed July 29, 1919. In the fall of 1929 the light service was purchased by Ottertail Power Company.

Dr. Melzer began practicing medicine in Woodworth on July 9, 1915. He was the only doctor for miles around and he delivered all of my brothers and sisters as well as me.

The homestead act of 1862 granted 160 acres of land to the man or woman (head of household) over 21 who would build a house on it and live there for five years, dig a well and cultivate a specified acreage. Non-citizens had to declare their intent of becoming citizens before filing a claim.
The act was modified many times. It became complicated and tied with so many requirements that it was impossible to live up to some of the conditions. For a time timber and stone quarters were allowed. The five year residency requirement was finally dropped to three and later to spending only 7 months of the year on the site.

After living on the land for 14 months a settler could buy land for $1.25 an acre or if the railroad owned it the cost was $2.50 an acre. Nearly half of the state of N.D. was given to the Northern Pacific in a land grant. As long as veterans lived on their homestead for one year they could deduct their military time from the residency requirement.

The railroad opened offices in foreign countries and advertised in foreign newspapers. Land speculators were often the chief beneficiaries of the law. Railroad officials preferred to have settler on the land. They felt that Europeans made ideal settler because of their industriousness and the similarity of Northern Europe's climate to that of North Dakota.

There were many abuses of the law when a settler appeared at the claim office to "prove up" his land. On one occasion the settler was asked if he had a well with water in it. He would reply, "there sure is water in that well; I just dumped a pail in it this morning."

In 1911 a lean-to was moved from section 10 to be added on to the house to accommodate the growing family. Ted was born on this place as were the rest of his siblings.

The Lyle Ingraham family occasionally went to visit the Gunder Johnsons. I remember one time when I was little (Willard) that part of their home had black tar paper installed on the outside of the house. I was about 3 years old then. I related this memory to my Aunt Louise Schuff and my Aunt Nora Steffens and they both said that there was never black tar paper on the Gunder Johnson's home but here below is the photo with tar paper on the front of the house just as I remembered it.

Aunt Louise cleared it all up when she said if there was tar paper on the house it would have to be while the house was under construction and apparently that was the time my family visited the Gunder Johnsons.

A few years ago I did an oil painting below of the Gunder and Laura Johnsons homestead where they all lived in Woodworth, North Dakota.

They sent to Sears and Roebuck for their clothing and other needed items. Gunder would take horse and wagon to Melville to haul supplies and get the mail. He would leave one day and return the next. At night the coyotes would howl and the wolves would come up to the house and the dog would bark and carry on alarming the children. Laura was relieved when Gunder would return as he would take down the gun and shoot into the air to scare the animals away.

The children attended the George Anderson school south of the Bah's and later the Wingire school. They sometimes went to the Seaborn store that also included a postoffice from 1907 to 1912 located at Woodworth, North Dakota.

179

Get togethers and dances were held at the E. Anderson Horse ranch about three miles east of Thosten Thompson's. Gunder had a button accordion that he played and furnished music for many dances around their area. He would get many musicians together for his little band and really put out foot

stomping music to dance and all had a good time.

Left is Laura and Gunder Johnson's 25th wedding anniversary photo.

The Fourth of July celebrations and chokecherry picking were also some of the highlights in that area. It was quite a great place for family gatherings and for many of the area farmers and ranchers.

In addition to farming the family was active in the Lunde church. They would drive the horses and buggy to church on Sundays. Later when there was no pastor at Lunde they attended the church in Woodworth. Gunder served on the township and school boards. The family was very musical and played for many area dances and had their own family orchestra.

Above is a photo taken in later years of eight of the now married family members of Gunder and Laua Johonsons 12 children.

L to R: Gena Ingraham, Louise Schuff, Nora Steffens, Ted Johnson, Lovida Snow, Hilda Schuff, Esther Sornson and Doris Rosenau.

Get togethers were common among family and friends and there were big attendances for their Lutefisk dinners. Lutefisk was a fish preserved in heavy brine described later. Most Norwegians love lutefisk. Also the Norweign fare included other famous Norweigen dishes and the families were always ready to have those dinners that were sure to bring all those delicious Norwegian dishes with Lefse that was a fried flat bread and many other mixed dishes that was to many to describe.

Of course when winter came it was also butchering time and they would get together for their famous krub feasts. Norwegians also celebrated the 17th of March but for a different reason then the Irish celebrated the event.

St. Patricks Patron Of The Irish.

They celebrated March 17th in commemorations of St. Patrick's great and noble deed in driving the Norwegians out of Ireland. It was centuries ago that many Norwegians known as Vikings came to Ireland to escape the bitterness of Norway's winters. Ireland was having a famine at the time and food was scarce. The Norskies were eating almost all the fish caught in the area leaving the Irish with nothing but potatoes. St. Patrick, taking the matter into his own hands like most Irishmen do, decided the Norskies had to go. Secretly he organized the Irish Republican army to rid the country of the fish eating Norwegians. The army sabotaged all power plants in hopes the fish in the Norwegian ice plants fish storage would spoil and force the invaders to a colder climate where the fish would keep.

The fish spoiled as planned but the Norskies, as every one knows thrived on spoiled fish. Faced with dismal failure the Irishmen sneaked into the Norse fish storage in the dead of night and sprinkled the rotten fish with lye hoping to poison the intruders. The hardy Norwegians thrived on the lye soaked rotten fish and called it lutefisk.

Matters became even worse for the Irish when the Norskies started taking over the potato crop and making lefse. Poor St. Patrick was at his wits end and finally on March 17th he blew his cork and told all the Norwegians to go straight to hell. It worked. The Norwegians promptly left Ireland and went to North Dakota where on March 17th they celebrated as Norwegian day and demonstrated not by the wearing of the green but the wearing of the fish by the sons of Norway.

Gena Alfea Johnson was the first born of Gunder and Laura Johnson. She married Lyle Jay Ingraham and I will write their life history later in this book as they are my parents.

One of the photos I like of my parents is below taken at the Oregon beach around the 1960s.

Louise Clara Johnson was the second daughter of Gunder and Laura Johnson. She was born in Evansville, Minnesota on July 19, 1903 and went with her parents to a homestead out of Woodworth, North Dakota. She grew up on the homestead until she met a good looking cowboy, Phil Schuff, from Miles City, Montana. They were married on Nov. 22, 1921.

Their wedding photo is at the left.

They farmed the Sunday farm located about five or six miles out of Woodworth, N.D. where their daughter Harriet Phyllis Schuff and son, Orville Schuff were born. In 1933 they moved to the Dittbenner farm about three miles south of Woodworth. Another son Donald Schuff was born there.

In 1934 they moved their family to the Jackson farm three miles west of Jamestown, N.D. where Phil Schuff went to work for the Stutsman County Road Department stationed in Jamestown, N.D.

Phil Schuff worked the rest of his life for Stutsman County Road Dept. as road foreman. Sometime in the 1940s they moved into Jamestown, N.D. He died Dec. 29, 1966 at Jamestown and is buried at Jamestown Memorial Cemetery north of Jamestown, N.D. Louise Schuff died April 1, 1994 and is also buried at Jamestown Memorial.

Above is photo of Harriet and Vernon Wahl taken 1992.

Harriet Phyllis Schuff was born July 6, 1926 at Woodworth, N.D. She grew up in Woodworth and Jamestown, N.D. where she met Vernon Arthur Wahl and married him Jan. 11, 1945. After their marriage Vernon or Short as everyone called him started farming with his parents out of Jamestown.

After some years Short and Harriet moved into Jamestown, N.D. and Short started to work for the Stutsman County Road Dept. When Phil Schuff retired Short took his place as foreman for the Stutsman County Road Dept. When Short retired he became a Stutsman County Commissioner. Vern (Short) A Wahl died on November 14, 2006 and is buried at the Highland Home Cemetery in Jamestown, N. D.

Short and Harriet had three children, Wayne Aruthur Schuff, Gene Orville Schuff and Brad Roland Schuff.

Orville Chester Schuff was born Nov. 11, 1929 at Woodworth, N.D. Orville went with his parents Phil and Louise Schuff to Jamestown, N.D. Orville met Beverly Guenther here and they married Sept. 18, 1949 at Jamestown, N.D.

The photo at the left was taken in 1999 of Orville and Beverly Schuff on their 50th wedding anniversary.

After their marriage they moved to El Cajon, California where Orville went to work for the city of San Diego, Ca. in the Engineering Dept. He was a surveyor for their road dept. They had four children, Gregory Marcus Joel, Karen and Roger Allen.

Orville worked as a surveyor until his retirement. Beverly Guenther Schuff died about 2003. Orville later married Gail and they reside in El Cajon, Ca. today.

Donald Schuff was born Dec. 11, 1934 at Woodworth, N.D. and grew up at Jamestown, N.D. He met Marlys Kose and they were married Feb. 14, 1951 at Jamestown, N.D. They had children, Debra, Brenda, Danny and Brent. Donald and Marlys moved to El Cajon, Ca. Donald went to work with his brother as a surveyor. Marlys and Donald divorced. Marlys died June 3, 1982.

Donald married Nelda after 1952 at El Cajon, Ca. They had two children, Deetta Schuff and John Philip Schuff. Donald divorced Nelda.

Donald married for the 3rd time to Maria after 1953 and again to Judy Sprague. She was born 1934 and they were married Mar. 25, 1995.

Above is a photo of Donald Schuff in 1992. Donald Schuff died about 2003.

Elenora Bessie Johnson was born Oct. 24, 1905 at Evansville, Mn. She was the third daughter of Gunder and Laura Johnson. She grew up on the Johnson homestead. Elenora met a young man, Arthur Henry Steffens. He was born May 30, 1901 at Pettibone, N.D. They married on Nov. 5,

1923 at Jamestown, N.D. Arthur's father, August Steffens was born in Osten, Germany. He came to North Dakota and married Elizabeth Bantkie. They had two children, Rosella and Arthur. They farmed at Bisby, N.D. Elizabeth died of cancer in 1904 at Bisby, N.D.

 August married a widow, Louise Kleese. She came with a son William Kleese. August and Louise moved to a farm near Pettibone, N.D. and they had one son, Edwin Steffens who was born Mar. 21, 1910. Edwin married Oleva Keaton Bellows. She was born on June 11, 1910. They later moved on the farm of his parents and lived there almost all the rest of their lives.

Arthur Henry Steffens and Elenora (Nora)Johnson (photo at left) had nine children. Arnold Burnell, Helen Marie, Gordon Henry, Rosella Loretta, Harry Raymond, Jerome Arthur, Gene Curtis, Shirley Susan and Margaret Elaine Steffens. Arthur and Elenora lived at Jamestown, N.D. until 1943 when they moved to Prosser, Wa. on a farm that Arnold Steffens and Willard Ingraham owned.

 In 1945 the family moved to Mabton, Wa. where Arthur worked for the Big Chief Hop Yards. Arthur Henry Steffens died Feb. 7, 1968 in a car accident at Mabton, Wa.

Eleanora (Nora) Bessie Steffens married James Manka. He died Jan. 6, 1972. Elenora (Nora) died Nov. 9, 2001 and is buried at the Mabton Cemetery. She is laid to rest next to Arthur Steffens.

Following is a story of her life written by Elenora (Nora) Steffens in 1991:

I was married November 5, 1923 in Jamestown, North Dakota., by Judge McFarland. After your father (Art Steffens) and I were married, we worked at Boynton Ranch 7 miles east of Wing.,North Dakota, for a few months. From there we worked for Patterson Land Co. on a ranch north of Wing which was managed by Mr. & Mrs. Ed Larson.

In May, 1924 I went to my parents place, as I was expecting Arnold. He was born June 16, 1924. That fall, Daddy (Nora refers to Art Steffens, her husband as Daddy) and I moved onto the Albert Turk place at Woodworth, North Dakota. Turk had a pool- hall in Woodworth. Daddy harvested the grain on his farm. From there we moved to Streeter, North Dakota. Daddy ran Mr. Swaggarts' farm one year. From there, Daddy got a job at the Stutsman County Farm at Jamestown, North Dakota. He was assigned to become Supt. at this place. Helen was born at this farm May, 1927. We were there until 1929. We moved to Vestal Cook's place, where Gordon was born in February, 1929.

In the spring, we moved to Section 13. Daddy worked for Chris Wingire. We lived there a couple years. There is where Rosella was born in April, 1931. After that we moved back to Jamestown.

We lived south of John Laurence, east of the stockyards. Arnold started school at the Washington School. During that time, until after a few years we lived in different houses. In 1934 we moved into the Kelly house. Harry was born in Trinity Hospital in 1934. From there we moved into the Larson house. We lived there until we moved west in 1942 - in a Model B car pulling a trailer. Daddy, - myself, Helen,

Rosella, Jerome, Gene and Shirley. Gordon and Harry rode with Norman and Willard Ingraham, and Arnold.

Arnold had come to Washington earlier - in-June of 1942 by train. He lived with Gena and Lyle Ingraham until he went into Service in 1943.

We lived in Prosser in Arnold and Willard's house for a couple of years. We moved to the Ranch House on Ellison Road in Mabton in June of 1944.

All my kids graduated from Mabton High School, except Arnold, who graduated from Jamestown High. Daddy worked for Yakima Chief Hop Ranches for 24 years. In Feb. of 1968 he was killed on Hi-Way in Mabton.

In a few years I married Jim Manka. He owned a grocery store in Mabton. He died from a heart attack June 6.

1972. 1 lived in his house, he willed me, until 1989. I moved to Sunnyside, Wash. October 24, 1989. As of now I'm living at the Sunnyside Manor. This is April, 1991. The photo at left taken about 1996 of Nora in front right and family l to r: Gene, Shirley, Arnold, Helen, Harry and Rosella standing by Nora.

The following was written by Arnold Burnell Steffens, the son of Nora and Art Steffens:

My name is Arnold B. Steffens. I was born on June 16, 1924 in Woodworth, North Dakota, on my Grandpa's farm - Gunder Johnson. My Doctor was Dr. Milzer, the only doctor in Woodwoth area at this time. My parents were Arthur Henry Steffens and Nora Bessie Johnson Steffens. I was the oldest of four sisters and four brothers.

I started school in a country school, called Wingire School. My mother and her sisters and one brother also went to this same school. I only went to this school a short time. We moved to Jamestown, North Dakota. I went to Washington, Roosevelt, and Franklin all in my first year. I finished my schooling in Jametown.

When I was growing up, it was during the depression. I spent my time with others during school vacation. In 1933 1 was with my Mother's sister Louise and her family. They lived on the John Dittbenner place outside of Woodworth, North Dakota. 1934-1935-My mother's brother, Theodore Johnson was married in 1933 to Irene Holtz, and they lived on the Albert Benson place outside of Woodworth, North Dakota. I was there for two summers. My Aunt Avis Johnson also stayed there. The two of us were together quite a bit of the time by ourselves. We did the milking, took care of the chickens. It was too dry for any crops to grow. No hay for the animals. Put up Russian Thistles for hay. I guess we got 5 cents a dozen for eggs at the Dittbenner store in Woodworth. At about this time Irene was sick a lot and she stayed quite a bit of the time in Jamestown. They had a daughter Lois born at this time. Uncle Ted would come and go a lot. He used to do repairs on cars. He liked doing this type of work. Avis was a joy to be with. Summer of 1936 I was with my Grandpa & Grandma August Steffens- they had a farm outside of Pettibone, North,Dakota.

My Grandpa Steffens came from Germany in 1895, plus or minus. He was a very strict person. When he showed or told you how to do something, he didn't think it was necessary to show or tell you how to do it the second time. My Grandpa never did drive a car or even own one. When he went to town or visited the neighbors he used his horse (Bessie) and buggy. One of my jobs was to harness Bessie and hook her up to the buggy for Grandpa. When I first got there, he showed me how to do all this. Well, the first time I tried to put the harness on Bessie I didn't get it on. A buggy harness comes in two parts, front and back. Grandpa got to wondering what was taking me so long to get the harness on, and he came and checked on me. What I had was all messed up parts. Grandpa wasn't too happy with me. We had a little schooling on how to put a harness on a horse. To this day I still remember how-a buggy harness goes on a horse. I never had any more problems the rest of the summer with buggy harness.

When I was very small, my folks operated the County Farm in Jamestown, North Dakota, where we lived. My sister Helen was born here. We moved back to Woodworth around 1929 when my brother Gordon was born.

We lived on a place Northeast of Woodworth, called Section #13 where my sister Rosella was born around 1931. I went to school at the Wingire School for a short time. I had two Aunties who were in this same school at the same time; Avis and Doris Johnson, my Mother's sisters.

Folks moved back to Jamestown where I went to school. 1932 during the summer I spent the summers on farms, starting in 1933. I was on the Dittbenner place at Woodworth that my Uncle Phil and Aunt Louise Schuff were on 1934-1935. 1 stayed with my Mother's brother Ted Johnson who lived on the Albert Benson place. My Aunt Avis Johnson also was there in the summer of 1935. I was on the farm when Ted's oldest daughter Lois was born.

In 1936 I-stayed with my Grandfather August Steffens' at Pettibone, North Dakota. 1937-1938 I stayed at the Jackson's farm where my Uncle Phil Schuff had moved to.

1940-1941 I was working on a farm in New Rockford for a Mrs. Daley. My Uncle Lyle Ingraham had a farm at the same area. I used to like to visit with my Ingraham cousins.

1936 - Aunty Louise and Uncle Phil Schuff and family moved from Woodworth, North Dakota to the Jackson Farm - west of Jamestown, North Dakota. I spent lots of my time at their home in the next two summers - I also did lots of baby-sitting during the years for Aunty Louise.

When I was there when Aunty Louise would fry chicken, it used to be kind of like a game who would get the breast of the chicken. Uncle Phil most of the time would eat his dessert first, before he ate his main meal. When we were kids, he would make you think he was going to get your dessert if you didn't watch him. All in FUN.

In 1939 I worked on Jensvold's dairy farm, located northeast of Jamestown, North Dakota. All the milking was done by hand. Milk was bottled by hand. All bottles were washed by hand. Milk was cooled by water, pumped by windmill. When there was no wind to operate the windmill I was on the end of a hand pump to keep cool water in the cooling tank. They used a car with the back seats removed to deliver the milk. No air conditioning at this time. Ice was used. They had around 50 to 60 customers at this time. Milk was delivered right to their door. At some places, milk was put right into the refrigerator or ice box. No one used to lock their doors then. Milk was sold for 5 cents a quart. Cream was 10 cents a pint. Milk was fresh every day.

1940-1941 - My uncle Lyle and Aunty Gena Ingraham and family lived on a farm outside of New Rockford, North Dakota. Uncle Lyle got me a summer job with a Mrs. Daley and her Grandson Everette Norton on a farm in the New Rockford area. The type of work was general farm work. About the only time we went to town was on Saturday night. We usually got our work done early on Saturday, so we wouldn't be too late. I would meet my cousin Willard Ingraham. We would walk the main shopping street, looking at the girls, talking over what happened during the past week and we would have a milk shake. We didn't smoke or drink. We just enjoyed each others company and made our own entertainment. That's the way it was then. Sometimes there was a Saturday night dance. Most farm folk did their shopping Saturday or Saturday night. Some would bring their eggs and cream in to sell.

Most of the time Sunday was a day off but you still had to do the milking and feeding calves, pigs, chickens, etc.

Everett Norton and I would take turns doing the milking on Sunday nights. We were milking 12 cows. I was getting $25.00 a month, room and board and long days.

In the fall of 1941 Uncle Lyle Ingraham sold out in New Rockford, North Dakota and moved west to Prosser, Washington.

1941 I was working for William Lees of Buchanan, North Dakota, on his farm for $30 per month. If it rained old Bill would dock you a $1. I think he was a Scotchman.

My cousin, Willard Ingraham, who was in Washington asked me to come to Washington. I went to Washington by train. My cousins Willard, and Norman were at the Prosser depot to meet me bout 1:30 in the morning. Next morning by 10:30 the Ingraham boys had me a job at the Grange Supply in Grandview, Washington.

My cousin Willard and I worked the same jobs. When one quit we both quit. We worked many different types of jobs- coal hauling, building of an elevator in Grandview, hops in Mabton and topping beets for White's in Prosser. We also worked picking up spuds in the Whitstran area – 10 cents we got for an 80 pound sack. We both quit this job, too hard on the back.

Most of the time we would go to the dances at the Wanita Grange on Saturday nights. My cousin Lorraine Ingraham taught me how to dance. Willard had the car, a 1937 Chevrolet. We could only travel 35 miles per hour - war-time speed. We used gas stamps to get gas.

I went to the Service in 1943. 1 served in the European Theater during the war 1944-1945. (Arnold below in uniform)

My cousin Willard Ingraham and I celebrated our 21st birthdays on the night of June 15, 1945 in Weisbodden, Germany. My birthday was June 16th and Willard's was June 23rd.

Separation Center was at Fort Lewis, Washington - November 14, 1945.

When I returned from the Service, most of my friends were returning about the same time. By the early part of 1946 most of them had returned. What I-noticed when I returned was how some people had aged, and how my sisters and brothers had grown-up. Some people had moved out of the area and some had passed on. It seemed like lots of the younger people were marrying and moving to the bigger cities on going to college. My service buddies and I had the same choices, we had to find jobs or go to college, even could marry - get ourselves back to a normal life.

In 1946 1 worked in hops in Mabton, Washington. I worked in Prosser, Washington at a concrete pipe place and worked on Sunnyside, Washington High School construction, Grandview, Washington Housing Project and worked on the construction of the Tea Garden plant, which is now the Safeway warehouse in Grandview, Washington.

On April 8, 1947 I got engaged to Lucille Williams, daughter of Charley and Minnie Williams who lived on a wheat ranch outside of Mabton, Washington, in the Horse Heaven Hills. I can remember going with the Williams' to the first family re-union in May, 1947 at Hood River Park in Oregon. This was the first time I met the whole Williams' family.

While at the reunion, "Pop" Williams came over where Lucille and I were. He asked us when we were going to get married, and he wanted to know this day and he didn't want any fooling around about it or he would not have anything to do with it. I was shocked, I asked Lucille, "What is your Pop doing, trying to get rid of you?" She told me "No, that's just Pop's way". He wanted to make plans for the wedding and to tell the rest of the family what would take place. Lucille and I set the date for September 13, 1947.

My cousin Willard Ingraham had his first date with Louise Williams at this reunion (Lucille's sister).

Before it was all over, we had cousins marrying sisters at a double wedding on September 13,1947 at the Charley Williams' Ranch in a new machine shed. The minister was trying to marry me to both sisters until Willard straightened him out.

When we first married we lived in Pasco, Washington at the River- side Homes. We were on the housing list in Richland, Washington for a house there. I was working for General Electric in the Hanford Area as a patrolman. Later Lucille went to work for G.E. and also worked in the Hanford Area.

We were still living in Pasco during the flood of 1948 - I had to fly to Richland; all roads around the river were blocked off, because of the high water. During the flood I stayed with the Birrenkott's. LeRoy Birrenkott was my best man at our wedding. I was able to get Lucille to Richland at a later date and she stayed with Ken and Louise Neil.

In 1949 we moved to Richland to 98 Cullum Avenue, on the South side of town.

We are the parents of four children: photo left is L to R; Jeff, James, Loretta and Janice.

We have six grandchildren at this time.

James Jay Steffens, born Sept 28, 1949. He married Janet Jacobs Sept. 8, 1953. They have two sons: Jeffrey David, born Dec. 22, 1978 and Eric James, born April 26, 1982.

Our second son, Jeffrey Allen was born November 18, 1951. He married Debra Scott April 3, 1993. Debra has a daughter Dieadera Scott, born October 10,1983. (They were later divorced)

Our oldest daughter, Loretta Ann Steffens was born May 23, 1954. She married Gene Douglas Rowlette January 29, 1972. They have two sons- Jason Lee born Sept. 14, 1972 and Gene Douglas born Aug. 26, 1975.

Our youngest daughter, Janis Marie was born Dec. 14, 1955. She married James Stewart McDonald June 1, 1974. They have one son, Scott O'Rian born Oct. 25, 1975.

We traded our two bedroom house at 98 Cullum for a three bedroom house at 102 Cullum in 1955.

Arnold wrote another article about one of his hunting trips as follows:

WEEKEND DEER HUNTING WITH WILLARD AND LOUISE AND THEIR DAUGHTER, CAROL INGRAHAM

In the past years, Willard and I had hunted together quite often. When you hunt with a person over a period of time you learn each other's ways. You know what the other person is going to do in the hunting field.

This week-end we decided we would hunt the White Creek area below Bickleton, Wahington. The area where we wanted to hunt and had seen deer was across Rasmussen land, below Dot. The Rassmussens' didn't allow hunting on their land. Two Rasmussen boys caught us while we were crossing their land and escorted us off..

When we got to where we wanted to be Willard, Louise and Carol hunted down a draw in a small canyon and I stayed up on higher ground on the side hill so I could watch if anything came out of this canyon. The only thing I saw was six doe. We got together a short time later and talked over what we would do. Willard said they would hit for the bottom of the canyon. I would stay on the hillside.

There are many small and large draws off these canyons. Lots of places for deer to hide and hunters can pass them up very easy. About a half hour after we had started I spotted what I thought was a buck deer coming off the hill and heading for one of those small canyons. I could still see Willard and wave them to head for that canyon. I worked myself higher up the hill and got myself between the hill and this canyon Willard was guarding. When I got into a position at the top of this draw I heard something start down the draw and hollered at Willard that a deer was on its way down this draw. At the present time I stayed right at the top of the draw and Willard started shooting down below me. He was firing slow. He shot five times and stopped. I hollered at Willard and asked, "where is the deer?" He answered, "You are not going to believe this but I missed him and I had all good shots." We found later after checking his gun that his sights were off. His gun must have gotten bumped.

We decided at this time that this deer had probably left the country. Willard started for the bottom of the draw and I was working my way alone along the hillside checking pockets of other small draws. I stopped to rest on a small knoll and could see these deer legs in the brush about two small draws from me. When it raised its head I could see it was a two point. When I shot it fell over backwards into the brush. When Willard got up to me we went over to check it out and no deer! We found some bone and a little blood. We started to check the brush and look for blood. Willard went down lower on the hill and I went higher up the hill. At the top of this small hill I spotted a two point buck that was shot in the hind leg. I shot and this time it rolled down the hill and ended up on top of a small rock pile.

I was so tired I just sat down and waited for Willard to come and check it out. When Willard came he checked this rock pile again, no deer! I just could not believe it. I knew I hit it again and saw it roll down the hill. We checked the brush around us and found no deer. Willard and I were arguing where the deer had gone. I kept telling him it was close by.

Louise and Carol were over across a draw from us. Louise called and said, "you two quit your arguing! Where do you want Carol and I to go?"

We decided to have them go to the bottom of this canyon and we would check on top. When Louise and Carol got to the bottom Louise hollered, "here it is!" Willard and I went to where Louise was and she was pointing. We still didn't see anything. Louise said, "no wonder you don't get any deer, you are both blind as bats!" The deer was there and covered with leaves. Was really hard to see it. It was still alive. Willard shot with his pistol. Willard tagged it and we dressed it out. Carol and I stayed with the deer while Louise and Willard hiked out to get Willard's tote-goat to pack the deer out with.

Carol and I waited quite sometime before they returned. Willard had a hard time getting the deer out even with the tote-goat. It had rained and all of the trails and roads were muddy. We got stuck a few times before we got to the top of the hill to the gate west of Dot going to White Creek.

The hunt was successful. Everyone was muddy and a little wet and tired. I think that if Willard would not have had his tote-goat we would have had a lot harder time than we did!

Arnold continues his life story as follows:

In 1950 1 got into an apprentice program for electrician with General Electric. While working in the Hanford Area, I worked most of the time in the 100 areas. I worked for General Electric for 18 years. In 1965 General Electric phased out of the Hanford Area. I worked for United Nuclear for 5 years in the late 60's and early 70's they started to close down the old 100 Areas. In June, 1971 I terminated from the Hanford Plants with 24 years of seniority. I went to work for Bonneville Power

Administration on construction Kime. 1971. While working in Montana in 1972 I got a phone call from my friend, Claude Drake - wanting me to bid on a maintenance job at Midway Substation, located along the Columbia River about 45 miles from Richland on Highway #240.

Lucille and I went and visited the Drake's at Midway. If you worked at Midway, you had to live there where they had houses to rent. While I was out there Claude introduced me to Reno DelCurto, who was the Foreman there, of maintenance. I put in a bid for the job and was the one selected for the job. I transferred from Bonneville Construction in June of 1972 to Midway Maintenance.

I became the last foreman there at Midway. I retired June 17, 1986 from Bonneville Power. All the houses have been sold and removed. Most of the people who were in operations or one of servicing groups now live in the Tri-City area and report to Ashe Substation. Many of the people have transfered to other areas or retired.

The first year after I retired we lived at Midway. Lucille was driving the school bus to Richland. June, 1987 was the last School Bus run from Midway. We bought a house in 1986 in the Granddview, Washington area and moved in June, 1987 to 1414 Summit Drive, Grandview, Wa. 98930.

In 1987 a group of us made a trip to Alaska. We had a good time; good fishing. We had a caravan of recreational vehicles. Others who went were: Glenn (Lucille's brother) & Audrey Williams; Frank & Aladine Rupert; Martin & Wilma Copenhefer; & Pauline Copenhefer, Cecil & Audrey Everett; and Walter & Marjorie Johnson.

September of 1988 we made a short trip with Mel and Betty Jacobs, to Lake Quinault Lodge. We stayed at Port Townsend, Washington one night, had a good breakfast at a small coffee shop at Port Town- send.

We also went to the Pacific Ocean. Sept., 1988 we went with Ivan & Hava Bates to Utah. Ike (Ivan) was born in Morgan, Utah. We all had dinner at a restaurant with his brothers and sisters while there. We visited the state capitol of Utah - Salt Lake City. We found Camp Kearns, where I was stationed during the war. We traveled to Bryce Canyon and down to Zion Park.

We traveled on to Las Vegas, Nevada. The Bates' had their camper and Lucille and I stayed in motels - except when we were in Ogden, we stayed with Ike's brother Carl. He was so good to us, made the best breakfast and showed us around the Ogden Area.

In 1989 - Trip to Europe 6-15-1989. Our counselor was Debbie Montgomery Rost. Lucille and I, Glenn & Audrey Williams and Martin & Wilma Copenhefer were on the same trip. Martin got sick at St. Louis, Mo. and had to be removed from the plane. He was in the hospital for a short time, and then they returned home.

Our trip started from Sea-Tac Airport, Seattle, Wa. 6/15/89. We stopped at St. Louis, Mo. then on to New York - then on to London, England. On 6/16/89 we stayed at the Barbican Hotel. Se saw St. Paul Cahtedral, the Clock Big Ben, Parliament buildings, the view of the River Thames. We saw the changing of the colors near Buckingham Palace. We saw the Queen Mother.

We took a ferry-boat outside of London to Aee-Brugge, Belgium. The only thing we saw in Belgium was the scenery from the tour bus, on our way to Amsterdam, Holland.

6-18-89 - Scenic view of City Amsterdam from tour bus. We went to a diamond factory, had a boat trip on the canal and went to dinner at Sea Palace Restaurant; it floats on the water - Glenn's treated.

From Amsterdam we went to Heidleberg, Germany 6-30-89, traveling on the Aut-Bon Highway. We stayed at the Scheid Hotel near Heidleberg, Germany. We toured the city by tour bus. We went to see the old Heidelberg Castle,--about'700 years old. Beautiful flowers around.

On our way from Heidelberg to Munich'6-21-89'we made a bus tour of the German Death Camp at Daghau; quite sad. While we were in Munich, we had a tour guide of the city, the famous beer gardens and world famous Glockenspiel. From Munich we were on our way to Venice, Italy 6-22-89. Nice scenery from the bus all the way to Venice. Venice is an island. No cars or buses. We took a boat there. We watched the glass blower and saw fancy shops.

We went to St. Marks cathedral and St. Marks' Square. We saw the Golden Staircase inside St. Mark's - lots of pictures. We stayed at Veranda Hotel Lido. The Adriatic Sea was in the-background.

From Venice we were on our way to Rome, Italy - lots of old history in Rome. We saw the Coliseum, old gladiator schools, the Arch of Constantine, the forum of the Trojan - scenic view of Rome by bus. We went to Vatican City, a city within. From St. Peter's Square we could see Egyptian obelisk 84 feet high. We went inside St. Peter's Church. While in Rome, we went to the Tivalli Gardens, June 25, 1989. 'We saw lots of olive trees, some over 600 years old. There were many fountains at Tivalli; organ fountains, avenue of one hundred fountains and bicchiorone fountains. They were all activated by the force of water, no pumps.

We stopped at St. Assissi. St. Francis's Church is there. We were on our way to Florence, Italy. While in Florence, June 26, 1989, we stayed at Hotel Arno. We saw the tomb of Michel Angelo and Gaulaeus-Gaulaello, statues of Hercules and David, many paintings of Michel Angelo.

From Florence', we went to Pisa, Italy, where we saw the leaning tower of Pisa. Lucille climbed to the very top. The Baptistry in Cathedral Square was beautiful, with alabaster vessels for baptisms. The doors were of elaborate bronze; acoustics are magnificent.

From Florence, Italy, we went to Alpentol, Switzerland 6-28-89. The scenery from the tour bus was out of this world. We stayed at Hotel Alpenhof outside of Lucerne, Switzerland, up in the Swiss Mountains. We made a tour into Lucerne. We saw the Lion Monument in Glacier Gardens. We went to the

St. Jetowich Church and walked across the Chapel Bridge. We
rode a cog-wheel railway, going up to Mt. Pitatus; 700 feet at
the top. The view was just beautiful.

June 30, 1989 we are on our way to see Paris. We saw
the Eiffle Tower, Notre Dame Cathedral. We saw the Louvre;
greatest art gallery in the world. Had a guided tour of Paris by
bus, and a walking tour of a perfume factory. We rode along
the side of the Seine River. Our hotel was the Fimotel. We saw
the Arch of Triumph and cafes along Champe-Elysees Street.
On July 1st, 1989 Glenn's and us ate our lunch at McDonlds!
We checked out some of the shopping areas.

On July 2, 1989 we left Paris for Madrid, Spain, going
by train. When we got to the Spain border, we had to change
trains. The trains in France travel at a high rate of speed, 100
miles per hour. The train we got on in Spain was like a cattle-
car. The compartments were small and they were crowded, six
persons in them. With luggage and carry-ons even more-
crowded. There were six narrow births, three on each side,
stacked three high. They were quite narrow, had a little pillow
and sheet. There was a urine odor in our compartment, and it
was warm and stinky. We opened the windows and it helped
some. We were traveling at night. Glenn & Audrey, Will and
Marge Gerlitz, and Lucille & I were in our compartment. We
were like fish in a can. We will remember this train ride. The
train arrived at the Madrid station around 9 am on July 3, 1989.
The temperature was over 100 degrees this day. We went by
bus to our Hotel Senorial. The air conditioning in our room
didn't work; the locals don't get too excited or in a hurry.
Their siesta is from 2 to 4 every after- noon.

We went to some shops close to our hotel. They were
very expensive. We stopped at a Burger King to have cokes.
Both Glenn and I had colds. 'My sister Rosella and husband
Kirk Kirkwood were also on vacation in Madrid. Glenn's and
us got together on July 4, 1989 with them. Rosella and Kirk
took us out to dinner at a Chinese restaurant. We had a nice
time with them. Their hotel was really nice, rated at 5-star.

Rating of ours was only 3-star and their air conditioning was working.

Arnold continues his story of their trips; the next trip was a driving trip across country with Willard and Louise and began as follows after reaching Colorado:

At Colorado Springs we went to the Air Force Academy, Garden of the Gods, Wind Caves, Will Roger Shrine, Seven Falls, the Hall of the Presidents, to Cripple Creek and to the Royal Gorge.

We went to Pueblo, Colorado. Saw the St. James Hotel at Cimarron. We stayed at Santa Fe, New Mexico. We also stayed at Albequerque, New Mexico. We stopped at the Meteor Crater, the Petrified Forest and the South Rim of Grand Canyon in Arizona.

In Jerome, an old mining town, we went to a yard sale. Willard had to use his 4-wheel drive to get to it. We drove to Phoenix and spent time with Mary Ann, Joe and Shannon Hicks. Mary Ann is Willard and Louises' daughter.

We went down to Old Mexico; visited Tucson, Arizona and spent the night there. We took in a few yard sales around Phoenix, Arizona. Mary Ann and Shannon went with us. On our way home from Mary Ann's we saw the London Bridge at Lake Havisu and spent one night in Las Vega, Nevada.

On March 14, 1992, the Steffens', - I, Lucille, Ma Steffens, Harry and Tip, Gene and Loretta and Shirley all flew down to Palm Springs, California to visit sister Rosella and Kirk, who live there, and sister Helen, and friend, Larry, who were wintering there from Holland, Michigan.
We went up on the aerial tramway; all had lunch there. We visited the Desert Springs Resort Area. Some of us went out to the Living Desert for a tour. Lucille and I visited the Gene Autry Resort Hotel. We saw many old Gene Autry pictures. We all went to the Palm Springs Follies. Performers were all over 60 years of age. I really enjoyed this. We all went out to a dinner and had BBQ ribs. They were really good.   Rosella and

Helen had good meals for us. They had a get-together over at
their Club-house, with a nice big dinner. Some of our cousins
were there - Donald Schuff and a lady friend; Orville and
Beverly Schuff, Eric and wife (Eric is Jerome's son) and their
two children. Eric was still in the army.

We played lots of pool over at their club-house. Some
of the ladies played cards. Lucille and I stayed with Dorothy
Buearegard, she had orange and lemon trees in her yard. When
we came home we brought some of the lemons back with us -
Thanks to Dorothy. We had a surprise birthday party for sister,
Shirley at Rosella's. Everyone had a good time. Dorothy took
some of us out to Indio, California to a casino. Lucille, Helen,
Shirley, Dorothy made a little on the slots. Larry and I watched

most of the time.
We returned home
March 19, 1992.
This ends Arnold's
own story of some
of his life. Left is a
photo of Lucille
and Arnold taken in
1998. Arnold
Burnell Steffens
was born June 16,
1924 at
Woodworth, N.D.
He died Dec. 15,
1998 at his home in
Grandview, Wash.
He was laid to rest
at Sunset Memorial
Gardens Cemetery at Richland, Wa.

Willard Ingraham gave the following memorial at Arnold's
funeral as follows:

MEMORIAL

TO ME ARNOLD HAS BEEN A COUSIN,
BROTHER-IN-LAW AND A FRIEND.
WE GO BACK A LONG WAY; IN FACT BACK TO THE
TIME WE WERE BORN IN A SMALL FARMING
COMMUNITY OF WOODWORTH, NORTH DAKOTA.
WE WERE BORN OF SISTERS, MAKING US BLOOD
COUSINS.

I RECALL ONE OCCASION WHEN ARNOLD
CAME TO VISIT US. WE WERE ABOUT 4 YEARS OLD
AT THAT TIME; ARNOLD IS ONE WEEK OLDER THAN I
AM. BACK OF OUR BARN THERE WAS A SMALL
KNOLL WE CALLED OUR MOUNTAIN; ON OUR
MOUNTAIN WAS SOME OLD RUSTED - OUT CARS
THAT WE COULD IMAGINE OURSELVES DRIVING ALL
SORTS OF INTERESTING PLACES. WE WOULD PLAY
BY THE HOURS AT THIS LOCATION.

ON THIS DAY, WE GOT TIRED OF PLAYING
WITH THE CARS AND VIEWED A BIG LAKE ABOUT A
QUARTER OF A MILE FROM OUR HOUSE. THIS LAKE
WAS ABOUT HALF A MILE ACROSS - SO TO US IT WAS
LIKE AN OCEAN. AN OCEAN THAT MY PARENTS
TOLD ME NEVER TO GO NEAR. BUT TODAY WAS A
BEAUTIFUL SUNNY DAY AND THERE COULD BE NO
HARM IN GOING DOWN TO WALK ALONG THE
SHORES OF THIS BIG BEAUTIFUL BODY OF WATER.

WE WERE HAVING SO MUCH FUN FINDING SO
MANY INTERESTING THINGS ALONG THE SHORE
LINE; BUT THIS WAS TOO MUCH FUN TO LAST. MOM
AND MY BROTHER, RAY, WAS HOT ON OUR TRAIL
LOOKING FOR US. WHEN THEY CAUGHT UP WITH US
I WAS TO FIND THE RESULTS OF DISOBEYING; FOR
ON THE WAY TO LOOK FOR US MOM HAD PICKED UP
A 3 FOOT LIMB FROM THE BUCK-BRUSH THAT

GROWS LIKE SAGE BRUSH HERE ONLY THE LIMBS
ARE LIKE WILLOW BRANCHES - NEED I SAY MORE!
      I FELT THE STING OF THAT LIMB ALL THE
WAY BACK TO THE HOUSE. ARNOLD TOLD ME
LATER HE GOT A COUPLE OF SWATS HIMSELF.
      THROUGH OUR GRADE SCHOOL YEARS
ARNOLD WOULD COME VISIT ME IN MY CLASSES AT
SCHOOL. WE COULD SHARE MANY EXPERIENCES
THROUGH OUR SCHOOL YEARS.
      WE WERE BOTH AGE 17 WHEN MY PARENTS
MOVED TO PROSSER, WASHINGTON. AFTER GETTING
SETTLED, ARNOLD CAME OUT TO LIVE WITH US.
      I BOUGHT A CAR GIVING BOTH ARNOLD AND I
A CHANCE TO GO TO WORK. WHEN WE APPLIED FOR
JOBS THEY HAD TO HIRE BOTH OF US OR WE WENT
ON TO LOOK FOR SOMETHING ELSE.
      WE WORKED TOPPING SUGAR BEETS, PICKING
POTATOES, WORKING FOR THE GRANGE IN
GRANDVIEW HAULING COAL OUT OF A RAILROAD
CAR TO A TRUCK THEN DELIVERING IT TO THE
CUSTOMERS TO THE BASEMENT OF THEIR HOUSES.
THIS WAS DONE IN 100 DEGREE WEATHER. ALSO AT
THE GRANGE WE WOULD LOAD AND UNLOAD
WHEAT SACKS TO WHERE WE COULD THROW THOSE
BIG SACKS OF WHEAT WAY OVER OUR HEAD.

      ALSO AT THIS TIME THE GRANGE WAS
BUILDING A BIG GRAIN ELEVATOR, WE GOT IN ON
HELPING TO BUILD IT.
      WE WORKED AT THE BIG CHIEF HOP RANCH IN
MABTON THROUGH THE HARVEST SEASON; THEN
CLEARING AN APPLE ORCHARD FOR FUTURE HOP
FIELDS. ARNOLD'S DAD WORKED HERE AT THAT
TIME ALSO.
      ARNOLD AND I WERE BOTH GOOD WORKERS
SO WE HAD NO PROBLEM GETTING JOBS OR GOING

BACK TO WORK FOR THE SAME PEOPLE IF THE OCCASION WOULD COME UP.

THEN WE GOT ADVENTUROUS AND DECIDED TO BUY A 10 ACRE FARM WITH PLANS TO BUY ANOTHER ONE AS SOON AS WE HAD THIS PAID FOR.

ARNOLD'S PARENTS WANTED TO COME OUT WEST SO THEY CAME AND MOVED INTO THE FARM HOME THAT ARNOLD AND I HAD PURCHASED.

WORLD WAR 11 CAME ALONG AT THIS TIME SO ARNOLD AND I HAD TO GO SERVE OUR COUNTRY.

ARNOLD WENT TO THE 2072 TRUCKING UNIT THAT SERVED THE ARMY UNITS. I WENT TO THE 526TH ARMORED INFANTRY UNIT. BOTH OF OUR UNITS SHIPPED OVER TO THE BRITISH ISLES BEFORE D DAY.

I WAS IN WALES, ARNOLD IN ENGLAND. AFTER D DAY BOTH OF OUR UNITS SERVED THROUGH FRANCE, BELGIUM, LUXEMBOURG AND GERMANY TO THE-END OF THE WAR.

AT THE END OF THE WAR IN GERMANY ARNOLD WAS STATIONED IN FRANKFORT, GERMANY AND I WAS STATIONED IN WISBAUDEN, GERMANY TO GUARD OMAR BRADLEY'S 12TH ARMY HEADQUARTERS IN THE TOWN OF WIESBAUDEN - AT THIS TIME GERMAN SOLDIERS WERE BEING RELEASED BACK INTO CIVILIAN LIFE AGAIN.

AT THIS TIME, ARNOLD AND I GOT TOGETHER TO CELEBRATE OUR 21ST BIRTHDAY AT WISBAUDEN, GERMANY, 1945.

SHORTLY AFTER THIS BOTH ARNOLD AND I WERE ON OUR WAY HOME TO BE DISCHARGED BACK TO CIVILIAN LIFE.   ARNOLD RETURNED TO MABTON, WASHINGTON WHERE HIS PARENTS THEN LIVED. I RETURNED TO PROSSER WHERE MY PARENTS LIVED. THIS WAS THE END OF 1945.

IN 1947 WE MET THE WILLIAMS GIRLS.
ARNOLD DATED LUCILLE WILLIAMS AND I DATED
LOUISE WILLIAMS. IN SEPTEMBER OF 1947 ARNOLD
AND LUCILLE AND WILLARD AND LOUISE
WERE.MARRIED IN A DOUBLE WEDDING CEREMONY.

THROUGH THE ENSUING YEARS WE VISITED
BACK AND FORTH COUNTLESS TIMES. ARNOLD AND
I WENT PHEASANT, DUCK, DEER AND ELK HUNTING
MANY TIMES.

ARNOLD WAS A VERY DEVOTED FAMILY MAN
WHO ALWAYS SPENT QUALITY TIME WITH HIS
FAMILY. HE WAS GENEROUS AND INCLUDED MY
FAMILY ON MANY OCCASSIONS.

WE WENT WITH HIS FAMILY HUCKLEBERRY
PICKING MANY TIMES AND ATTENDED THE WORLDS
FAIR IN SEATTLE AS WELL AS GOING TO NEHO BAY
ON THE UPPER COAST OF WASHINGTON WHERE WE
WOULD GO OUT ON THE BOAT FISHING FOR
SALMON. WE ALL WENT SMELT DIPPING WHERE WE
WOULD GET THOSE LITTLE FISH BY THE DOZENS
PER DIP. WE WOULD ALL HAVE A GOOD FEAST OF
SMELT.

LUCILLE IS A TOP NOTCH COOK AND ARNOLD
LIKED TO BARBERCUE IN HIS BACK YARD, MANY
TIMES MY FAMILY AND I ENJOYED THEIR
HOSPITALITY.

AFTER OUR CHIIDREN WERE RAISED ARNOLD
AND LUCILLE AND LOUISE AND I TRAVELED MANY
PLACES THROUGH OUT THE UNITED STATES,
ENJOYING EACH OTHERS COMPANY IN MANY
HOURS OF COMPANIONSHIP.

IN 1997, ARNOLD, LUCILLE, LOUISE AND I
CELEBRATED OUR 50TH WEDDING ANNIVERSARY
TOGETHER WITH ALL OUR FAMILIES AND MANY
RELATIVES AND FRIENDS ATTENDING.

OUR RELATIONSHIP HAS WELDED VERY
CLOSE TIES THROUGH THE PAST PACE OF LIFE AND
FRIENDSHIP HAS BONDED EVEN CLOSER AS THE
YEARS HAVE PAST; BUT NOW WE MUST RELEASE
THAT FELLOWSHIP TO ANOTHER EXISTENCE OF
TIME WHEN WE WILL MEET AGAIN IN A JOYOUS
HAPPY LIFE.
IN OUR EXISTENCE OF TIME WE ARE
SADDENED AT SUCH A TIME AS THIS BUT ARE ALL
HERE TO SAY IN OUR OWN WAYS TO SHARE A BOND
OF TIME WITH THE LOVE OF OTHERS TO SHARE.
ARNOLD'S SOUL GOES AWAY BUT CARRIES
ON THROUGH OUT TIME, BUT CLEARLY, TO SAY,
THAT TIME DOES GO ON TO RELATE THE LOVE THAT
HAS BEEN LEFT TO GROW FOR OTHERS TO KNOW.
I NOW BID YOU FAREWELL ARNOLD; WHERE
THE ANGELS HAVE SURROUNDED YOU AND TAKEN
YOU TO THE WONDROUS PLACE OF GOD; WHERE HE
WILL TAKE CARE OF YOU AND GIVE YOU FUTURE
ASSIGNMENTS IN NEW AND GLORIOUS EXISTENCE.

SO LONG FRIEND,

WILLARD INGRAHAM

Lucille Williams was born April 9, 1928 at Mabton
(Glade) Yakima County, Wa. She died Nov. 19, 2004 at her
daughter Janice's home at Richland, Wa. She was laid to rest

at Sunset Memorial Gardens Cemetery next to her husband Arnold.

Lucille's sister, Louise Ingraham gave Lucille's memorial at her funeral at the Luthern Church in Richland as follows:

PAGES OF TIME
By- Louise Ingraham 11/26/04

'This is very difficult for me to talk about because the hurt of loosing someone special is there. Lucille was your mother and grandmother and friend; she was my sister. She left behind many loving memories that each of us have of her. It is in this way that we will keep her close for all our lives.

If you also believe as I do that the soul lives on forever and never dies then you can believe it is possible to listen and hear thought messages through the soul. If we desire and ask in this way Lucille can reach out through our thoughts answering our personal needs.

I wrote a book about this subject and discussed it with Lucille. She had her own strong beliefs in the power of' the lord and did more than talk it; she lived it in her daily life by how she touched all of us in loving ways. Her presence is felt today all around us. I can almost hear her say, "it is alright to share memories but just get it right." My answer to her is, "I will try."

We were sisters and more. We laughed together and cried together. Pop as we called our father called us sissy because he said we looked alike. Maybe that was true but even then Lucille had her special ways. She was gentle in her thinking and learned to cook and sew at an early age. She was more like our Mom in actions and personality than any of the rest of us in the family.

Lucille's first paper connection with church was probably the Cradle Roll that our Mom entered our names into when we were very small. I can remember seeing the document but mostly I remember being told what it meant to believe in God and Jesus.

Living on a ranch far from town there weren't many opportunities to attend church. Lucille and brother George though found a way to attend a church function when they were going to high school in Mabton. The ranch was 15 miles from town and too far to go back and forth each day so they stayed in town in a rented house. The Methodist church in town had a youth group that met each week. I would guess it was the fellowship that they were seeking when they began to attend but what they learned was more. I can remember their discussions about the bible with our Mom when they came home for the week ends.

There is much more I could say about my memories of Lucille but I will leave those to be entered into the family book I am writing. Our Mom wrote poems and often clipped others writings that meant a lot to her. I found the following clipping taped inside the back cover of her family photo album and would like to leave you with those thoughts:

A BENEDICTION

God keep thee in the busy day,
And in night's lonely hour;
Though storms may gather round thy way
Trust His protecting power.

God guide thee; May his wisdom shine
Unclouded o'er thy soul
And lead thee by its light divine
To the eternal goal.

God bless thee!
On this earth below
And in the world above

A rich inheritance bestow
His everlasting love.

The Nora and Arthur Steffens family story continues as follows:

Helen Marie Steffens was born May 25, 1927 at Jamestown, N.D. She married Bernard Smolen and he was born at Wahurn, Wi. on Nov. 13, 1921. Helen and Bernard

(Ben) Smolen were married on July 17, 1949 at Prosser, Wa. the photo above is of the family; Ben with Earl on his lap and Helen with Gary on her lap. The two children were, Gary Smolen was born on May 4, 1954 at Richland, Wa. and Earl Smolen was born July 26, 1956 at Holland, Mi.

Ben worked at the Hanford project at Richland, Wa. in the early 1950s then they moved to Holland where Ben worked

214

for the United States Postal Service. Benard (Ben) Smolen died Jan. 29, 1983 at Holland, Mi. and that is where he is buried.

Gordon Henry Steffens was born Feb. 16, 1929 at Woodworth, N.D. and married Grace Maurantonio. She was born Sept. 13, 1931. They were married on Oct. 15, 1955 at Great Falls, Mt. They had four children. Angela Kay Steffens was born April 28, 1957. Shirley May Steffens was born July 19, 1958. Thomas Arthur Steffens was born April 9, 1960.

Joseph Edward Steffens was born Feb. 11, 1965. All children were born at Great Falls, Mt.

Family photo left is: back L to R: Angela, Tom, Shirley and Joe between Grace and Gordon in front.

Gordon graduated at Mabton High School. He joined the United States Air Force and retired in 1972 as a Chief Master Sargent in the Air Force. Gordon Henry Steffens died June 26, 1984 at the age of 55 at Great Falls, Mt. from a heart attack. He is buried at Great Falls, Mt. His wife Grace still lives there.

Rosella Loretta Steffens was born April 8, 1931 at Woodworth, N.D. and married Carl Durwood Kirkwood. Carl was born Dec. 26, 1913 at Flat Rock, Crawford Co., Il. Rosella and Carl (Kirk) were married Dec. 22, 1950 at Richland, Wa.

Photo at left:
Rosella and Carl Kirkwood

I (Willard Ingraham) was there at the time of Rosella's birth on that farm several miles from Woodworth, N.D. My mother Gena Ingraham was the mid wife who brought Rosella into this world. I remember that Uncle Art Steffens took all of us children, Arnold, Helen, Gordon and myself, Willard and sister Lorraine Ingraham out to the barn at the time to play games.

Carl (Kirk) Durwood Kirkwood worked at the Hanford Project at Richland, Wa. Rosella and Kirk then moved to California. Kirk died Jan. 28, 2000 at Cathedral City, Ca.

Harry Raymond Steffens was born on Mar. 12, 1934 at Jamestown, N.D. He married Edna Elizabeth Tipman. Photo of Tip (Edna) and Harry on wedding day.

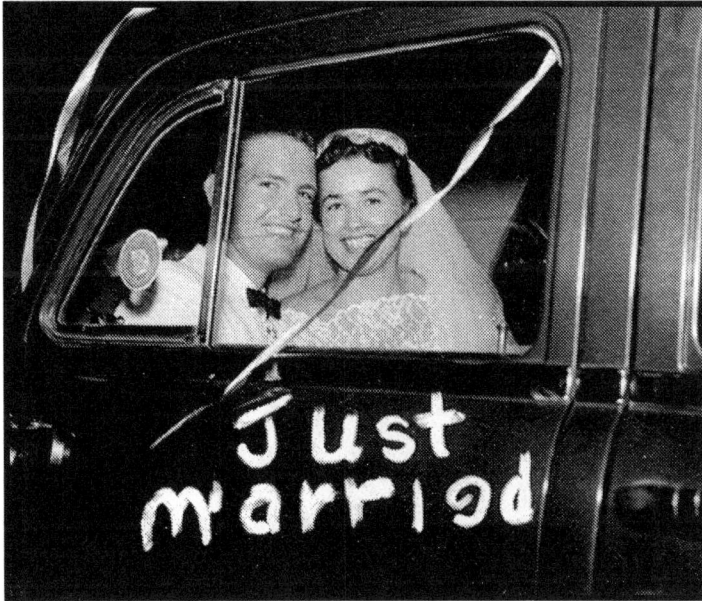

Tip was born on Feb. 20, 1933 at Stettler, Alberta, Can. Harry and Edna (Tip) were married on May 4, 1956 at Pearl Harbor Naval Base, Hawaii. Tip as most people call Edna was

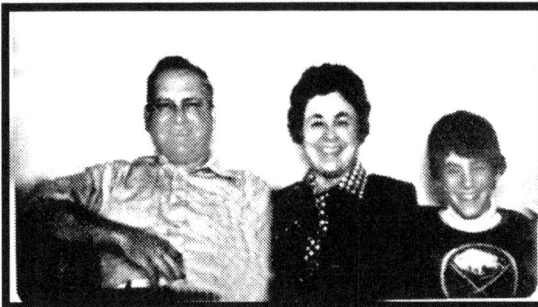

a registered nurse at Leahi, Hawaii at that time and Harry was in the Navy serving that area at that time.

They have one son, Michael Eric Steffens. (family photo above) Michael was born on May 12, 1962.

Harry served as a fireman in the Granview, Wa., Yakima County and Zillah, Wa. Fire Depts. He then moved to Sunnyside, Wa. and there he served as a police officer and then went to work for the Sunnyside Fire Dept for 17 years with the last four years as their fire chief. Harry's photo as fire chief. He retired in 1982. Harry Raymond Steffens died March 14, 2007 and is laid to rest at the Lower Valley Memorial Gardens, Sunnyside, Wa.

HARRY R. STEFFENS, above, today was appointed Chief of the Sunnyside Fire Department by City Manager John Bingham. Steffens, who has served as Acting Chief since the March 1 retirement of former Chief Don Smith, was selected as the top applicant from a field of 10 who were recruited statewide. Steffens is married to Edna Steffens, R.N., who works with Dr. Maling. They have one son, Mike, a junior at Sunnyside High School.

Jerome Arthur Steffens was born Jan. 30, 1937 at Jamestown, N.D. He married Reba Harriet Fisher in 1958. She was born June 6, 1932. They had two children. Vickie Lynn Steffens. She was born Feb. 2, 1958 at Elkins, W. Va. And Hazel Kathleen Steffens who was born on May 22, 1961 at Elkins, W. Va.

Jerome Arthur Steffens was divorced and he married Irene Callaway. Their photo is below. Irene was born Sept. 5, 1933 at Pineville, Md. They were married on Nov. 9, 1963. They had one child, Eric Jerome Steffens. He was born on Mar. 7, 1964 at Lynnwood, Ca. Irene had three children from a previous marriage and Jerome adopted the children. They are Carrie Maraine Copeland Steffens who was born April 19, 1957, Angela Fern Copeland Steffens who was born April 15, 1958 and Michael Theodore Copeland Steffens.

Jerome was in the service (Army) when he met his first wife. He met his second wife in California and later Jerome and Irene with family moved to Mt. Vernon, Wa. Jerome Arthur Steffens died Dec. 28, 1988 at Mt. Vernon, Wa. and is buried at Hawthorne Lawn Mem. Park, Mt. Vernon. Irene Steffens died June 19, 1995 at Long Beach, Ca. She is buried at Hawthorne Lawn Mem. Park, Mt. Vernon, Wa. next to her husband Jerome.

Gene Curtis Steffens was born Jan. 10, 1939 at Jamestown, N.D. His first marriage was to Plyllis LaBarge (divorced) and his second marriage to Loretta Ellison. Loretta was born on Oct. 26, 1946 at Richmond, Ind. They were married Oct. 13, 1968 at Connersville, Ind. Loretta and Gene's photo is above. After their marriage they settled in Kennewick, Wa. Gene worked for

the telephone company and Loretta worked for the Benton
Public Utility District. When they retired they moved to
Indiana and that is where they are as of 2006. They had no
children.

Shirley Susan Steffens was born Mar. 27, 1942 at
Jamestown, N.D. Below is photo of Shirley in high school.

She married Roger Baraja.
Roger was born Jan. 31, 1938 at
Worland, Wy. Shirley and
Roger were married on April 10,
1960 at Coeurd'alene, Id. They
have two children. Randy
Curtis Barajas was born on Feb.
13, 1961 at Sunnyside, Wa.
Sandra Eleanor Barajas was
born Sept. 7, 1963 at Sunnyside,
Was.

Margaret Elaine Steffens
was born Nov. 21, 1945 at
Mabton, Wa. and died at birth.
She is buried at the Mabton
cemetery.

Gladys Hilma Johnson was born on the Ole Bah farm
northeast of Woodworth, N.D. on Feb. 16, 1908. She was the

fourth daughter of Gunder
and Laura Bah Johnson.

Claus Steffen and
Gladys Johnson were
married Feb. 4, 1928 at
Fargo, N.D. They had
four children. Left is
Claus and Glady's
Johnson's photo. Claus
Henry Steffen was born
Sept. 5, 1900 at Esensee, Germany. He immigrated to the

United States from Hamburg, Germany on Aug. 20, 1923. His parents were Jurgen Heinrich Steffen. Claus died on July 1, 1980 at Sioux Falls, S.D. Gladys died on July 21, 1982 at Sioux Falls, S.D.

Claus's father, Jurgen Henry Steffen and Arthur Henry Steffens father, August Steffens were brothers. They got into an argument and decided not to have the same last name and that is why Claus's last name is Steffen and Arthur's last name is Steffens.

Claus and Gladys Steffen children were:
Harold James Steffen-M-Louella Louise Petratz
Dorothy Rebecca Steffen-M-William Raski and later
Dorothy Rebecca Steffens-M-Kenneth Clare
Donald Eugene Steffen-M-Marie Christine Swanson
Robert Clayton Steffen died in Germany

Theodore Orville Johnson was born Aug. 21, 1911 at Woodworth, N.D. His parents were Gunder and Laura Bah Johnson. He married Irene Elizabeth Holtz on Mar. 15, 1933.

Photo above all related: back L to R, Lyle Ingraham, Claus, Marie and Gladys Steffen, and Ted Johnson. Front L to R. Lorreine and Gena Ingraham and Irene Johnson, Ted's wife.

Theodore (Ted) and Irene had seven children as follows; names are highlighted:

Lois Mae Johnson-M-Curtis Burkhardt. Curtis was born on Nov. 12, 1931. They had three children. Curtis died on Oct. 1, 1960 in a head on car collision. He was a police officer. Lois and Curtis had three children as follows:

Ennis Ray Burkhard b; July 8, 1954, Jamestown, N.D. married Gloria Geyer b-Now. 15, 1951 and they had two children: Kaylin Elizabeth b-Sept.22, 1986 and Tierney Wynne b-May 22, 1989

Corrine Elizabeth Burkhardt b-April 3, 1958 and married Dan Walter Vahle Dec. 12, 1986. Walter was born April 16, 1958.

Cheryll Renee Burkhard b-September 18, 1958, Jamestown, N.D. and she married James Allen Bratvold. James was born Sept. 25, 1956.

Lois Mae (Johnson) married Duane Allen Knudson. Below is Lois and Duane's photo taken about 2006. Duane was born on Oct. 22, 1934. They had one child: Craig Allen Knudson –b-July 23, 1963. Craig married Maureen Lakovsak b- Aug. 27, 1961.

Lois and Duane Knudson reside in Jamestown, N. D.

Duane Orville Johnson-M-Adeline Schielke. They had three children.

Charles Burnell Johnson-M-Delores Meyers. They had three children.

Quentine Darle Johnson-D- Mar. 23, 1980. He was single.

Jerald Dean Johnson-M-Luanne Orner

Glen Alan Johnson-M-Leona Murchie. They had six children.

Sandra Lee Johnson-M-Joel Dahlke. They had three children.

Ted and Irene Johnson farmed the Benson farm near Woodworth, N.D. for several years. Ted then moved his family to Jamestown, N.D. where he went to work for the Stutsman County Dept. as a mechanic. It was the same place that Phil Schuff worked. Theodore (Ted) Johnson died on Feb. 22, 1974. Irene died on May 26, 1979. They are both buried at Jamestown Memorial Cemetery.

Left photo is all brothers and sisters of the Johnson family L. to R: Charles and Glen Johnson, Lois Knudson, Duane and Jerald Johnson and Sandra Dalke.

223

Lovida Massie Johnson was the sixth child of Gunder and Laura Bah Johnson. She was born on Jan. 7, 1914 at Woodworth, N.D. She married Harold Holtz at New Rockford, N. D.on Aug. 25, 1935. They had no children and divorced. Harold was the brother to Irene Johnson whose husband was

Theodore Johnson. Harold died at Portland, Or.

Lovida married Mike Aloyus Snow on Mar. 3, 1973. Their photo is at left. They adopted a son, Dean Alan Snow.

Mike Aloyus Snow died on Mar. 3, 1973 and is buried at Great Falls, Mt. Lovida Snow died on Jan. 15, 1989 and she is buried at Great Falls, Mt.

Hilda Amanda Johnson was born on Jan. 2, 1916 at Woodworth, N.D. She was the seventh child of Gunder and Laura Bah Johnson. She married Harry Victor Schuff on June 21, 1933. Their photo is at the left:

They had six children:

Deloris Louan Schuff-M-Donald Brown
Opel Maye Schuff-M-Wayne Baus
Donald LeRoy Schuff-M-Tana Thompson
Eugene Allen Schuff-M-Sharon Bedwell
Leonard Dean Schuff-M-Maria Biggs
Larry Keith Schuff-M-Linda Johnson

Harry Victor Schuff died on July 4, 1965 at Great Falls, Mt. Harry was the brother to Phil Clifford Schuff of Jamestown, N.D. Harry and Hilda Schuff were divorced and Hilda married Elmer Christ Schaber on Oct. 17, 1958. Elmer Schaber died on Mar. 3, 1985. Hilda Amanda Schaber died on May 20, 1994 at Great Falls, Mt.

Esther Grace Johnson was born on April 16, 1918 at Woodworth, N.D. Her parents were Gunder and Laura Bah Johnson. She was their eighth child.

She married Lloyd Sorenson on Aug. 15, 1937. Lloyd was a farmer at Buchanan, N.D. They moved to Jamestown, N.D. where Lloyd was a railroad engineer. He passed away on Oct. 13, 1983 at Jamestown, N.D. Esther is the only one yet living of the Gunder Johnson family as of year 2006. Lloyd and Esther adopted one girl, Linda Sorenson. Linda, Esther and Lloyd's photo is left.

Linda married and divorced Rodney Jordon then married James Townsend.

Olga Johnson was born on April 16, 1918. She died at birth and was a twin to Esther Grace Johnson

Avis Lillian Johnson was born on Oct. 27, 1920 to Gunder and Laura Bah Johnson at Woodworth, N.D. She was the tenth child. She married Daniel Vincent Glowac. Their photo is below.

They had four children:

    Robert D. Glowac-M-Marilyn J. Topp
    Phyllis Jeanne Glowac-M-Charles Christ
    Phyllis Jeanne Christ-M-Dennis L. Dallman
    Phyllis Jeane Dallman-M-Warren Rex Hokana
    Diane Glowac_M-Ronald Hobgoss Sr.
    William Glowac-M-Kathy Hahn

Daniel Vincent Glowac died on Dec. 14, 1983. Daniel and Avis lived at Jamestown and Fargo, N. D. Avis died Aug. 5, 1983. She is buried at Lunde Cemetery at Woodworth, N.D.

Doris Evelyn Johnson was born on May 27, 1923 at Woodworth, N.D. to Gunder and Laura Bah Johnson. She was their eleventh child. She married Raymond Ervin Rosenau and they had three children:

Gary Lee Rosenau-M-Lois Henrietta-Krabbenttoft
Rodney Gene Rosenau-M-Vicki Ann Voldahl
Susan Kay Rosenau-M-Kerry Howard Peuser

Ray and Doris lived on the farm with his parents for a while when they moved to Jamestown, N.D. where they continued to live. Their photo is below taken 1992.

Doris died on Oct. 1, 1999 at Jamestown, N.D. She is buried at Sunset Memorial Gardens, Jamestown, N.D. Raymond Rosenau died June 13, 2006 at Fargo, N.D. He is buried at Sunset Memorial Gardens in Jamestown, N.D.

Gordon Johnson was born at Woodworth, N.D. on Sept. 15, 1925 to Gunder and Laura Bah Hohnson. He died on Aug. 31, 1926. He died from scarlet fever and is buried at Lunde Cemetery at Woodworth, N.D. He was the twelfth child of Gunder and Laura Bah Johnson.

CHAPTER IX   10th GENERATION
LIVING THROUGH HARD TIMES

Gena Alfea Johnson-b-Dec. 1, 1900 at Evansville (Elbow Lake), Mn was the first born of Gunder and Laura Bah Johnson. In 1907 Gena and sisters Louise and Nora were the only children that Gunder and Laura Johnson had when they left Evansville, Mn. on the train traveling to Melville, North Dakota to live on their homestead that Gunder owned. Gunder's homestead was about ten miles southeast of Woodworth, N.D.

A short distance from Evansville, Mn. Gena's family had her picture taken when she was a small child. Her photo is below.   They lived at Erdhal, Mn.

In 1907 Gena moved with her parents to Woodworth, N.D. where her parents homesteaded a 160 acre farm. The first year there, Gena entered a one-room school about three miles from their home. The school was called the George Anderson School.

Gena was seven years old then and her picture was taken below with her school chums (caption under photo). It was 1907 at that time. Later the Johnson children attended the Wingire School

Woodworth school district #3. Back row: May Townsend, Alice Johnson (Sunday), Cara Johnson (Schilling). Front Row: Gena Johnson (Ingraham), James McDonald, Willard Townsend, Mazie Townsend, Gladys Hames (Derickson), 1907.

Gena as the oldest of the family and had a lot of practice in how to handle small children. There eventually would be more sisters and brothers in the family; a total of ten in all. Gena loved children and in turn they loved her. She also helped her Dad, Gunder with chores outside of the house. There was milking cows and field work.

Below is a photo with Gena Johnson sitting on the upper top of the hay rake. By this time, she was well versed on operating a hayrake as she had many opportunities to operate one.

Gunder wanted all of their children to marry Norwegians but time would prove that none of their children did. Gena was very fluent at speaking the Norwegian language. In fact she was the only one of the children that was confirmed in Norwegian. She also learned how to read music by note when she played the piano and organ. With this ability she chorded on the piano when her father, Gunder played his button accordion. She chorded on the piano when her father and his little musical band played for dances.

Gena attended the Woodworth school district #3. As she grew to be a teenager she helped her mother with the birth of many of her ten siblings coming into this world.

As a young lady playing the piano in her fathers band at dances she noticed a young man that tugged at her heart strings; it was his unusual laugh that attracted her. This young man was also musical and played the violin in good old time fiddle music with his father Chauncey Ingraham's band. Both families were musical so they certainly had something in common.

231

This young mans name was Lyle Ingraham and he started to date Gena but her parents protested because he was not a Norwegian. They wanted their daughter to date only Norwegians. Gunder and Laura tried many things to break this young couple up but to no avail, they were in love with each other. Gena's parents got desperate and ordered Lyle not to come to see Gena again. That did not stop Lyle from coming and Gena did not listen to her parents. Her parents gave up and allowed them to finally date each other. Gena was the oldest daughter of Gunder and Laura so in essence she paved the way for the rest of her siblings. She was now age nineteen and she thought she was old enough to make her own decisions. In time this young couple Gena and Lyle would become my parents.

Lyle Jay Ingraham was born January 30, 1897 at Mantorville, MN. He was the son of Chauncey and Myrtle Ingraham and grew up on their homestead. As a young man World War I came about and he wanted to go serve his country. He paid his way to Jamestown, N.D. where the local board was located to sign up for the army. Above is his photo at that time.

On June 5, 1918, he registered. I have the notice of his registration certificate that states in accordance with the proclamation of the president of the United States and in compliance with LAV, Lyle Ingraham, Woodworth, N.D. has submitted himself to registration and has by me been duly registered this 5th day of June 1918 under the supervision of the local board on July 18, 1918.

Lyle got a notice of classification that was A. Then on August 5, 1918 from the local board at Jamestown it certifies that Lyle Ingraham, order No. 113, serial No. 71 has been finally classified and recorded in class one. Lyle received an order of induction into military service of the United States signed Oct. 14, 1918 that Lyle Ingraham, order Number 113, Serial number 71 will therefore report to the local board named

below at Jamestown, N.D. at 10 A.M. on the 21st day of October, 1918 for military duty. He was inducted into the army and sent to Fort Winfield Scott, California.

Then he was discharged from the draft; copy on the left: it read that Lyle Ingraham, army serial no. (4576245) C.A.C. is hereby discharged from the military service of the United States by order of the president dated November 11, 1918. It said Lyle Ingraham was inducted into the service from the jurisdiction of the local board for Stutsman County, Jamestown, North Dakota on the 11th day of November 1918 by order of Colonel Marsh and E.G. Abbott, Major, CAC Adjutant. World War I is over and now people can begin to get their lives together again. Lyle served about a month in army life before being discharged because the war ended.

Lyle then turned his mind into how he wanted to direct his life from this point. He got together with his brother Lee and they decided to start a drey business in Pettibone, North Dakota. It was a small town about five or six miles west of Woodworth, N.D. The drey line was a delivery service where they hauled and retrieved material, grains and machinery all by horse and wagon along with many other services oriented work.

Jan. 7, 1919 Lyle Ingraham and Gena Johnson went to Jamestown, N.D. and got married (photo above)

They rented a small house in Pettibone, N.D. and settled in the small town.

Gena made herself busy helping others. When someone got sick or needed a mid-wife to deliver babies she was there; she had a lot of practice. Gena was always good with children and the children liked her.

It was on August 21, 1919 that Raymond Lloyd Ingraham was born to Lyle and Gena. He was a premature baby and so small Gena could put her ring around his little wrist. Raymond was so small they had to hold him with a pillow under him.

I have a photo of him on the left at two years old standing

in the yard across the street   where they lived in
Pettibone.

The drey business was dissolved and Lyle and Gena moved to the George Anderson farm at Woodworth, N.D. where Norman, Jerome Ingraham was born on Sept. 11, 1922. Before Norman's birth Gena lost two babies at their birth, Charles LeRoy Ingraham was born in 1920 and LeRoy Norman Ingraham was born Sept. 9, 1921.

Dr. Melzer was our only local doctor and he played such an important part in our families and others lives I have included a long

Dr. Simon W. and Beatrice (McDaneld) Melzer

Simon W. Melzer, the son of Simon and Mary (Otto) Melzer was born April 4, 1886 at Mayville, Wisconsin. When he was fourteen years old he began hunting the famous Horicon Marsh area which he and his friends hiked several miles to reach. After high school, Simon was a year too young for medical school, and, he was short of money too, so he taught a backwoods school six miles from home. He earned $40 a month and paid $8 a month for room and board. He also trapped mink, raccoons and muskrats. He worked as a "pusher" pushing millionaire duck hunters through the marsh in duck boats, setting decoys, and retrieving birds. At age nineteen he entered medical school at Northwestern U in Chicago. Four years later he began an eighteen month internship at Cook County Hospital. Here he met and married Beatrice McDaneld, the daughter of Noah and Lillie (Wilson) McDaneld. Beatrice was born November 14, 1885 at Marion, Iowa. She was a registered nurse at Cook County Hospital. They were married at Kensington, Minnesota December 31, 1911.

After practicing medicine only a few years in Kensington, a friend told him of a possibility in a little N.D. town, Woodworth. Kensington was a Scandinavian community. Dr. Melzer was German so he had some difficulty communicating in Kensington. When he went to Woodworth he said, "They didn't have a doctor, and it was a good duck hunting country. I liked what I saw, you bet." "Oh the town was a boomer — two banks, two liveries, two of everything — six or seven groceries." Dr. and Mrs. Melzer moved to Woodworth the last week of July 1915. Woodworth then boasted a population of 450 people. Their first home was on the site where Donald Johnsons now live. That house later burned.

Melzers had two sons. Simon (Sim) was born November 30, 1913. Laurence was born July 13, 1915.

It wasn't long until Melzers built their house across the street from the Lutheran Church on the north end of main street. Ben Bryan was the contractor or builder. (This remained Dr. Melzer's home until a couple years before his death.)

Melzer's first office is today a museum dedicated to his memory. The building contained two rooms.

Dr. S.W. Melzer

prior

Story is continued from page

It was 25 feet square. He rented it for $10 a month to begin with. He later built an office just south of his home. (Chester Thompson's home today) While he practiced downtown he also built the drug store that Clarence Uggen owned and operated for many years.

Dr. Melzer practiced only minor surgery, setting bones, lancing boils and stitching lacerations. He got $25 for a tonsilectomy, $10 for a fractured wrist (many broken by a backfiring Model A engine crank), and 50 cents for extracting a tooth. Later, of course, prices increased.

Mostly on Sundays, Doc and his hunting buddies, Albert Hanson, an area farmer, and Jesse Nygaard, a Jamestown banker, took to the field and welcomed thick clouds of waterfowl. Doc later said, "We had it all to ourselves — right here in Woodworth there weren't three or four hunters." When Doc's boys got older, they joined in the hunting. They'd be out hunting by daylight and quit at 1 pm. Several times in the fall the wives would show up with a picnic lunch and spread it out near a haystack. (Trees were scarce.) Someone's waving a white flag or handkerchief was a sign that Doc was needed somewhere. Doc's wife not only helped with his medical practice, she also picked his ducks. He says, "She wouldn't let me pick any." He made it sound as if he were denied a good part of the hunting experience. His favorite waterfowl was the canvasback.

Many of his early calls were made by horse and buggy, but this was the beginning of the automobile era, and he made many calls by car on prairie trails and very poor roads. Between 1915 and his retiring in the 50's, he delivered over 2000 babies in the Woodworth and surrounding area. The 1918 flu kept him moving all hours of the day and night for weeks. He made calls where the entire family, in one case eleven people, was laid out with the flu. He often fed livestock and did essential chores that family members were no longer capable of. He was seldom ill. He was able to avoid the flu, but in 1936 he got typhoid fever. He was treating four or five cases at the time. This bout kept him in the hospital for seven weeks. Before that he'd had headaches and some sinus trouble. The Doctor who tended him when he was in the hospital said, "I think that typhoid burned everything out of you." Doc says, "I think he was right." After the typhoid he was no longer bothered with the headaches etc. He enjoyed very good health for many years.

Once after a delivery, the new father asked, "How much do I owe you?" Doc said something to the effect, "Why do you ask? I know you can't pay me now." This was during the 30's.

Some of Stuart Thompson's best memories of growing up in Woodworth include those warm afternoons when sitting in the shade and listening to Doc tell stories. One story is about a notorious dog that Doc bought from Sam Shipstead, a brother of Senator H. Shipstead of Minnesota. "Rex" was an excellent hunting dog. He would ride along on the running board of Doc's Model T. Once while hunting, Rex fell off the running board and caught a leg in the spokes. Doc had to set and wrap the leg. Rex was a good retriever. If a duck dived, so did Rex. Once Doc got two cows as payment from a farm family. A farmer on the south edge of Woodworth kept the cows for Doc, and got the morning's milk. Doc had C.D. Unruh make a harness for Rex. Doc built a sled. In winter his boys could use the dog and sled to pick up the evening's milk. The dog wasn't without fault. He would fight any dog that came near him, and he hated cats. Rex was sometimes gone for days at a time — picking fights. One time Ben Bryan called Doc from Edmunds saying Rex was there, fighting any dog that dared to cross his path. Once while Rex was chasing the neighbor's cat, she jumped through a hole in the screendoor. Rex followed, enlarging the hole, and killed the cat on the living room floor. To keep peace with the neighbors, Doc thought it best to get rid of Rex. He called Senator Shipstead who gladly accepted such a fine hunting dog. The Senator was pleased with the dog, but its guessed that his enthusiasm faded when Rex "licked" President Calvin Coolidge's dog on the White House lawn.

Continuing Melzer's story.

Beatrice Melzer died April 16, 1948.

Simon Melzer graduated from Woodworth High School in 1932. He received his B.S. from Northwestern U of Chicago. He also attended De Paul U where he completed a graduate study program. He married Loa Reeser at Woodworth June 2, 1940. In 1945 they moved to Canby, Minnesota where Sim owned and operated the Melzer-Reeser Motor Co. In 1957 he began teaching in Canby High School. He retired from teaching in 1978. He was active in church and civic affairs in Canby. He was also an amateur radio operator. Sm and Loa had two daughters, Beatrice and Barbara. Beatrice lives in Minneapolis and Barbara in San Antonio, Texas. Simon died March 12, 1985.

Laurence graduated from Woodworth High School in 1933 and the School of Mines at Golden, Colorado. Laurence married Dorothy Brooks of Kansas. He is a geologist and has a position with the government. They have four children. Mary Ann Staib is married and has four children. She and her husband live at Plano, Texas. Betty Moore is married with two children. They live at Midland, Texas. Martha Savage lives in Brooklyn, New York. She and her husband have one child. Steven Melzer is married and has two sons. They live at Midland, Texas.

On May 6, 1949 Doc married Sara (Sadie) Uggen. She was in poor health for several years. She died October 22, 1956 in Jamestown. She is buried in Gem Cemetery.

Many people remember Doc for his love of the outdoors. He was an avid hunter and even in his 80's, he was one of the best shots around. After his eyesight began to fail, he started fishing, and he too did this with enthusiasm. He often said, "I had a wonderful life in N.D. with all the fine people around Woodworth and west to Pettibone and Robinson. I also lived in the most wonderful time this Nation will ever have." He saw the first cars, radios and televisions, and the development of a great farming area.

Doc's first wife, Beatrice, worked hard with the

Stutsman County Welfare Office during the Dust
Bowl days of the early thrities.
   Dr. Melzer died May 11, 1983 in a nursing home
in Canby, Minnesota. He lived to be 97 years old.
He and Beatrice are buried in Gem Cemetery.
   (Some of the material for this story was taken
from the "North Dakota Outdoors" magazine of
September 1978. Ted Upgren wrote the story for the
magazine.)

Final excerpt of Melzer article.

I was born, Willard Stanley Ingraham on June 23, 1924 on a small farm outside of Woodworth, N.D. at either the George Anderson or George Benson farm. At that time there were no hospitals and only one country doctor (Dr. Melzer) available to care for all the people of the community. When Dr. Melzer was called for my birth I was an anxious baby who could not wait for him so I entered this world with Dad (Lyle Ingraham) as my doctor. By the time Dr. Melzer arrived, I was fussing and already satisfying my appetite for which in all my life I have not lost my appetite for food.

In May or June of 1925 Dad heard of the big money to be made in Wyoming working in the oil fields. He knew it would be dangerous work but wages were good and he wanted to buy a farm that they had their eyes on. He packed up the family and moved to a small town out of Casper, Wy. The work he was assigned to do was to replace any missing bolts or tighten any loose bolts on the oil covered oil derricks. Many workers got hurt or killed when they stepped out on a cross brace only to find out that it was only the thick oil on the brace that was holding it in place. The weight of walking across on the cross brace would give away on one end and down would go the worker.

I don't remember my parents saying how long they were at Casper but I would venture to say maybe less than a year. They moved back to Woodworth, N.D. to the Bullock farm.

On August 12, 1926 Lorraine Jainett Ingraham was born. A short time after Lorraine was born our family was hit with scarlet fever. Lorraine was so sick and Mom told me the only thing that kept me happy during the day was to put a Sears and Roebuck catalog in my lap and I would sit there looking forward as my neck must have been too sore to turn. She said I would sit there and continually turn the sheets in the catalog hour after hour.

Norman said he remembered turning pages on that catalog also. He also remembers our family moving earlier in 1926 to the Bullock farm that was located not far from the Gunder Johnson homestead. All of us children were so sick with the scarlet fever at this time. Raymond had to wear glasses after he got well because of the scarlet fever.

My mother Gena's brother Gordon Johnson died from scarlet fever during those years of epidemic.

In 1928, Lyle and Gena bought the farm that was located about three miles south of Woodworth, N.D. by Dittbenner Lake. We referred to it as the Len Fish Place.

In 1928 there was always excitement around home as Dad had wild horses that he would break to drive and ride. How Dad kept from getting killed by those wild horses was a mystery but it seems he had a way with animals. The rest of our family soon learned to be very careful around the barn when the horses were there.

It was fun to go down and play with the colts and I thought that would be safe enough until one time a colt kicked me in the stomach and almost knocked me out. We kids were mostly content in breaking the young calves to ride. We soon had those calves tame enough so we could ride and chase the cattle back to the barn.

My parents also raised ducks, geese and chickens. When the geese nested by the barn in a lot of straw the male gander would stand guard and if he caught any of us half way to the barn he would come grab us by the seat of our pants and whip us with his wings all the way back to the house as we tried to get away. I was about five years old then.

The chickens were turned loose during the day and penned up in the chicken house at night. The coyotes got so brave they would come during the day and if they caught a chicken far enough away from the chicken coop they would have their dinner.

Also the big hawks would swoop down and get a chicken every once in a while until Dad bought a couple of ginny hens and they guarded the chickens with their shrill cackle that was a warning before the chickens got caught.

There was no electricity to the farms at that time so when Mom got a washing machine with the agitator protruding down from the underside of the lid it was hand crank power that was used. The agitator had three rounded pieces of wood about two inches in diameter and eight inches long that went down into the clothes. The agitator would turn back and forth in the clothes as the outside crank was turned cleaning the clothes. On the top of the machine were roller wringers that we turned the clothes through to get the water removed from

241

the clothes and ready to hang on the clothes line for drying. It still was a lot of work but it beat the old scrub board and wringing the clothes by hand.

Left: Photo of Gena and Lyle. My father was an old time fiddler and Mother played the piano so we grew up having lots of music around. My parents played for countless barn dances and house parties. Many nights we kids curled up on a bench and slept until the dance was over in the wee hours of the morning.

How often I think back to 1929 when I was five years old and I saw the first black and white silent movie we attended at the community building in Woodworth, N. D. At that time to me seeing a moving picture was unbelievable. Of course, there was no sound with the picture and you must know that this was the time before radio and electricity in small communities like Woodworth, N.D. This great evening ended up with a Christmas tree and Santa Claus passing out Christmas presents to all the small children.

It was kind John Dittbenner, the owner of the Dittbenner grocery store that always made sure a sack of candy was thrown into the groceries for us kids. He always made sure we had a piece of candy before leaving his store.

I (Willard Ingraham) was playing in an old car body on a knoll beyond the barn. Cars were just starting to come to our area so I am sure that old car body was an old model T Ford. We kids would play for hours here at times.

One day I looked at that big lake that was about half a mile wide and it looked very tempting even though my parents warned me never to go near that lake. Below is this forbidden Dittbenner Lake, Woodworth, N. Dakota.

As my cousin, Arnold Steffens and I played, we got closer to that lake until we were close enough to investigate all the new things along that vast body of water. Our minds were on nothing but seeing more of the shore line. All of this was too much fun to last because it seemed all of a sudden there were my mother and my brother Raymond hot on our trails. My mother picked up a three foot limb of buck brush as she came looking for us. The buck brush grew wild there and was about four foot tall. These bushes had limbs like a willow tree. Need I say more, because I felt the sting of that limb all the way back home. Arnold said he got a couple of swats also.

It seemed that this was the time of learning my boundaries because during the following fall Mother took Raymond Norman to school; in fact, she took all the children to school along the way. Lorraine and I were too young to go to school yet so we were playing cards at home and decided we wanted something more exciting. We called our pet dog in from outside and shut the door to make the dog run around the table that was in the center of the kitchen. I picked up the broom, Lorraine picked up the mop and around, and around the table, we went chasing the dog.

We were having a lot of fun when the dog decided that was enough. The low window was about two foot above the floor and it had a storm glass in it. The other window was about four foot above the floor and it only had a single glass in that window. The dog picked single glassed window and jumped on the trunk under it and

243

out through the window she went with about a five foot jump to the ground outside.

Wouldn't you know it; my Dad was just coming by the house leading a couple of horses that he had taken to drink down by the well. When he looked up he saw the dog coming out of the house through that window.

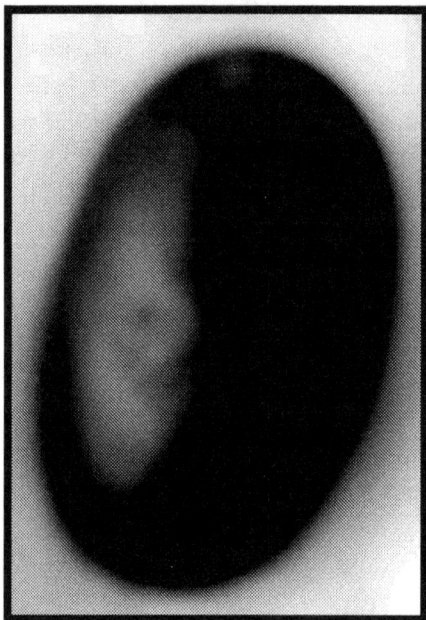

Lorraine and I were busy playing cards when Dad came directly into the house. I guess you know I got another good lesson in discipline by my Dad's hand. My butt was pretty warm for a while when I sat down.

There was no money to buy toys so we had to improvise our own way of playing. We took string and made a play pasture; for the fence line we used a group of pegs and then the string for a two wire fence. We used round rocks about an inch in diameter that we found about and used them as our horses. The rough small rocks were our cows and smaller rocks were our calves and colts.

Norman found two black round rocks with one that had a 22 marked on it. Below is a photo; one can if looking closely see the 22 yet this day many years later.

That was always his favorite because he was born in the year 1922. That rock held a special meaning for him through the years. When he grew up and had his own family he told them about this special rock and wished that he had kept it.

Unknown to Norman through all those years I had kept a little calumet can and in it I kept those two black rocks with some agates I had collected when I was little. It was the only thing I had kept from my own childhood days.

About the year 2000 Norman mentioned the black rocks and how he regretted not keeping the little black rocks because one had the year 22 marked on it representing 1922 the year he was born. To his surprise I told him that I still had those rocks and they are yours. Norman now has his special rocks and one can see a picture of them above in this book.

During the year of 1929 our family was still living on the farm that our parents Lyle and Gena had purchased. On the day indelible in my mind was a day that it was rainy with dark blue clouds in the sky. It was a refreshing day as the rain had cleaned everything leaving a fresh smell in the air with very little wind blowing.

The rain had stopped and there were a lot of little green frogs hopping all over the place. Our family all went outside the house looking to the direction south. Blue clouds were hanging on the lover side of the sky and it was very enjoyable to be outside and observing the beauty of everything around us. It made us all feel very secure with all the family standing there together and enjoying what God was displaying for all of us. As we looked south at the low hanging blue clouds we were surprised that there in the clouds were beautiful white buildings with house, barn and all the normal other farm buildings scattered all through out the farm. All the buildings were white. The strangest thing to all was that we were seeing white barns and most of the barns in this area were all red.

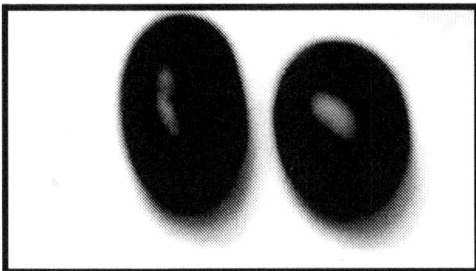

Our parents told us what we were seeing was known as a mirage. Dad and Mom were well acquainted with all the farms in the surrounding country side and did not know any farm that looked like the mirage we were looking at in the sky.

I am today almost eighty three years old and I have thought back to that mirage in the sky in my mind but have never experienced anything like what our family saw so many years ago.

My Mother always liked to raise a big garden but with a big garden there was also a lot of weeds to be removed from the rows of vegetables that she grew. One warm day my Mother decided to weed; this was in the summer of 1929. She pulled the stone bolt out near the garden then turned the stone bolt on its side, bracing it up to cast a lot of shade for Norman, Lorraine and I (Willard) to lay on the blankets and have our naps while Mother and brother Raymond were busy weeding the garden.

All three of us kids were sleeping soundly and did not know that the pigs had become curious and had come to the stone bolt. They were rooting all around us until our Mother noticed them and she soon dispersed them out of our area.

In 1930 I would walk up a knoll east of the garden and sit on this knoll looking out into the distant watching the prairie grass sway and roll in the wind. It resembled the ocean waves in a big ocean. My scope of the world at this time was Woodworth with a population of about 350.

My grandparents, Gunder and Laura Johnson's home was located about ten miles east of our farm. About five or six miles north of Woodworth were my other grandparents, Chauncey and Myrtle Ingraham living on their homestead. Both grandparents had proved up on their homesteads that they had obtained through the Homestead Act.

My little mind at that time would have been amazed to

have known that through my life I would visit most of the states in the United States and also be fortunate to travel to many of the countries of the world and in each of these places I would come away with another interesting story to tell. When I was little I remember looking out over all the miles of prairie grass from one special knoll I sat on and wondered what my life would be like and how many of these wonderful things I was seeing now would I see again. From this same knoll I watched a train about five miles in the distance lumbering along with the billowing black smoke shooting out of the smoke stack of that train. The land around me was all flat land so I could see for miles. The train was working its way toward Woodworth. A photo of that train is above.

Just down the hill from the house near the marsh that all the pussy willows grew Ray, Norman and I would play along the edge of the marsh. We noticed bunches of fair sized rocks were placed in circles. We wondered why they were placed in a circle with selective rocks. Years later, I found out that this was an Indian encampment and the Indians placed their tepees. The rocks were placed around the outside of the tepees to hold the bottom of the tepees down so the wind would not blow through the tepee.

The big fear in this country was a possible prairie fire that would roar along at a fast speed destroying everything in its path. North of our farm was a big marsh land covered with pussy willows that extended for about a quarter of a mile and about a mile beyond the marsh land was a farm called the

247

Dittbenner farm because John Dittbenner had lived there and later moved into Woodworth to be near his grocery store.

I remember looking out over that marsh land at night was the most mysterious sight that anyone could behold with the millions of fire flies that would appear to twinkle their fire lights off and on. We used to collect them in a fruit jar and pound a bunch of small holes in the lid then watch them light up.

We got a chance to observe them and see what made them light up. Did you know that the fire fly is also called the lightening bug? It is characterized by a soft body with a light producing organ at the rear of the abdomen. There is also a variety that is known as the glow fly and glow worm but they are the wingless variety. If you see the fire flies light up across a large area twinkling in the night it looks like a big metropolitan city in the distance. Back in 1930 there was no electricity in that area so a display of lightening bugs was quite a novelty to us.

A gathering place for a lot of families in the summer time was at a lake and place to swim. The water though was full of blood suckers that would cling to your skin. When I was five years old and came out of the lake in very shallow water there was a bunch of those blood suckers hanging on my skin. It scared the heck out of me until my mother took them off of me.

The families held big picnics along Dittbenner Lake located on Lyle and Gena Ingraham's farm that was less than half a mile from their house. We picked chokecherries that grew on small trees along the water. They were also known as June berries because it was in the month of June that the berries were ripe and ready to pick. These berries made the best jelly that anyone would want to eat. Photo below of the lake; I (Willard) was in the group somewhere.

In Dec. 22, 1930 our little sister, Gerada Agnes Ingraham was born. It was late in the afternoon when Dad went to Woodworth in the sled pulled with a team of horses to

get Dr. Melzer. He was the only doctor in the area for miles around. While Dad was getting the doctor Aunt Rose, (Ralph Ingraham's wife) put Raymond, Norman, Lorraine and I (Willard) to bed.

The doctor came and delivered a bouncing baby girl, Gerada into the world. Everything seemed alright with the birth and all. While Dad took Dr. Melzer back home something apparently went wrong because our little sister died. She was such a beautiful baby with long black hair. All of us children got to see her.

Photo is at left. She was buried at the Woodworth cemetery north of Woodworth. There was only a little metal marking at her gravesite.

When I retired in 1978 I took my parents back to North Dakota to visit many of our relatives and friends at Woodworth, Jamestown and New Rockford, N.D. We made a stop over at Laurel, Montana to visit the Claude Ingraham family and the Ralph Ingraham family and also to Billings, Mt. to visit my grandma Myrtle Ingraham. She was in a nursing home and was 105 years old at that time. She could neither see or hear but I was so blessed when I put my face on hers with my mouth next to her ear, speaking softly to her she understood every word and knew that all of us were standing around her. My parents tried to talk to her but she could not hear them but from hearing me she knew all of them were there and how very happy she was to know we were all there.

At the time of our visit to Jamestown my Aunt Esther Sorenson (my mother's sister) offered to make sure that our little sister, Gerada Agnes Ingraham would have a gravestone at her grave site if I would cover the costs. I was thankful she wanted to see that our little sister had a proper grave stone in place. Our little sister, Gerada has a nice colonial rose granite gravestone placed at her gravesite; photo below.

Going back to April 8, 1931 my mother took Lorraine and I (Willard) over to Uncle Art Steffens home. After we were there for a short time my Uncle Art took my cousins Arnold and Helen and sister Lorraine and I out to the barn where we played games. After a while we were told why we had been taken out to the barn. My mother, Gena was a midwife to many births and on this day she helped Aunty Nora deliver Rosella Loretta Steffens into this world and we got to see this little baby girl.

In September 1931, I started to school in Woodworth in the first grade. Miss Hough was my teacher. She made us learn our phonics very well so we would know our alphabet sounds that helped us all to read well. My (Willard Ingraham) first grade classmates in the photo above were back row left to right Everett Deede, Eugene Nygard, Morris P. Morrison, Jean Gwenn, Lois Loosey, Samuel Beck and Wallace Wilson. Front row left to right is Corley Wright, I (Willard Ingraham) and Oliver Graves.

To the left is the Woodworth School. My brothers Raymond and Norman were already attending this school.

During the winter we were in school when a blizzard came up.

All of us children that lived out of town had to go stay over night with another family living in Woodworth. Raymond, Norman and I stayed with our Uncle Ralph and Aunt Rose Ingraham. Uncle Ralph was the custodian of the school. In 1932, I was in the second grade with the same classmates.

Photo below (all relatives) taken 1932: back row l to r, unknown, Ray Ingraham, Esther Johnson holding Gordon Seffens, Avis and Doris Johnson. Front row l to r: Norman and Willard Ingraham, Arnold Steffens, Lorraine Ingraham and Helen Steffens.

Above is a 1932 photo of the Ingraham family l to r: Ray, Norman, Willard and Lorraine in front.

I was five years old when the depression hit but I can remember the hard times. My parents, Lyle and Gena Ingraham had purchased the farm where they raised enough food to eat but there was never any extra money for other necessities including money to operate the farm. It was in 1932 when they lost their farm.

Herbert Hoover was president of the United States in 1929 during the great disastrous depression. It was under his administration that the economic system of America collapsed. The stock market crash created panic that preceded a nation wide depression. Bank closures took place everywhere. There were no Federal Insurance Guarantees that protected people from loss. In effect what happened was shutting people out by closing the banks and retrieving money that was the peoples.

In rural America the farmers were unable to borrow money for operating costs due to the bank closures. Outstanding loans were called in from lack of none payment. Foreclosures on farms ran rampant. To make everything worse the whole country was in a draught.

In the year of 1933 Franklin Roosevelt became president of the United States. He established the Works Progress Administration known as the WPA. This program gave jobs to many. The Social Security Act passed and that helped elderly people to survive as did the Unemployment and Old Age Compensation Act. With the work programs in place and people back to work money began to flow and families could eat regularly. Hope for a future of families in the United States rose.

My Father (Lyle) at first would work over 200 miles from home to get on the WPA. He was lucky to get home once a month. It was rough for everyone but there was enough money from his work that we were all eating regular meals. If lucky, we children might even get a pair of shoes without holes in the toes.

Lyle and Gena Ingraham lost their farm in late 1932 but managed to stay on the farm until school was out in the spring of 1933. They then moved to a town of Goldwin that was located about 10 miles south of Woodworth. The farm was about a mile west of Goldwin. The first thing Lyle did was get a bunch of wild horses from the hills of Montana and with the help of his brother-in-law Phil Schuff they proceeded to break the horses to drive and ride.

Believe me all of us children were very careful when we went to the barn area with all those wild horses running around. Lyle and Phil broke all of the horses and did pretty good money wise doing so.

Phil Schuff was a cowboy from Miles City, Montana; he married my mother's sister Louise Johnson.

Out of the bunch of horses, a good bunch of workhorses were produced and a selective few were broke to ride making some good saddle horses and they brought a good price.

The farmhouse we lived in was located on a hill above the barn and over looking the pasture and marshland. Again we had a beautiful view of all those lightning bugs at night.

In the fall of 1933 all four of us children, Raymond, Norman, I (Willard) and Lorraine attended the school in Goldwin. We walked to school which was about a mile from home.

After the fall harvest all three of us boys would herd the cattle in the harvested fields around the straw stacks. While sitting on the straw stacks watching the cattle we would braid halters and reins that we put on the steers and broke them to ride. We used the steers as horses to herd the cows and ride instead of walking to get the job done.

The string we used for the halters was in the straw piles in abundance as this was the string that had been used to tie the bundles of grain stacked together before it was threshed.

About November of 1933 we moved to a farm approximately six miles southeast of Woodworth and we attended the school at Woodworth. Lyle was still breaking wild horses to drive and to ride. He got a blazed face chestnut gelding about a three year old that was the prettiest horse I had

ever seen up to that time. Dad broke it out as a saddle horse.
When the principle of Woodworth schools saw that horse he
just had to buy it. His name was Professor Reginald Hoidal.

Russel Deede was going to high school in Woodworth.
He lived with his parents Mr. and Mrs. Gottilip Deede and they
lived at the end of the school bus line that is why Russel Deede
was driving the bus. It was on March 15, 1933 on the way
home from school on the bus that Russel saw a pond that was
frozen over just off the main road. He decided to have some
fun with the bus; the bus was going in circles sliding sideways
and having all kinds of fun until Russel slid the bus too fast and
the bus ended up too close to the edge of the pond and got
stuck in the mud.

The big problem was that Lyle and Gena were waiting
for us to come home from school so they could go to Mom's
brother Ted Johnson's wedding to Irene Holtz. It was quite
obvious that the bus was not going any where but soon parents
of the children on the bus came to see what had happened. The
bus was pulled out and we were all delivered to our homes.
My parents were not very happy with Russel, our bus driver.
Russell never did tell us what discipline he received from his
parents for his escapade with the bus.

The farm that Lyle and Gena Ingraham leased was a
small farm that barely had pasture enough to feed the thirty
nine head of cattle and six horses. Along with little pasture and
the draught in the country and lack of land to grow and harvest
any hay. Because the neighbors had either bought or leased all
the land for miles around and no one was selling any hay they
owned Lyle and Gena decided that with no way to raise enough
feed for their animals they would have to sell out and move.
They set their sale date for April 17, 1934.

Dad had a pet goose and if Dad was any place on the
farm and he called Pete the goose would go to where Dad was.
The day of the sale Pete knew something was wrong and with
the large crowd at the sale the goose was right on Dad's heel.
If Dad went into the house that day old Pete was there never

leaving Dad out of his sight. The auctioneer Ben Gilberts was so impressed with the goose that he bid on Pete, the goose and bought him.

A copy of the sale flier is below.

AUCTION SALE

I will sell the following described personal property at my farm, located 2 miles east, 2 miles south and 1 mile east of Woodworth, on

TUES. APRIL 17

Sale Starts at 1:00 o'clock P. M. sharp   *1934*

6   Head of Horses

1 Gray mare, weight 1025 pounds, 4 years old

1 bay colt, coming 2 yrs. old

1 sorrel mare, weight 1200 pounds, 9 years old

1 Yearling colt

1 Sorrel mare, weight 1100, 7 years old

1 black mare, weight 1100 pounds, 7 years old

39 HEAD OF CATTLE

10 Fresh Cows;   4 coming fresh
1 Pure-bred Polled Angus bull
5 Heifers, 2 year old, fresh in summer
9 Yearlings
10 Spring Calves

3 Turkey Hens
2 Hogs   2 Geese   6 Ducks
1 Stock Saddle   15 chickens

Kentucky double disk, 11 ft. drill; John Deere plow; P & O breaking plow; Deering mower; McCormick Rake; boss harrow; 2 wagons and racks; wagon box; sled: cultivator

HOUSEHOLD GOODS AND NUMEROUS OTHER ARTICLES

TERMS OF SALE: CASH

LYLE INGRAHAM

Ben Gilbertson, Auc't.   - -   G. W. Nygaard, Clerk

Thank goodness the sale went better than they figured it would thus giving Dad a chance to get a house ready in Jamestown, N.D. by school time next fall.

Statement of Lyle Ingraham Sale,
Held Apr. 17th., 1934.

Purchaser	Article	Amount.
Aug. Krenz	Trough, gas engines	.75
C.H. Thorson	Water tank	1.00
Den Voth	Chicken coop	1.50
Aug. Krenz	Wheels	.30
Gott. Schelske	Scrap iron	.25
" "		.25
Elmer Larson	2 bars	.25
Otto Koenig	Iron bar	.50
Fred Bitz	Eveners	1.55
Geo. Retzlaff	Cab	1.00
Aug. Krenz	Poles	3.00
Den Harr	Fork	1.10
Gott. Beck	Fork	.75
" "	Fork & Bbl.	1.00
Otto Koenig	Nests, etc.	.50
Gust Liberda	Wagon, rack, wheels	5.25
Aug. Krenz	Lumber	2.00
Gust Liberda	Drag & cart	1.50
Helmer Bah	Gang plow	6.00
Aug. Krenz	Cultivator	2.50
Gust Liberda	Mower	6.00
Elmer Larson	Sulky plow	3.50
Fred Hochhalter	Wagon box	5.25
Aug. Krenz	Bob-sled	1.00
Wm. Reich	Steel, eveners	2.00
Otto Koenig	Stone boats	1.00
Henry Friedholm	Hay rake	5.00
Gott. Schelske	Red & white cow	17.00
" "	Black & white cow	12.00
" "		18.00
Andrew Deede	Blue roan cow	15.00
John Shay	Black & white cow	18.00
Gunder Johnson	Red cow	13.00
G.W. Schelske	small red & white cow	17.50
	Red & white cow	15.00
John Shay	Red cow	19.00
G.W. Schelske	Roan cow	18.00
Phil Schuff	Bull calf	8.50
John Shay	9 calves @ $5.00	45.00
And. Deede	Angus cow	16.00
And. Deede	2 red cows @ $15.00	30.00
" "	Roan heifer	12.00
" "	6- 2 yr. old heifers @ $14.50	87.00
" "	8 yearlings @ $8.00	64.00
Dave Scott	Angus bull	16.00
John Shay	Grey mare	37.50
Gott. Beck	Sorrel mare	28.00
D.G. Wilson	Harness	8.00
Wm. Reich	Harness	4.50
Phil Schuff	Harness	1.25
A.C. Heinrich	Sorrel colt, yearling	17.00
Dave Scott	Bay colt, 2 yr. old	14.00
Rud. Goter	Saddle & bridle	4.75
Elmer Larson	Sow	6.00
Phil Schuff	Trough	1.00
Gust Liberda	3 turkeys @ 1.50	4.50
John Shay	Gobbler	1.00
Ralph Ingraham	14 chix @ 45¢	6.30
Ed. Stebner	6 ducks @ 35¢	2.10
Ben Gilbertson	Goose	1.75
Phil Schuff	Wagon & rack	12.00
Gott. Deede	Pump (5.50)	5.00
John Shay	Cream can	2.00
J.W. Deede	Cream can	1.25
Henry Friedholm	Barrel	.50
Gust Loose	Goose eggs	1.00
Frank Stoppleworth	Duck eggs	.35
Otto Struxness	Turkey eggs	1.60
Jacob Sohl	Lantern, etc	.50
Peter Hemitz	Kerosene stove	.50
Henry Deede	Cot	2.00
Dave Scott	Baby crib	2.25
Gust Loose	Bed & spring	4.50
Chas. Costello	Cream Separator	3.00
Andrew Deede	Sewing machine	6.00

I have inserted copies of the sale items and the amount each brought. Even though the statement is difficult to read one can see that the prices each item brought in 1934 were considerable lower than one would receive now although the amount was considered good for 1934.

As one continues to view, the sold items and amounts it seems the household items sold for pennies compared to today prices but Gena and Lyle were happy with the amount they got from the sale.

```
               Lyle Ingraham Sale, continued.

Purchaser            Article                    Amount.
Gust Loose           Phonograph                   1.50
Phil Schuff          Library table                2.50
Don Sunday           4 chairs                      .60
John Shay            4 chairs @ 45¢               1.80
G.W. Nygaard         Guitar                        .40
Geo. Challberg       Violin                       3.00
Phil Schuff          Table                        6.50
Rudolph Peda         Dresser                      4.00
Gott. Deede          Large jar                    1.75
George Retzlaff      Smaller jar                  1.25
Gott. Deede          2 boxes fruit jars           1.00
Henry Friedholm      "    "    "    "             1.30
Gott. Deede          Roaster etcs.                 .50
Wm. King             2 boxaes fruit jars          1.30
Gott. Deede          Jars & glasses                .75
Otto Pieske          Pan & glass ware              .60
Gott. Deede          Pail                          .30
    "      "         Jugs, jars, bottles          1.00
    "      "         Can & pump spout              .50
Albert Deede         Scoops                        .50
Fred Bitz            Spades                        .60
Frank Stoppleworth   Wire stretcher               1.30
Hugh Dickinson       Traps                         .50
Gott Deede           Door & hoes                   .80
Fred Hochhalter      Junk                         1.05
Wm. Holmes           Collar                        .75
Fred Bitz            Clevises                      .90
Tom McCurdy          22 rifle                     3.00
Elmer Larson         Shot gun                     4.25
Ed. Stebner          Mantle lamp                  3.75
Helmer Bah           Plants                        .25
Fred Hochhalter       "                            .25
Ed. Stebner           "                            .15
Gott. Deede          Range                       10.00
Ralph Ingraham       Heater                       8.50
                            Gross Sale - - - - - $ 730.40
Expenses:
Auctioneer, Ben Gilbertson, 2% - - 14.60
Clerk, G.W. Nygaard,        - - - - - 7.00
             Total expense  $ 21.60               21.60
             Net to Lyle Ingraham            $ 708.80

Received copy of above sale:
                                       Nygaard
                                          Clerk.
_____
Owner.
```

After the sale Raymond being the oldest went to work for the Monsons for the summer. They were located about nine miles east of Woodworth. Norman went to work for Uncle Phil and Aunt Louise Schuff. Mom took Lorraine with her and she went to work for Amicks. I (Willard) went to Uncle Harry and Aunt Hilda Schuff who lived on a farm about six miles east of Woodworth and Dad went to Jamestown to get a house together for all of us by the time school would start in the fall.

Because of our family situation Mom got all of us children out of school for the rest of that school year with all of us passing to the next grade for the fall term.

I (Willard) was ten years old then, they had a Shetland pony on the farm at Uncle Harry, and Aunt Hilda's that was not broke to ride so I immediately proceeded to break it to ride. That little Shetland pony and I became good friends. Every day I would ride him most of the day.

The photo at left is of me (Willard) with that little pony I enjoyed so much.

They also had a collie dog that became my good friend. We would play tag and I would go up in the hay loft and hide under the hay. The dog would always find me. With two friends like these my summer went pretty fast.

One Sunday during the summer Uncle Harry and Aunt Hilda wanted to go visit someone so they sent me to a neighbors home where there was about four children all of whom I had never met. Their parents went with my uncle and aunt. It was about a mile walk to go to their farm and when I got there the two youngest girls had baked some cookies that they gave me. The two guys tried to be friendly but I did not seem to fit in so I bid them goodbye and walked back to Uncle Harry's place. To my surprise Raymond had walked three miles to come and see me. He had just gotten there. We had a wonderful visit before he had to go. He left and walked back before dark. I don't remember when my uncle and aunt returned.

I rode the little Shetland pony all over herding sheep, looking for turkey nests that I found sometimes half a mile from the farm. Regardless of where they would go and hide my little Shetland and I would find them.

Dad stopped once during the summer and picked me up and we went to see Grandpa and Grandma Chauncey and Myrtle Ingraham who at that time still lived on the old homestead. When Dad took me back to Uncle Harry's place he told me to hang on that he was working on a home and we would all soon be all together again. What he had done was to buy two lots in Jamestown and bought a railroad refrigerator car and had it moved onto the lot then remodeled it.

He put windows and a door in it and made a bedroom on each end of the refrigerator car with a big room in the center. Believe me it was as snug as could be in the winter and the summer.

It was sometime in August of 1934 that Raymond left Monson's and Norman left Uncle Phil's place. They both went to Jamestown to help Dad work on the house he was remodeling to be ready for the rest of the family by the time school was to start the first of September.

During that summer in 1934 I was 10 years old when I stayed with Uncle Harry Schuff and Aunt Hilda. In late August I was taken over to stay with Aunt Louise Schuff.

They had a big sale and it was mid afternoon and the sale was all over. The auctioneer and all the people had already left. Uncle Phil was already working in Jamestown working for the Jackson Construction Company. He was to come the next day to pick up Aunt Louise and children,

Harriet, Orville and Donald along with whatever they had
saved from the sale. My Dad (Lyle) was also to pickup Mom
(Gena) Lorraine and me (Willard) the next day and we would
go to our new home in Jamestown.

Uncle Ted Johnson was at the sale and had purchased a
wagon, a team of horses and enough grain to fill the wagon.
He now had a problem for he had a team, a wagon full of grain
and a car to get to his farm which was ten miles away. It was
getting late so he had to drive home to do his chores. This left
me to the driving the team of horses with the load of grain to
his place ten miles away. I wasn't even sure exactly where his
place was located; I had only visited there once. The dark
night set in long before I got there. It was quite a challenge for
a ten year old boy and when I got there I thought that I had
turned into the right drive way. As I turned in it really
concerned me to drive the horses on this dark night into a
narrow driveway without tipping the wagon over. After I got
in the yard Uncle Ted came out of the barn to direct me to the
granary where he unhooked the horses and took care of them.

After the horses were cared for Uncle Ted drove me
back to Aunt Louise's where I was to spend the night. Aunt
Louise let us kids stay up extra late that night but soon Harriet,
Orville and Donald were all played out and were put to bed. I
was all tired out also from that long trip with the horses but
Aunt Louise asked me if I would stay up with her.

She turned the kerosene lamp off and we set on the
floor looking out of a low window. She opened the window so
we could see down the long drive way that came into the farm.
Aunty Louise seemed really nervous about something so I
knew something was wrong.

After a time a car turned off the main road at the
beginning of the drive way and immediately turned off their car
lights. After a period of time we heard Aunt Louise's
Sheppard dog hit a fence up towards the car and give out a yip.
It was then that I realized why we were sitting all night by this
open window because Aunt Louise kept saying I don't have

any of the sale money with me. As afraid as she was it was evident to me even though I was only ten years old that she for sure had the money from the sale with her that night.

We continued watching out that window until about four o'clock the next morning until the car finally left. We both laughed and both agreed that the car must have been some lovers parked up by the drive way.

I asked Aunt Louise about that night sixty years later if she had that sale money in the house that night. She told me yes that she did and that is why she was so afraid. I told her I had been sure she had the money all the time.

The next day her family moved to Jamestown, North Dakota to a farm about three miles west of Jamestown. Uncle Phil was working for the Jackson Construction Company and there were a lot of big trucks and heavy equipment parked in the big barns on that farm. We always referred to their place as the Jackson farm.

The same day Uncle Phil picked up Aunt Louise and their children my Dad picked up Mom and Lorraine and came and picked me up from Aunt Louise's place and we were on our way to Jamestown and the home that Dad had made ready for us.

It was later in the evening before we got there and was it ever a joyous time to all be together again for the first time since the farm sale in April at the farm out of Woodworth. It was late at night but Dad had to show us the park across the river from our house but we could only go straight across to the park unless we swam the river. We then walked three or four blocks up the river until we crossed a bridge into the park.

In the park they had slides, swings and other fun things to play on. In Jamestown we experienced a new kind of life; we were living next door to people a hundred feet apart and we had sidewalks and street lights. It was a far cry from roaming around our farm. It did not take long to learn that the sidewalks and our own yard was the best place to play. Living in town did give us an opportunity to gain many friends and the park was just across the James River from our place.

We could swim in the river and take the short cuts to the park. A big hill was a short distance east of our place that we could walk up several blocks with our sleds and slide for several blocks down in the winter time.

I made good use of the public library that had millions of books. I was an ardent reader so I always had books checked out to read. I remember one winter we had a three day blizzard and I discovered one of my books was over due. I walked a mile in the blizzard to return the book only to find the library closed due to the storm; what a disappointment that was.

In the fall of 1934 Norman, Lorraine and I (Willard) went to the Lincoln school about six blocks from home. Raymond attended Junior High a mile walk from home. Norman was in the sixth grade, I (Willard) was in the fourth grade and Lorraine in the second grade. Dad was working for the WPA.

It was in 1935 and we were visiting Uncle Art and Aunt Nora across town from where we lived in Jamestown when we went out to play. Arnold, my cousin, had a coaster wagon that Norman was using on the sidewalk in the front of their house. Norman had one leg in the wagon and the other leg pushing the wagon fast down the sidewalk. He was having a good time. The wagon axel had an attached wheel with a nail holding it in place on the axel. Norman ran that nail into his ankle. His ankle was bleeding and Norman saw a wash tub on the porch that had a lot of dirty water in it but he dipped his foot into it anyway to wash the blood off his foot. The results of that was Norman got blood poisoning in his leg. He was taken to Doctor Surtness who told Mom that Norman's foot would have to be removed. When Mom got Norman home she said that she was not going to let that happen to Norman.

About six blocks from our house there lived a retired nurse that Mom was acquainted with. She went to her house and discussed Norman's problem. The nurse came to look at Norman and she said that it was very bad but there was a chance if Mom wanted to try what she would tell her. She told Mom that she was to get Norman up every hour day and night and soak his foot in as hot water as Norman could stand for a length of time then change to cold water. She was to do this every hour until the swelling and poison started to recede. It was through Mom's perseverance to save Norman's foot that she succeeded by her care and the constant soaking. Norman's leg was saved and it left him with a healthy leg to use for all of his life.

It was later in 1935 that Dad got sick with an ulcer and had to have an operation. Dr. Surtness told Mom to get a bag of ice and put the ice on his stomach and bring him to the hospital the next day and he would be operated on. All the directions were followed and Dad was operated on successfully but he then had pneumonia that put him near death. When he coughed the nurses were afraid that he would tear his stitches loose. For about two or three days it was touch and go with Dad but finally he pulled out of it and recovered.

The nurses were not watching him very well as per Dad telling Mom he had not had a bowel movement for three days and felt sick. That is when Mom had a talk with the nurses and things began to get better for Dad. You must know though that in those days there was not the technology that people have available as in the present times.

The hospital was located across the road from the Lincoln school so Norman, Lorraine and I would run across to see Dad every day at noon.

Times were tough at home then because Dad was laid up and the money had stopped coming in. Mom got a job at Peterson Biddick Company on their assembly line picking feathers off turkeys as they were moved down the line. It was hard on Mom but we were all still eating.

Dad got out of the hospital and he did the cooking while he was recovering. After he was well enough to work

Dad traded the car in for a truck, built a box on it and went to the Red River Valley and collected a load of potatoes. He sold all the potatoes to people wherever he could find buyers. He did very well doing this and besides this gave him a chance to get income until he was completely healed from the operation.

In the summer of 1935 at the age of eleven I (Willard) went to work for a farmer near Woodworth, N.D. He was a friend of my parents; his name was Vestal Cook. He sent me to raking hay with a team of horses. Vestal rented many acres of hay ground in New Rockford, North Dakota which was sixty miles from Jamestown. This was a time when we put all the hay up in stacks. I worked there for three weeks.

There were two other men with our crew of four. When the mowing and raking were completed then came the stacking of all the hay that had been mowed and left in raked winrows across the field for curing in the sun. After a few days of curing in the sun and the hopes that no rain would come we stacked all those win rows of raked prairie and clover grass and put it in haystacks. The stacks would end up about twenty foot high and about twelve foot by twelve foot wide.

Then they would use a bull rake which was about eight to ten foot wide with six foot long protruding wood teeth laying on the ground built six inches apart and eight foot wide; they hooked a horse on each side of the bull rake leaving the horses working alone about ten foot apart. By driving the two horses with each horse straddling each side of the winrow of hay the protruding teeth on the bull rake would scoop up the hay until full and the driver sitting on a long plank with a seat on it would set on it and lift the loaded hay off the ground and then drive the load to the location of the hay stack where there was a hay stacker.

With the stacker it would grip the protruding wood teeth like the bull rack leaving the stacker teeth flat on the ground. The bull rake would push its load of hay onto the stacker teeth. Then the driver would back the bull rack away from the stack of hay on the stacker teeth and go back to the field after another load.

The stacker was called an over shot stacker. To stack the hay they would take a team of horses and pull the loaded stacked teeth of hay up that protruded about twenty feet tall; hit a stop guide and throw the hay into the hay stack up to twenty foot tall.

The team of horses would back up letting the over shot stacked teeth to come back slowly to the ground. This routine was repeated many times until the stack would reach a heighth of twenty feet and round off the top to shed rain and that completed a hay stack.

I helped a man build those stacks from the ground to the finished stacks reaching the wanted heights. In that process many times we would almost get knocked off the haystack as the hay would fall down on us. I worked at this job for three weeks for fifty cents a day. To me at that time it was more money than I had ever seen.

With the money I thought I could buy my school books and new enough books that would have all the pages in it. I did not want or need a new book but it sure was nice to have a book with all the pages in and not marked all up. Also now with some money I could finally buy myself a new shirt. Believe me being the third boy in the family I always got hand me downs to wear.

Left is a photo of my new best friend and me (Willard) at that time.

Norman worked the summer for Pat Parson and carried water by hand for his lawn for ten dollars a month. Pat Parson had a red headed son Calvin that was about two years younger than I was. We became best of friends while we lived in Jamestown. They lived the fourth house north of our house.

In September of 1935 I was in the fifth grade in our school. My teacher was Miss Churness that taught the fifth grade. She was also the principle of the school that was a two story brick building with six rooms. There was one room for each grade of the six grades. The classes were from thirty to forty students per grade. I liked the teacher very much. One day in about mid term she was calling selected students into her principles office and some came back to the class room crying. She called me into her office and believe me I was sweating about that time wondering what I had done now. She began with how did I like school and many more questions concerning my school. She ended up telling me what a nice boy I was and I was doing fine in school. When I returned back to my classroom with a big smile on my face everyone had that surprised look on their faces.

For the summer Raymond went to work for the Rickfords who had a son Kermith that was about five years older than Ray. Ray slept in the attic of the house and he said one night when he saw a white figure come and stand at the foot of his bed it scared the day lights out of him but that figure would come back now and then until he got used to it and he did not pay much more attention to it.

Maybe it was his guardian angel because one time in the summer Ray was shocking grain when the lightning was cracking all over every where. A bolt of lightning headed for him and something told him to throw the pitch fork he was carrying away from his body. The bolt of lightning hit the pitch fork and guess what would have happened if Ray had not gotten that pre-warning.

Kermith's father was a heavy man so Kermith and Ray did almost all of the farming that summer. Ray was about sixteen years old then.

CHAPTER X

HOPE FOR BETTER TIMES

In September of 1936 all of the children of Gena and Lyle Ingraham headed for school. Ray was now in high school. Norman was in the eighth grade, I (Willard) began the sixth grade and Lorraine was in the fourth grade.

Unknown to the rest of us Dad's love was farming and he yearned to get back on a farm. Well he should because he was a good farmer. We had lived in Jamestown, N.D. about three years and in October of 1936 Dad found a farm at New Rockford, N.D. that needed someone to run it on shares. The owner of this farm was W.C. Schwoebel that Dad had met with and they formed a satisfactory contract agreed upon by both parties that Dad would farm as a share farmer.

It was the last of October of 1936 that the Lyle Ingraham family moved to New Rockford on the W.C. Schwoebel farm; (photo below). The farm had a couple of

sections of land, forty-five head of cattle and enough machinery to adequately farm all the land there. Bill Schwoebel owned the John Deere Machine Company at New Rockford.

Raymond Ingraham was now seventeen years old and he soon got well acquainted with running the John Deere tractor preparing the land for new crops to be seeded.

After living in town this farm seemed like a blessing to all of us. It was a large farm and there were plenty of chores for all of us to do each day. Our day started at 5:30 A.M. each day, seven days a week. Even with all of this work we all seemed much happier. The harvest time was the busiest time of the season.

These were the days before combines so all the grain had to be cut with the binder and the straw and the grain heads were then made into bundles by the binders and left in the field in winrows. Raymond was following up and putting all those bundles so the grain could cure in shocks and left in shocks until the threshing rig would come in and set up in the field to start the first straw pile. The thresher separated all the grain from the straw and it was taken into the storage bins on the farm or into the town elevator to be sold.

To get the bundles of grain to the thresher there were about six hay racks with a team of horses and a driver who loaded the hay racks full of bundles to take the load to the thresher and unload the bundles in the thresher.

The thresher was powered by a tractor that then extracted the grain from the straw. The straw was left in big straw piles that were fifteen to twenty feet tall.

Going back to the cutting time with binders Dad would be driving the tractor, pulling two grain binders. I (Willard) would operate the first binder and Norman the second binder. I was thirteen years old at that time and Norman fifteen.

The days were from 4:30 A.M. to 10 P.M. every day except Sundays. Work days were very long but like the saying goes "you make hay while the sun shines." The days were very hot, many over a hundred degrees and the binders were made of iron so the metal would get so hot that we could hardly touch it. The iron seat that we sat on did not get that hot only because we were always seated on it.

The first school year on this farm was 1936 – 1937. The little one room schoolhouse was just across the road from the Schwoelel farm where we lived (photo below). One teacher taught all eight grades. Being that we were close to school made it nice to be able to come home each day to hot lunches.

Miss Genevieve Sauser (photo left) was our teacher and she boarded at our home for the first school term. For the second and third school term Miss Eikom was our teacher. Our big yard was like a baseball diamond so it made an ideal place in the summer time (on Sundays) for many of the neighborhood boys to get together and play baseball.

271

During the winter months, the neighbors would get together on Friday nights to play cards. The game of Whist was played and it was the favorite game at that time.

We played either cards or Dad was an old time fiddler and Mom played the piano so they furnished the music for the good old home dances. Of course at many of these social gatherings there would be a basket social where the man would bid on the basket and if you bought the basket the lady that brought it was your social guest and you shared her basket of goodies and ate with you. There were usually community event that the money was collected for.

As our parents were both musical there was always a lot of music in our house. It made for many happy times at home and we still hold many happy memories.

On January 7, 1939 the neighbors surprised Lyle and Gena Ingraham on their 20th wedding anniversary. There was a mock wedding performed by Judge Hodges of New Rockford with many other games that made the evening into the night a very happy event. Many neighbor friends came and lots to eat at the end of the evening and into the wee hours of the morning.

The one room schoolhouse across from the Schwoebel farm had only sixteen students (photo below). They were

Carol Jane Starkey, Billy Starkey, Pete Klocke, Loverne Klocke, Reynold Christ, Sigrid Anderson, Joe Anderson, Edgar Duda, Delores Siebold and her younger brother LeRoy, Norman, Willard and Lorraine Ingraham, Richard Krause and younger sister and a Stap child.

It was agreed between Dad and Bill Schwoebel that Dad could buy and keep some milk cows, chickens and a few pigs to feed the milk to on the farm at the time we lived there. In 1939 Dad decided to rent a farm and temporarily we moved to a small farm three miles west of New Rockford. During the winter months Lorraine and I attended New Rockford school. My class, the eighth grade had forty two students. It was a far cry from the one room school with sixteen students in all eight grades.

In March of 1939 Dad leased a farm and started farming on his own. I (Willard) painted an oil painting of this farm pictured below.

At this time Dad could not afford a tractor so it was fun attending the sales where he purchased eight head of horses and machinery to farm with. Dad was always handy around machinery so some of the pieces he purchased were not in the best of shape but after Dad got the machinery home he soon had it fixed to operate like new.

At this time I was fifteen and was introduced to the gang plow; a plow that turned over two fourteen inch furrows of black soils every round. The plow was pulled by six horses.

It amazed me how when starting to plow a large field a mile long that it took one hour per round. Soon thou I would see the field begin to turn black.

Working long hours in the field was the only secret to accomplishing the job. This farm was located ten miles southeast of New Rockford and another town Brantford, N.D. that was located six miles further southeast of the farm. So when a breakdown occurred it meant longer periods of time to get parts. Most of the time except at harvest time if we had a breakdown we could normally improvise or fix it ourselves.

The small one room school that was a mile from the farm was again eight grades taught in one room. Lorraine and I walked to school every school day. This was the third school that Lorraine and I attended all in the same school year.

I was the only eighth grader. We had a young teacher and two months left of that school year so when it came time to take my final test to graduate the eighth grade they sent me back to the school across the road from the Schwoebel farm where we had once lived. Miss Eikom was the teacher and there were two eighth graders, Delores Siebold and Sigrid Anderson taking the test. I passed fine and finished the test early.

My diploma is on the left. The superintendent of County Schools sent my invitation for graduation to be held at New Rockford, N.D.

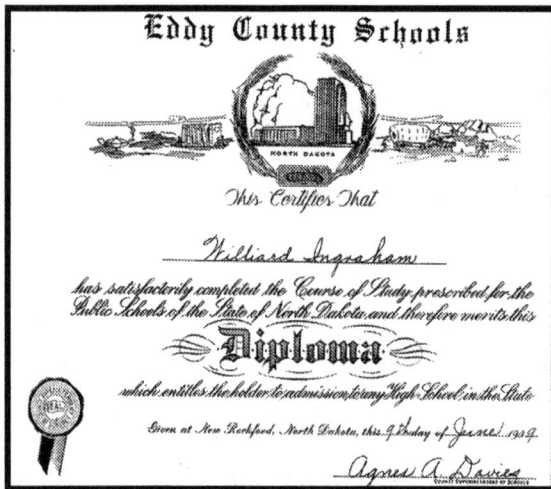

274

Raymond and Norman got a job working away from home at two different farms so that left me to help Dad do the farming. After the plowing was completed then I hooked up four horses to the disk and run it over the field to smooth out the furrows. After that I used four horses hooked to a drag unit that was built with a lot of spike iron pegs to break up all the clods of dirt leaving the fields smooth and ready for drilling the wheat seed.

The seed drill machine had a big trough like box built about four foot high and 12 inches x 18 inches x 12 foot long to hold the seed grain with a 6 foot in diameter wheel on each end of the box under the trough. It was these controlled feeders that let grain move down into a metal hose placed 4 inches apart and disk wheels that went into the ground to plant the seed in controlled depths and into rows.

The field was one mile long and there were markers at the end of the drill that marked the ground to follow in to make the next row. Also on each end of the mile there was a white flag pole that also was a guide to make straight rows in the field. I stood on top of the grain box as I guided the four horses from end to end of the field.

In 1939 and 1940 there were good crops. In the fall after harvest in 1940 Dad purchased a tractor and every thing was looking great. The crops were good, stock was increasing and we were now milking about ten cows. In fact Dad even offered to buy the farm from the owner who lived in Canada but he did not want to sell.

During the school year of 1940-1941 Lois Johnson stayed with our family and attended school. She fit in our family and became our little sister. Lois is the daughter of Ted and Irene Johnson.

On the north end of the pasture, one half mile from the barn there was a small river that cut across the corner of the pasture. The cows always liked the other side of the river so I would have to wade almost knee deep every night across that river to get the cows and drive them back to the barn to milk.

My little black terrier, Tippy with a white stripe on her chest always followed me so I would carry her over the river and back across. She liked that. I am holding Tippy in photo below.

Many times, I would sit across the river with Tippy and watch a den of red fox play outside of their den. After a while the fox got used to me and let me get very close to them but never close enough to pick one of the little fox up. They were always so cute to watch them play. The only thing bad about them was once in a while if they found a chicken far enough away from the chicken house they would catch it and have a feast for their family.

We always had a large vegetable garden and sometimes two big gardens so there was always a large selection of vegetables for Mom to can. She always kept the pantry shelves full. It was mostly Mom and I that raised the gardens.

The crops were good in 1940 so during harvest time that year Dad let me have a team of horses and a wagon with rubber tires that made the hay rack lower to the ground. It was easier for me to load. I was sixteen years old and felt I could do any thing that the men could do.

The threshing crew consisted of young boys like me except maybe a little older. It was about a three week tour going around with the threshing machine to many local farms to harvest grain. When they were threshing away from home, the threshing crew slept in the hayloft of the barn in the hay. Mice would run across our blankets during the night but we were too tired to worry about such a little animal.

Every morning there was a wash pan by the pump and we would wash up for breakfast. Threshing was into late fall and sometimes there was a frost and ice would form in the wash pan. But did we ever eat once we got to the table as all North Dakota women were good cooks and always had plenty to eat that we hungry boys took advantage of.

Above is our family in 1940; L to R Willard, Lorraine, Gena, Ray, Lyle and Norman Ingraham.

Almost at the end of the threshing season a dreaded rain came so we knew it would be a few days before the grain could be threshed so we went home. Dad had just come down with Yellow Jaundice and the rest of the family got it except Norman and Mom. We were so sick and turned yellow like a Chinaman. When Dad went to the doctor he was told just to go home and eat a lot of honey. That is what we did and all of us got over it but I still felt the effect of the Yellow Jaundice for at least five years later.

Our crop that year was one of the earlier crops to have been threshed so we were lucky but that was the end of our threshing tour for that year.

None of the farms in that area in the 1930s and the 1940s had electricity unless they had a Delco system. Consequently with no electricity there were no inside toilets. The outside toilets were built about three hundred feet beyond the house and even now I think about what a task it was in the winter when we had to at times tramp through two foot of snow to get to that toilet then open the door to find a foot of snow on the toilet seats. After clearing the seat with our gloves we had to clear more snow to find the Sears and Roebuck catalog. Can you imagine sitting on those seats in 40 degree below weather with a blizzard going on outside?

Light in those times there were kerosene lanterns that we took with us at night to show our way. The trick was to keep the lantern burning until we got where we were going without the flame in the lantern blowing out from the strong winds. Getting back to the house was difficult without getting blown off course.

In one of those bad blizzards that winter Dad, Raymond, Norman and I went to the barn to do the milking and chores. Mom set the Aladdin Kerosene lamp by the window facing the barn so we would not get lost coming back to the house in that blizzard. The snow and wind was blowing so hard and it was so cold that we had to use the collars of our coats to warm the air before breathing it or the cold air would take our breath away. The strength of the wind easily could blow us off coarse and we would never find our way back to the house. In blizzards like that we heard of farmers that went to the barn and were found the next day frozen to death.

Growing up in North Dakota was not always difficult. Dad played old time fiddle music and Mom played the piano. There was always plenty of music in our home. Mom could read notes also besides chord and would read and play many religious hymns.

In 1940 we had a battery operated radio. The radio was just coming in as a standard household item. We had our favorite radio programs such as Alley Oop, The Cave Man, Jack Armstrong, The All American Boy, One man's family, The Shadow Knows, Little Orphan Annie and we also listened to boxing with Joe Louis decking most of his opponents.

Grandpa Gunder Johnson lived in Jamestown, N.D. and once a week he had a radio program of his own with his little band playing dance music. He played a button accordion and sometimes he played Norwegian pieces and played and sang the songs in Norwegian.

We all enjoyed Major Bow's Amateur Hour and the many contestants on the show were great entertainers that each reached their own status of fame. Major Bows was respected in how he helped introduce many entertainers and they would go on to great wealth. When Major Bow's committed suicide Ed Sullivan took over the Amateur Hour and narrated it for many years. When Ed Sullivan left Ted Mack narrated the program for many years.

There is quite a story about Major Bows and his personal life that many people are unaware of. At the beginning and the end of his amateur hour program he would recite the most beautiful poems and some were quite lengthy. This was the time of World War II. Many of our troop ships going to Europe to fight the Germans were blown up in the middle of the Atlantic Ocean.

It seemed that the German submarines would know when these troop ships would be traveling. The captain of our ships were not allowed to open their route orders until they were underway a day out from the US shore but still it seemed the German subs were always there waiting to blow them up. The FBI knew that the message must be getting to the Germans by radio but what radio station and how. After a time with much intelligence work the FBI narrowed the source down to it coming from Major Bow's Amateur Hour; but how?

Finally they broke the code and found that the poems Major Bow was giving at the beginning and end of his program was coded. The messages were getting to the German submarines directly from that amateur hour program. Like many German officials when they were about to be caught they carried a poison pill that they then took and in this case taking it was the end of Major Bows.

I was one of the soldiers on one of the troop ships that got attacked by six German submarines. I was in a fifty ship convoy heading for the German War and D-Day. The soldiers were standing on deck with our life preservers on and when I looked out the side of our ship I could see a missile coming straight at our ship.

My thoughts at that time was; it looks like we are going to have a wet bed tonight but the captain of our ship skillfully maneuvered the ship and the missile traveled on by our ship about three foot from it. In a fifty ship convoy there is also a destroyer and air planes that were catapulted off some ships that dropped ash cans on the German submarines. Also many of the ships in the convoy were tossing ash cans over board. We saw debris off some submarines that floated to the top of the water. We heard later that of the six German subs that attacked our convoy five was destroyed.

I am getting ahead of my story to describe how treacherous Major Bow's radio program against the safety of our troop ships. It was in 1941 that there were tremendous changes in the lives of the Lyle and Gena Ingraham family. In the spring of that year our family survived a devastating tornado that affected more than a dozen farms in our area in N. Dakota.

In later years, I wrote a book, "Farm Boy To Soldier" that contains the story of the tornado but I thought it worthy to repeat how our family lived through a tornado in this book. Our whole family, Dad, Mom, Raymond, Norman, Lorraine and I (Willard) were sitting in the house on our farm relaxing after lunch. We looked out of the window and we could see the wind begin to blow the dust across the fields.

Dad was watching the weather change very abruptly and he knew that something was about to happen. He had lived through a tornado as a young boy. What he saw was reminding him of the tornado long ago. We all watched as the storm increased in intensity. Some objects outside started to move across the yard pushed by the force of the wind. Suddenly the clouds were boiling like a hot tea kettle on a stove. The clouds were dark and rolling in the sky and on the ground our hayrack started to move across the barnyard all from the force of the wind.

Dad shouted, "it's a tornado, everyone to the basement." We all made a dash to the basement door except Mom. She thought that she must get her purse that was in her bedroom. Raymond and I chased after her to make sure she got to the basement. Mom retrieved her purse and we were just going down the basement stairs when the full force of the tornado struck. The rest of the family had already made it to the basement. The house began to shake like it would come apart any minute. Objects from the force of the wind blowing were hitting the side of the house like a bunch of bullets peppering the side of a building.

The storm probably only lasted a few minutes but it seemed like a long time and then the wind suddenly stopped. Everything got very still except it was now raining. The storm was over and it was safe to go outside to check the damage. Many strange things had happened. The house had holes in the roof. The house had been peppered with small sticks and straw that stuck out of the side of the house.

The barns were built big in North Dakota so that the loft storage space would hold a winter supply of hay to last until spring. We found one 12 inch by 12 inch by 18 foot timber that had supported the loft structure of the barn one half mile from home in our wheat field lying all by itself. We had a small amount of hay left in the loft of the barn that was still there and intact.

We had a rabbit pen in the loft of the barn with an empty pail that we used to get corn for our pet rabbits sitting on top of the rabbit pen. The pail was still there unmoved throughout the storm even thou the top half of the barn had been destroyed and was gone.

Just the barn was destroyed by the tornado; all the other buildings needed only minor repair (photo below).

Norman had recently purchased his car and he had insured it at the time of the purchase. There were three cars standing in the yard and only Norman's car had insurance on it and his car was the only one damaged.

It took a while to clean up the mess that was scattered for half a mile stretch but we got it cleaned up. A new barn was built over the existing barn with a new gable roof instead of a hip roof like the old one thus making the barn look cheaper.

We seeded our wheat and barley crops and planted about thirty acres of corn. All the crops looked very good and we waited for harvest time. Raymond and Norman were still working out on other farms.

In 1941 the combine was introduced into our area so at harvest time the crops had to stay in the fields for about a week longer to be really ripe before they could be harvested. The combine finally moved into our field and the golden wheat just rolled out of the combine.

Dad had an old truck that I drove to the combine and emptied the hopper into the truck periodically. When the truck was full of wheat I drove to a little town called Brantford, N.D. six miles from our farm and unloaded the wheat into the big elevator. I hauled several loads of wheat to the elevator the first day and we were all happy with the good crop we had.

But things changed as that first night after we started our combine harvest a big hail storm came in and totally destroyed all the rest of our crops. What a disappointment! After the tornado and now total destruction of most of the crops Dad cinched up his belt and tried to make some logic out of what to do next. Another fact that was weighing on his mind was that Raymond and Norman were already working out away from home and soon I would want to go make some money on my own.

Dad figured it might be best if he got a smaller place and he could handle the work on his own with Mom's help and make the change before the family was scattered all over. One night he went to bed thinking about all of this and the next morning woke up and informed all the family that he was going to Washington State and buy a small irrigated farm that he could handle. Three days later he was in Prosser,

Washington. He bought a 20 acre irrigated ranch and informed the family to get ready for the sale because as soon as papers were all completed he would catch the train and be home soon.

Raymond, Norman and I (Willard) lined all the machinery up and everything else that would sell all in a row across the barnyard ready for the auctioneer and sale day. We also got some paint in red and green colors according to their design and made that row of machinery look pretty sharp.

When Dad got back October 22, 1941 was set for the sale date and anybody that knows North Dakota realizes that we took a chance that late in the fall. The sale flier is at the left.

We lucked out, a nice sunny day was awarded us, and many people came. A very good sale was enjoyed that day.

SALE!

I will sell at Public Auction at my farm 3 miles south, 4 miles east, 2 miles south and ½ mile east of New Rockford and 5 miles northwest of Brantford on

WEDNESD'Y Oct. 22

Commencing at 11:30 Sharp

1941

LUNCH SERVED AT NOON BY LADIES' AID

The following described personal property, to-wit:

29 Head of Cattle 29

15 head Milch Cows, some to freshen in few days — — — 13 head Young Stock

SHORTHORN PUREBRED BULL WITH PAPERS

11 Head of Horses 11

7 Work Horses — 4 Colts — — Ages from 1 to 12

Weather Lamb — 4 Turkeys — Some Chickens — 19 Head of Hogs

FARM MACHINERY

John Deere triple Plow; Deering Mower; John Deere Binder; John Deere Field Cultivator, with Tractor Lift; International 8-foot horse Disc; John Deere Gang Plow; John Deere Corn Plow; Bradely Corn Plow; John Deere Mower; Hay Rocker; International Hay Stacker; 2 Wagons and 2 Hay Racks; John Deere Tractor; Brand New International Corn Binder; Van Brunt Drill; John Deere Pump Engine and Jack, new last fall; Deering Hay Rake; Boss Harrow and Cart; Wild Oat Cleaning Fanning Mill; Washing Machine Engine; 5 sets Britchen Harness; Water Tank; International 10-inch Burr Feed Grinder 1½ ton Whippet Truck; Good 4-wheel Trailer and Box; Hay Rack; and many other articles too numerous to mention.

Potatoes and Vegetables — 30 Acres Corn — About 1,000 Bushels of Oats

HOUSEHOLD GOODS

Brand New Coronado Washing Machine; White enamel Pressure Gas Stove, and many other household articles.

TERMS OF SALE:— Sums of $25.00 and under, Cash. On sums over $25.00 time will be allowed to October 1, 1942, on acceptable paper bearing 7% interest. Anyone desiring terms must make arrangements with clerk before the day of sale. No property to be removed from premises until settled for.

LYLE INGRAHAM, Owner

Before sale date, Dad purchased a new 1941 three quarter ton pickup, (photo below is that model).
He built a rack on the back of the pickup, and had it all ready to go by sale day.

1941 Chevrolet Pickup

There were only personal things kept from sale and loaded onto the pickup and into the trunks of Raymond and Norman's cars. After the sale the three rigs caravanned together Washington bound with all six family members aboard.

We first headed for Jamestown, N.D. where many of Mom's relatives lived. We stayed with Phil and Louise Schuff and family while in Jamestown. We had to see Grandpa and Grandma Gunder Johnson, Uncle Art and Aunt Nora Steffens and family, Uncle Lloyd and Aunt Esther Sorenson, Aunt Avis Glowac and Uncle Ray and Aunt Doris Rosenau as well as Mom's brother, Ted and Irene Johnson and family. After visiting everyone, the caravan was on the way again headed for Edgar, Montana where Uncle Ralph and Aunt Rose Ingraham and family lived at that time. We stayed overnight and were on our way again heading for our new home in Washington.

On November 5, 1941 we arrived in Prosser, Washington. The temperature was in the 80s and not a cloud in the sky. It was hard for us to believe because before we left North Dakota we already had snow and really frosty nights since September.

Dad had purchased a 20 acre farm (photo below) about 4 miles west of Prosser so now we again began attending sales to purchase a tractor and all the equipment. Farming was different here as all of this land had to be irrigated and that meant new type of farming tools had to be implemented.

The winter of 1941-1942 was an open winter with no frozen ground so Dad's choice to immediately buy a tractor was a good choice because he immediately went out plowing fields for farmers and had more jobs than what he could do.

Mom was busy cleaning house and arranging the furniture that was purchased to replace the furniture that was sold at the sale in North Dakota.

Raymond and Norman went out looking for jobs. Lorraine signed up for school. I did not sign up for high school at that time. We just started to get settled when the Japanese attacked Pearl Harbor on December 7, 1941. President Roosevelt not only declared war on Japan but also joined England to fight the Germans. President Roosevelt gave his famous speech saying, "this day will live in infamy and there is nothing to fear but fear itself." He assured everyone that everything would turn out alright. When all of us in the

Ingraham family heard that famous speech by our president on the radio that morning all of us boys knew it would not be too long before all three of us would be fighting in the war.

Below is a photo of our Ingraham family at Prosser, Wa., 1941: L to R., Ray, Norman, Willard and front row Gena, Lyle and Lorraine.

In the spring of 1942, I got a job with an elderly couple, Mr. and Mrs. E.J. Appel to farm their 40-acre farm. They were neighbors to my parents in Prosser, Wa. My first purchase was a new bicycle. Now I was able to ride back and forth to my job. This lasted for a short time then I was just itching to buy a car. I found a 1929 Model A Ford coupe for $35.00; a photo of my car and bicycle above.

It needed some fixing but in about two weeks you would not have recognized that Model A as the one I had purchased because now it sported a new paint job, a new rumble seat and it purred like a kitten. I painted the car black with yellow orange spoke wheels and silver trim, headlights and hub caps. Pretty sharp; sometime in the summer months of 1942 Dad heard of a ten acre farm for sale with a two bedroom house, a barn, and a new chicken house that would handle 500 chickens. It was all irrigated land and was only about two miles from my parent's home. My older brothers Raymond and Norman were talking to Dad as my cousin Arnold and I were walking up to Dad. Dad had just asked Ray and Norman who had said they were not interested in buying a farm. As I

stood listening to Dad talk about the farm I decided I wanted to purchase it. Arnold Steffens (my cousin) was staying with us then he wanted to buy the farm with me.

Farm at left:

Arnold and I did buy and Arnold's parents Art and Nora Steffens and five children were living in Jamestown, N.D. at that time so Arnold and I offered if they wished to come to Washington and live they could on our farm for just keeping up the farm payment, utilities, irrigation water and taxes on the farm. They could live there until we wanted the farm because Arnold and I were planning on buy another farm as soon as we paid for this one.

Uncle Art and Aunt Nora decided to take us up on our offer and came to live on our farm until the summer of 1943 when we sold the farm because both Arnold and I were going into the Army. With the war going on and our future not known we decided to sell the farm that we had already fully paid for. We doubled our money on our investment.

In the fall of 1942 at fruit harvest time, I went to work for a fruit packing plant in Grandview, Wa. We were able to work all the hours we wanted. This seemed just right for me. I was working 18 hours a day until my parents made me stop the long hours and go back to a 12 hour day. I had worked enough overtime to pay for my 1937 green, 4 doors Chevrolet that I had purchased when Arnold came out from Jamestown to stay with us. The photo below is my new car.

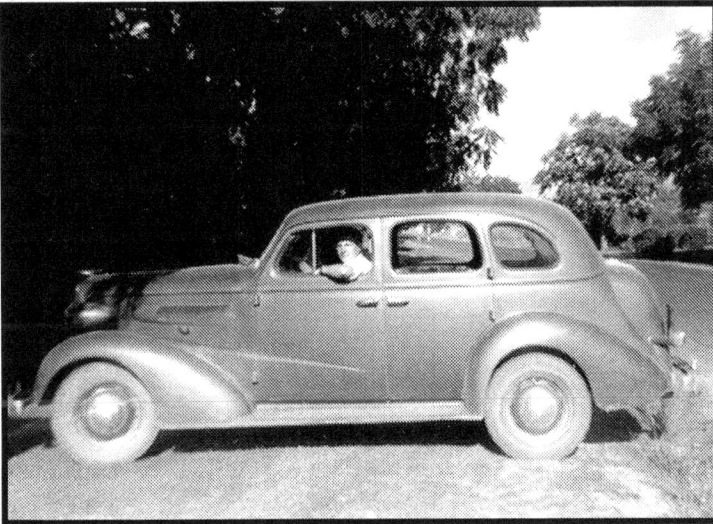

Arnold and I were inseparable; anybody hiring one of us would have to hire both of us or we went on to a place where we both could work at the same place. We were both good workers. We had no problem getting jobs or going back to jobs where we had worked.

In September of 1942 Norman received his notice to enter the army in November. Knowing that all of us boys would soon be in the service we decided to return to North Dakota for a visit. My cousin, Arnold Steffens, Norman my

brother and I all drove back to North Dakota to see our
relatives and friends. We rode back with Norman in his 1935
tan, 4 doors sedan car. When we got back to New Rockford,
N.D. we discovered that the farmers were feeling the pinch of
the war to the point they needed help to harvest their grain.
The farmers talked to all three of us about helping them harvest
their grain. We had not planned on helping but finally we all
agreed to help them out for a few days. Below is Arnold
Steffens standing by Normans' car and behind is the threshing
machine we all worked on.

Left is Norman watering the horses before putting them away for the night.

Before leaving for Washington we drove to Jamestown, N.D. to visit our relatives and grandparents that lived there. Our grandfather Gunder Johnson told us as we said our goodbyes that he would never see us again. He was right because he died in 1943.

The November date for Norman's entrance into the army arrived and off he went to camp Gruber, Oklahoma. (photo left)

Norman was assigned to the 88th Infantry Division.

My cousin Arnold Steffens, my brother Raymond and I (Willard) all went to work at the Yakima Chief Hop yards in Mabton, Washington. We helped in their harvest of hops and after that all through the winter we worked clearing apple orchards for more hop fields.

In December 1942 I was 18 years old I thought it was about time for me to go to serve my country. I went to Prosser Selective Service Board to volunteer to go into the air force. My thinking was that the air force would train me to become a pilot. No such luck, their quota was filled for the air force. It did not take them long to call me for the army and on December 9th of 1942 my greetings came and I was to go to the local doctor to get a check up to see if I was physically fit to go to serve. On March 18, 1943 I was inducted into the army at Fort Douglas, Utah. Then I was sent to FortKnox, Kentucky where I was assigned to the Company A 2nd Platoon 526th Armored Infantry Battalion. Above is Willard Ingraham at Fort Knox, Kentucky for basic training.

On April 15, 1943 Arnold Steffens was inducted into Kerns Air Force Base, Salt Lake City, Utah and assigned to 2072 OM Trucking Co. His photo is below

On December 25, 1943 my sister Lorraine Jainette Ingraham married Lester Mott. (photo right)

He was born September 12, 1919, New York. Lester was living at Clovis, California and then worked at the Hanford Project near Richland, Washington when Lorraine met him.

After their wedding they moved to Clovis, California where Lester was working with his parents on a dairy and fruit farm. Clovis is near Fresno, California.

On January 9, 1944 many friends and neighbors surprised Lyle and Gena Ingraham to celebrate their 25th wedding anniversary which was on January 7, 1944. A fun evening was had by all with a lot of pleasant conversation and like always a lot of good food.

On May 17, 1944 Raymond Ingraham joined the Army Air Force, Hqd 1504 AAS Base unit. His photo is below. At this time all three of us boys were in the service for World War II.

Lyle (Dad) still did custom work with his tractor. He had a lot of customers. He had rebuilt his barn to have big hay storage in the middle separating the two sides of the barn where one side was all concreted out and stanchions installed to hold ten cows for milking. Oh, yes there were also at least ten cows to milk two times a day, seven days a week.

It was in 1954 that Lyle and Gena decided to sell their 20 acre farm four miles west of Prosser. They purchased a home in the town of Grandview, Wa. (photo below) that had about an acre of land. Dad kept himself busy raising a big garden and Mom still canned a lot of fruit and vegetables. They also played for dances whenever they decided to do so.

In 1957 Lyle and Gena Ingraham accepted a job to be custodians of the Benton Public Untility District in Kennewick, Washington. In 1959, they purchased their home in Kennewick, Wa. at 1107 E. 6th St. (photo below)

Whenever it was possible they loved to take some vacation time to drive to Jamestown, N.D. and to Laurel, Mt. to visit their relatives and friends that were located there. In January of 1969 some 75 friends and relatives attended a reception at the Benton City Odd Fellows Hall honoring Lyle and Gena Ingraham on their 50th wedding anniversary (photo below). They are holding their wedding photo.

Hosts were Ray and Anna Ingraham of Benton City, Wa., Norman and Verdell Ingraham of Prosser, Wa. and Willard and Louise Ingraham of Longview, Wa. with their daughter Mary Ann. Lyle and Gena Ingraham had been married on January 7, 1919 at Jamestown, North Dakota.

Other relatives present for the party were Ronald and Dorothy Rideout and children Debra and Jeanie; Norman, Verdell and children Jerome, Janette and Jacquelyn; Lester, Lorraine Mott and children, Sherri, Kimberlee Ann and Lori from Clovis, California. Other relatives Vern and Harriet Wahl and son Brad of Jamestown, N.D., Ralph and Rose Ingraham and daughter-in-law of Laurel, Mt. and Arnold and Lucille Steffens and daughters Loretta and Janice of Richland, Wa.

At that time everything in the west was iced over; planes were shut down at the airports and the highways were covered with ice leaving bus travel almost impossible. I

(Willard), Louise and daughter Mary Ann were living in Longview, Wa. at that time. We finally got seats on the train to Kennewick to celebrate my parents Golden wedding but it certainly was not easy. The night of the celebration the roads were all iced over and Benton City is about 20 miles from Kennewick so I drove Dad's car to Benton City. We managed to stay on the road but it was one slippery road.

Our return trip to Longview was another problem. Our train was supposed to leave Pasco at 3 A.M on Sunday morning but when we called the station the trains were running late and they told us to call back in an hour. My Uncle Ralph and Aunt Rose were staying at the folks in Kennewick and I told them they should all go to bed because it was not fair to have them stay up. The delays continued until 5 A.M. and I asked Dad if he would take us to the Pasco train station and we would wait it out there. Louise, Mary Ann and I waited until 6 A.M in the station and we were informed that the passenger car was on the track but was not connected to an engine so there was no heat until an engine was hooked onto the car and on the way. They told us they would give blankets to keep us warn while waited in that train car for the engine.

We waited until 9 A.M. when here came the engine and we were soon on our way. It was crowded because everybody was trying to get home. We got to Vancouver, Wa. and everyone was crowding to change trains going north. I got to the train door with only Louise and Mary Ann boarding the train and they told me that all seats were taken with nothing more available. I explained to them my family was already on board and we were getting off at Longiew; I told them that in a situation like this who needs a seat I will stand because my stop is only 45 miles away and I would sure appreciate it if they would let me in and I would be glad to stand all the way. I got on and did stand the rest of the way. Louise said that Mary Ann and she also had to stand.

We got to our home in Longview about 7 PM that Sunday night and we were very happy about that because we had not been to bed since Friday night.

In 1975 Lyle and Gena Ingraham decided to retire from their job at the Benton County Public Utility District where they had worked since 1958. They had kept the main building and the service center building both always looking like new buildings.

In 1979 Lyle and Gena Ingraham were honored on their 60th wedding anniversary with an open house and family dinner at Willard and Louise Ingraham's home in Kennewick where they were now residing. Their photo is below.

Many friends and relatives enjoyed the 60 years of memories related by different persons that attended the party. Lyle and Gena at that time had four children, 11 grandchildren and 16 great grandchildren.

Lyle Jay Ingraham passed away on July 21, 1982 at the Kennewick General Hospital.

LYLE J. INGRAHAM

Lyle J. Ingraham, 85, died July 21, 1982, at Kennewick General Hospital. He was born January 30, 1897, at Mannsville, Minnesota.

Mr. Ingraham was a retired custodian of Public Utility District No. 1. He worked at the PUD from 1957 to 1965. Prior to that he lived several years in Grandview, where he moved from a farm west of Prosser.

He was a member of the United First Methodist Church in Kennewick and active in Buena Vista Grange in Prosser. He was a musician and played the fiddle at many dances with his wife, Gena, at the piano.

Mr. and Mrs. Ingraham were married January 7, 1919, in Jamestown, North Dakota.

He is survived by his wife, Gena; three sons, Raymond of Benton City, Norman of Prosser and Willard of Kennewick; one daughter, Lorraine Grebeldinger of Pasco; four brothers, Lee of Gig Harbor, Ralph and Claude of Laurel, Montana, and Floyd of Alleene, Arkansas; one sister, Edna Patno of Chicago, Illinois; 11 grandchildren and 19 great-grandchildren. He was preceded in death by two sons and a daughter who died at birth, his parents and a sister. His mother, Myrtle, passed away in February at the age of 108.

Services for Mr. Ingraham were Saturday, July 24, at Muellers Tri-Cities Funeral Home and burial followed at Desert Lawn Memorial Park in Kennewick.

He had been born on January 30, 1897 at Mantorville, Minnesota. Lyle had been staying at the Kennewick Life Care Center for the past two years. He was laid to rest at Desert Lawn Memorial Park Cemetery at Kennewick, Washington.

The obituary is at the left.

My mother, Gena was staying alone for the past few years but the time came for her that she needed some help so she was placed in a retirement home where all meals were furnished. She stayed there for about a year then her daughter,

Lorraine Johnston took our Mom to her home and took care of her until she died on August 19, 1986 at Pasco, Washington.

She had been born in Evansville, Minnesota. She was laid to rest at the Desert Lawn Memorial Park at Kennewick, Washington. She would have been 86 years old in December.

Her obituary is left:

It was during those busy years that Lorraine was going through that our Mother needed extra help and could no longer live alone that Lorraine insisted she was not going to send Mother to a nursing home. Lorraine made it work for her by taking in our Mother and two other elderly women in her home to care for. She cared for all three of the women until they passed away.

We all know that it had to have been a hard three and one half years for Lorraine with all the care these women needed. It was Lorraine's kindness and generosity in care giving during these years that the rest of the family had much to be thankful about. We are all grateful for Lorraine's kind and considerate services during that time of need. She served as a caregiver without complaint and we give you Lorraine a great big thank you.

Gena Alpha Ingraham

Gena Alpha Ingraham, 85, Pasco, died Tuesday at Our Lady of Lourdes Hospital.

She was born in Evansville, Minn. She lived in Prosser and Grandview, moving to Kennewick in 1958.

She was a member of the Buena Vista Grange in Prosser, Prosser VFW Auxiliary, Prosser Homemakers Club and First United Methodist Church, Kennewick.

She and her husband, Lyle, played for many dances through the years.

He died in 1982 after being married for 63 years.

Survivors include sons Willard, Kennewick; Norman, Prosser; Raymond, Benton City; daughter Lorraine Johnston, Pasco; 11 grandchildren; 21 great-grandchildren; one great-great-granddaughter; seven sisters.

Two sons and a daughter died previously.

Funeral services will be held at 1 p.m. Monday at Mueller's Tri-Cities Funeral Home, 1401 S. Union, and burial will be in Desert Lawn Memorial Park.

I t seems appropriate to have a photo in memory of our
parents, Lyle and Gena Ingraham and their final resting place
at Desert Lawn Memorial Park cemetery at Kennewick, Wa.
The photos are below.

CHAPTER XI
RAYMOND, ANNA INGRAHAM AND FAMILY
By: Willard Ingraham

Raymond Lloyd Ingraham entered the U.S. Army Air Force May 17, 1944 and was sent to California to Fairfield Air Base, HQD 1504 AAS Base unit. He was sent to Florida then to Trinidad and from there to Italy. When the war was over he was sent to Camp Roberts, California.

In June of 1946 Raymond was discharged at Fort Lewis, Washington and returned home to Prosser, Washington where his parents Lyle and Gena lived. Photo below

It was on July 12, 1946 that Raymond Lloyd Ingraham and Anna Rose Crosby borrowed my car to drive to Lewiston, Idaho where they got married. Upon their return to Prosser they built a new home about five miles northeast of Prosser and completed it in 1946.

In the years that followed the family grew to three children. There was Dorothy Jean, Linda Rae and Lloyd Raymond. All three children were born at the Sunnyside hospital.

Family photo below, back l to r; Dorothy and Linda; l to r; Ray, Lloyd and Anna in front

In 1950, the couple sold their home north of Prosser that they had built. Ray's (Raymond) employers, Joe and Nick Foisy transferred him to Royal City next to the Grand Coulee Dam that was under construction to manage their pinball business there. Royal City was thriving with all the contractors and employees working on the great Grand Coulee Dam at that time. It was a time that the federal government was harnessing power from the Columbia River with the construction of the dam. When completed there would be water control on the great Columbia providing electrical power to a greater part of the northwest.

Ray and family lived at Royal City for several years before they moved to Benton City, Washington.

Ray worked for Campbell Grocery Market as the manager at their Richland store. Below is Ray presenting a customer a check for winning the bonus card promotion.

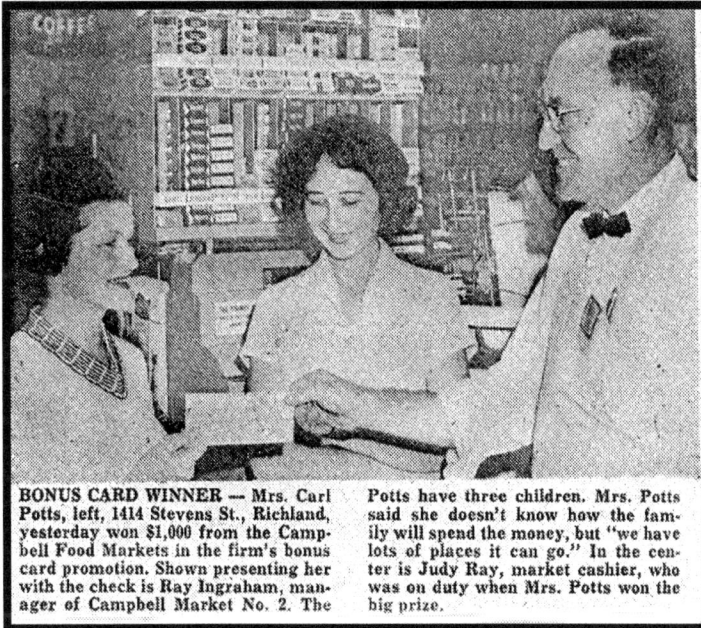

BONUS CARD WINNER — Mrs. Carl Potts, left, 1414 Stevens St., Richland, yesterday won $1,000 from the Campbell Food Markets in the firm's bonus card promotion. Shown presenting her with the check is Ray Ingraham, manager of Campbell Market No. 2. The Potts have three children. Mrs. Potts said she doesn't know how the family will spend the money, but "we have lots of places it can go." In the center is Judy Ray, market cashier, who was on duty when Mrs. Potts won the big prize.

All was going good for the family then another job change took place when Campbell Market was sold. Ray went to work for Albertsons Grocery chain at their Store in Richland.

At this same time, Anna Rose had gone to work for the Benton City School District in the school cafeteria. It wasn't long and she became the supervisor.

It was in 1955 when the Benton City School District held a big public banquet at the school to raise money for the school. It was Anna and her staffs' responsibility to organize and serve that big banquet and others that would follow. Having attended several banquets I can personally vouch for the wonderful food that was served at those banquets. I

remember one that they specialized in serving Norwegian fare
and it was marvelous.

All three of Ray and Anna's children, Dorothy, Linda
and Lloyd attended the
Benton City schools. Those
were active and busy years
but never too busy to be a
close knit family. Later
Dorothy, Linda and Lloyd
took their school year turns
and each graduated at the
end of their senior year at
the Benton City High
School.
Dorothy left graduated
1964.
Linda below graduated
1965.
Lloyd below graduate 1966

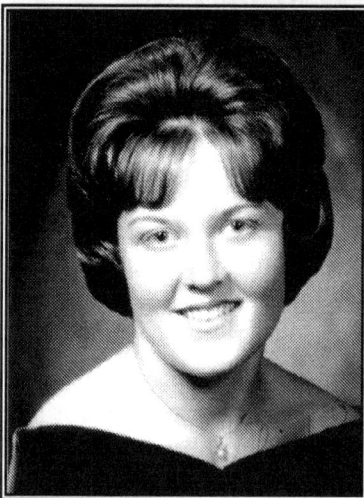

RAYMOND, ANNA INGRAHAM AND FAMILY

Ray retired in 1984. It was then time to look forward to vacationing in a motor home. It was in 1985 that Ray and Anna bought a new motor home. There were many short trips and many times with a boat in tow for fishing. Photo below was taken on one of those camping trips in 1993.

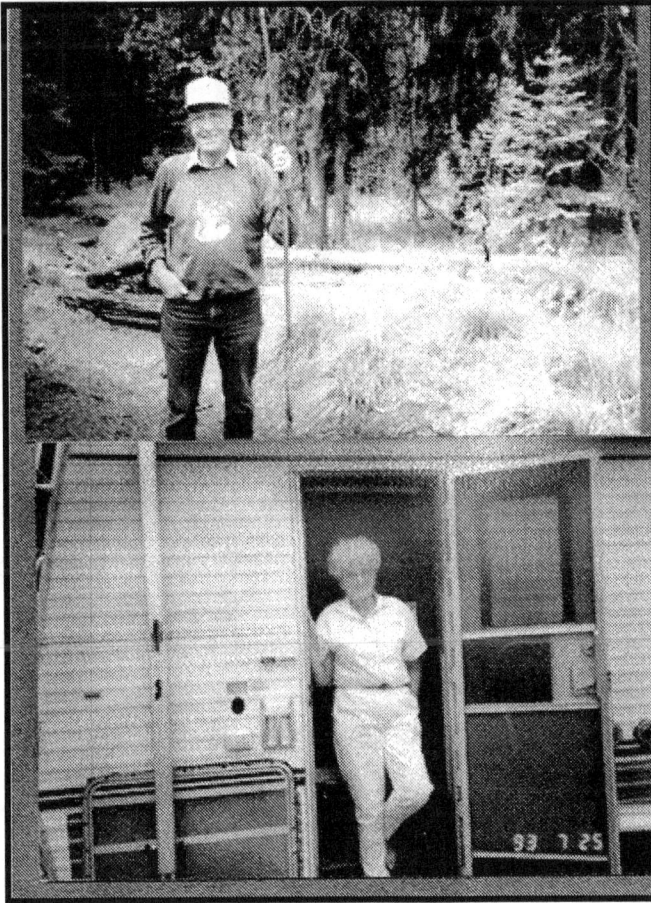

It was in 1987 that Anna retired from the Benton City School District. They loved motor homing and became one of those Arizona snowbirds. In 1988 they spent the winter in Yuma, Arizona in their motor home at a lovely campground. They had many friends and there were camp parties with lots of dancing and card playing and many excursions across the border into Mexico.

They made use of the hobby classes offered and Ray fit zipper art into his agenda; photo below is Anna and Ray with Ray's zipper art in the background.

Anna took classes that interested her. They repeated these winter trips every year through the winter of 1999.

It was in 1996 that Ray and Anna Rose Ingraham celebrated their 50th wedding anniversary at their home in Benton City.

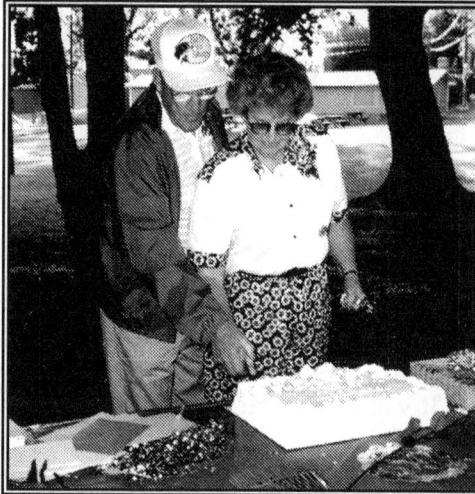

RAYMOND, ANNA INGRAHAM AND FAMILY

It was in 2004 that they sold their home in Benton City and moved to Prosser into one of their daughter and son-in-law, Linda and Dan Gile's park model homes at Prosser, Washington.

On July 12, 2006 Ray and Anna Rose Ingraham celebrated their 60th wedding anniversary (photo below)

Anna Rose had heart surgery in late November, 2006. She remained in the hospital until her passing on April 1, 2007. The family celebrated Anna's life on April 6, 2007 with Reverend Larry Howell, a friend of the family, officiating. The services were held at Prosser; Anna's grandson Byran has a beautiful voice and he sang in remembrance for his grandmother.

Anna's son, Lloyd showed family slides. Lloyd also wrote a wonderful heartfelt story in memory of his Mom, "What it means to be a "A Perfect Mom." that was read by his uncle Willard Ingraham: Lloyd's story follows:

A PERFECT MOM

By: Lloyd Raymond Ingraham

If you were to ask me what are the requirements to be a perfect Mom I would simply think about my Mom and say, "Mom always loved each of us unconditionally; she was patient and understanding. She was wise when she gave advice.

Mom always tried not to be judgmental when we made mistakes; but she was always interested in how we were going to fix the problem.

Mom taught us if we can not say anything nice about someone then it's best not to say anything at all. She told us to think about what we wanted to say before hurting someone else's feelings. She would say to treat people the way that you would want to be treated.

When I was 3 years old I came down with polio which started the crippling of my feet. Mom and Dad did not have a lot of money however they always found a way to make ends meet.

They both knew it was important for me to get help while my bones were in the forming stages so Mom would drive me up to Yakima for treatments 2 or 3 times a month year after year.

As I was growing up and had to wear braces to keep my legs straight school kids often made fun of me. Mom always comforted me and told me not to worry about what others said. She told me I had to be strong. Mom taught me to meet life head on. She said, "sometimes you have to fight for what you want out of life." Because of what Mom told to me in those days made me who I am today.

Five months ago Mom had to have open heart surgery and ever since then her health has slowly depleted and it hurts because I can not help her. She was always full of life and enjoyed every minute of it. This beautiful lady that gave me life cries out in pain and lord it's hard for me

to let go but I know Mom will be in a better place; free
from pain.

Over the years Mom has always been my rock; she
was always there, she was my best friend. She always
willingly gave of herself. She never asked for anything for
herself. Mom is going to be truly missed by all of us that
loved her.

Willard wrote his message for the family in
remembrance of Anna:

I would like to add this: by Willard Ingraham
In a time like this it is only natural to feel sadness.
We all feel a lot of emotional feelings of sadness but I asked
of you, who is it really do we feel sadness for? Is it Anna we
feel the sadness for? I don't think so. I think Anna is
looking down on us with a big smile and would be saying to
us, "I now feel the full force of God's eternal love and
Jesus' shining light to guide me. I feel no pain and with the
light of God's abundant understanding and forgiveness and
happiness for all; I feel whole and happy. I love all of you,"
Anna

Anna's son, Lloyd designed and gave a beautifully
orchestrated slide presentation of Anna at different times in her
life.

Byron Ingraham, Lloyd's son and Anna's grandson has
a beautiful voice and he sang the song, "Where You Are" in
memory of his grandmother Anna.

From the graveside services the group was invited to a
luncheon prepared by her family and given in honor of Anna. It
was a time of sharing over a wonderful luncheon and plenty of
photo taking. We all know that Anna as she looked down was
pleased with the send off.

DOROTHY JEAN (RIDEOUT) WOLTERS AND FAMILY

Dorothy Jean Ingraham is the daughter of Raymond and Anna Ingraham. She married Ronald Chapin Rideout. Ronald was born Jan. 5, 1941 in Brewer, Maine. He joined the US Air Force in 1960 and was stationed at Moses Lake, Washington.

It was while Ron (Ronald) was stationed at Moses Lake that he met Dorothy Jean Ingraham. They were married in Benton City, Washington on June 27, 1965 and made their home in Kennewick, Washington. Ron worked for Boise Cascade.

RAYMOND, ANNA INGRAHAM AND FAMILY

The couple had four children above; l to r back row, Michael, Deborah, Phyllis and front l to r; Dorothy, Ron and Kevin.

The children are as follows:

Deborah Ann Rideout; born July 4, 1967 at Richland, Wa. She married Mark Thomas McCollum who was born Sept. 27, 1963 at Tyronza, Ark. The couple was married on Nov. 23, 1984 at Benton City, Wa.

They had two children(family photo above taken 2007):
Left; Mark, Deborah, Mandy and Scott.

     Amanda Lynn McCollum, born Nov. 17, 1985 at
Richland, Wa. and Scott Thomas McCollum, born Sept. 8,
1991, Richland, Wa.

     Deborah, Mark and family made their home at Benton
City until recently they moved to Prosser, Wa. Mark works for
the Burlington Railroad Co.
     Phyllis Jean Rideout: born June 1, 1966 at Richland
Wa. Phyllis now lives at Twin Falls, Id. (photo below).

M

ichael Dean Rideout; born June 10, 1969 at Richland, Wa. He
married Mireya. This couple had two children; Matthew Dean
Rideout, born Aug. 7, 1992 and Brandon Michael Rideout,
born Nov. 16, 1994. Both were born at Twin Falls, Id.
Michael divorced and married Amy Chambers; they had two
children, Nicholas Rodney Ray Rideout- b- Dec. 10, 2001;
Tashyanna Mary Jo Rideout-B-Jan. 9, 2003. Both children
born at Twin Falls, Idaho.

Michael divorced and remarried as he says "to the love of his life, Mindy Mullen." Their photo is below.

From this marriage the couple had two children Nicholas Rodney Ray Rideout born Dec. 10, 2001 and Tashynna Jo Rideout born Jan. 9, 2003.

Michael Dean Rideout works at P.W. Sugar Factory.

Kevin Chapin Rideout, born Sept. 20, 1971, Richland Wa. He now lives in Tin Falls, Id. and works at Twin Fall Sugar Factory.

Kevin's photo
left taken in 2007.

Ronald Rideout had worked for Boise Cascade for fourteen years and in 1979 they moved to Twin Falls, Id. Ronald was injured in a motorcycle accident at Twin Falls. He was hospitalized and later passed away. He was buried on Oct. 27, 1987 at Twin Falls, Idaho.

Dorothy Jean Rideout married John Wolters on November 5, 1989. They reside at Twin Falls, Id.

DOROTHY JEAN (RIDEOUT) WOLTERS STORY
By: Dorothy Wolters

I am the oldest of Anna and Ray Ingraham's children. I remember when I was very young being with Dad as he milked cows and then running up to the house to see Mom bathing my baby sister at the kitchen window. Daddy used to let me ride the cows. This was when we lived in Whitstran.

We moved to Grand Coulee before Lloyd was born. Dad worked below the house and Mom used to walk us to the store with Lloyd in his stroller. One time when we came out of the store Lloyd had a vase stuck on his arm. Boy was Mom upset with him.

We used to catch fire flies and put them in jars. We thought we could make a light that way. Dad got a job in construction; he drove the water truck.

We moved to the Richland Y and lived in a camp trailer. Linda and I shared an army cot. We slept foot to foot. Lloyd had his own small cot. We weren't there very long before they bought the place in Benton City and I started 1st grade and Lloyd got polio.

I learned to dance the polka on Grandpa Lyle Ingraham's feet. He would come home from work at the PUD and we would meet him at the kitchen door. He would put us on the toes of his work boots and dance around the kitchen on the farm in Prosser. He taught us to milk the cows. The cats used to line up and he would squirt milk on them.

We had a wonderful childhood. Many Sundays were spent at Grandpa and Grandma Ingraham's house with them and our uncles playing music. They would play for grange dances. One time they put me on a box behind Grandpa and I rubbed his shoulder so he would keep playing.

RAYMOND, ANNA INGRAHAM AND FAMILY

When Grandpa and Grandma Ingraham moved to Grandview Great Grandma Ingraham came to visit. She put all the great grand kids at her feet and told us stories about Indians coming to their homestead and how she always had to bake extra bread because she HAD to give them some.

My children still talk about the music when they were young and my Grandparents lived in Kennewick. Ron and I spent many hours with them. Ron felt like they were his Grandparents too and loved them dearly. We had them to our house in Kennewick every chance we could. They liked it best when we came to their house. You could not be in their house 5 minutes without Grandma giving you coffee and cookies. She always said "have you eaten?" She could fix a big meal with nothing in the cupboard. We thought she was magic. Grandma taught us to can fruit and to cook. She always said, "be the labor great or small; do it well or not at all." She told us her mother would tell her that. She taught me to knit and crochet and also to tat. I still have one of her tatting shuttles. She tried to teach me the piano; all I got was the cows.

One of our fondest memories of the farm was milking with Grandpa and Grandma letting her parakeet (Teddy) fly around the house and allowing him to sun himself on the front porch every day.

Going to my own family; I met Ronald Rideout in the spring of 1963. We became engaged on Christmas day, 1963. Ron was from Maine and was in the Air Force stationed at Moses Lake, Wa. A friend had brought him down to date one of my friends. It was love at first sight.

We were married June 27, 1965. We had 4 beautiful children. Deborah Ann was born July 4, 1966, Phyllis Jean born June 1, 1967, Michael Dean born June 10, 1969 and Kevin Chapin born Sept. 20,

1971. We lived in West Richland, Richland Y, Richland and in April 1971 we moved to Kennewick and lived there until we moved to Twin Falls, Id. in 1979. Ron worked for Boise Cascade Paper Mill from June 1965 until August of 1979.

After moving to Twin Falls, Idaho Ron worked in a barite mine head. He ran the mill plant that separated the barite from the other rocks and in the summer of 1980 I worked in the lab running test samples on the ore. I got a job as a teacher's aide in Oct. of 1979 working in the Jr. High School resources room teaching reading and math.

In the summer of 1981 Ron went to work at the Longview Fiber Box Plant; he was the oilier for the whole plant. He worked there up until his motorcycle accident March 11, 1987. Ron laid in a drug-induced coma for 3 months while in Boise Hospital. My parents, Ray and Anna Ingraham brought their motor home to Boise for me to stay in while Ron was in the Boise Hospital.

One or the other parent was with me while Ron was in Boise. During that time in Boise I really got to know my Dad. We went for many walks and had the time to converse while we walked.

Then Ron was moved to the nursing home in Twin Falls, Idaho and lived another five months. He communicated by blinking his eyes. He passed away Oct. 24, 1982.

I married John Wolters Nov. 5, 1989. He was a long time friend of Ron and mine.

Deborah married Mark McCollum of Benton City. They have 2 wonderful children:

Amanda Lynn who was the apple of her grandfathers eye and Scott Thomas.

All my other children are named on the preceding page.

RAYMOND, ANNA INGRAHAM AND FAMILY

Below is a photo of John and Dorothy Wolters taken 2007.

LINDA RAE GILES AND FAMILY
By: Linda Rae Giles

I (Linda Rae Ingraham) am the daughter of
Raymond and Anna Rose Crosby Ingraham. I was born in
Sunnyside, Wa. I lived and attended school at Benton City. I
married Danny Lee Giles on August 5, 1967 at Benton
City.

Dan and
Linda Giles
wedding
photo is at the
left.

RAYMOND, ANNA INGRAHAM AND FAMILY

Danny's parents, Mr. and Mrs. H.W. Giles lived at Prosser, Wa.

Danny was employed by the Pacific Northwest Bell telephone company in Portland, Oregon. We made our home in Vancouver, Wa. at this time.

Dan transferred with Pacific Northwest Bell Telephone Co. to Yakima, Wa. Their two children were born in Yakima. Michelle Lynn Giles was born Sept. 11, 1969 and Michael Lee Giles was born April 27, 1971.

With our family, we moved to Omak, Wa. where Dan worked as a lineman for Pacific Northwest Bell Telephone Co. He had worked in Omak three and a half years when we decided to buy a one-acre farm in Spring Coulee, Wa. It was here that we purchased and operated the Western Farmers Association store in Okanogan.

Later we (Danny and Linda) moved to Eureka, Mt. where Dan took up logging. I (Linda) and our family moved into a log cabin at the end of a lake not far from town. But the wilderness was still calling so we moved to Skagway, Alaska.

Together we started up a janitorial service and Danny became a bush pilot. He hired out to take hunters over select areas to find the best place to hunt for big game. He would then fly them into remote hunting camps. Because of the expense of living Danny had to take on a third job; this time in a logging mill. After the mill closed down we decided it best to move back to the Yakima Valley; this time to Kennewick where Danny went to work at General Telephone Company as a lineman.

A short while later we decided to move back to Montana, this time to Whitefish where we started up a construction company.

Even though our children were young, Michelle and Michael started working along side us and the four of us became roofers. Business was good and before long we had 29 men on the payroll. We were roofing hotels, schools, condos, hospital, homes, etc.

Because of the workload, Danny came down ill and as a hub of the family, I (Linda) decided, it was enough.

One more move was on the horizon and our family moved to Prosser, Wa. where we where roofing contractors as a family again. It was then that we started our cattle herd. It was also then that we had the opportunity to open a tire store in Prosser. By then Michelle and Michael were old enough to work beside us so Dan's Discount Tires became a family operation.

After selling that business, we bought our first used semi-truck and Dan drove for Union Pacific Railroad hauling their piggyback trailers. After short time we bought a new truck and started hauling fish from coast to coast.
After a trucking accident, we started building new homes as well as remodeling homes. We also contracted and built commercial buildings. It was then that I (Linda) decided to get out of construction and started working as a cook at the Prosser School District along side my daughter, Michelle.

During this time my family also started constructing a senior mobile home park just north of the Prosser Airport.

After selling the park, we built a five unit strip mall on the property adjoining the park that includes a successful family operated car wash, operated by Michael and a café operated by our daughter Michelle and our daughter-in-law Jodi.

(Note): A newspaper article of the café opening is on the following page. The business is located north of Prosser near the airport. They have a drive in window as well as plenty of indoor seating.

Photo of Michelle and Jodi below in their cafe

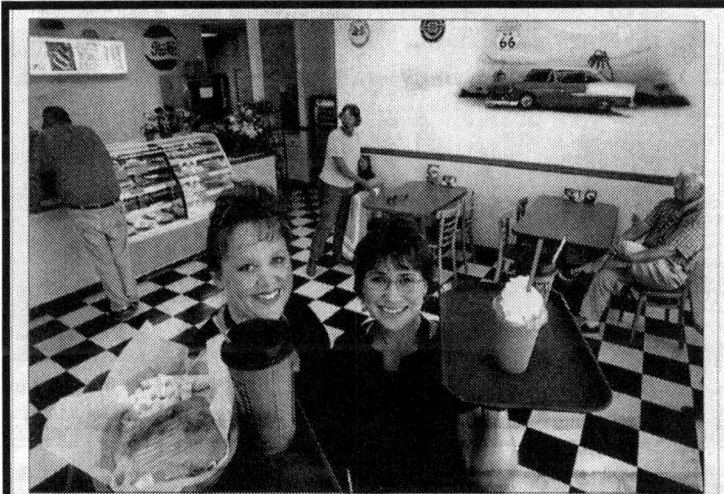

Michelle Pleake, left, and Jodi Giles are co-owners of the Speedway Cafe in Prosser. The cafe has a classic car Americana theme.

Herald/Paul T. Erickson

In the family fastlane

By Cara Fitzpatrick
Herald staff writer

PROSSER — Jodi Giles and Michelle Pleake kept it all in the family when they married each other's brothers.

Now the two Prosser women have taken it a step further by going into business together.

Giles and Pleake opened the Speedway Cafe a week ago at 413 Wine Country Road in Prosser.

The "hip-hop 1950s" cafe fulfills Pleake's lifelong dream of owning a restaurant, and it naturally evolved into a family project.

"She has cooking experience, and I have business experience," Giles said.

In their day jobs, Giles is the administrative assistant to the Benton County Commissioners, while Pleake has been a cook in the Prosser School District for more than a decade.

Despite having full-time jobs and raising several children each — all age 10 and younger — Giles and Pleake

Prosser sisters-in-law open Speedway Cafe

jumped at an opportunity to open their cafe in a vacant spot in the brand-new Wine Country Plaza.

The plaza is owned by their father/father-in-law Danny Giles. And Jodi Giles' husband, Michael, owns the Pit Stop, a car wash in the strip mall.

"It's truly a family operation," Jodi said, laughing.

The cafe's theme originally was intended to go along with the Pit Stop so the two businesses could operate side by side. But Giles and Pleake also wanted a drive-through, which worked best in a corner spot.

The cafe was moved, but the theme stayed because it fit the family atmosphere they wanted to create. Electric yellow walls with red trim and a black and white checkered floor were meant to be eye-catching and inviting to children and adults.

"We wanted a place where we could take our kids," Giles said.

But they also wanted a variety of food, drinks and desserts to appeal to all ages. The menu includes deli and panini sandwiches, wraps, espresso, milkshakes, root beer floats, cookies, cheesecake and cinnamon rolls. Breakfast options, such as waffles, pancakes and biscuits and gravy, also are planned for the future.

Pleake said most of the products, such as the tea and espresso, come from Washington-based companies and many of the food choices are intended to be a healthy alternative to fast food restaurants.

"We wanted something that isn't necessarily available in Prosser," she said.

The cafe is open from 5:30 a.m. to 8 p.m. Monday to Friday and from 7 a.m. to 8 p.m. Saturday. For more information, call 786-1005.

■ Reporter Cara Fitzpatrick can be reached at 582-1542 or via e-mail at cfitzpatrick@tri-cityherald.com.

Of coarse as a very united and busy family as we are this is not the end. We not only run cattle, we also have a vineyard in Sunnyside, a Payday Loan store in Pasco at Road 68, an embroidery company, rentals, 4 semi-trucks (two running the 6 northwest states and two that haul local) and at the same time all three of the girls in the family, myself (Linda), Michelle and Jodi work at the Prosser School District.

When asked what the best thing in our lives are, we answer, "the best thing in our life is the fact that our two children and their mates live within a stones throw from us and that we get to see them and our 5 grandchildren each and every day."

Dan and Linda center above with Grandpa Ray next to Dan and our children and grandchildren are as follows:

Michelle Lynn Giles married William LeRoy Pleake III on May 6, 1989 at Prosser, Wa. This couple had two children; Josephine Morgan Pleake born June 9, 1994 at Richland, Wa. and Benjamin Bruce Pleake born June 24, 199 at Richland, Wa. The Pleake family is above on the left.

Michael, Jodi and family above on the right.

Michael Lee Giles married Jodi Elizabeth Pleake on July 31, 1993 at Prosser, Wa. This couple had three children. Emilee Alexis Giles born Feb. 26, 1995 at Richland, Wa., Baylee Nicole Giles born Nov. 18, 1977 at Richland Wa. and Natille Rylan Giles born Dec. 23, 2002 at Yakima, Wa.

MY FAMILY

By: Lloyd Ingraham

Several years ago my Dad met my Mom through his sister Lorraine. Mom and Lorraine became best friends so Lorraine introduced Dad to Mom. From there love seemed to blossom and grow. Dad asked Mom to marry him and she accepted his proposal.

They wanted to start a family right away so they did. The first child born was Dorothy Jean then a year later Linda Rae was born. Dad wanted a boy so 16 months later Lloyd Raymond joined the family.

Our folks brought us up with good values, respect yourself and others. Treat people the way you would want to be treated. They taught us the differences between right and wrong. They showed us the importance of family and the true meaning of love.

Dad has loved Mom from the first time he met her and for both of them this love has grown throughout the years. Dad felt that family time was very important. They always guided us in the right direction.

Dad and Mom enjoyed camping with the whole family. We often went to the Oregon coast where we would walk on the beach. Mount Saint Helen was another place our folks liked to go. We were told to always be on the lookout for bears in that area.

Our family was very close; we always enjoyed each others company. The folks would enjoy all the family functions when we would bring our families together. The kids would go play and we all would sit by a campfire and discuss days that had gone by.

In Dorothy's junior year at Kiona-Benton High School she met Ron Rideout who was in the air force at Moses Lake, Washington. Ron would come to visit her every weekend. Sometimes he would even have to hitch-hike down because he did not have the money for gas.

In Dorothy's senior year Ron told the folks he wanted to marry D.J. They told both of them to wait until she finished high school so they did. The following year they became man and wife. And for me Ron was the brother that I never had. Ron had a gift with mechanical things; he would take them apart just to see what made them work.

Ron and Dorothy had 4 children, Debbie was the first then came Jeanie, then Michael and last but not least Kevin. Ron was killed in a motorcycle accident in 1987. He laid in a coma for 8 months and Dorothy never left his side. Now Kevin reminds all of us of Ron because he is a lot like his dad.

Dorothy is now married to John Wolters and they live in Twin Falls, Idaho.

Linda met Danny Giles when they were both going to Columbia Basin College. Danny had a high performance 56 Chevy and they would often sit in front of Mom and Dad's house with the motor idling until the early morning hours. You can only imagine what they did all those hours.

Dan (Danny) was and is a man that enjoys life. He loves to talk with people and we always find his stories very entertaining. Danny went to California to work for General Telephone. He would often drive back on his weekends just to be with Linda. She has always felt that the sun sets and rises with Dan. While Dan was in California he was diagnosed with appendicitis and they wanted to do surgery on him there. Dan wanted to be with Linda so against their suggestion he left for the Tri-Cites. They told him his appendix could rupture before he got to the Tri-Cites. His first stop was our house to see Linda and then to the hospital. Thank God everything worked out. They were married shortly after; they moved to Yakima where Dan worked for the phone company.

Linda and Danny had two children, Michelle and Michael. Danny has been a General Contractor. He even built their own house where they now reside. He has built several other houses for other people in this area.

RAYMOND, ANNA INGRAHAM AND FAMILY

Dan and Linda have also owned and still own their trucking company. They often hire 2 to 3 drivers to operate their fleet of trucks. Danny and Linda live in Prosser.

I (Lloyd) was married three times. My first wife Christine was probably the mistake of my lifetime. I was married to her for 2 years. I got the divorce.

Then 10 years later, I (Lloyd) met Tammy Dixon; we married and had a son named Bryan who is now 23 years old. Bryan wants to become a firefighter.

Bryan's photo is at left; taken 2007

(note from Willard) This young man has a voice for singing that is professional.)

I (Lloyd) met and married my present wife Patty; we have been married for 20 years. Below is our photo taken 2007. I (Lloyd) believe this woman should be given a medal for putting up with me for so many years. I work for the railroad and Patty works as a nurse at Lords Medical Center.

Patty and I bought 5 acres in Pasco, Wa. We have a big yard and Patty really works hard to maintain it.

Over the years all of us try to stay in touch; we do enjoy visiting with each other. We are still a family because of our folks and the values they shared with all of us.

Four months ago Mom's health started failing; Linda did not like what she saw. She took Mom to her heart doctor in Richland. This doctor felt if you are in your 80's you have had a good life. Linda did not like what the doctor said and moved Mom to another heart doctor.

He thought Mom should undergo open heart surgery. She made it through the surgery but her recovery has been rough. She is having problems with her circulation every since. It hurts to see her health slowly being taken away and the pain increasing inside her legs. She is slowly running out of options; her body is getting weaker.

Dad is hanging on just to be with Mom; however his health is affected because of the stress he feels. This is hard on the Alzheimer's that is slowly overtaking his brain. Our goal was and is today to get Mom well so she can be with Dad. Dorothy, Linda and I had to make the hardest decision we have ever made. We decided to place Dad in an assisted living facility where he could get the care that he so badly needs. Our goal is to get Mom healthy again so they can be together.

Linda takes Dad up to see Mom everyday and Dad sits there by her side until Mom has to go for dinner. They often hold hands just to reassure each other; for now that has to be enough.

For me this is the hardest thing I have ever had to do; to see the two people you love most in the world hurting inside. I totally feel helpless, empty and my heart is heavy.

Note: After this writing Anna Rose Ingraham passed on April 1, 2007. Presently Raymond Ingraham remains in the assisted living facility at Prosser, Washington.

LIFE WITH MOM AND DAD
By: Lloyd Ingraham

When we were younger my sisters and I would have some pretty gruesome battles. My sisters would team up together thinking they would show me who the boss was. Dad and Mom would let us know when we had over stepped our bounds.

I can remember one day when I threw that trump card out there only to be grabbed up by Mom. I said, "If you do not let me go I am going to run away." She said, "I am tired of you threatening me with that; so let's get your bags packed and I will show you to the door." As she threw some of my clothing into my suitcase she started telling me about the kind of people I better look out for. She also asked me what I was going to live on. As she is walking me to the door I am starting to think that this is really a bad choice. I started backing up; making statements like Mom I really don't want to go. She first told me that was too bad that she had enough of my threats. Then I started stomping my feet and yelling, "Mom I really don't want to go." Now she had me; she said and I remember it to this day, "You have to do 2 things for me before I agree to let you stay."

I am thinking to myself; OK Mom anything. She said, "you have to tell me like you mean it that you are really sorry." I answer, "Okay Mom that's easy; I am sorry," boy you know I was sorry.

Mom continued, "and then secondly you have to agree to never threaten me with that statement again." I answered, "Okay Mom you have a deal." Well I guess you know Mom won that round.

I came home from school one day and Mom must have had a bad day at work. She asked me a question and I must have said the wrong thing, or just smarted off at her with what I thought was funny. However she didn't see it that way because she started using my head as a basketball. She starts hitting me on both sides of my face.

Then like fool, I said, "are you done now?" This however was the wrong thing to say because it was time for the second round; Mom won again.

Afterward Mom had some time to think about it she really felt bad. Now I am no fool; I can use this for special treatment. So she gave me a hug and said she was having a bad day. Every once in a while I like to bring this story up to her. You know Mom and I get a good laugh about that story today.

Dad and Mom liked to camp and because it didn't cost a lot of money back then we often went. We always liked the Oregon coast and Mt. Saint Helen.

It wasn't until all of us kids got out on our own that Dad and Mom bought their first motor home. They often went to Moses Lake with their best friends Howard and Betty Hornvett.

Then all 4 of them started going to Yuma, Arizona for the winter; they became snowbirds. They would leave after Christmas and come back home at the end of March.

One day after Mount Saint Helen blew her top Mom and Dad were camping and they got stuck at Fish Trap for about a week before they could get out. They had to shovel off the roof of their motor home which was covered by ash. They were on their way home and decided to stop off at Lake Warden to fish and stay the night.

Lake Warden looked like a big bowel of milk and the fishing was no good. They decided to leave for home and Dad backed the motor home into the boat ramp so he could place the boat onto the trailer. He left the engine idling and went around the front of the motor home to help Mom load the boat.

They both heard a loud pop and the motor home went into reverse. Mom got knocked off her feet and managed to crawl into the clear. Dad jumped back behind the wheel of the motor home only to go down with the motor home as it fell into 11 feet of water.

Now Dad wasn't much of a swimmer and Mom thought he was going to drown. He went down 3 times then a voice told him to pull himself up along the side of the motor home. He then managed to get on top of the motor home where Mom maneuvered the boat over to him. He got inside the boat and she pulled him to shore. I believe that my folks were touched by Christ that day.

They did however loose their little dog Bonnie; she drowned in the motor home and Mom grieved like it was one of us kids.

The motor home was a total loss; Dad thought he had lost everything. We told him they still had each other and the motor home could be replaced. They later did buy another motor home which they enjoyed for many more years.

RAYMOND, ANNA INGRAHAM AND FAMILY

CHAPTER XII
    VERDELL, NORMAN INGRAHAM AND FAMILY
By: Willard Ingraham

When Lyle and Gena Ingraham moved to Prosser, Wa. in 1941 Ray, Norman and Willard had jobs but all were living at home. Lorraine was going to Prosser School at that time.

Norman loved horses and bought a beautiful bald faced bay called Champ. In his time off from his job you would see the two together with Norman playing his new guitar serenading his horse. What a pair they were with Norman riding his favorite horse or parked somewhere and Champ listening to Norman do what he loved, playing his guitar. (Photo above taken 1942)

All of us boys knew how to shoot the 22 caliber rifle very well so we would go rabbit hunting in the Horse Heaven Hills where there were an abundance of wild rabbits running around that the farmers were only too happy for us to thin the rabbit population down. If that wasn't enough hunting for us we drove up to the city dump at night and shot the rats. Photo: Norman and a prized shot.

In November of 1942 Norman Jerome Ingraham was inducted into the army from Prosser and was sent to Camp Gruber, Oklahoma. He was assigned to the 88th Infantry Division at Camp Gruber where he took his basic training which included many long hikes and very grueling training. Norman's photo is at the left.

He was taken to the firing range where he learned how to shoot many different weapons the army way. From that training they made him the instructor to teach many recruits how to shoot the army way on the firing range. Because of this daily shooting at the firing range Norman's hearing became very impaired so they assigned him to the QM detachment 1881 unit at Camp Gruber.

Back in the 1940s during W.W.II there were no earmuffs used on the firing line or any other place in the army.

Norman's job (photo right) now was driving the camp officers around and was assigned to drive the camp bus.

VERDELL, NORMAN INGRAHAM AND FAMILY

In 1944 Norman was assigned to Co.D 1919 S.C.U. at Hollywood, California where he worked in the postal department to sort the big influx of army mail.

Later Norman was assigned to Firestone Tire Company in Los Angeles, California to make tires for the army.

Then in January or February of 1946 he was discharged through Fort Lewis, Washington and returned back home to Prosser, Washington. (Norman's photo is below)

Shortly after returning home Norman Jerome Ingraham, son of Lyle and Gena Ingraham married Verdell Noble.

Verdell was born Dec. 4, 1927 at Van Buren, Arkansas. Her parents Chester Lee Noble and Ethel Cox Noble lived at Grandview, Washington. Verdell is the third child of eight children; five girls and three boys.

Verdell and Norman were married at the Methodist church in Prosser, Wa. on July 27, 1946. Willard Ingraham was Norman's best man at the wedding.

Above is a photo of Norman and Verdell, 1954 with children Jerome and Janette. Left is daughter, Jacquelyn age 11 years. Their children were all born at Prosser. Jerome Jay Ingraham was born May 26, 1951 at the Prosser hospital. Janette Marie Ingraham was born November 18, 1953 also at the Prosser hospital and so was Jacquelyn Ingraham born on August 28, 1955.

VERDELL, NORMAN INGRAHAM AND FAMILY

Norman worked for Hall and Atwater constructing a school building in Prosser. In 1950, Verdell and Norman bought a 20-acre farm on Buena Vista road west of Prosser. The couple purchased some milk cows, a tractor and machinery. They drilled a new well on their property and remodeled their home.

In 1964, Norman went to work for Valley Ready Mix in Grandview, Wa. Everyone liked Norman to deliver concrete to them because he would put those big concrete trucks any place the contractors wanted them to be. Not only that Norman delivered to individual customers; he wasn't afraid to help them with the pour. Norman was requested by many of the customers to make their delivery. He worked there until his retirement in 1984.

It was in 1967 that Verdell decided to go to work for the Safeway grocery store in Prosser. Verdell worked there until she retired in 1985.

The years living on the farm were working years. The family milked cows but they also raised beef cattle. Norman bought young stock, pastured them on their land for the summer months and sold them in the fall of the year so they

did not have to buy hay for the winter months

After retirement, it was time to slow down so in 1999 Norman and Verdell sold their farm that they had lived on since 1950 and moved to town. They purchased a new home in Kennewick, Washington. Verdell and Norman above at home.

NORMAN INGRAHAM'S ART GALLERY

With extra time on his hands after retiring, Norman decided to try his luck at oil painting of animals and scenic pictures on canvas. He has pictures displayed in his home along with carvings he has done. Below; photo is Norman and one of his paintings.

Norman painted in colored oils; as you can see even the black and white reprints shows that Norman has great artistic talent.

Photos on this page and following are some of Norman's art.

VERDELL, NORMAN INGRAHAM AND FAMILY

What follows is an art gallery of some more of Norman's work.

Some of the frames were removed to adjust to the close quarters and the angle of the photo that was taken. In all cases, the works were kept intact and are as painted by the artist.

Some of Norman's carvings are below

Above is only a few of Norman's carvings. The top photo is a likeness of the cement truck that he drove for years in his work. The top shelf on the lower photo has several likenesses of the cement truck as well as other carvings as does the bottom shelf. Norman liked to carve horses, birds and animals also.

All of Norman's work is good and his children have some on display in their own homes.

Norman celebrated his 80th birthday on Sept. 11, 2002 at their daughter Janette's home (Photo below). Most of their family was there including grandchildren and nine great grandchildren. Guests included brothers Raymond and wife Anna, Willard and wife Louise; also sister Lorraine.

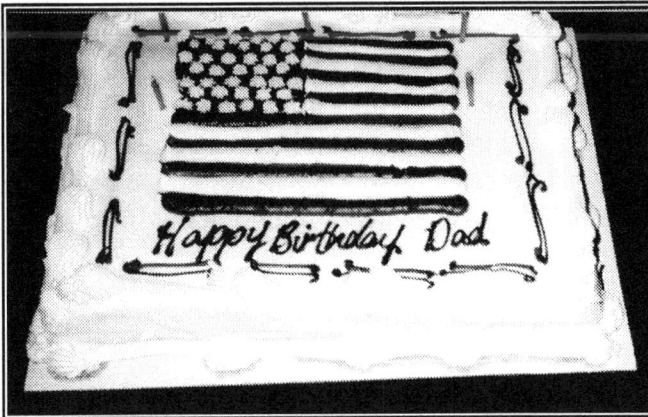

The birthday cake had a special meaning from family honoring their Dad with an American flag and the Happy Birthday Dad.

VERDELL, NORMAN INGRAHAM AND FAMILY

Below is Norman and Verdell standing center with family.

From left to right each family group is clustered together as follows: Stephani and Doug Cooper and mom Stephani holding Conner and down front is daughter Jasmine standing in front of Grandpa Norman. Next on the left are Randy and Tammie Peters with mom Tammie holding Jaden. In the back row next, are Mckenzie and Scott Garberg; next Janette Burgess and friend standing behind Verdell; behind Norman is son Jerome and Lisa Ingraham. To the right are Johnny and Shannon Santoy with Mom holding Mercedes and Andre in front.

Not everyone could be present. Verdell and Norman's daughter Jacqueline (Jackie) Turner resides in Florida. She is a production manager for an upscale residential construction company and could not leave at that time.

Jackie could not be present at the next celebration time for her parents Norman and Verdell but she put into motion plans that made the occasion special as follows.

Norman and Verdell celebrated their 60th wedding anniversary on July 27, 2006. Their daughter Jacqueline Turner of Florida arranged via phone to host a dinner party at a local restaurant and included in the celebration, Anna and Ray's Ingraham's 60th anniversary, Willard and Louise's 59th anniversary and sister Lorraines 80th birthday.

Photo below left to right: Lorraine Johnson, Louise and Willard Ingraham, Anna and Ray Ingraham and Norman and Verdell Ingraham.

Time has a way of making a gathering an important milestone in the lives of people. This occasion was no exception with Jackie's kindness in including with her parents 60th celebration also including Anna and Ray Ingraham in the celebration of their 60th anniversary. It was the last gathering of all the Ingraham brothers and wives and sister as it was in November of 2006 that Anna had major heart surgery and passed away in April of the next year.

VERDELL, NORMAN INGRAHAM AND FAMILY

PHOTO GALLERY OF JEROME JAY INGRAHAM

Jerome Jay Ingraham, son of Norman and Verdell Ingraham born May 26, 1951. He married Sharon Miller on Feb. 20, 1971, Kennewick, Wa. Sharon was born Dec. 30, 1973 at Walla Walla. They had two children:

Robert Jerome Ingraham son of Jerome and Sharon Ingraham was born August 29, 1973, Portland, Oregon. He married Roberta Wagner on Nov. 26, 1993 at Coer'D'Alene, Idaho. Their photo is below. They had three children all born at Prosser; Casey Marie Ingraham b, April 25, 1997, Corry Ann Ingraham born Feb. 15, 1999 and Cody Ingraham born May 12, 2002.

Kelly Ingraham, daughter of Jerome and Sharon Ingraham. Kelly married Donald Allen Brown. They have two children. Ashlynn Lea Brown, b, Oct. 5, 1999, Richland, Wa. and Deegan Andrewer Brown, B. May 4, 2001, Prosser, Wa.

Jerome Jay Ingraham, son of Norman and Verdell Ingraham married Elizabeth Anne Cook on Sept. 14, 1990 at Clarkston, Wa. They have one child:

J.W. Ingraham, B, June 30, 1999 at Clarkston, Wa.

The family photo is below: Elizabeth (Lisa), JW and Jerome Ingraham

Jerome is a building contractor of Commercial and Residential properties. At this writing, Jerome has three commercial and residential construction contracts in process.

VERDELL, NORMAN INGRAHAM AND FAMILY

JANETTE BURGESS STORY AND PHOTO GALLERY
By: Janette Burgess

My parents bought a small farm in 1950 on Buena Vista Rd, Prosser, Wa. We had a beautiful view of Mt. Adams and those beautiful Horse Heaven Hills.

Mom and Dad ran a modest dairy which filled many week ends with "bucking hay," chopping corn and hay and working cattle in every aspect. My father also drove truck for Valley Ready Mix, 33 years to be exact. My mother was a homemaker and Dad's right hand man. She also worked at Safeway Stores and later retired after 18 years.

Mom and Dad had three children, Jerome, Janette and Jackie. Here on this modest farm these three children flourished.

My parents were remarkable people; they loved each other and they loved us. They were an uncrackable force. They were strict but fair and loving. Our lives were rich with travel, faith, hard work and fun times.

They were handsome people; both of them. My parents were respected and I was and am extremely proud of them. Both parents were excellent horsemen and this is where I developed my love and appreciation of this noble animal.

My husband, Yancey and I built a large horse barn in Benton City, Washington where we boarded, trained and showed registered quarter horses and thoroughbreds.

We raised two daughters, Shannon and McKenzie. Both are excellent cattle women and horsewomen.

Shannon married John Santoy in 1997 and they have two children, Andre and Mercedis. They live in Benton City.

McKenzie married Scott Garberg in 2005. They live in Benton City.

We all love our life, our land and live in peace.

JANETTE BURGESS FAMILY

Janette Marie Ingraham, daughter of Norman and Verdell Ingraham married Edward Allen Hall, June 17, 1972 at the Methodist Church, Prosser, Washington.

They had one girl:

Shannon Marie Hall, born April 21, 1974, Prosser, Wa. Shannon married Johnny Santoy on Sept. 26, 1996. They have two children:

Andre Santoy, Born April 30, 1998, Prosser, Wa. and Mercedes Marie Santoy, born April 4, 2002, Richland, Wa.

A 2002 family photo is below Johnny, Shannon and children Andre and Mercedes Santoy.

Janette Marie Ingraham Hall married Wesley K. (Yancey) Burgess on June 2, 1979 at Benton City.

Below is Janette and Yancey, 2002.

They had one girl: McKenzie Lesley Burgess

McKenzie Lesley Burgess, born Oct. 17, 1985
Richland, Wa. McKenzie was married on Nov. 19, 2005,
Prosser Wa. to A. Scott Garberg, Benton City, Wa.

McKenzie and Scotts wedding photo is below.

W.K. (Yancey) Burgess passed away on March 11,
2003.

JACQUELYN TURNER'S STORY
By: Jacquelyn (Jackie Turner)

When I was a little girl, I remember all of the family gathering playing cards and always enjoying a wonderful meal together. It was what "family" was all about.

I remember hearing all the laughter coming from around the table as the adults played cards, doing their best to "outwit" Grandpa Ingraham, which rarely happened. I remember Grandma's lefsa, lutefisk and krube on holidays that we shared. Oh and don't forget her date filled sugar cookies. Then there was Grandma crocheting while she was falling asleep her fingers never missing a step. Let's not forget Grandpa's fast step as he danced his "jig" and laughed. They played the violin and piano together and continued to make music for over 60 years! I honor Grandpa and Grandma's memory.

Their children and spouses are special also. Look at the milestones they have accomplished! Three couples celebrating sixty years of marriage, birthdays ranging from 86 to 75! Just think about it, how often does this happen? You are all amazing and very dear to me!

Laughter has always been a special part of our family; we need to do more of it. Thank you all for your love and kindness.

JACQUELYN TURNER'S FAMILY

Jacquelyn (Jackie) Ingraham, was born Aug. 28, 1955 at Prosser, Washington and is the daughter of Norman and Verdell Ingraham. Jacquelyn married to Robert Wayne Haley, Sept. 15, 1973, Prosser, Wa.
They had two children:
Tammie Waynette Haley was born Sept. 23, 1974 Pasco, Wa., daughter of Jacquelyn and Robert Haley.
Steffani Ann Haley was born March 26, 1978 at Richland, Wa. daughter of Jacquelyn and Robert Haley.
Tammie Waynette Haley married Daryl Brown. Daryl was born Oct. 26,1964. They had one child:
Nate Lucus Brown born Dec. 10, 1998
Tammie Waynette Brown married Randy George Peters, Sept. 3, 2004, Richland, Wa. They have a son:
Jaden Skyler Peters was born Nov. 17, 2005, Yakima, Wa.

Family photo: Tammie, Randy, baby Jaden and Nate

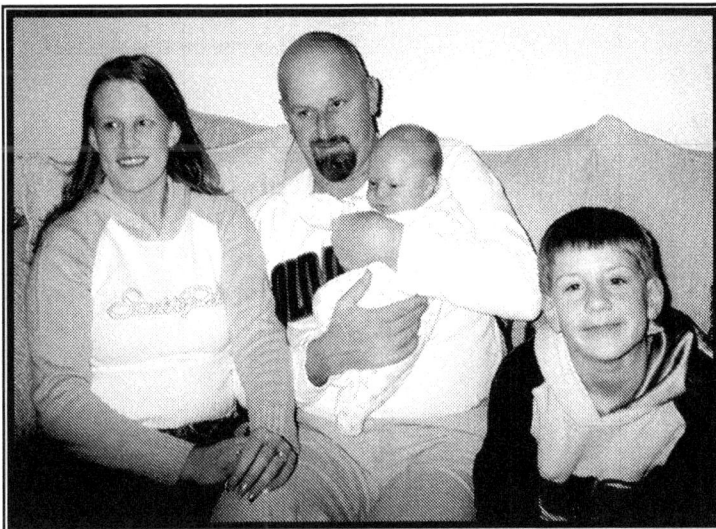

Steffani Ann Haley, daughter of Jacquelyn and Robert Haley, born March 26, 1978, Richland, Washington and Douglas Cooper have two children:
Jasmin Wikcole Cooper was born Oct 1, 2003, Richland Wa.
Conner Cooper born August 4, 2005 Richland, Wa.

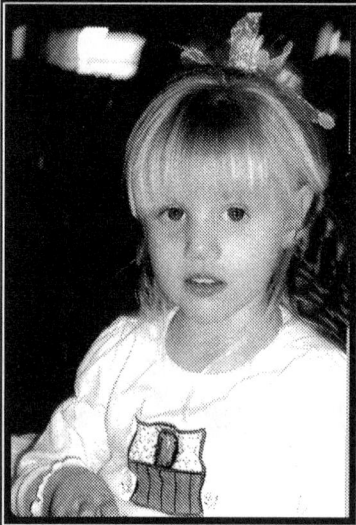

A family photo taken 2006: Above is Doug and Stephani with mom Stephani holding Conner and left is a photo of Jasmin.

It was October 2005 that Louise and I (Willard) were invited to join Verdell and Norman for a trip to Panama City Beach, Florida to visit their daughter Jacquelyn (Jackie) Turner. Jackie was a wonderful host and took time off from her job as a production manager for upscale homes to take us on tours of the area. Jackie's photo is left. (Her dad's oil painting is behind her) Jackie's home is pictured

below.

CHAPTER XIII:
LOUISE, WILLARD INGRAHAM AND FAMILY

BACK HOME FROM WORLD WAR II
Willard Stanley Ingraham-WWII; I am a veteran of the
Army from March 18, 1943, - December 29, 1945.
I was inducted in the army at Fort Douglas, Utah and was sent
immediately to Fort Knox, Kentucky for my basic training and assigned to A Company 2nd Platoon 526th Armored Infantry Battalion, Fort Knox, Kentucky. I served there for six months doing my basic training. Willard's photo is at the left.

In September of 1943 our unit moved by train to Camp Bouse, Arizona. We were taken twenty miles into the desert from Bouse, Az. where we set up camp in tents in tent city that we called Happy Valley to the tune of about ten thousand soldiers. We received our maneuver and special training here

Beginning in October of 1943 mail was censored and given an APO address. Soldiers were not allowed to leave camp except in small groups led by a non-commissioned

357

officer or an officer. Soldiers were sworn to secrecy and threatened with death if they disclosed anything about the Gizmos or our training with them. We called these tanks Gizmos or man made moon light tanks.

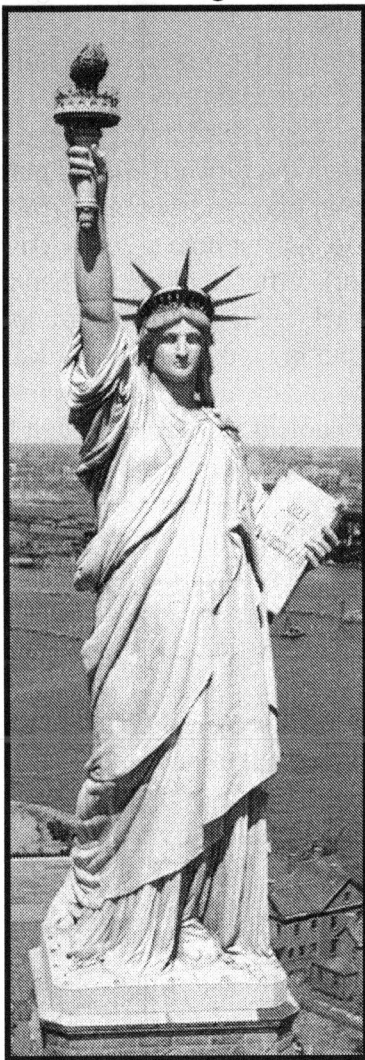

In March 1944 it was time to move again by train to Staten Island, New York port of embarkation for over seas.

We were also the night protective guards at the railroad tracks to see that no one came around the Gizmos in any way while being loaded onto the trains and onto the ships once we got to Staten Island.

We had orders backed up clear to the president that if anyone messed around our secret tanks and would not listen to our commands we were to shoot them with no hesitation. We had eighteen days and nights in New York. We used both while there between our duties before being shipped out to Swansea, Wales to await D-Day, the invasion into France against the Germans.

Above is the last view of the New York harbor and the Statue of Liberty as the troops saw as we were shipped out; it was an impressive sight to remember as we faced the unknown.

I have four battle stars for Participating in Northern France, Ardennes, Rhineland and Central Europe across France, Luxemburg, Belgium and Germany. I also fought in the Battle Of The Belgium Bulge.

One night in January of 1945 A Company was holding a defensive position somewhere near Malmedy. It was snowing and very cold at night. Kenneth Murvine, Cleve Collins and I were selected to man the forward control point about three hundred yards in front of our defense line. We took a phone and strung a line to our fox hole (already dug) from the rear C.P. (control point). After hooking the phone up we now had communications back to the rest of our group. This fox hole was quite a way out in no man's land. It was located somewhere between the enemy and our front line of defense. By sitting up in the foxhole it was large enough for all three of us. I took some candles with me and some writing paper planning to write some letters while there making the night go faster. The candle was bright enough to write a letter.

I was thinking of my parents so I started to write to them. The fox hole had a cover over the top of it so light would not drift out of the fox hole and give the enemy a chance to kill.

As I started to write the letter seemed like my mind turned into poetry. My letter turned out to be a poem. I simply called it Fox Hole Poem. This was on the night of January 13, 1945. After the poem was written I pulled my mouth organ out of my pocket and started to play a few tunes. Ken and Cleve began to sing. We thought that was not too bad so we opened the circuit up back to the rear control point and called ourselves the Ingraham, Murvine and Collins Broadcasting Company.. We tried to not be too loud with our singing etc and stir up the enemy camp. The time went very fast that night.

Note: The Fox Hole Poem was inserted on the following page. The poem was published in the Stars and Stripes. Also inserted is another poem Willard wrote.

This page was dedicated to Willard's poem.

SON WRITES "FOX HOLE" POEM

Mr. and Mrs. Lyle Ingraham received the following letter written January 13, 1944 in rhyme by their son Pfc. Willard, now at the fighting front. It gives a glimpse of life in the fox holes and of what the boys "over there" are thinking:

As I sit in my fox hole tonight
and I think of home,
I know for sure I'll never more
want to roam.
I have a dim light to write
this by,
As a big light would show into
the sky.
And with the enemy right over
the hill,
A big light would give them a
chance to kill.
I have two buddies now by my
side,
But this fox hole is big enough
for us to hide.
One's name is Cleve and the
other one Ken,
And in my opinion they're both
good men.
Another buddy, Boyce who is
just up the line,
Who you know I think of as
fine, he was up to my fox hole
to see me today---
But doesn't come often as he's
quite far away.
We both send our love, from us
today
And hope soon to come home and
stay.
He's a very good buddy, who is
very true
And helps me out when I'm
terribly blue.
It's now zero weather and
plenty of snow,
But we stay on the line and
fight the foe,
I think of the furlough I so
long ago had,
But then here's the enemy which
makes me so mad.
You folks were so good to me
when I was home,
So over here I feel quite
alone.
Your letter I receive with lots
of cheer,
and to me none other can be so
dear,
I hear from Lorraine, Norman
and Ray,
But it's your letters Mom that
I get most every day.
The Yakima place is the best
place to be,
But it's far from England with
all it's tea,
France and Belgium are farther
away yet.
But you go where you're taken
and take what you get.
So with this little fox hole
poem,
You know dear folks I'm
thinking of home.

By: Willard Ingraham

Below is the second poem Willard wrote.

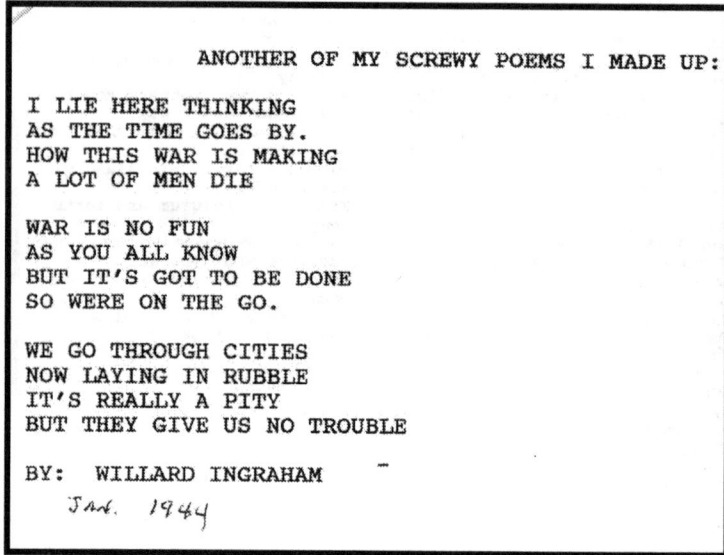

```
           ANOTHER OF MY SCREWY POEMS I MADE UP:

I LIE HERE THINKING
AS THE TIME GOES BY.
HOW THIS WAR IS MAKING
A LOT OF MEN DIE

WAR IS NO FUN
AS YOU ALL KNOW
BUT IT'S GOT TO BE DONE
SO WERE ON THE GO.

WE GO THROUGH CITIES
NOW LAYING IN RUBBLE
IT'S REALLY A PITY
BUT THEY GIVE US NO TROUBLE

BY:  WILLARD INGRAHAM
    Jan. 1944
```

The 526th Armored Infantry Battalion soldiers were recognized for their battle abilities; the ones I am referring to are the Battles Of The Belgian Bulge at Stavelot and Malmedy. The fierce fighting against superior German enemy forces occurred in December, 1944 and January 1945. From these battles the 526 A.I.B. gained the nickname Battleaxe. The 526 Armored Infantry Battalion was authorized to add the word Battleaxe to the 526 Armored Infantry Battalion shoulder patch.

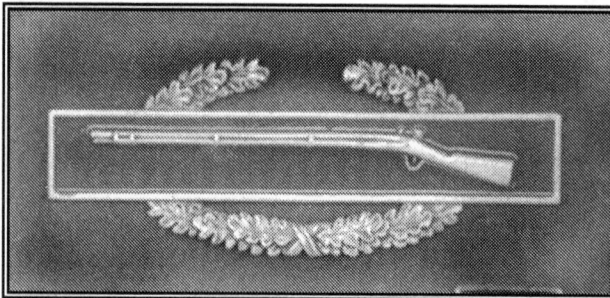

I was issued the Combat Infantry Badge; photo is at left.

I was also issued the Bronze Star; photo below.

The 526 Armored Infantry Battalion holds the distinction of being the only separate Armored Infantry Battalion in the army that worked with the T Force of the 12th Army Group Task Force and Counter Intelligence as special troops.

The 526th Armored Infantry Battalion would often work separately by companies. Yes also sometimes as individual squad units in order to reach our objectives and missions assigned to them. Our 526 Armored Infantry was not only working with T Force (task force) but also with Counter Intelligence called C.I.C. (Counter Intelligence Corp).

General Eisenhower was the supreme commander of the European allied forces. Toward the end of the European War the 526 Armored Infantry was sent to Wiesbaden, Germany under General Bradley, 12th Army Group where General Bradley's headquarters were located. They wanted the 526th as a combat unit to guard the town while German soldiers were being released back into civilian life again.

On May 8, 1945 the European war was over and in September of 1945 the war was over after the atomic bomb was dropped on Japan. Then in November of 1945 we got our orders that we were going home.

We loaded up in cattle cars on the railroad to ride to Antwerp, Belgium. At Antwerp we loaded onto the Liberty Ship called the S/S Irvin Mac Dowel headed for Boston, Massachusetts. Then we were transferred to a train for a five day ride ending up at Fort Lewis, Washington. There I was processed for discharge with my ruptured duck December 29, 1945.

The Ruptured Duck was an honorable discharge symbol insignia attached to our army uniform. When this insignia was placed on our uniform, we had 30 days to get back into civilian clothes. Willard's photo is on the left where one can see the insignia on his uniform.

At the Prosser, Washington railroad station I left my army duffel bag at the station and walked down town to Riches Café that was still open to find

someone I would know but no luck and with no taxis I wasted no more time but took off walking the four miles to my parents Lyle and Gena Ingraham's home.

I was in good shape so I walked and ran those four miles in no time. My parents had just gotten home from playing for a dance and had gone to bed when I walked in. There was so much to say but it had been a long day but Dad drove me back to Prosser to collect my duffel bag and when we came back home again we talked the rest of the night.

I just gave you a glimpse of the almost three years that I served our country in World War II. Sixty years after the war my family persuaded me to write a book of those World War II experiences. "Farm Boy To Soldier" has been published and is available.

One of the first things I did when I got home was to go to the photographers and get a picture of me in my army clothes and one of me in civilian clothes again. Willard on right in civilian attire taken in 1946.

LOUISE, WILLARD INGRAHAM AND FAMILY

At first when I got home from the service I felt worn out and did not feel like doing much of anything except to rest. After a couple of weeks of resting it was time to start thinking of what direction I wanted to take with my life from that point of time.

I had saved my money from the sale of my farm and car when I had entered the army life and had purchased bonds during the service knowing that on my return home from the war and back in civilian life again I had made myself a promise that I would treat myself by buying a new car.

On checking with the dealership in town for a new car the agent at the garage snarled and told me, "don't you know there was a war going on and we have had no new cars to sell since the war?" My comment to him was tell me about it, as if I did not know about the war. After learning that I was a veteran just returning home he immediately informed me how they would take good care of all the veterans.

Since I could not buy a new car my thoughts turned to the purchase of an 8 cylinder Pontiac convertible just completely overhauled and they would give me my choice of paint. I thought this car would do me until new cars became available again. The photo of that car is below. My mistake was in paying cash for the car before the work was completed.

The car turned out to be a lemon with a complete overhaul this 8 cylinder Pontiac would only get 40 miles an hour on the road. I immediately took the car back to the garage but they would do nothing to fix it. I insisted on trading it back to them to get a car that would work right. They told me I couldn't do that; I asked why not and they told me I would loose money on the trade.

Finally they got in a 1940 black sedan Chevrolet that I purchased from them. The car had a couple of flat tires on it and they told me they could not get any new tires. By the end of that day thou I had gone to several towns and ended up with four new tires. To make a long story short; the 1940 Chevrolet I bought turned out to be a good one (photo below).

I kept it until 1949 when I traded it off and bought my first new car, a 1949 sedan Ford. I bought from another dealership because they were shafting other veterans coming home also. We had a strong V.F.W. club in Prosser and guess what that Ford dealer that shafted me and others went out of business.

After all this hassle I felt like getting a beer; when I ordered it they asked if I was old enough and they had to see my driver licenses. After spending three years in the army with two of those years overseas on the front lines and then to have someone ask if I was old enough to have a beer shocked me. After the server explained he could loose his license if he served someone underage I would understand and enjoyed my beer they served as I was 21 years old.

My cousin Arnold Steffens returned home from the service about a month before I got home. Norman, my brother got home in about January 1946 and Raymond my other brother returned home in June of 1946. We had all made it back from the war safely.

In the spring of 1946 I made a decision to make farming my next adventure. I was single and living with my parents so Dad suggested I help him finish the other side of his barn as it could accommodate ten cows in stanchions for milking and he would let me use it for my cows after I bought them. That is what I did; when I bought my milk cows the barn was equipped so that milking machines worked on either side of the barn. Below is a photo of Dad and I hauling hay.

There was a nice 20 acre farm with an old style house on it with a screened in porch along two sides and a nice barn. An elderly man by the name of Ole Grambo owned the ranch and was living there by himself. Ole was 89 years old.

Ole Grambo's photo is below.

I always liked that place and I like Ole Grambo very much. I would take his mail to him often. One day as I visited him I told him if he ever sold his farm I wanted him to give me first chance to buy it. He said he would think about it. A short time later he did decide to sell. A price was set and I took him into town where we signed the papers and then I went to the bank and got the first GI loan that they had processed and the farm was mine.

This 20 acre farm was located at the corner of Buena Vista and Wilgus road. A photo of this farm is below.

The acreage also had about half an acre of concord grapes with two grape plants of very sweet red eating grapes. I was still staying at home with my parents and this left the farm house vacant so I rented the house to Norman and his wife Verdell. I farmed the land.

In May of 1947 I had my first date with my love, Louise Williams at her families family reunion at Hood River Park, Hood River, Oregon. Louise's photo is below.

Arnold Steffens my cousin was dating Lucille Williams who was Louise's sister. Arnold wanted me to drive to the reunion and told me Louise was available that day and she would be my date. I told them that would be fine with me. I drove to Mabton to pick Arnold up then we drove up to the Williams ranch to pick up Louise and Lucille. After that we drove on to the Hood River Park to meet the girls' family.

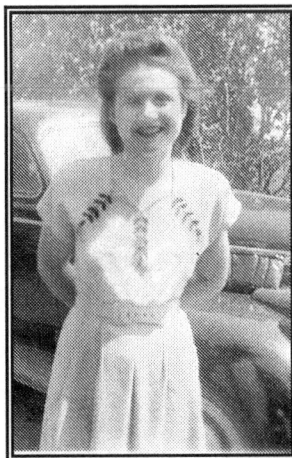

After the reunion Louise and I started dating steadily. Later that summer it was decided that all four of us were going to get married. Charley Williams, Louise and Lucille's father told us if we would have a double wedding he was building a big machine shed and the double wedding could be held on the ranch in the new machine shed. We all agreed to that so on Septmeber 13, 1947 Arnold Steffens and Lucille Williams and

Willard Ingraham and Louise Williams were all married at that time. Louise and I (Willard) are at the right.

Lucille and Arnold's photo is at the left.

There were over 400 people attending the wedding. The only

369

hitch was when the minister tried to marry both the girls to Arnold. I had to step up to him and correct him. After all no one was going to steal my bride.

Both couples went on separate short honeymoons. Arnold and Lucille then went to Richland, Wa. to live. Arnold was working at the Hanford Project as a guard.

Willard and Louise went to Willard's farm on the corner of Wilgus and Buena Vista Rd. at Prosser, Wa. to live.

When Louise and I returned from our honeymoon, there were a lot of things to be done. Before the wedding my sister and her husband Lester Mott had come up from California and had helped me paint the inside of my house. That was a big help. Now I had to get my cattle to my farm from my parent's farm. I had it made when milking my cows at Dad's because he had milking machines. Now I had to milk ten cows twice a day, seven days a week all by hand for all 365 days a year. My day started about 5 A.M. in the morning.

In October of 1947 a month after getting married I

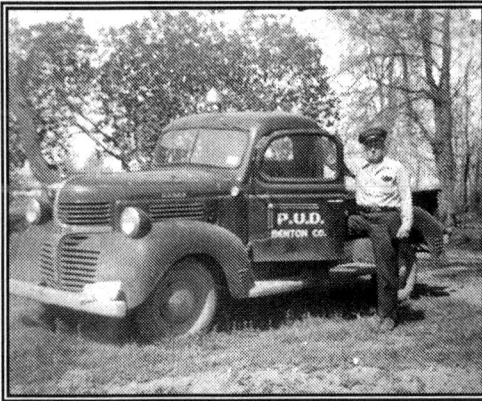

heard of a job opening for the Public Utility District in Prosser. Upon applying for the job I was immediately hired.

Below is the PUD truck I was assigned to use.

The grape crop was now ready to pick so I asked Louise if she would hire some pickers to come and pick our crop. Back then it wasn't a problem because neighbors usually helped pick grapes for each other. Mostly the women picked.

I took care of placing the grape boxes and collecting the full boxes at night after I got home but Louise did a good job of getting the grape job done. You know I think the pickers liked Louise as their boss better than they did me.

The first two winters living in our home was rather cold because the house was an old farm house with no insulation and the wind would blow the curtains back inside the windows. I knew many changes were needed and it would be cold soon.

In 1948, I was assigned as meter reader for the Benton County Public Utility District and one of my jobs was to read the electric meters in Benton County every month.

In the spring of 1948, I signed up for training to become a pilot of small aircrafts. I received my private airplane license on June 6, 1948. A copy of my pilot licenses is below.

I was working for the P.U.D. at that time and had an hour lunch break so decided I would get a little flying time in at that time. The wind was blowing a fairly good gale but nothing to be concerned about so I thought. I got the airplane checked out at the Prosser airport and headed for the end of the run way and

preparations for the take off. The photo of that plane is at the right. I revved the airplane up keeping the brakes on to get a good fast push on the take off. As I raced down the runway a big side wind rolled down over Horse Heaven Hills and caught me half way down the runway as the plane lifted off the ground. The wind pushed the plane over the airport office building just missing it and the trees around the office.

Unknown to me the airport had just received word to ground all planes but it was too late as I was already going down the run way for the take off. Those airplanes at that time had no radio communication installed in them. Once in the air I thought I might fly high enough to get above the wind storm but no luck as the wind storm was deeply set in so then I decided that I had flown this plane up here and one way or another I was going to get the plane back on the ground.

I circled the airport for a landing pattern to land and to assess my options for getting the plane on the ground. The wind was very strong with dust flying very heavy. There was only one run way at the Prosser airport so I had no choice but to land that plane with those strong cross winds.

All my instructions that my instructor had given me in training I recalled very clearly. The instructor had advised me in training if caught in a situation like this to dip the wing into the wind as I landed and pray that the plane would settle back straight and not tip over the other way and send me rolling.

Two men met the plane halfway down the runway as I landed to catch hold of the plane wing tips as I landed. Their timing was perfect as each man standing on each side of the run way grabbed hold of the wing tips to keep the plane from being blown over. They hung on tight as I taxied the plane back to the tie down spot to secure the plane in place. As I maneuvered the plane in place for the tie down ropes in order to reach the exact spots other men came out to hold the plane down while ropes were being secured. The lord was with me; it was another safe landing.

Millard Hileman brought his plane in about five minutes after I landed. He also brought his plane in safely. We had taken our flying instructions at the same time from

372

Jean Larson as our instructor. Jean Larson had been a fighter pilot in WWII and was also a good friend of mine.

Sometime later I was still flying and enjoyed my time doing so up among the clouds. Every time I took the plane up I practiced my 720's and purposely stalled the plane. I watched it climb then the plane would stall out and took a sudden dip toward the ground as I pulled the plane back to level flying again. It was fun to gain higher altitude then put the plane into a tail spin. It was fun spiraling the plane down in a fast tail spin.

I remembered my instructor, Jean Larson, telling me what to do if my plane was going into a power dive. Jean would never take me into a power dive but he showed me what to do in case it ever happened to me. Jean warned me to make sure to have a lot of altitude if I ever attempted one. I felt good about my flying so I thought why not try one to see what it was like. I took the plane up over 5000 feet and put the plane into a power dive. As I came down the plane was going so fast it started to vibrate as I cross controlled to bring the plane out of the dive. As I tried to pull the plane out of the dive the wings started to shake and vibrate so hard that I well knew if I pulled the plane out of the dive too fast the wings would break off the plane. I looked at the ground coming up fast and I kept my cool and gently forced the plane slowly to come out of the fast power dive. At this point I did not think I would be able to bring the plane up in time before the ground came up to meet me.

Slowly, slowly, the plane now shaking like it would shake apart I pulled harder on the stick and the plane responded and suddenly the plane dipped out of the dive into a long swoop and it was out of the dive. By the time I pulled out of that dive I had less than 800 feet left before hitting the ground. I never entertained the idea of ever putting the plane into another power dive after that.

I believe it was in 1950 when the airport called and said there was a plane down in the Blue Mountains. They were organizing all the planes and people to search for a down plane. They wanted me to go along as an observer with a dust crop pilot. I did and as we were flying over the rugged tree covered mountains a radio call said that the plane had been spotted and they gave us the location.

We headed for that location and saw the pilot standing outside by his plane. He had landed in the only clearing that was there for miles around. The dust pilot I was with said that the field looked pretty good and we would go down and cheer the downed pilot up and give him some candy bars that we had with us.

It was open forest land and the landing was pretty rough but we made it down. The downed pilot was very shaken up after spending all night in the plane and in cold weather with nothing to eat. He was not hurt and his plane was alright. We pushed his plane to the further end of the clearing and prepared him for a take off. The dust pilot I was with said that we would take off first then we would watch the downed pilot take off and both would fly to the Pendleton, Oregon airport.

We took off and the plane in that high altitude would not lift off fast enough. The big trees at the end of the field came up fast making it look like our plane would soon be floating in the tops of those big trees. The dust pilot told me to hang on because we were going. I may have imagined it but I thought I heard the tree tops scratch the bottom of our plane. Once we were up we circled to watch the downed plane take off. As I looked out my side of the plane I told the dust pilot what I saw happening.

I told him the downed plane is now airborne and looks like he will make it. Oh No I exclaimed he is setting the plane back down again. Guess he decided to stay. WE both commented that if he had time to set that plane down again he sure would have been able to have flown the plane over those tree tops. Apparently the tree tops scared him out.

We saw that the pilot on the ground was OK so we left and flew to Pendleton Airport. After we landed and informed everyone of the problem they immediately organized a ground party to pick up the pilot.

They did pick up the downed pilot but it was a couple of months later before they got the plane out. I heard they had to take the plane apart and haul it out of that location. The downed pilot had said that when he landed he had noticed a railroad track not far from where he put his plane down. He thought maybe if he followed the track he would find someone but after walking in that cold a while he decided to go back to his downed plane. He told everyone that was the longest night he had ever experienced in that dark forest in the mountains.

As a matter of information, I want to tell you what happened to my good friend and instructor Jean Larson. Jean also had a crop spraying business at the Prosser Airport in the early 1960s. One early morning Jean took off from Prosser with a loaded plane to spray fields near Kennewick, Washington. His plane crashed and Jean lost his life doing what he loved to do, flying airplanes.

There were a lot of things that happened in Louise and my life in 1948. On April 5, 1948 we were so happy when we became parents of Carol Jean Ingraham. Now we were a family and very proud to have a little girl in our house. We both loved children.

Our family photo is at the left.

May of 1948 we got some warm weather in the mountains that made the Yakima and Columbia Rivers' overflow their banks. All up and down the Yakima Valley the Yakima River was flooding. I jumped in the plane at Prosser and flew over the flooded land. It was so unbelievable the

375

amount of farms that were under water. Our farm was on higher ground so we had no problem with the flood conditions.

This is photo of a flooded area at that time along the Yakima River.

On December 28, 1949 we were blessed with another girl, Mary Ann Ingraham born at Sunnyside, Washington. What a tax deduction we got that year!

I brought Mama and baby home on the 30th of December just in time because the temperatures dipped to 28 degrees below zero and it came with what they called a blizzard. It was nothing like the blizzards I had known in North Dakota. This winter of 19491950 was abnormally cold and it held on for about six weeks. Most people had frozen water pipes to thaw out continuously.

Our house was so cold that we closed off our bedrooms and moved into the front room where the oil stove was. We put the baby crib next to our heater to keep warm.

With the water pipes frozen outside I had to chase my cattle down to my parent's farm every morning and night to water them. Yes I was still milking ten cows morning and night, keeping the house going and still working out at the P.U.D. Eight hours a day and more because power lines were also going down in this cold weather so overtime work was also required on the job. We had cold weather but at least in our home we did have an inside bathroom and electric lights.

That winter of 1949-1950 was the coldest weather recorded and it was the first time that the mighty Columbia River froze completely across ¼ of a mile between Pasco and Kennewick, Washington.

After a winter like that we knew it was time to remodel our home and make it more comfortable. Our home was a two story house with a screened porch on two sides of the house.

In remodeling the porches were torn off, (photo below with porches removed). The second story was cut off and the house was extended to make a 1600 square foot modern home with new kitchen, washer and dryer, a new forced air oil furnace system was installed and all outside walls were insulated as well as new sheet rock through out the house. New insulated siding was installed outside of the house. This was not done all in one year.

The photo at right is of Carol on left and Mary Ann taken July, 1950.

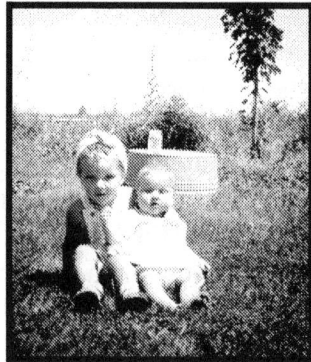

I did the remodeling except for the removal of the second story roof and installation of the new roof. There was a working bee week-end when a lot of our relatives and friends came to work on the roof. What a

377

blessing to have the whole house enclosed and I could do the rest as I had time. Louise got tired helping me to move sheet rock from room to room but when it was completed we had central heat and were snug as bugs in a warm house. The finished remodeled home is below.

Our 1940 black sedan Chevrolet that I had purchased when I got out of the service in 1946 was getting older and Louise and I decided it was time to get that new car I

had promised myself. We purchased a 1949 grey sedan Ford. Above is that new car loaded for camping.

LOUISE, WILLARD INGRAHAM AND FAMILY

Louise and I enjoyed our girls and always included them in everything we did. Louise had come from a family of 11 children and at the once a year family picnic there would be new cousins to meet for our girls to play with. The Williams family was on fast tract with the addition of new family members. All the Ingraham families continued to grow also.

In December of 1945 when I was on my way home from the service in Boston, Massachusetts I had seen a 7 inch lighted screen they called television. It was something few knew anything about and it was predicted that within 10 years the television set would be standard in most homes in America.

When I had told what I seen and heard to others that was called a T.V. no one thought such a way of communication was even possible. Guess what; in 1954 we purchased our first television set; an RCA with 17 inch screen and sat it in our front room on the left in the corner.

On June 15, 1955 I had just entered the main office of the P.U.D. building just before noon to pick up some more meter books to take with me for the afternoon meter readings. One of the girls in the office was on the phone and she called me over and told me I had a phone call. It was she told me my wife and she was very upset and wanted to talk to me. When I answered the phone Louise told me she had just gotten a call from her family that her father had suffered a stroke and was taken to the Yakima hospital. I told her I would take some time off and be right home. At that time we were living on our farm four miles west of Prosser. We made arrangements with my parents Lyle and Gena Ingraham to take care of our girls Carol Jean and Mary Ann and for Dad to milk my cows in case I did not get back.

This was the second stroke Louise's Dad had. The first stroke he had was earlier that year in January. It had been on his right side and he had been bedridden for all these months.

When we arrived in Yakima at the hospital nine of her brothers and sisters were there with their spouses. Louise's Dad was in a large single room and the attendants were generous by letting all of us into the room even setting up chairs for everyone. We all sat there into the late night and just before midnight Charley Allen Williams passed on.

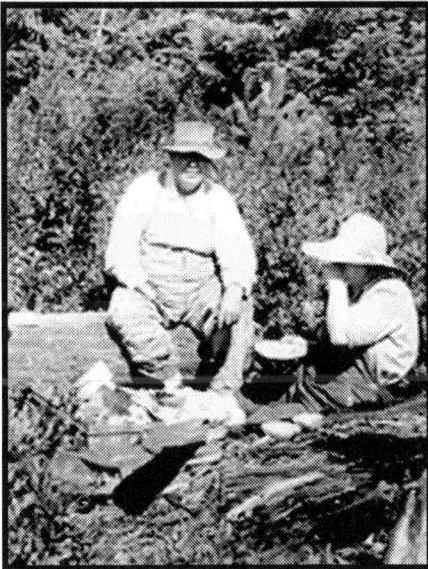

Funeral arrangements were made and Charley Allen Williams was laid to rest on June 18, 1955 at the Grandview, Washington cemetery. Charley was a much-respected family oriented man.

The photo on the left is of Charley in the huckleberry fields. He and Minnie are having their lunch. Camping in the Mt. Adams area and picking berries was one of Charley's favorite yearly trips. Picking berries was a serious business for Charley and he scouted out the best picking areas with all hands picking gallons of berries every day. Minnie canned lots of huckleberries in the evenings but it was the campfire gatherings that Charley instigated for fellowship. Telling

stories and eating the sweet fruits, mostly watermelon he
brought from home was a highlight for him.

Below is a family photo; Mary Ann left, Willard, Carol
and Louise taken in 1955.

In 1955 I sold all our milk cows and bought some
Hereford beef cattle; no more milking cows. That same year
we finished remodeling our house and now we had a double
garage and work shop. I had also allowed for a little shop area
where I sat up an electronics ICS shop.

I was interested in electricity and I also wanted to learn
more about radios and the new field of electronics in television
that had just been introduced at that time.

I built many of my own testing instruments. I was also
taking a home study course in electronics.

In 1955, the main P.U.D. office at Prosser was
transferred to Kennewick as that area was now growing faster
and the public demand was to move the main office of the
P.U.D. to Kennewick.

In 1957, I was transferred to Kennewick, Washington and became an apprentice meterman in the Meter Dept. I was under a three year apprenticeship program to learn to test, repair and install meters of all types and also test and repair relays and all related sub-station instruments in our district.

We sold our farm in Prosser and moved to Kennewick.

It was the beginning of a new type of life for all of us. We purchased an all brick home in the newly built south part of Kennewick. Photo left. Carol and Mary Ann are standing out front.

I set up my electronic shop in the basement area. Photo right is of my electronic shop in Prosser before we moved.

LOUISE, WILLARD INGRAHAM AND FAMILY

Soon we had many new friends and wonderful neighbors. We now had more leisure time and Louise and I planned our lives accordingly.

Louise decided to go to work and worked chair side and also did the bookkeeping in a dental office. Louise in dental uniform and my photo is below. After working there for two years, she decided to go to college and major in business administration. She enrolled in daytime college classes and worked at the college bookstore part time.

Both our girls, Carol Jean and Mary Ann were in grade school. Their lives were full of activities. I enrolled in college to get all the credits possible from night courses. This meant hard study time and long hours after work but in the long run I knew it was worth it.

For recreation, Louise and I joined a square dance group where we learned many kinds of square dances and round dancing. Our photo is right in our dance attire.

To me these years were great years and I cherish the memories of each of those years.

Our neighbors got together once a month for a

good party of bridge playing. At this same time we purchased
a 1958, 15 foot camping trailer and this became an advantage
to get away on weekends and on summer vacations. We
traveled all over the northwest, up and down the west coast,
through San Francisco, Oregon and Washington exploring the
ocean costal areas and visiting relatives. It was also great to
take the trailer to the mountains and pick huckleberries that we
then would can them right there in our camp; sometimes as
many as 50 quarts a season. We enjoyed the pies and sauce in
the winter months.

We also covered
the primitive areas of
Idaho and Montana
searching out semi-
precious stones for my
collection and hobby in
rock and jewelry making.

In 1959, we bought
a new Chevrolet green station wagon and installed a hitch on it
so we could hook onto our green camping trailer. Photo is
above. Now with the station wagon two more people could
have a nice place to sleep inside.

In 1959, my Dad decided to build a new block garage at
their home in Kennewick. I had some experience building with
concrete block so I helped him build the garage. Norman
helped with the roof and the shingling of the roof. It happened
that shingling was done on a very cold day but we got that
garage finished.

The grade school was giving music lessons so in 1959
Mary Ann decided she wanted to take violin lessons. One
night when walking home from school she was carrying her
violin when she her friend started playing around and Mary
Ann fell hard on her violin and broke it. She was in trouble
and she wrestled with what to do. That night after dinner I
went into the living room and sat in my favorite chair reading
the Tri-City Herald when Mary Ann came in and stood next to

me with a tear running down her cheek with a troubled look at what she was going to tell me. Finally she related to me what occurred on the way home from school and when she finished her story I asked her, "Did you mean to do it?" She told me no and how sorry she was. I told her because she came to me and told me the truth and that she had not meant to break her violin I would not punish her. Years later she told me that she had surely learned a lesson from that episode.

In 1959 the P.U.D. built a float to be entered in the parade in downtown Kennewick and Mary Ann was asked to ride on the float. She really added beauty to the float.

In 1960 Louise and I had a private music teacher come to our home and give Mary Ann piano lessons and Carol Jean piano accordion lessons. This private teacher was teaching other young children in various types of instruments so he put them all together to form a band to play. They really got good and played all different types of tunes. The band went to different benefit programs, Christmas programs and even played on some T.V. programs.

We were friends with Howard and Gladys Brightman who had two boys who played in the same band. Often to entertain the family it was Carol Jean on the piano accordion, Mary Ann on the piano and Mike Brightman on the clarinet and Dennis Brightman on the trumpet. That quartet really could play some beautiful music together.

In 1962 Carol Jean Ingraham started a science project that involved having two white rats in our home in a cage. The rats really got to be quite friendly with all the handling that Carol did with them. She bathed them every day and brought them out of their cage to set on her lap and petted them. In the experiment she used with the rats they got so they would do anything that she wanted them to do.

On March 24, 1962 Carol Ingraham, an eighth grader at Park Junior High School in Kennewick was named grand prize winner of the Junior division at the Mid Columbia Science Fair in W. Richland, Wa. Her exhibit was on antibodies from human saliva injected into rats. During her experiment she had to take her rats to a medical office where they drew blood and tested it in a centrifuge. After winning the local award Carol represented the Mid Columbia Fair with her experiment at the Inland Empire Science Fair in Spokane, Washington the following month.

In 1962 Carol Jean, Mary Ann, Louise and Willard Ingraham and Louise's mother Minnie Williams all loaded up in our 1959 Chevrolet station wagon with destination Chicago, Illinois with a lot of stops along the way visiting with relatives we had not seen for a long time. There were many new cousins that we had never met before. The first stop was in Laurel, Montana to see many relatives there. We stayed with Uncle Claude and Aunt Lorreine Ingraham and their children Cenra and Bob Weatherford and son Denel Ingraham.

Our Uncle Ralph and Aunt Rose Ingraham lived across the street so we saw them but their seven boys were away from home and we did not see them at that time. My Grandma Myrtle Ingraham was staying with Claude and Lorreine at that time so we had a good visit with her.

We left Laurel, Montana and headed for Jamestown, N.D. a one day drive away. We got to Uncle Phil and Aunt Louise Schuffs fairly early in the evening. The next day we visited Harriet and Vernon (Short) Wahl and family, Lois Burkhardt and children, Doris and Ray Rosenau, Esther and Lloyd Sorenson and my Grandmother Laura Johnson.

The next day we were on our way again with one night at a motel then to Chicago, Ill. We headed for Harriet and Glen Drawn's place. They had informed us before hand to not try to come direct to their home but phone when we got near Chicago and they would come and direct us to their place because people that lived in Chicago even got mixed up with directions.

As we entered Chicago I got into a street that led into the central area that had about eight streets with stop lights headed eight different directions. About that time I was thinking that I should have taken Harriet's advice; the surprise of such complicated street patterns was the worst. Quickly getting over the shock my mind was going a hundred miles an hour and logically I picked the street I hoped would take us the direction we needed to go. Luck was with us; the right street was chosen and when we showed up at Glen and Harriet's house she couldn't believe it.

Harriet Drawns my cousin drove us around the rest of the time we were in Chicago. Harriet's mother, Aunt Edna Anklam lived in Chicago also and we stayed one night with her. I had an Aunt Esther and Uncle Otto Warnke living in Chicago also. They had two boys and five girls also living there so we all decided to have a picnic at the Chicago Park to meet everyone. We met Gustave and Genevieve Warnke and family, Marvin Warnke was killed in Europe in WWII. Lois and Clarence Kunstman and family, Deloris and Robert Stamp and family, Donna Warnke, Arlene and Albert Sawicki and family and Carol Mar Warnke were all at the park. It was great fun meeting a lot of the cousins I had never seen before.

The next day Glen and Harriet drove us up to Holland, Michigan to see my cousins Helen and Benard Smollen and family. We had by now met many of our relatives and we were back on the way home via South Dakota to see more relatives. We stopped in Sioux Falls, S.D. to visit Aunt Gladys and Uncle Claus Steffen and family.

They have a daughter Dorothy Raski and family that live in Stockton, Ca. and a son Robert Steffen who died in Germany while serving in the army after WWII in a truck accident. Two other boys, Harold and Louella Steffens and family and Donald and Marie Steffen and family took us all out to dinner at Sioux Falls that night. We had a very enjoyable time visiting and fellowshipping that night.

We stopped over in S. Dakota and took in the Passion Play. It was at an outdoor theatre street setting and it was raining really hard. We did not notice how wet we got from the rain we were so engrossed in the re-inaction of Jesus taken to the cross on the hill.

From there we visited the Yellowstone Park and then stopped over again in Laurel, Montana at Uncle Claude and Aunt Loreine's place in Laurel, Mt. Louise's Mom had such a good time visiting with Grandma Mrytle Ingraham that they corresponded regularly after that.

Our next stop was Great Falls, Mt. to see more relatives. Gordon Steffens, son of Art and Nora Steffens of Mabton, Wa was in the army air force and his family lived in Great Falls at that time. Gordon was away that night but we stayed with his wife Grace and family.

Also living in Great Falls, Mt. was Uncle Harry and Aunt Hilda Schuff and family. We went to visit their family that night. Early the next morning we left to go home via Glacier National Park.

We had been away from home about 2 weeks by this time. Every where we went the women went to bed earlier but each of the families we visited wanted to stay up to talk until after midnight and by then I was running out of steam from loss of sleep and having done all the driving. Once in a while I would stop at a beautiful stream. Carol and Mary Ann would get hungry for a milk shake or a banana split and would prompt me to get going and find a Dairy Queen stop.

We got back to Kennewick about dark that night. Our trip left all of us with a lot of wonderful memories.

It was 1966 and it was time to review our goals and make changes. We had lived in Kennewick by now for nine years and a lot had already happened. My three year apprenticeship at the PUD had ended in 1960 when I became a Journeyman Meter man. I had continued my college night courses recording many credits and I felt good about that. I was now comfortable with all the phases of meter and relay work plus substation instruments and installation.

I was looking back at the 19 years I had worked with the Benton County Public Utility District and knew I certainly had a good job for the rest of my working career but I also knew that if I remained in this job I had no opportunity for higher promotions. The big decision was do I leave a good job of 19 years or do I venture out into new territory with risks.

At this time the Cowlitz County Public Utility District at Longview, Washington was advertising for a Meter Technician that I was qualified for. I talked it over with my family, Louise, Carol Jean and Mary Ann about how this job change pursuit would mean a big change for every one of us in our family.

Louise was working for Washington Mutual Bank in Kennewick and had a good job, Carol Jean had just graduated from high school and Mary Ann was in her Junior year in high school. In our family discussion no one was too thrilled about a move but in the end they all agreed to back me if I decided to make the change.

I answered the job offer by sending my application and requested a meeting with the management. I got an immediate response and a meeting was set up in Longview. After meeting with their present Meter Foreman, their Superintendent of the line department and their staff member that reviewed application for new hires I was told that the job was mine if I would accept.

I asked to meet all the Meter Department employees and visit the Meter Department before I gave them an answer. They said that it was a fair request and a time was set. Along with the visit I had asked for some personal requests if I made the move and some other requests concerning the Meter Department functions.

I knew there were many changes needed in the department that I could help them with. We reached an agreement and in October of 1966 I bid goodbye to the PUD at a going away party. On the following Monday I reported to work at Cowlitz County PUD at Longview, Washington.

It was an easy transition for me personally because I had brought my camping trailer to live in. When I arrived that

Sunday evening I had gotten a space at a trailer court about half a mile from the PUD service center and the Meter Department. That same Sunday evening after getting settled in the trailer court I went to eat and then to the Safeway grocery store to get a local paper so I could check the ads for rentals for my families move. As I purchased my paper a lady standing behind me in the grocery line overheard me say that I wanted a rental apartment. She told me she knew of a vacant rental but would have to go home to get the telephone number. We agreed I would drive her home and she would give me the number and let me use her phone.

The number I called was a business number and the man there offered to meet me at the rental site to show me the vacant apartment. I took him up on his offer and he showed me a very nice clean apartment in a good location. The apartment came with an overhead open garage that I could back my trailer along side my pickup. It was a two bedroom apartment and I felt it would be adequate for my family until we could build a new home what Louise and I had already discussed. I rented the apartment that night.

After my first day on the new job that evening I moved the trailer to the apartment and settled in. I planned to go back to Kennewick on week ends until I could move everyone to Longview.

Mary Ann wanted to stay and finish her Junior school year out in Kennewick so we boarded her at her friend Joyce Clingers home. Carol Jean was to come to Longview with Louise and I.

On my first week-end back to Kennewick my parents returned with me and stayed with me in the apartment for the week. When I returned to Kennewick the next week-end I found Carol had other ideas than coming to Longview; Carol and Garry Rosson wanted to get married. It was on December 19, 1966 that they were married and made their home in Kennewick.

LOUISE, WILLARD INGRAHAM AND FAMILY

After Louise came to Longivew there was no Washington Mutual at that time to transfer to so she went to work in the Business Office of the Longview School District. We both signed up for night college courses.

During that first winter we also designed our plans for a new house that we planned to build. By spring of 1967 we had purchased a one acre view lot overlooking Longview, Mt. St. Helens and the Columbia River. We also selected a building contractor.

The lot was full of trees that had to be removed to enhance the view so my job was cut out for me. I wanted trees so I left the cedar trees that did not interfere with the view. It was a major job clearing and cleaning all the brush but it had to be done before we could build. I spent many late evenings after work and week ends rain or shine working on that lot before it was cleared. I felt like before I was done I could compete with a logger on a tree clearing project.

The view opened to one of the most beautiful view sites imaginable and we had the house built placing the structure to take it all in from a row of windows all along the south side of the building using the design we had drawn. From the living room in our new home we could see Longview, Kelso, the Columbia River, Kalama, Mt. St. Helens and Mt. Hood. It was just like a big framed picture looking out from our living room window.

I had left the vine maple trees when I cleared the ground and in the fall of the year those trees gave a splash of red and yellow leaves that were stunningly beautiful among all the other greenery.

By June of 1967 after eight months as a Meter Technician I was promoted to Meter Forman in the Meter Department at Cowlitz P.U.D. My work load expanded as we fabricated and installed all the instrumentation and controls of 19 new substations and remodeled 8 old substations plus installing telemeter, trend metering and all central controls at substation switching from a central point. It was challenging and fun to be involved in all of the modern day technology in the electrical field.

I also enjoyed many hours perfecting my rock and wood working hobbies. I made tables from black walnut tree wood and inserted slabs of petrified wood rocks and semi precious stone with crushed rock all embedded in casting resin one and one half inches thick for my table tops.

The photo below is of three matching tables that I made from solid walnut wood with the inlaid rock tops. We still have them today in our living room.

On August 28, 1967 Jon Garry Rosson our first grandson was born. Garry and Carol Rosson were living in Seattle at that time. It was in 1969 that they got a divorce; it was after the divorce that Jon came to live with us. Jon's photo is left.

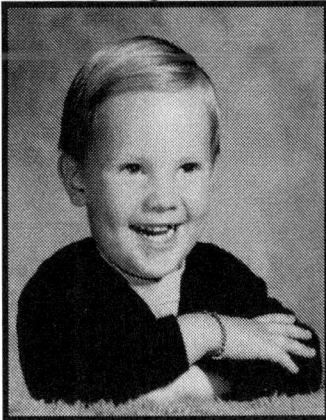

He was about 2 ½ years old and he fit into our lives perfectly. We loved having him living with us. At his age he already had a vocabulary that was unbelievable for 2 ½ yrs.

Louise was working at the school district so we signed Jon up for kinder garden at a church school. At night after work when we picked Jon up to go home it was pure pleasure how he brightened up our lives with all that energy.

Louise found out that it was different raising a boy then it was the girls. The girls would sit still playing with their dolls dressing and undressing them and talking to them.

Jon loved playing outdoors and when he came into the house his favorite was to walk the length of the davenport and jump down before he was caught. Louise would grab him to check his dirty feet out for mud and also inspect his pockets. One day she put her hand in his pocket and found nothing then went to the second pocket and let out a screech when her hand hit a live frog. I told her boys are a little different than girls.

Another morning Jon was sitting at the kitchen counter on a stool and grandma was in the kitchen talking to him. I was in the bathroom getting ready for work when here came Jon running down the hallway as fast as he could and into the bathroom. I asked him if he was having a problem that morning. Jon said, "No, grandma is talking and I am not listening."

We often took Jon to the coast on week ends in our trailer and camped out. In season we would dig for clams and other times we just walked up and down the beautiful sandy beach that ran for miles along what was called Long Beach.

We all loved watching the waves come in and out as the different sounds echoed. The sounds were especially great at night when the tide was moving to and fro continually with such a huge body of water and the continuous movement it made mystical sounds in the darkened night.

We had Jon for about two years and his father wanted to take him. Louise and I had a big decision to make because we did not want to give him up but knew if we kept him there would be a fight and Jon would probably resent us for not letting him go with his father. Hopefully we told ourselves that we had made the right decision. It was the most difficult thing to see that little boy go.

I kept busy with the new house; there were many things that had to be completed after we had moved in that fall of 1967. I installed all the wiring with special lighting effects. I also did much of the finishing inside as well as all of the landscaping outside.

It was September 1967 when Mary Ann enrolled in the Longview high school for her senior year. She was not a happy camper leaving the Kennewick school but she was a good sport and accepted the move as necessary in her life; she handled it just like she does every change she makes.

In September 1967 the Cowlitz P.U.D. signed me up to teach metering at the University of Washington in Seattle, Washington for one week. Louise went to Seattle with me for a little vacation and in the evenings we tried different restaurants. One night my cousins, Fern and Jim Goemmer from Tacoma joined us at a Chinese restaurant that they knew about. It was great and their visit added to our enjoyment.

In 1970 we bought a new Oldsmobile car; it was the only car I ever drove right out of the show room; (photo is below).

Good things were happening from our move. In 1970 Washington Mutual Bank built a branch in Longivew. The personnel office of Washington Mutual in Seattle located

Louise and offered her a job at the new branch. She accepted leaving her job at the Longview School District. In less than two years she was promoted to Assistant Manager at the Longview branch. Louise's photo is below.

By now Mary Ann had graduated from high school and went to work for a credit union in Longview.

By now it was 1972 and Louise and I (Willard) celebrated our 25th wedding anniversary. The photo is below.

We all needed R & R and we purchased a 1972, ¾-ton pickup to pull our 15-foot trailer that we still owned. It was ideal; we loved the ocean beaches at Long Beach, Washington and pulled our trailer down there for long weekends on sandy beaches.

We liked visiting the beaches so well we purchased a building lot that we could later build on but at the present time use to park our trailer on the weekends and vacations. The lot had running water piped to it and just across the sand dunes was the ocean. It was really up town living there next to the ocean on weekends and at night, we could listen to the roar of the ocean.

We had become good friends with Howard and Carm Williams. They were in our bridge group and also in our dance group. Howard was the main office supervisor for the Cowlitz P.U.D. In our conversation we had learned that both couples liked to travel and especially liked the great outdoor. Howard knew some one at a travel agency in Longview that had a

In raft on Colorado River

MAY 28TH, 1973

Longview couples 'shoot rapids'

By Kay Green
Daily News Staff Writer

Shooting the rapids is a great way to spend a vacation.

Or so Howard and Carmelita Williams and Willard and Louise Ingraham of Longview report after "shooting the rapids" on the Colorado River in mid-May.

The two couples were among 35 persons from throughout the United States who went by rubber rafts down the mighty Colorado River from Page to Phantom Page near Bright Angel Creek on the south rim of the Grand Canyon.

The 87¼-mile trip took four days in 25-horsepower motor-driven crafts that look like giant-sized life rafts. All provisions were stored in rubberized bags in water tight compartments on the rafts.

Each craft had a pilot and an assistant who were capable, knowledgeable persons, Williams said. If there were questions as to safety of a rapid at any time, they'd stop at the sand bar and check the rapids before taking the passengers through.

The boats are pliable — when the back goes up, the front goes down, etc., Williams noted. "You are wet all day long, but you dry out rapidly because of the dry weather," he added.

"We did hang up on one rock at which time the metal compartment got dented," the Cowlitz PUD building supervisor said. "Usually when we hit the rapids we went right through them." The water was calm between rapids, which numbered 31 on their trip. The rapids are rated from 1 through 10, from mild through rough. This group hit one at an intensity of 8 plus.

The river is emerald green until it is joined by the muddy Little Colorado, at which time the Colorado turns manila folder color. The canyon has sheer rock walls from which an occasional water-

fall emerges.

It depends on river conditions how fast the rafts travel. The guides know the river from A to Z and consider safety at all times, Williams noted. The travelers wore life jackets at all times.

Meals were eaten and night stops made on the sand bars. Portable chemical toilets, erected beside tents, were the first item put up when the rafts stopped. Wastes went into the toilet and paper into sacks. When the group departed, the sacks were burned and the balance buried and marked on the beach. "You lost your modesty the first day out," Williams quipped.

The sand bars were left clean — there wasn't even a match stick left behind. Williams said all litter was carried out of the canyon and disposed of properly. The tour sponsor, Sanderson River Expeditions Inc., says "Take only pictures, leave only footprints."

The second day out a woman broke a leg when she stepped off a rock ledge into the sand and it gave way. The only communication with the outside world is radio and then only when a plane is flying overhead. It was a day later before a helicopter flew in to pick up the accident victim, Williams said.

The trip ended at Phantom Ranch where the two couples stayed for the evening. The following day they took a dragout mule 7.3 miles, a five-hour

trip, out of the canyon. The next day they flew to Page.

The trip down river took four days, the flight back 45 minutes. "We took pictures from the plane of the area we'd come down only hours before," Williams said.

The Williams learned of the excursion through television and when they visited the area last year, made arrangements to receive literature.

River travelers provide only their personal clothing and items, the excursion arranges everything else including food, cots and sleeping bags. Cost of the trip only is $185 per person, but well worth it, Williams declared.

The 35 included an 86-year-old woman from San Francisco, four high school students from North Carolina, a Chinese girl from Los Angeles, an IBM program analyst from Chicago, a doctor from Phoenix and a secretary from Georgia. Ingraham is meter department supervisor at the Cowlitz PUD.

Memories are recorded on film, but "the experience is one we'll never forget," Williams concluded.

vacation trip we were all interested in. It was through this agency that the four of us; Howard, Carm, Louise and I

(Willard) booked a trip to vacation by shooting the rapids of the Colorado River in rubber rafts. We all drove to Page, Arizona and stayed one night in a hotel. The next morning we were bused to Lees Landing at the head waters of the Colorado River. There were 35 people on this adventure and we all loaded into two rubber rafts with pontoons strapped to two sides..

The weather was cool but the sun was out and that was good because for the next four days we would be wet from the river ride as much as we would be dry. We knew that from Lees Landing there would be no way out of the canyon until we reached Phantom Ranch. Our night stops would be on beaches along the river.

Our pit stops for bathroom relief would have to be occasional stops on beaches along the way. Everyone was modest but stopping for a bathroom break was a must. Every two hours if a sand bar was available our guides would dock our rubber rafts for a break. The guides would holler out, "women to the left and men to the right" or reverse the call. Many times the travelers would get mixed up and women and men went the same direction on shore.

Once I was standing there doing my thing and looked to my right and there was a woman squatting; she looked up at me and said, "what the heck; who cares."

At night they would stop at larger sand bars and night camp would be set up with cots for sleeping that they had brought on the raft. It was surprising how good the meals were; we had steaks for dinner and pancakes and eggs for breakfast. All the food had been brought with us on the rafts. The motto was, "leave nothing but our foot print," so when we embarked each day everything we brought with us had to be taken back out.

The chemical toilets were set up at each camping spot at night. We were traveling with Sandersons River Expeditions Inc. and they insisted on another rule to take only pictures and leave only footprints behind. We rode rafts with pontoons tied to each side for 87 ½ miles and we went through many wild rough rapids on the way. Sometimes we rode on the pontoons of the raft and hung onto ropes as we traveled through rapids; it was like riding a bucking bronco.

One early morning one of the passengers got up from her cot early to make the chemical toilet before the crowds came and as she walked in the dark she misjudged the terrain. She stepped off an embankment and messed up her foot. She was in deep pain so the guides tried to radio for help but the canyon was too deep at that spot for a signal.

We stayed at that campsite for another night. We had a doctor aboard but the only pain killer the good doctor had was scotch. That poor lady was kept on scotch for the rest of her ordeal. The next morning the guides decided they had to move her further down the river in order to pick up a radio signal for help and that is what we did.

All of us moved down river to a better open site and a big beach where the guides finally made radio contact. Shortly a helicopter came in and picked the injured lady up. They flew her to Phoenix, Arizona and just before they landed she went into shock. The later report that we got was that she had broken a bone in her foot that was almost protruding out of the skin but after a prolonged stay at the hospital she was released and had a full recovery.

After four days in the open we finally ended up at Phantom Ranch at the bottom of the canyon along the Colorado River. We stayed in tent barracks with the women together in one building and the men in another building.

The next morning we were fed breakfast and our guides lined us up and we mounted the mules we rode out of the canyon up a narrow trail. On the ride up we could look down from our mule perch and see the phantom ranch getting smaller and smaller as we went further up the side of the canyon. If those mules made a misstep we could easily tumble hundreds of feet.

On the way up the trail there was an eighteen year old boy riding in front of me. He was from Chicago and was scared to death of the ride. He pulled back hard on his reins and his mule started coming back onto mine. If he continued backing up we were both going to go over the edge of the trail mules and all. I hollered at him to drop the reins and at the same time I slapped his mule on the butt to move it up. By that time his mules was next to me and I was able to jerk the reins out of his hands and give his mule another slap at the same time. I was relieved when the mule moved forward; there were a few anxious moments for a little while.

As we got close to the top that day the boy from Chicago hollered up at some one telling them I had saved his live as he pointed at me.

We knew from a story we heard at Phantom Ranch that night before we rode out that it could be a treacherous ride out of the canyon. We had been told that the mules spooked and mules and riders had gone over the edge a few days before; all met their death on that trail.

We rode the mules for 5 hours without dismounting until we got to the top of the canyon which was the south rim. We were ready for the nice hotel and hot showers and a good meal that night. The next morning after breakfast the four of us, Howard, Carm, Louise and I were ready to take our charter flight back to Page to pick up our cars.

We boarded a small plane and the pilot took off over the canyon. He flew close and showed us the route we had taken down the Colorado River. He gave us an extra touch with this over the canyon panoramic view and the Colorado River from the air. It made us a little nervous wondering if that small plane had enough power to get us back up out of that deep canyon. The pilot did not have to give us a tour but was doing it for an extra touch and it was much appreciated by all of us.

When we got back to Page, Arizona each couple went their own way to finish the vacation. Louise and I headed for

California. We crossed the Mahove Desert and headed for Los Angeles. We decided to visit cousins, Melvin and Laura Thompson at Lancaster, California. They were surprised but happy to see us and we spent our time there catching up on family news before we had to leave for home.

In 1975 we purchased a bigger trailer; a 22 foot making our excursions to Long Beach where we had an ocean front lot at Surfside Estates more enjoyable. Our trailer slept seven people and there were times we stretched the space for 9 people. Depending on the weather, we had campfires either on the beach or on the lot near our trailer. Photo of the trailer and pickup is below.

Sometime during the summer of 1976 I found out how quickly things can change. I had always thought my life was blessed with good health but one Friday night when I came home from work it all began with one of the worst headaches I have every had. I suffered all week end with a sharp headache that would not let up. I had very little if any sleep and by Monday morning Louise was able to get me a 3 pm appointment with the doctor. The doctor told me I had acute thyrodiditis. By the time I saw him I had also lost my voice and had lumps on each side of my neck the size of golf balls. The doctor prescribed citromil to bring the swelling down. The pills worked for one side but not the other side.

Then the news from the doctor was that I needed to have an operation to remove the swelling from the other side. Louise and I were scheduled to take a group to the Holy Land on a tour and we would loose our investment in the tour if we canceled. I finally convinced the doctor that I should be allowed to have the surgery when I got back even though by this time I was so weak it was difficult to walk across the floor.

I went home to rest and by early fall when we were scheduled to leave I felt well enough to take the trip although I had learned a lesson not to take my health for granite. I consider health a gift from God and I had observed first hand how quickly it could be taken away.
September 21, 1976 we met our group at the Portland airport in Oregon and boarded our flight to Chicago, Ill. And from there on to New York to catch our international flight to Athens, Greece.

In Athens we visited the Acropolis at a time that the original statues still were standing in their respective places. In later years because of weather erosion the Greeks moved the originals to a museum and put up replicas.

Another visit was to Corinth the place named in the bible. The ruins were crumbled but walking and viewing in the area gave the impressions of what that city must have been like in ancient times.

Athens had so many interesting things to see; it was quite an experience to see Constitutional Square sitting like a spoke in a wheel with 8 different street meeting at the center spoke. It was an over exemplified version of what we are calling round-about in parts of Kennewick that streets are intersecting.
On that tour we flew off to Amman, Jordan which was called the city of Philadelphia in the bible. From Amman we bused south then rode on horseback into the old city of Petra.

While in Jordan we also visited Moses well where Moses struck the rock and gushing waters came forth. Moses had said to his people, "how many times do I have to help you." It was as if Moses thought he was doing the wonderful miracles. We went to Mt. Nebo where Moses viewed the Promised Land but God would not let him enter it because of Moses way of thinking.

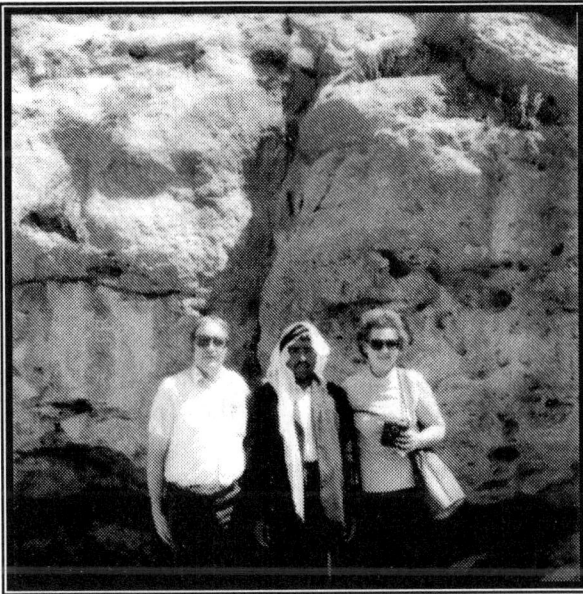

At the left is a photo of Willard and Louise taken at Moses well with a Bedouin.

From Jordan we went to Capernaum, Israel where we took a boat ride from Tiberius across the Sea Of Galilee to Capernaum. We viewed the site where Jesus had talked to the multitudes. They were wonderful experiences including our trip to the Jordan River where many of our group was baptized including Louise and I.

In Jerusalem we visited the Garden Tombs and upper room where Jesus held the last supper. One day we went to the Mt of Olives and the place of ascension where I had the privilege of leading the whole group gathered there in prayer. There were seven ministers in a group but the guides asked me to give the prayer. I instantly froze thinking I cannot do this.

then I remembered in the bible where it said walk up in faith and I will be with you so I did walk up to the mike and thought I am now in your hands. As I stood there in front of all those people, I had the most peaceful feeling come over me and I began to quote scriptures in prayer; God was giving me the words and all I had to do was open my mouth. I felt that my soul was full of the Holy Spirit and my mind was wondering what it might have been like when Jesus ascended with all the people watching him.

Willard is at left standing in front of the place of ascension pictured above.

Later some of my group (pictured below) told me that what they had heard me say was not from me; I admitted that the lord had given me the words. It was at this same time I felt my health problems were gone; I knew I was completely healed but I told no one until I got home.

Our next stop was the Church of Nativity in Bethlehem where Jesus was born. Later that day we visited the Dome of the Rock with the sacred rock of Abraham's sacrifice on Mt. Moria.

It is only a short 25 miles from Jerusalem back to the Dead Sea and that was the next place we visited. This is where the Dead Sea Scrolls were found. It was only a short distance on our way back to Jericho and an interesting stop there at the site with all the ruins.

Later that day when we got back to the hotel I looked for the citramil pills that I took every night and could not find them It was like they had disappeared. I never found the pills until I got home but I felt good without taking them and the swelling on my neck had disappeared.

We returned home via New York City and had an opportunity to tour there. When we got back home I had an appointment with my doctor. The doctor asked me how the trip was and I told him great and I am healed. He did a double take and asked me if I had gone to some faith healer then he examined me. I told him what had happened on Mt. of Olives and he just continued with all the tests he could think of. He shook his head in disbelief; he said to me, "well you had it when you left and it is gone now."

I can attest when the Lord heals he does a complete job because that was in 1976 and today into year 2007 I have never had a sick day since I had the problem with headaches and the lumps on my neck.

It was on Tuesday, January 25, 1977 when we got a sad call from Louise's sister, Nora May Nelson that their mother had suffered a stroke and was in the Prosser Hospital. The two sisters agreed to meet and drive up to see their mother yet that day. It was late when they got to the hospital and they found there mother was still in a coma. Some of the family was with her so later that night they agreed that some would stay and some go get some sleep and come back in the morning.

Louise and Nora May went to their brother Earl's in Mabton but had no more than gotten into bed when the call came that their mother had passed away.

Louise called the next day to tell me the funeral was to be held on Jan. 29th. I drove up on Friday evening to be with Louise. All the family was there for the funeral and Minnie Williams was buried at the Grandview Cemetery next to her husband Charley Williams. Minnie was a very special person and was loved by many.

Our lives were full and always packed with busy times. With the routines and heavy responsibilities at work I began to think about other meaning to life. I prayed for priorities and studied the bible with a more serious way of viewing the passages for meaning. It changed my life and my way of thinking. It was just like the blinds had opened up to the wisdom of understanding. Our social life changed as we took more time to study the bible.

Each year for vacation we traveled as we had become tour hosts and the doors kept opening to continue hosting overseas tours; we made the Holy Land our specialty. During those years we took seven different tours featuring the Holy Land. We purchased group tickets and made sure we booked flights to Israel with stop-overs going and coming. Each tour included Israel but the stop overs were all different. We visited them all, Amsterdam, France, Rome and the Basilica of St. Peter and the Vatican, the Roman theatre and trips to the Isle of Capre.

  I can not forget Vienna. A delight at Vienna was watching the Lipizzaner horses go through their paces then a visit to Schonbrunn Palace where Napoleon's life and home was on display.

  We made sure we visited Greece again and the old city of Corinth where Paul preached. It was easy to bus on to Delphi and we saw the temple of Apollo and the cuneiform that marked the center of earth. Oh yes a highlight for both of us were the Greek Island tours we took. It was like stepping back in time as our ship took us to the islands Hydra, Pores and Aegina.

  We never missed seeing Cairo, Egypt and took trips up the Nile. The camel rides to the pyramid of Gesa were a must. We got to visit the St. Sarquius church that was built over the cave where the holy family Joseph, Mary and baby Jesus had stayed while in Egypt. The island of Cypress was on our agenda where Lazarath went after Jesus resurrected him from the dead.

  Jordan was an important stop over and on one trip there we stopped at a place in the desert near where Sadom and Gomora were located before God destroyed them with fire and brimstone. We were able to pick up small samples of fire and brimstone rock that I still have.

  You don't go to Israel unless you visit the Church of Nativity, the tomb of Lazarus, the hill where Jesus was crucified, the Old City of Jerusalem and so many other stops.

  There was Masada and Beerasheba, the Baptist Monistary where John the Baptist lived and studied; Nazareth and Cana in Galilee where Jesus made wine from water, Megiddo, the place of Armageddon. It was all thrilling and our guides were so informative. We visited this area so many times that the guides remembered and would arrange that their bus would find us during our tour on another bus just to say hello. We included England and all of Ireland and Scotland in some of our stop overs. There were other places, too many to name but we always saw so much and there was so much to do. We have so many memories and are so thankful for the opportunities we had as tour hosts.

Louise and I had discussed the possibility of her employer, Washington Mutual Bank transferring her to a larger branch bank in Seattle. I knew I did not like or want to live in Seattle but we both knew that sooner or later the subject or an official request would be forth coming. Sure enough one day when I was in an important meeting with three of the engineers discussing coming jobs my phone rang.

Guess who was on the other end of the line; you guessed it. It was my wife, Louise and she asked if I would take time to talk. I told her I had a meeting couldn't it wait. She quickly told me it was about a job offer elsewhere and she had to give them an answer in half an hour. I wanted more time but she told me that was impossible as the corporate bosses were pushing her for an answer. We agreed to meet at a coffee shop near by.

I excused myself from the meeting telling them I had an emergency and I would get back to them as quickly as I could. I met Louise and we ordered coffee and she brought me up to date on what the bank was asking of her.

It was a transfer offer to either Seattle or Kennewick and they needed an answer now; I asked her if she realized what she was asking of me? In reality I had about 20 minutes to make up my mind to retire from my job, sell our home and relocate.

Bank officials wanted her to pack and move immediately. There was need for her services either in Seattle or Kennewick. I felt I needed to evaluate the pluses and minuses so I used a piece of paper and under two headings I wrote down the pluses if we moved and the minuses or stayed.

We both prayed about making the right decision and carefully evaluated the list of plus and minuses. I already had a full retirement pension earned but I had a good job and could work there for many years yet I also knew Louise needed to work additional years for her retirement.

Seattle was out for both of us. The Kennewick branch was an assistant branch manager position; it was the same position she held at Longview only the branch was larger with a bigger staff and of coarse the income was bigger. On management moves the bank bought the employees home and paid all the moving expenses so that was a plus.

I asked Louise how she felt about the change and she said I had to make the decision. It still was a tough decision but we both knew it was the right decision to accept the move to Kennewick. Below is our Longview home.

Even though I was only 53 years old retiring was only part of the options. I had many things I could still do with my life only in a different way. I had a very peaceful feeling about moving and looking closely at Louise I said, "Let's do it."

I think under it all Louise was relieved even though we both loved our home and life there in Longview, Wa. So it was Louise went back to the bank and accepted the appointment if they would give her two weeks before reporting in Kennewick. They wanted her to go immediately but finally accepted the timetable.

For me; I went back to my office and said nothing to anyone until that night I wrote out my resignation. The next morning was as usual with all the men assembled for their daily orders when I asked them to lock down so we would not have any interruptions from other departments. It was the look on their faces that told it all; "what now?"

I proceeded to tell them I was holding a resignation in my hand, they were the first to know and I would be retiring February 28, 1978. I did explain the reasons but my retirement news was a shock to all of them.

Louise left on schedule for her new job in Kennewick and I had to work with the realtor to list our home. We had gotten appraisals and the bank had agreed to buy for the appraisal price if the house did not sell in a few weeks.

The first weekend after Louise left I loaded up my ¾ ton truck with incidentals and went to Kennewick. The bank would make the big move in a moving van. Louise had arranged for a realtor that we knew to show us homes over the week end. We viewed homes all day with no luck of seeing anything that we were interested in until about 5 P.M. that Saturday. We liked south Kennewick and the realtor after rechecking found an empty brick home in the area we liked.

The house was empty as the owners lived in Idaho and had been renting but the renters had moved out. Irony was that this home was only a few blocks from where we had lived in the 50s before we moved to Longview. We both liked the neighbor hood and the all brick homes in the area. Louise did not like the kitchen and the basement was not completely finished. I promised I would remodel the kitchen with more cabinets and finish the basement if she would give me enough time to do the work myself. I liked the idea of remodeling as it was the kind of work I liked and we could make it into what we both liked.

The renters had left the house in disarray and everything needed to be painted and updated with carpets etc. It was a solid brick home that could be upgraded with some changes and a lot of hard work. We agreed to purchase and I turned to the realtor with an offer $7,000 under the asking price with no negotiations or dickering; just a yes or no. If they said no we would look for another home the next day.

The sellers did try to talk to us but our realtor was firm with the offer and it stood. By 10 P.M. that Saturday night we had a signed faxed agreement with keys to the house and were able to unload my truck with what I had brought from Longview into the garage.

I went back to Longview to finish my days at the P.U.D. and make ready for the move. There was a lot of work getting ready for the movers to come in. I did much of my own crating; especially of the big mirrors. It was determined that not one moving van would be needed but two vans would move us. We had a big home in Longview and it was full of furniture, collectables and personal items.

Meantime in Kennewick Louise with the help of Mary Ann began the clean up and painting job in the evenings.

The Cowlitz P.U.D. employees gave me a big going away party that included a cake and a 30 year employment plaque. They had taken up a collection and really did a bang up job with a send off party that included celebration of the 11 plus years I had worked with them.

I think back at that morning on the 7th of March, 1978 that two big moving vans parked in the drive of our home in Longview. It took all day to load even though I had a lot of things in crates. I asked them to leave my bed out that night so I would have a place to sleep. The two vans were full and they had to tie my motorcycle onto the bumper of one of the vans. I also had my truck full of my expensive hand tools etc.

Below they are loading the vans for moving.

It was the morning of the 9th that we all took off for Kennewick. I was in Kennewick by noon but the vans were slower and it was an hour later before they arrived. They had about 8 employees to unload. I had gone through the house and made signs numbering all the rooms through out the house. As the men unloaded I stood by the door and directed them to each room that their items were to be placed. By evening it was all unloaded and even the beds were set up so we had a place to sleep that night.

There was still lots to do and there were days of arranging and installing as well as doing all the finishing touches down to even wall papering in some rooms. I enjoyed all the remodeling and cabinet building as I went along. I engineered and installed my own yard and garden automatic sprinkler system through out our yard to plant the garden I loved to see grow.

We think of all we went through with that move and how much help we had. Our time will come again one day and we will have to reduce the overload in our home. Not knowing the time table though we can begin anytime and make it easier by unloading many of the items not used.

We had really settled in by September, 1978 and
planned a trip to the Holy Land. Our daughter, Mary Ann
agreed to go with us for a two week trip through Israel and
include Switzerland. We were so happy to have her go with
us; to that date none of our family had accompanied us on any
of our overseas tours.

On September 25, 1978 we departed via New York and
on to Amsterdam, Holland for stop over and then took a flight
to Israel. We were met by our tour guide and bused to
Netanya, Israel. We checked into the Blue Bay Hotel at
Netanya along the Mediterranean Sea. It was beautiful there.
The sea was blue green and beautiful with little pollution in
those days.

From there we toured Caesarea founded by the
Phoenicians that was later incorporated into the Hasmonean
Kingdom. After the fall of the second temple Caesarea became
the Roman capital of the country.

Our trip this time was different and exciting in a
different way because we had our daughter viewing it for the
first time. We traveled by bus to Megiddo in the Jezreel Valley
where the big battle of Armageddon will be fought one day.
Above is a photo of Willard, Louise and Mary Ann at
Megiddo.

In Megiddo we viewed the place of Solomon's stables and stopped at Canna. (below). As the bible, verse John 2:1-2 on the third day there was a marriage at Canain, Galilee and the mother of Jesus was there. Jesus also was invited to the marriage with his disciples and it was here that Jesus preformed his first miracle by turning water into wine.

So much to see and time went too fast. The church of the Multiplication still stood near where Jesus

took two loaves of bread and fish and fed many thousands of people. It overlooked the Sea of Galilee. Next was the Mount of Beatitudes, (photo above) and it was there that we boarded a boat to cross the Sea of Galilee to Tiberius. It was here on the sea that Jesus had walked on water. It was a favorite spot of

413

ours that the motors of the boat would be stopped and there would be a time of prayers. One could imagine the times long ago when the fishermen in boats were a normal scene on the sea and that it was near this area that Jesus spoke to the crowds on shore.

Tiberias is always a fun place to stay overnight and if you are brave you can have the traditional Sea of Galilee fish served to you with the head still on. With a refreshing nights rest we were ready to move on in the morning. We were bused to the River Jordan and the place of Jesus' baptism.

We stopped at Jerico and on our way to Jerusalem we viewed the Mt. Temptation. Our accommodation in Jerusalem was at an Israel owned hotel and considered a five star. It was clean and very comfortable but not anything like a five star would be in the U.S. Our food was adequate and the meat on the menu was always called "bef". We wondered at the authenticity of beef sometimes!

Biblical history abounds in this area and we toured all the major sites. One of the first was the Good Samaritan Inn located a short distance from the church of Nativity in Bethlehem. This was the birthplace of our lord, Jesus. Above is the photo of the Church of Nativity in Bethlehem.

414

We entered the nave of the church where three different religious alters exist in adjoining areas. The Greek Orthodox, the Roman Catholic and the Jewish alter. It is always impressive to go down the stairs into the grotto area and see the spot where Jesus was said to be born (photo below). One can not be sure of the exact spot as displayed but one knows it is in that area. Our tour then took us to the tomb of Rachel near Bethlehem. Afterward we visited Lazarus tomb at Bethaney (photo right) where Jesus resurrected Lazarus from the dead. The tomb was located in a cave and it was here that the spiritual energies seemed very strong.

Near the Mt. of Olives was the Dome of the Rock. We were instructed to remove our shoes before we entered this sacred building of the Arabs' and the ladies had to keep their heads covered as well as their shoulders out of respect.

Just across the courtyard and down some steps we entered on the level of the sacred Waling Wall of the Jews. There were Jewish guards between the Dome of The Rock and the Waling Wall because of the sanctity of both places.

Jerusalem, Old City

Above is a photo of Jerusalem and the Dome of the Rock to the right and across the courtyard from the Dome is the Waling Wall; one can also see part of the walls that encircle all of the old city of Jerusalem. The photo is impressive and was taken across the Kidron Valley looking at the Old City. There is so much history within these walls it is unbelievable. Also it holds Arab populations who live in the old city and have small stalls along the streets where they sell their wares. Housed within the walls are the Armenians who fled Turkey under rule to Israel. The Greek Orthodox Church has a section within the old city also. It is remarkable that one church in the old city has two different religious claims to the place Jesus was nailed onto a cross and yet their beliefs are so different. Each different nationality has their own section within the old city that they live and yet they co-mingle in their daily lives.

LOUISE, WILLARD INGRAHAM AND FAMILY

We walked through the streets in the old town of Jerusalem. That was interesting as we visited the spot the Romans had kept Jesus overnight. The rock floors were just like they had been centuries before; even the games the Romans played were etched into the stone.

We followed along the seven stations that Jesus had walked with the cross. The street was right through the main part of the old town so as we walked there were open fronts for stall after stall of merchandise and foods sold by Arab store owners. The smells in that tight woven area was close and pungent but again it was more meaningful because of how it all appeared to us and the pavement we were walking on Jesus had walked on dragging that cross.

We stayed at the International Hotel in Jerusalem from September 28th to October 3rd so we became well acquainted with all of our surroundings. It was near the hotel one day that Mary Ann and I took a camel ride; I told Mary Ann (photo below) to be careful that it was a long way up there on the top of that camel.

We had come back from our tour early that day that
Mary Ann rode the camel. As our bus stopped near our hotel
there was a man with a camel and offering rides on the camel,
of course Louise and I had just seen Mary Ann riding this
camel. There were two camels standing there now and Mary
Ann would not get on her camel unless I would ride the other
camel.

After riding the camel we went to our hotel room to
freshen up; Louise wanted to rest but Mary Ann and I wanted
to walk down towards the wall of the old city of Jerusalem
where there was many little shops full of interesting things.
The shops were about six blocks from the hotel and we had
walked about half way when a bomb went off in a post office
about a half block to our left making a lot of smoke. Mary Ann
and I continued walking and shopping anyway. The sun was
now on its way down so Mary Ann and I thought we had better
get back to our hotel to be on time for the dinner hour. We
found out later that a Palestinian had set a bomb but that it had
not hurt anyone except the building.

One day we visited the Shrine of the Book, the Garden Tomb, Golgotha, the place of the skull.

Above is a photo of the place of the skull.

We saw a close up of the Waling Wall, and King David's tomb. These tombs were real and all the commercial aspects of our tour left our minds when we entered these sacred places.

They bused us to the church of St. John at Ein Karem where John the Baptist was born. It was six miles from Jerusalem. I took the picture of the location of the burial place within the church. A really serene feeling came over me and I felt the spiritual warmth being close to some one with such

spiritual power having been buried there. The photo is below.

The Dead Sea was one of our tours. One day we met up with a man by the name of Carlton Roberts with was interesting when we found that he owned four McDonald restaurants in Arkansas. It brought a little of our U.S. culture back in our thinking.

We stopped that day at Qumran where the Dead Sea Scrolls had been found. It was interesting because we had gotten to see the original scrolls that had been preserved by the

Jews and all under glass in a temperature controlled cave back in the outskirts of Jerusalem.

Below is a photo taken during a rest stop at the Dead Sea; left to right is Mary Ann, Louise and I (Willard)

Our day was not done and we stopped at Masada, the fortress of Jewish Zealots in 70 A.D; photo is above. Afterward our bus took us back to Beersheba. Not much there in the middle of a sandy desert. The only thing we saw moving in the desert was a woman herding a band of goats.

Hebron is an Arab occupied town and it was here that we visited the mosque of Abraham where Abraham, Sara, Isaac, Rebecca, Jacob and Leah are all buried. Biblical reference Gen: 35; 29; and Gen: 49; 31 and Gen: 50; 13.

The mosque of Abraham is pictured below.

King David was born in Bethlehem and often referred to as the city of David. It was there in Hebron where David became King David and established his kingdom. When David died they buried him in a tomb located on the top of the Mt. of Olives that we also visited in Bethlehem.

One day back in Jerusalem we met the man who spent 15 years building a miniature city of Jerusalem as it was in the time of our Lord Jesus Christ. He built a replica of Solomon's Temple where the present Dome of the Rock stands.

Our tour ended in Israel and we flew to Switzerland and checked into the Victoria Jungrau Grand Hotel at Interlaken, Switzerland. The food was excellent where ever we ate in Switzerland. Their hot chocolate drink the most delicious I have ever drunk.

We took a train ride to the top of Jungfrau Mt. On the top of Mt. Jungfrau there was a building that we entered from inside a tunnel from the train. It was freezing cold and fogged in up there but inside the building it was warm. They had an outside balcony though if you wanted to step out into the weather. Mary Ann and I were brave enough to step out at that 11,750 foot altitude and below zero weather. The altitude and cold took our breath away so we did not stay long.

The photo below is Mary Ann and Willard on the balcony; visibility on top of that mountain was gone that day, wrapped up in fog.

The trip back down the mountain on the train was great; we came down out of the fog and could see the terrain of the mountains change from the higher altitude to lower but still we were in mountainous areas when we debarked at the bottom. We saw how families attached their barns to the houses and we could see why; no one would want to move around out of doors in the winter months.

LOUISE, WILLARD INGRAHAM AND FAMILY

THE ECLIPSE OF 1979

On Tuesday, February 27, 1979 at 8:17 A.M. the sun was in total eclipse over the Tri-Cities in Kennewick, Washington. This would be the last total eclipse of the century that would be visible from the continental United States. Looking back it seems funny how the end of the century seemed so far away in 1979.

The eclipse track passed through Washington, Idaho, Montana and North Dakota. The moon moves in front of the sun and Baily's beads appear just before the corona of a total eclipse. Sequence of exposures showed the moon covering the sun moving from left to upper right in total solar eclipse. Exposures were made at seven minute intervals; photo below.

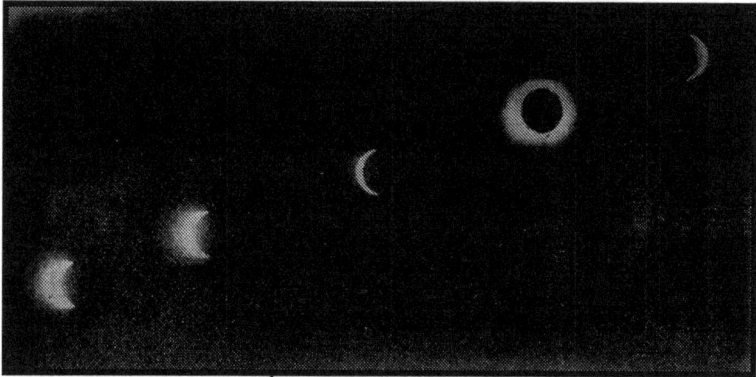

That morning of the 27th it was a beautiful sunshine day with no wind and just as still as it could be. When the moon passed over the sun everything had a weird silence fall over the area.

It was a worth while experience and the Tri-City Herald had a nice write up explaining the eclipse that went like this:

Tri-citians today got a sensational view of the last total eclipse of the sun in North America this century.

We saw just about everything you could hope to see said Battelle Astronomer Jerry Stokes who was on the top of Rattlesnake Mountain west of Richland.

Below is a photo Willard took that simulates the eclipse as a jewel; it was a well sought after frame and to have captured it on a home camera was phenomenal.

In down town Kennewick two women whooped and gasped in amazement as the sky began to darken when the moon made it west to east march across the sky plunging the Pacific Northwest briefly into darkness. Reports showed that thousands of ground sky watchers in the Pacific North West peered in vain today as clouds turned their view into the greatest cosmic disappointment since the comet KoHoutek turned tail and disappeared into the heavens five years ago with hardly a peek at its ballyhooed brilliance.

Hundred of Tri-City school children viewed the eclipse – most of them with homemade viewing boxes with teachers and parents supervising the students. As totality approached

Karla Kerbaugh, a third grader at Westgate school in Kennewick, pulled her viewer box tight around her head and watched the reflection of the moon pass in front of the sun. "It's pretty neat; want to look", she asked, peeking out from under the box.

However school officials reported attendance was down in all Tri-city schools; especially in Pasco and Kennewick. At Highlands Middle school in Kennewick only 100 out of 720 students were in their early morning classes. "Parents had the option of keeping their kids home and most of them did," said a school official.

Repeated warnings not to look at the sun during the period of the eclipse may have been ignored by some. Two Tri-City ophthalmologists said that they began receiving phone calls within minutes after it began getting light again at 8:19 A.M. People were saying they think they had looked at the eclipse wrong and were worried if they had damaged their eyes. One eye clinic reported ophthalmologists as saying if eclipse watchers have black spots and if the eyes hurt they should be checked.

The skies were saturated with air traffic as observers went aloft to beat the clouds with a view from above. At the Tri-City airport in Pasco several light planes loaded with eclipse watchers took off between 7 and 7:30 A.M. a Tri-Citians and visitors worried about the cloud cover and tried for a clearer view. About 40 persons clambered onto the roof of the Clover Island Motor Inn to watch including two men who had traveled to the Tri-Cities from Japan. They cheered, whistled and clapped as the moon finally edged over the last of the sun at 8:17 A.M.

At the Red Lion Motor Inn in Pasco breakfasters watched from the window as the moon moved slowly between the sun and earth dipping in and out of the clouds. About 50 persons, many with cameras lined the shore of the Columbia River at Richland's Howard Amon Park. Many were visitors staying at nearby motels. On the gravel road leading to the

Benton and Franklin County Fairgrounds in Kennewick about
8 cars and 18 people were lined up to watch the eclipse.

Cy Gengelback, Portland said that he had watched the
1918 eclipse and was among those at the fairgrounds on this
day to watch. Another visitor, Bob Brown, Bellevue, a 1962
graduate came supplied with a telescope, binoculars, camera
with telephoto lens and sheets of aluminized mylar that he gave
out to people who had no eye protection. "I came all the way
over here to see this and there are people right here in the Tri-
Cites that wouldn't even get out of bed to see it," said Brown.
"It was a thrill of a lifetime and should not have been missed."

Small groups of people were lined up along highway
395 to witness the eclipse. Most came well equipped with
viewing devices.

Tri-City Herald reporter Mary Jane Lewis said, "I
watched the eclipse very carefully. I was a second grader at
Longfellow in 1931 when I watched a partial eclipse and
burned my eye. I did not take any chances today. I looked
through the same eye."

One eclipse watcher said, "the geese were flying in
every odd direction after the eclipse was over in Kennewick."
Another observer said that roosters crowed loudly during the
totality.

LOUISE, WILLARD INGRAHAM AND FAMILY

HOLYLAND, PETRA, GREECE AND EGYPT

All of our tours were first class with five star accommodations and I have already explained the 1976, 1977 and 1978 tours. From this point on I will only pick out the highlights of the following tours so that it will not become repetitious.

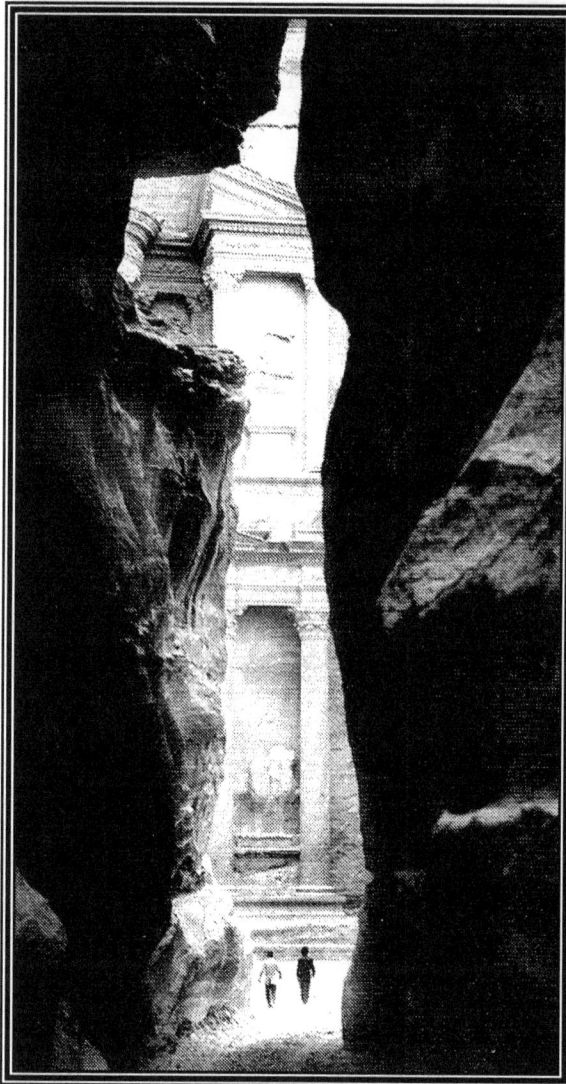

On the 30th of April 1979 we departed with twenty five anxious travelers on a 22 day tour from Portland via Chicago and on to Amsterdam, Holland, Rome, Italy, Athens, Corinth, Greece, Cairo and Luxor, Egypt.

We visited Amman and Petra, Jordon. A photo left is the entrance to Petra through a canyon lined with rock. . There was five hundred feet of rock walls of straight cliffs looming on each side of the trail for about three miles. At the end of the trail all of a sudden the scene opened up to the beautifully carved buildings in rock that exploded into view to the surprise of all travelers going there. Petra lies 165 miles south of Amman, Jordan passing through the biblical kingdoms of the Ammonites, Bashamites, Amorites and Moabites then to reach Petra, the ancient capital of Edom known as Siloh, the hidden city we had only one way to view it and that was to ride horses down the narrow trail. Our ride down the canyon by horses was an unforgettable experience but the highlight was when the trail broke out into the open and there in front of us was what was left of what was once the center of Petra.

Our tour took us into Israel and to Jerusalem, Bethlehem, Jacobs Well, Sea of Galilee, Capernaum and later to Istanbul, Ismir, Ephesus, St. Johns' tomb and Turkey. There are many things to tell about this tour but I will highlight a couple of places

.On the 18th of May, 1979 we flew out early from Tel Aviv, Israel to Istanbul, Turkey. We settled into our beautiful International Hotel in Istanbul.

We were up early next morning to fly on to Izmir, Turkey and bus on to Ephesus. Izmir was a surprise with their one million people with their houses with red tile roofs; we noted there were many storks nesting on the chimneys. As we traveled we also noted some fields with red poppies growing that they told us they used for their medicine.

We were told we passed the small house that Mary, mother of Jesus, lived in while she was there. We also saw the place where Mary was buried. Jerusalem also claims the buriel tomb of Mary, mother of Jesus. We have seen both places and they both could be right because we know that when Jesus was on the cross he looked down at John, his disciple and said, "John take care of my mother."

We know that John went to Turkey later and St. John and St. Luke are also buried there. Mary was probably buried in Turkey and sometime later her body could have been moved to Jerusalem. We also saw the Basilica of St. John and the tomb of St. Luke there. A photo is below.

Our tours to the Middle East were like passing through history and viewing it as it once was. I (Willard) taught a series of Bethal bible classes at our church for a number of years and my studies and presentation of the material I would be teaching was made much easier having toured the areas we were teaching about.

It was dreams come true for me to look back on having hosted seven tours into biblical history. I learned so much and saw how it must have looked in the time of Jesus and before. I am forever grateful of the opportunities we had to travel this great country; it is those trips that now has helped me in constructing the story of mine and my families lives into book form.

AN EXPLORITORY TRIP THROUGH MEXICO

Louise and I had already hosted many tours throughout the world and had never hosted a tour down through Mexico so in November of 1979 we decided to take a thirteen day trip on our own to explore the country of Mexico for future tours we would be putting together for our clientele to enjoy a "Maximums" enjoyable trip.

The trip from Pasco through San Francisco to Mexico City was no problem as long as one had passports and we did. There were many things in Mexico City to keep everyone busy for two or three days like the old and new Basilica of Guadalupe. A photo of Mexico City is below.

Our guide stopped to show Louise and I a cactus plant. To the Mexican people the cactus is very important plant for commercial use. This plant is a Maguey Century plant that has many uses. Examples are as follows: they use it for making paper much like the Papua plant seen in Egypt. The needles on the plant are very sharp and strong and they are used for sewing. The juice from the plant is used as a drink.

A believe it or not story was, "near the Maguey Century plant a man had a jackass that liked beer; the man would uncap a bottle of beer, set it on the ground and the jackass would immediately pick the bottle of beer up in his mouth, raise his head up and drink the contents from the bottle (photo below)."

The next stop was the great compound of Quetzalcoatl where we saw the Temple of Quetzalcoatl, the city of the Gods ruins at Teotihuacán with the temple of the sun and temple of the moon. When the Aztecs arrived in the valley of Mexico, Teotihuacán had long since been abandoned according to Aztec mythology it was in Teotihuacán that the Gods met to create the sun and the moon. There they built two pyramids so that the Gods Nanauatzin and Teotihuacán by casting themselves from the pyramid summits into a huge bonfire in an act of sacrifice would be resurrected as the sun and the moon; hence the names of the two pyramids.

Teotihuacán was one of the most advanced cultural centers of all Mesoamerica; founded in the north of the valley of Mexico. At its height (500-600 A.D) it was then one of the largest cities in the world as well as an example of urban planning. The city was laid out on two main streets; one north – south (the avenue of the Dead) and the other east – west; all the principal building in the center of the city. The city grew to such size it encompassed the surrounding towns (photo below).

Some sections consisted of over 176 interconnected rooms beneath one roof. The size of the population is still in doubt with estimates ranging from 5,000 to 250,000. Of course on festive and religious occasions the population was many times that amount. The Ciudadela alone can hold 60,000 people at one time. After all is said and done we still do not know who the Teotihuacán were, where they came from, where they went or even why. The Aztecs call the spot Teotihuacán, "the place where one became a God." It had disappeared from history by the time they arrived on the scene and only legends and the vast ruins were left to impress them with the greatness of the builders.

We went back to Mexico City to overnight and the next day we went to a bull fight. It was the first and last bull fight we wanted to see. We then went to Taxco, a silver mining town that was a good place to shop for silver items.

We flew on to Oaxaca but got bumped off the plane by a popular Mexican hosted tour the day we had planned to fly out.

There was a lot to see at Oaxaca and we saw the largest tree in the world; 160 feet tall, 160 feet in circumference.

In Mitla we visited Mitla Palace of interior with very intricate unique mosaic construction. At Mount Albon I walked through a very dark passage way inside the observatory building and almost knocked myself out by hitting a protruding knob rock at the end of the tunnel that was head high intended for that purpose. At the end of this dark tunnel there was only a three foot hole to crawl out of.

Coyoto Pec a few miles from the airport is where the famous black pottery is made. We saw demonstrations and I got a picture of Dona Rosa, the owner and founder of the famous black pottery; she was doing very well for a person 100 years old. Louise bought two small signed vases.

Then we visited an Indian trading market held on Fridays about 15 miles from Oaxaca. It was Thanksgiving day and since we hadn't been able to leave on our scheduled flight to Chichen Itza we had our Thanksgiving dinner at our hotel and French onion soup was the entrée of the day.

The next day we flew from Oaxaca to Chichen Itza; it was a cloudy day so we flew through the clouds to try to find the small airport with no radio communications in the plane. The pilot was flying about 800 feet above a very swampy area looking for the airport; we knew something was wrong flying this low in a DC9 Boeing plane. The stewardess was looking out the plane windows to locate the airport. I was looking out the window and saw a runway with a small airport and told the stewardess but the plane traveled on; soon it turned around and landed at that airport. As we had been flying over that swampy area Louise commented, "oh no not here." There was a British passenger on the plane and when he saw the swamp he told us afterward that he was ready to nip under the seat!

Our hotel was close by but we had to walk two miles to get to the pyramids of Chichen Itza to visit the ruins. There was one pyramid that was located half a mile down a jungle path. I wanted to go see it but Louise would not go with me. She stayed with the guard that was standing guard at the head of the jungle path. I knew there were tigers and other wild animals back in that jungle but I wanted to go down and see this pyramid. There were times I was wishing I had eyes in the back of my head because I could feel the danger around me. I did see the big observatory pyramid which was different than the other pyramids.

The Mexican air line that bumped us off the plane in Oaxaca must have felt badly for doing so because the next day someone sent a private car to take us all the way to Can Cun which was on a 20 mile strip of sand, ¼ mile wide jutting out into the ocean. There were many big and beautiful hotels built along on this man made peninsula of land. We slept in luxury in one of those hotels.

The next day they took us to the ruins of Tullum about two hours from the hotel along the coastal area. It was a great trip and we enjoyed seeing the ancient ruins. For others this was a very touristy place for those who wanted to scuba dive and spend leisure hours drinking in outdoor thatched bars.

We had one more night in the very luxury El Presidente Hotel before they took us to catch our plane for home. By this time we were armed with huge amounts of information for putting tours together that we planned to host coming back to Mexico.

LOUISE, WILLARD INGRAHAM AND FAMILY

MT. ST. HELEN ERRUPTS IN WASHINGTON STATE

Mt. St. Helens a magnificent beauty as photographed below but everything changed when at 8:32 A.M. pacific daylight time a magnitude of 5.1 erupted on Mt. Saint Helens on May 18, 1980. It set off rockslides and avalanches on St. Helen's north side of the mountain that caused pressures and major pumice of ash eruptions from the mountain.

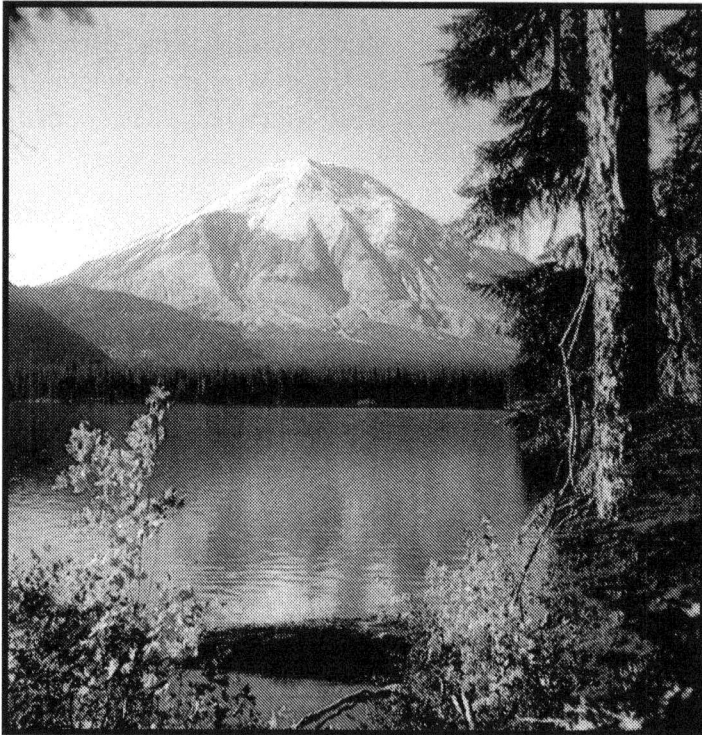

The explosive eruptions was seen for many miles away. Thirteen hundred feet of the top of the mountain collapsed and blew outward that covered twenty four square miles of debris and obliterating 250 square miles of recreation timber and private timber lands. An estimate of 200 million cubic yards of volcanic debris was blown down by volcanic mud flows into the rivers causing mammoth damage along the way including taking out bridges as the mud flow and trees were pushed at a high rate of speed as the flow progressed to the lower areas. The column of smoke and ash erupted 12 to 15 miles into the sky. Below the eruption of Mt. St. Helens, 1980.

My par ent s Lyl e and Ge na Ing rah am and Lo uis e and I wer e tra veli ng up the Yakima Valley to Prosser about two hundred miles as the bird flys from the mountain. It was a beautiful sunny morning. We were on our way to celebrate a 25th wedding anniversary for Earl and Erma Williams in Mabton. As we drove along we suddenly noticed the change in the weather. It began to get darker and looking up into the sky there was a lot of dusty looking puffy clouds that were rolling and reminded one of boiling dirty water in a tea kettle.

My parents and I talked about the memories of the North Dakota tornado we experienced years ago. We did not know what was happening until we got to Mabton and they told us Mount St. Helens erupted into a volcanic blast. The volcano ash covered some of the places near the mountain into 20 to 30 feet of ash. Fifty-seven people were near the mountain that day that lost their lives.

Years later the timber, bushes and flowers are returning (photo above). The scientists are letting the land evolve on its own to study what happens. The elk herds have returned as well as fish in a new lake that was formed. There is a visitor's center that was built near Mt. St. Helen to show a close up of the vast top of the mountain that disappeared in the eruption. The visitor's center held a wealth of information that was there for years but has now been closed and relocated at Castle Rock, Wa.

July 1, 1980; Kennewick resident Louise Ingraham has been promoted to Bank Manager of the Grandview Branch of Washington Mutual Savings Bank.

A Washington Mutual employee beginning in 1956, Mrs. Ingraham has served in a variety of capacities including assistant manager at Longview, Wa. branch and also the Kennewick Branch her most recent position.

Louise Ingraham attended Columbia Basin College and Lower Columbia College majoring in business administration. She is active in the National Association of Banking Women and the United Methodist Northwest Conference as well as other community organizations. Louise's photo is at the left.

Later she went on to manage the Richland branch of Washington Mutual for 4 years and returned to the Kennewick branch as manager until her retirement.

LOUISE, WILLARD INGRAHAM AND FAMILY

GRAND EUROPEAN, OBERAMMEGAU PASSION PLAY

On July 7th, 1980 we began a 22 day journey, "Grand European Holiday and Oberammergau Passion Play," from Kennewick, Washington via Seattle airport SeaTac and New York, JFK airport and on to London, England, three days of seeing many sights such as changing of the guard, Cleopatra's needle, Big Ben, The British Museum etc and on to Paris, France. We visited the Eiffel Tower, the Obelisk from Karnack, Egypt and the Louve. Our tour took us to Switzerland, Milan, the leaning tower of Pisa, Rome, Florence, Venice and Naples. On our visit to the Isle of Capri we boarded a hydrofoil that took us to the famous cave Marine Cathedral, "The Blue Grotto." A photo is below.

This is one of most beautiful phenomena's we have ever seen.

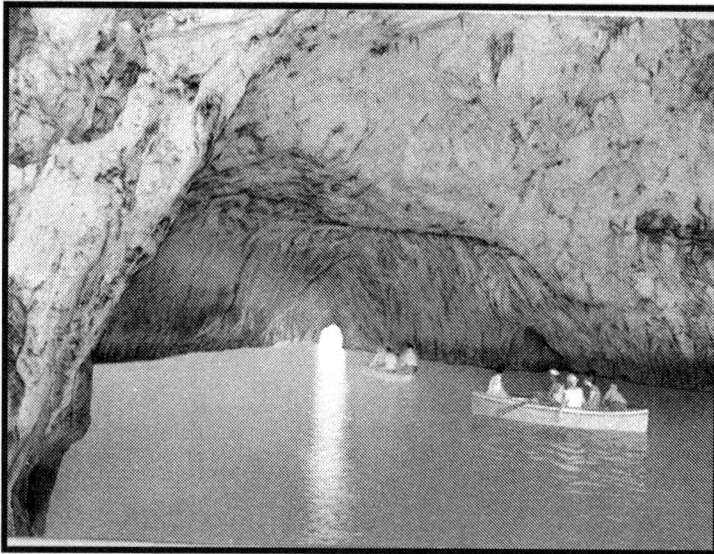

The blue of all blues reflects everywhere. It can be viewed only 65 days of the year because of seasonal hazards.

We were transferred there by small rowboats for four people to a boat; we entered through a narrow fissure and found the magic spectacle of the Grotto. The Grotto receives light which has passed underwater; this light freed from the water colors the walls, roof and stalactites with intense blue. The light makes the water opalescent and anything submerged in the water appears silver. In the Grotto we discovered the secret fascination that is Capri.

We rowed back to our hydroplane and boarded it for the return trip to Naples. We were all speechless in awe of what we had just witnessed.

Our tour now took us to another of the highlights of our tour, a small village in the Bavarian Alps that is famous for its wood carving industry. In 1633 Oberammergau was stricken by the black plague and thousands of people died through out Europe. The people of Oberammergau all prayed for and end for this tragic sickness. The black plague by passed them; the sickness ceased and as an expression of gratitude for the end of the scourge the villagers vowed to enact the Passion of Christ

every ten years. A photo from the play is above.

The first performance took place in 1634. It was after 1674 that the dates for giving the play were changed so as to fall on decimal years. From 1680 on the play has been given regularly every ten years except during a ban on religious plays in the 1770s and during also at the time of the Second World War.

The text has been rewritten several times. The play takes almost eight hours to perform and the 124 speaking pieces are acted by inhabitants of the village. The stage is an open air platform and the audience is seated in a closed roof auditorium which holds 5,200 spectators. A special bonus on our tour was that in Oberammergau where Joe, Mary Ann, Louise and I stayed was at Rudi Zwink's place. He was the one who played Christ in the passion play.

We took the delightful cruise up the historic valley of the Rhine River to Cologne, Germany where we visited the famous cathedral of Cologne. It was here that in WWII I stood guard at the outside door of this cathedral. We were the first Americans to enter Cologne; no lights and all buildings around the cathedral were bombed out. The German soldiers crossed back over the Rhine River. My job was to see that no destruction or looting happened to the cathedral.

GRANDDAUGHTER SHANNON WAS BORN

It was December of 1980 that Louise and I flew down to Phoenix, Arizona to visit our daughter Mary Ann and her husband Joe Hicks to enjoy Christmas with them. They had purchased a new home in Tempe, Arizona that is a suburb of Phoenix. While visiting at Christmas we discovered, "Louise and I" that we would soon be grandparents. Shannon Ann Hicks was born on April 27, at 11:10 P.M, 1981 at Tempe, Arizona. Shortly after that time we got a call from Mary Ann that we were now grandparents of a dark haired, brown eyed, bouncing healthy baby girl with strong lungs.

She is our first granddaughter and we were very happy. We were also grandparents of three grandsons, Jon, James and Paul.

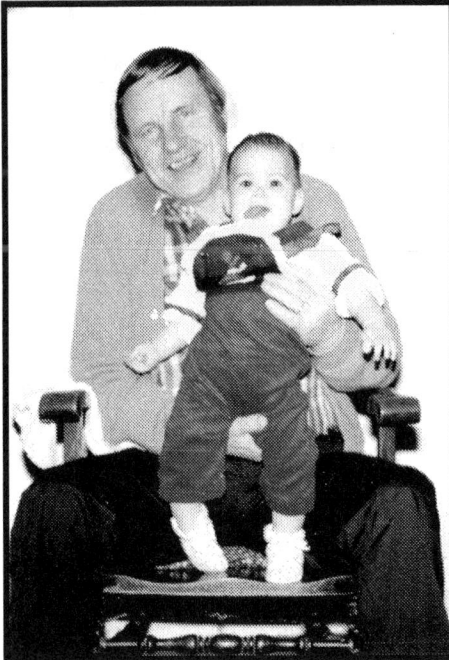

After a few months we went back for another visit to Phoenix and this time is was grandpa's joy to get acquainted with our new grand daughter Shannon Ann Hicks. Shannon and grandpa's photo is at the left.

LOUISE, WILLARD INGRAHAM AND FAMILY

While we were visiting in Phoenix Louise and I purchased a 22 foot Travel Craft motor home. We packed up the motor home for a week end excursion to Tuscan, Arizona. Little Shannon sure liked traveling that way. The weekend went too fast but Mary Ann and Joe had to get back to go to work. It was time for us to leave for home; Louise and I put our suit cases in the motor home to drive it back home to Kennewick, Washington (photo below).

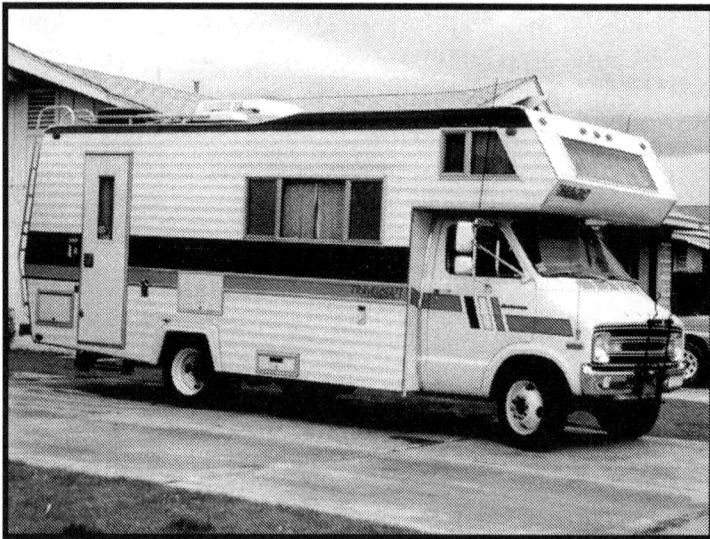

TEACHING BIBLE CLASSES

It was on September 20, 1981 Willard Ingraham was given a certificate of completion from the Adult Christian Education Foundation that he had completed two years of intensive studies of the old and new testaments and was thereby qualified to teach the adult bible classes known as the Bethel Series that are the stories of the bible.

I (Willard) was one of the bible teachers that taught two years of classes to the United Methodist Church members in Kennewick, Wa. After teaching these classes I took another year of study to teach the Kerygma Program; a study in depth of the people of God which is the study of the prophecies of the bible. After completion, I taught this program classes for two years. Louise attended all of my classes.

Above is a photo of our Methodist Church in Kennewick. Our girls Mary Ann and Carol both are members of this church and attended bible studies here when they were growing up.

LOUISE, WILLARD INGRAHAM AND FAMILY

MEDITERRANEAN CRUISE

Oct. 26, 1982 our group took off on a 20-day tour of the Holy Land and Copenhagen with a seven-day Mediterranean cruise via Seattle, Washington, Copenhagen, Denmark, Greece, Kusadas, Istanbul, Myknonos, Ephesus, Turkey then on to the Mediterranean cruise. Our first stop was Santorini, a city at the top of a huge volcanic mountain that we rode mules to the city.

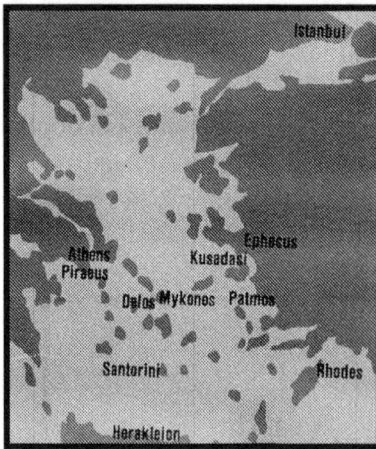

It is also the island of the mythical place called Atlantis. Look at the map left and you can see most of the Greek Islands.

Especially note the steep terrain in the photo below of Santorini. It is up that steep winding trail you see on the right that we rode mules to the top and walked down.

Below are photos of Willard and Louise on their mules during the ride.

Then we went on to Knossos, Crete the capital of a 4000-year-old Minoan civilization. The Minoan civilization exited in the northern part of Greece at one time. This civilization is related the Bronze Age culture. They flourished in Crete from about 3000 to 1000 BC.

We have also visited the site of the Minoan civilization in the northern part of Greece. It is remarkable that this culture is also believed to have been the first existence on the now fabled Atlantis that some say that its existence and location was in the Mediterranean off the coast of Greece. There is a great deal of history written about this civilization that perhaps will be researched by those reading what I wrote.

Our next stop was on to the island of Rhodes where
John the Apostle built a fortified city, which now is the best,
preserved of its kind in the Mediterranean.

Next we travels to the island that was dominated by the
famous monastery on the tiptop side of the mountain; it was
here on the island of Patmos that John the Apostle was
imprisoned and exiled in a cave when he wrote the book of
Revelation that we read in our bible.

Photo above is of Patmos; please note that there is a
crack in the ceiling on the photo in the upper left. This crack
has a great significant as they had an earthquake at the time
that John lived in this cave. The earthquake split the ceiling
into three parts with cracks as you can see. The way one sees
those cracks is per John's version it indicates the trinity.

We went on to Damascus, Syria and toured through the
Omayad Mosque where they had an orientated tomb enclosed

in a glass case where they claim the head of John the Baptist's head is entombed. We walked down the street called Straight.

From here we traveled to Jordan where we toured Ammon and Petra as well as other sites. Then we crossed the Jordan River where we toured dozens of important sites in Israel including the Sea of Galilee, Masada and other sites.

After the tour through Masada we bussed back to Jerusalem where we overnighted and allowed our group the next day a free day to do as they wished. Five of us, Willard, Louise, Helen Dennis, Enid Koch and Mary Ellen Bromley took a special chartered small plane to Mt. Sinai.

It seemed that we landed out in no man land in the desert but as pre-arranged a small bus and driver was waiting for us to take us to St. Katrina. It was not a long drive but was a winding road in the bottom of a canyon with mountainous rocks on each side of the road. At the end of the ride, the road appeared to break out into a more open space and there before us was the famous St. Katrina. The photo is below. It was a

fortress that had stood time for centuries but still occupied by monks.

LOUISE, WILLARD INGRAHAM AND FAMILY

It was exciting to tour the place of the burning bush; a bit of a disappointment that the area pointed out to us was but a small bush up on the mountain behind the monastery.

The grandeur of the monastery perhaps was in the many artistic works and portraits hanging on the walls that were ancient and priceless. Here in this stark land to find a fortress and such beauty in ancient art was astonishing; one only reads of such things in history books and we had the privilege to see it all.

What we saw next was disturbing to see for all of us to view the place of burial of the monks. It was in a building that was sacred but the bodies of the deceased monks lay resting in a single open tomb as a memorial to fit their religious beliefs. For a monk anything but a prayerful mood was not acceptable. For us touring this open grave and sanctuary one had first to pass by the smells that emanated in such a building before feeling the rapture it held from those monks gone on. One could not help but think of all the good works that was done by these souls when they walked this earth.

After our tour of St. Katrina we were transported back to Eilat for lunch. Eilat is on the shores of the Red Sea and it was our pleasure to visit the Underwater Observatory and Aquarium for a close-up view of exotic fish and tropical corals. It was a wonderful way to end our day before our return trip to Jerusalem.

Our day was one that gave us time to reconstruct in our minds what it must have been like at St. Katrina centuries ago. We had flown in on a small passenger plane and been whisk along the road by bus. Had we been traveling in an earlier century we would have counted our trip by days and weeks to take such a journey from Jeruselem to St. Katrina. Our journey would have been across the desert and by camel or on foot. The hardships would have been many and there would have been no exotic luncheon at Eilat on the shores of the Red Sea. When we snuggled back in our comfortable bed at Jerusalem we had thanks in our prayers for what we had seen so easily.

We left Israel by bus down through the Gaza strip. We crossed the Suez Canal by ferry and were taking to the border of Cairo where we changed to an Egyptain bus and were bused to Cairo and after riding camels to the basee we went up ramps and steps inside the pyramid of Geza. Below is a photo of our group by Alabaster Sphinx. Louise and I (Willard) are on the left.

Below is one of the camels ridden at the pyramid.

While in Egypt we also visited the Museum in Cairo.

Another successful tour and ended too soon. We returned home from Egypt via Copenhagen, Denmark, Seattle and to Pasco.

LOUISE, WILLARD INGRAHAM AND FAMILY

A TOUR GROUP THROUGH MEXICO

Louise and I took an exploratory trip to Mexico November 1979 to prepare a future Mexico tour. It was on November 14th, 1983 that we had worked out a tour that we were sure all tourists would appreciate. We left Pasco, Wa. with our group via Los Angeles, Ca. to Mazatlan, Mexico; Mazatlan had a population of 350,000 and was famous for it's shrimp. The Mexicans say that Iguana legs are better eating than chicken. We do not know because they did not get any takers from our group.

From Mazatlan on the 17th we flew a short pleasant flight to Guadalajara where they had a population of 3 million. Our Mexican guide told us that 25% of the people of Mexico are uneducated.

Below is a photo of the butterfly-net fishermen from Janitzio Island. They truly looked like butterflies with their nets spread out.

At our next stop we boarded a bus with a guide that would be with us for the rest of the tour. On Nov. 18th we traveled by bus to Pascquarro about 200 miles.

451

    We had been gone four days and our group had just experienced a lovely day and felt a close unity among each other in the group.

    On Nov. 19th we stopped in Morelias; population 500,000. The hospitals in Mexico are called social security hospitals with socialized medicine. We were told Mexico has 600 dialects and sometimes there are 60 dialects in one community.

    It was Nov. 21, 1983 that we arrived in Mexico City; a population of 21 million. We saw sights in Mexico City too numerous to mention although some of the highlights was the theater play we attended and the ruins just outside of Mexico City.

    We left the city for Teotihuacán; I wrote earlier about this city in our exploratory trip to Mexico. From this stop we went to Taxco where the group liked the shopping for silver keepsakes. Our next stop was Pueblo where we found the whole town was flooded with about 6 inches of water because of the rains. We stayed at a very nice hotel but none of the toilets would flush because of the floods; we left all of this behind traveling through the mountains and tobacco growing country. We reached the chief seaport located on the Gulf of Mexico. This seaport was founded in 1519 and was the first Spanish settlement in Mexico. Our beautiful hotel was located

on a sandy beach about 10 miles out of Veracrus. (photo is left) They serenaded us with beautiful steel drum music.

LOUISE, WILLARD INGRAHAM AND FAMILY

We bused the group from Veracrus back to Mexico City where we boarded our plane via Houston, Texas and back home to Kennewick, Washington. The entire group really enjoyed the places they saw and visited in Mexico.

SHIPPING AND MAILING SERVICE

In 1982 Joe and Mary Ann decided to leave Tempe, Arizona and move to Kennewick, Washington to start a business. We all decided Allied Services would be that business. It was a shipping and mailing business service oriented with UPS, Federal Express, Airborne, money orders, notary services and a small gift and food department. We offered ice cream, cookies and snacks. We started the business from scratch which required a lot of PR work to get it going to full speed. The intention was for Joe and Mary Ann to handle the business but the business took off and more help was needed so the three of us, Joe, Mary Ann and I (Willard) ran the store; pictured below.

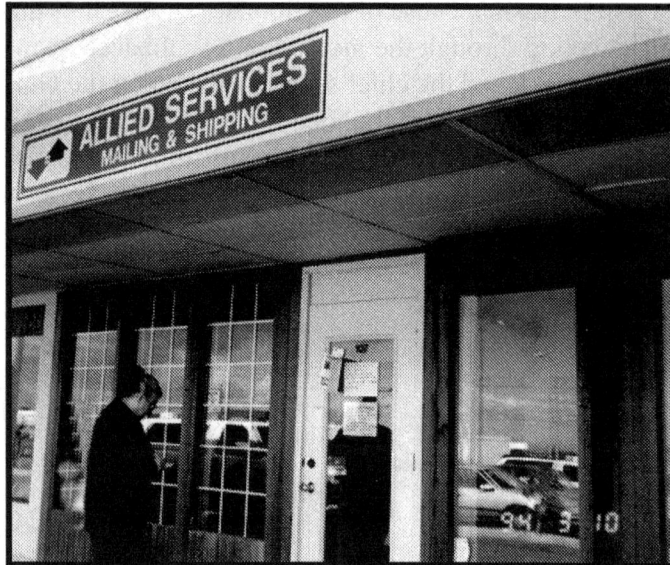

THE HOLYLAND; PASSION PLAY AT OBERAMERGAU

On August 29, 1984 our tour left Pasco, Washington to the Holy Land with the passion play at Oberammergau plus Austria, Egypt, Greece and Turkey. We traveled via New York to Vienna, Austria where Mozart, Beethoven and many other famous people are buried. We attended an orchestrated string instrument rendition of all the favorites at a dinner in Vienna. Another highlight was the Spanish riding academy that featured the magnificent Lipizzaner horses. They put on a great performance.

Another thrill was visiting the well known church with a painting depicting the death of a royal by knife in a love affair. The church was in the mountainous area outside of Vienna and it was our privilege to have an overnight stay at a palace turned into a hotel. It was a beautiful setting for a wedding and as luck would have it there was one scheduled for that night. Louise and I went to the ballroom to check out the dancing and were enjoying watching the bride and grooms dance party when we were asked to join in on the dance floor. It was special dancing on that lovely marble floor to the tunes that only eminent at a formal Austrian wedding celebration. They must have noticed that we were a little different; perhaps it was our language accents or was it just the charm of having American guests; nevertheless Louise and I will never forget this memorable evening in the company of an Austrian wedding party.

On our way from Austria via bus our tour took us through the lovely country side of Germany. At one point our guide pointed out to us that we were passing by the road that led to Berchtesgaden, Hitler's Eagle's Nest. This was the hiding place for Hitler during WWII. It was not on our tour to take this side trip to the mountain top structure but we could see it from afar and could visualize why he choice such a secluded place to hide.

As we traveled along our bus took us across the Ammer Mountains to Oberammergau. Ober means over and gau means area hence Oberammergau. Our destination was Oberammergau and the passion play. The Oaberammergau Passion Play is only shown once every 10 years and we had toured here in 1980 so we were very fortunate to tour it again in 1984 when they had a special celebration of 250 years from the first program in 1634. Our group really enjoyed the thrill of seeing and hearing such a renowned play even if it was all spoken in German; the acting depicted the scene in a magnificent way. A photo of Oberammergau is below with the passion play theater at the top.

Our next stop was Amman, Jordan and Israel that took us to many religious places including Hebron outside of Jerusalem. Hebron is an Arab occupied city and the tensions run high here between the Jews and Arabs so there are times a tour can not go there although it is the sight of the burial place of well known biblical persons and a stop one wants as a memory.

Our visits always included all the historical sites in Egypt and Greece as well as Istanbul, Turkey. We toured the Blue Mosque (pictured below) and St. Sophia Museum in Turkey.

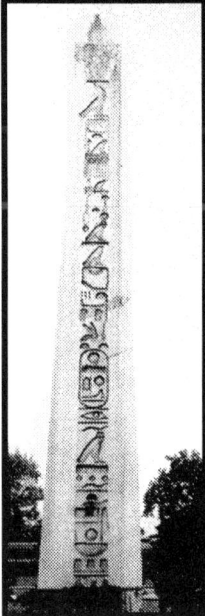

We saw many other important sites one of which was one of the original obelisk near Cairo (pictured left). There are four obelisk in all. Each weigh 80 ton. Besides the Cairo site there is one in Istanbul, Turkey , one in London England and the other one is now a question of where. We have seen three of the obelisk.

It is a good luck and assures a return to Egypt is one takes a boat ride on the Nile at sunset. We did just that and if we never return we shall always have fond memories of another tour. All too soon we boarded our plane for the USA and home.

LOUISE, WILLARD INGRAHAM AND FAMILY

MOTOR HOME CARAVAN; 4 STATES AND CANADA

On June 14, 1986 with Ray and Anna Ingraham in their motor home and Louise and I (Willard) Ingraham in our motor home we were on our way to Laurel, Montana to pickup Claude and Lorreine Ingraham in their motor home to all caravan several states and Canada for 28 days.

Our first stop from Kennewick, Wa. was to overnight at Missoula, Mt. The next day we made it to Laurel, Mt. where Ray parked his motor home in Claud and Lorreine's driveway. I parked our motor home in Cenra and Bob Weatherfords drive as they lived next door to Claud and Lorreine and were Cenra's parents. Pictured below: Willard and Louise left, Anna and Ray and Claude and Lorreine.

Just across the street our Uncle Ralph and Aunt Rose Ingraham lived. It was an evening of relatives enjoying each others company long into the night but the next day we left Laurel now with three motor homes caravanning that included Claud and Lorreines motor home on the way to Jamestown, North Dakota. There were stops along the way; one was at Medora, N. Dakota that is in the Badlands. This was Theodore

Roosevelt's favorite stomping grounds. As we entered Medora there was a sign that read, "welcome to Medora, 103 years old."

Left is a photo of all three motor homes lined up at a rest stop.

We got in late that afternoon to Woodworth, North Dakota but we had reservations in a field that they opened up just for Woodworth, North Dakota's 75 year celebration. Above is a photo with everyone at rest.

The founding of Woodworth was in 1911. Claud, Ray and I (Willard) were all born at Woodworth. Arnold and Lucille Steffens arrived in their motor home from Washington. Arnold's mother, Aunt Nora was with them. Also Arnold's sisters Helen from Michigan and Rosella Kirkwood from

California arrived. My Aunt Gladys Steffens was also there from Sioux Falls, South Dakota.

On one of the days during the celebration we went to the Woodworth cemetery where Uncle Claud and Lorreine have a son, Delton Dean buried. Ray and I (Willard) have a little sister, Gerada Agnes buried here also.

We took time to drive out to Chauncey Ingraham's homestead and took pictures of what was left of the house. Our next stop was the Lunde Church Cemetery where Grandpa Gunder Johnson and Grandma Laura Johnson are buried. The Johnson's have two daughters and a son buried there, Olga Johnson who was a twin to Aunt Esther and a son Gordon Johnson and a daughter Avis Glowac.

I (Willard) have two brothers buried here, Charles LeRoy and LeRoy Norman Ingraham.

Some things were not the same; one was the school building that Ray and I had attended had burned down and a new building stood in its place.

From Woodworth we all went to Jamestown, N.D. where we got a good place to park our motor homes. Our caravan had gotten bigger as Arnold and Lucille had joined in along with their guests, Aunt Gladys, Aunt Nora, Helen and Rosella. In Jamestown there were many relatives to see. We were invited to Duane and Lois Knutson's home for a buffet. Duane and Lois had gotten all the relatives together from Jamestown so we were able to see and visit with Aunt Louise Schuff, Esther Sorenson, Harriet and Vern Wahl. Aunt Doris Rosenau was in the hospital but Ray Rosenau joined the group.

The following day after the buffet Ray Rosenau offered to drive Ray and Anna and Louise and I (Willard) up to New Rockford where Ray and I used to live with our parents. We saw school friends Joe Anderson, Bill Starke and their wives. After our visits with them we went to see the farm we had lived on before moving to Prosser, Washington. We took photos and after stopped in next to our farm to see Pete Klocke and some of his family.

Afterward we went on to New Rockford and met another neighbor Erma Christ who lives in town. She had lost her husband Amile some years before.

It had been a great stop over at Jamestown but the next day the three motor home caravan, Claude, Ray and Willard were on our way again to Fargo, N.D. We turned south into Minnesota where we soon saw a road sign that indicated Evansville, Mn. coming up. This was the place where my grandparents Gunder and Laura Johnson lived before moving to North Dakota on the homestead years ago. Also it was where my mother, Gena Johnson Ingraham was born. We drove through town and on our way again.

A couple three hours later we were in Mantorville, Mn. where my grandparents, Chauncey and Myrtle Cowles Ingraham used to live before moving to North Dakota on their homestead. Lyle Ingraham, my dad, was born here at Mantorville, Mn.

Below is the historic opera house in Mantorville.

We saw many Ingraham and Cowles names on tomb stones in the West Concord Cemetery a few miles from Mantorville. The famous Mayo Brothers Hospital is a short driving distance from Mantorville. Then we drove north along the Mississippi River to Duluth where we boarded the Vista Queen for a cruise on Lake Superior.

Our next motor home caravan stop was Thunder Bay, Canada and after entering Canada we stopped at the Kakabeka Falls.

The highway north of the border from Thunder Bay to Edmonton, Canada was a good straight road and surprisingly flat instead of mountains as I had expected. In Edmonton we visited the world's largest fashion shopping mall, fun and entertainment centre. It also had the largest water park, man made lake with waves and beaches and 17 giant slides. It boggled the mind; the size and quantity of what was displayed in the mall.

There were over 700 stores and among them many ice cream stores. We had fun with the coupons that were offered for ice cream cone samples. I don't know how many times we sampled but there were more than a few.

Since this time another covered mall has been built at the twin cities in St. Paul, Minneapolis, Mn. that is said to be larger than the Edmonton mall.

We drove to Calgary, Alberta, Canada where we visited Heritage Park; it has 60 acres that represents an authentic portrayal of life in Western Canada prior to 1915. Our last stop was the Calgary Stampede and the rodeo with the famous chuck wagon races. It would end our planned high light before beginning our return trip home. I am glad we saw the chuck wagon races but one could see the race was dangerous; we were told that sadly one of the wagons overturned a few weeks later killing one of the drivers.

Our way home took us via Banff and Lake Louise, Canada. It is a beautiful lake setting in the mountains. We stopped to enjoy the view while we had lunch at the Banff Hotel there on the shores.

Traveling through the mountains to the Washington border we were surprised at a large herd of mountain goats in our pathway. It was quite a sight but they bounded out of the way and we continued to the border. This had been a 28 day memorable trip.

VANCOUVER CANADA WORLD FAIR 1986

August 21 -22-23 and 24th Louise and I (Willard) put
together a tour to go to the Worlds fair, Expo 86 at Vancouver,
Canada. We filled up a bus with 45 passengers fully escorted
to and from Kennewick, Washington by Willard and Louise
Ingraham including lodging aboard the SS Prince George ship
anchored three miles from the fair location.
Below is a poster advertising the world fair in 1986.

THE 1986 WORLD EXPOSITION.

Our lodging included buffet breakfast every morning
that we were there and the monorail was only a half block from

the ship that took us right into the fairgrounds. I escorted the group the first time as a guide to show them the way then left everyone on their own traveling back and forth from the ship to the fair so they could come and go as they pleased. They had free monorail passes and the monorail ran 24 hrs. The group loved the convenience and freedom they had as some did not want to be at the fair every day and all day long. To break up going to the fair everyday we added a mini tour of Vancouver as part of the tour package. One afternoon we took those that wanted to go to a 3D movie showing in Vancouver.

The group was always kept busy and entertainment even on the long bus ride home. We played question games like how many provinces in Canada and etc. A wonderful trip enjoyed by everyone.

THE GREAT CHINA WALL TOUR

On the 23rd of Oct. 1986 our tour group gathered at Pasco to begin our 17 day tour with focus on China via Seattle, Wash. to Hong Kong then China. Louise and Willard below.

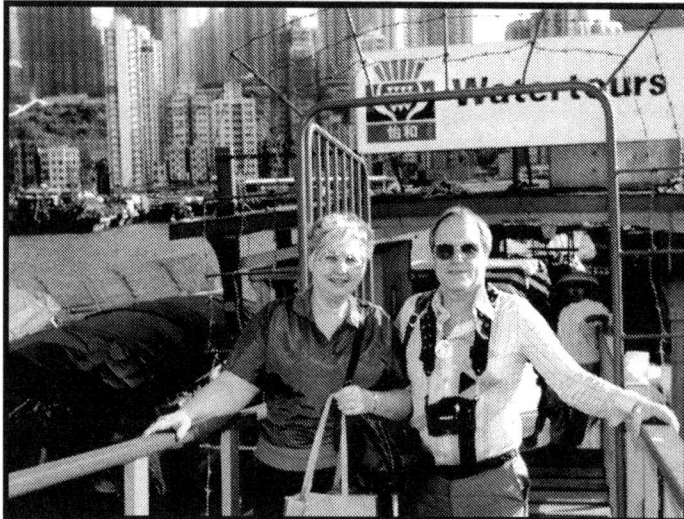

Hong Kong was a hustle bustle modern city that has many things to see and explore. We took the cable car ride to the highest point and enjoyed the skyline scene. There was time for a lot of shopping for all. Famous maker suits for men and women were available. Besides shopping our group took a 2 ½ hour cruise around the Kowloon Peninsula and harbor while eating our dinner aboard.

On day five we were transported to the train station (Lo Wu) where we boarded and were on our way to Guagchow. Our first night we were served a 10 coarse dinner at the Bei-yuan restaurant; we stayed at the deluxe Garden Hotel. The next day we flew to Gullin and stayed at the Rong Cheng Hotel; next we took a cruise on the LiJiAng River. We passed by mystical peaks that had countless pinnacles on pointed hills jutting up all over like they grew into big mountains of dirt; skinny like tree mounds. A photo is below.

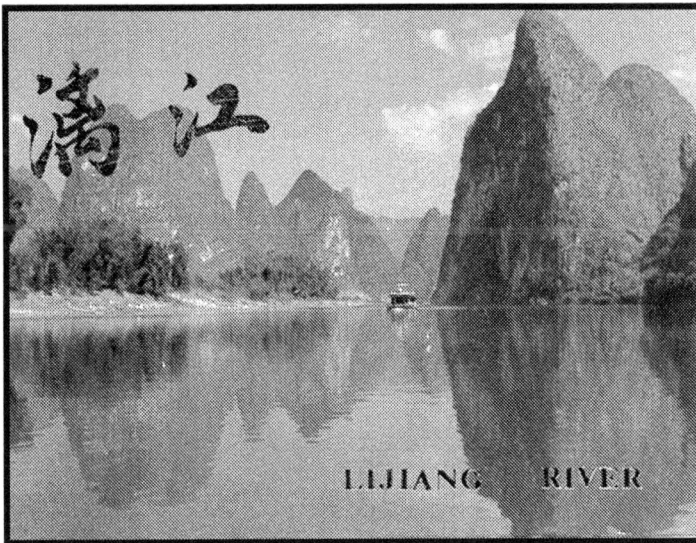

漓江

LIJIANG   RIVER

One of our extra entertainments on that river trip was our guide who professed to be a palm reader. He had a great audience with our group and willing hands held out to know their secrets.

The next day we flew to Xian which was the largest city in the world in the 7th century. We checked into the Xian Hotel and the following day we were taken to the museum of the Qin terracotta figures. Qin Shi Huangdi's Mausoleum and the museum of the Qin dynasti terracotta warriors and horses lies about 36 kilometers east of the town of Xian at the foot of the Li mountains. A new road leads to this large museum complex which houses over 7,000 terracotta statues of soldiers and horses over 2000 years old. The first pit containing terracotta figures was discovered in early 1974. In 1975 the state council decided that a museum be built over the original excavation site and after four years exhibition halls and several auxiliary buildings had been built. The other pits with figures had come to light in 1976. The museum was open on Oct. 1, 1979. The museum covers an area of two million square meters. Below is a photo some of those terracotta figures.

Qin Shi Huangde was the first emperor of China. He became king of the state of Qin in the area around present day Xian in 247 BC at the age of thirteen. At this time China was divided into many contending states or kingdoms hence the

465

period is often referred to as the warring states. By 230 BC seven states had achieved dominance and the next decade Qin, under the ruler ship of the young king, conquered the other six to unify China in 221 BC.

On day 10 we took the flight from Xian to Beijing where we checked into the Lido Hotel. The smog was so thick that most of the people on the street were using nose and mouth masks. The next day we toured the Imperial Palace museum, Temple of Heaven and Summer Palace. That night we all enjoyed a western dinner at our hotel. The next day we walked up on the famous Great Wall of China. The wall starts at Shanghai Pass in the East and ending up at Jiayu Pass in the west. The Great Wall traverses up and down over numerous mountains and valleys in five of China's northern provinces and two autonomous regions. It extends over a distance of more than 6000 Km. It is a symbol of intelligence of the working people of old days. Construction of the wall first began in the 7th century BC after Qin Shi Huang the first emperor of the Qin Dynasty (221-206 BC) after Qin Shi Huang. The first emperor of the Qin Dynasty (221-206 BC) achieved the unification of China in 221 BC. He had the fortification walls of the kingdoms Qin, Zhao and Yan linked up to be a continuous wall extending more than ten thousand Li (a Li = ½ KM) or about 5000 KM which formed the essential size of the present day great wall. Since then the later dynasties restored and reinforced it during the Ming Dynasty.

The next day we flew to Hanzhou, a pleasant tree filled city on West Lake. Here they raise silk worms. We toured a silk worm factory where they extracted the silk from silk worms then cast the worms into pails and ate them. It was an interesting process.

We went by train to the beautiful Shanghai Hotel in Shanghai. The next day they took us by bus to a show by the children at a Chinese school. It was rewarding when we got off the bus there was a line of small Chinese children that shook our hand and each child greeted us with an English hello, hi or some other greeting. We were ushered into the school where we enjoyed the very talented show presented to us.

We were allowed to shop in a Chinese section of town. It was interesting to note that whatever we Americans looked at and or bought the Chinese would flock to that area to view our cultural interests and if we bought some of the Chinese were sure to also buy what we did. We visited a park where there were many Chinese University students and they surrounded us to practice their English on us. Their highlight was to have an American signature on paper they pushed at us.

It is also noted that all the tour was controlled by government. The buses, the planes and even the guides all were under the control of the government. The same Chinese guides were with us for the entire time. We were never too late or too early for a flight or the train or bus because everything was government controlled.

We were not allowed to offer our Chinese guides any tips. Louise did though at the end of the tour leave her hair drier with our young guide. She was thrilled with this token gift and it came under approval to give her this item from her government.

During the entire tour we were accompanied with an older lady whose job was to value the services of the hotels. We were told that in China a young person is assigned a job by the government that they will perform for the rest of their lives. There is no choice of employment by the individual.

We were also told that the Chinese wanted boy babies not girls. They would give extra compensation to a parent that had a boy but not if they had a girl. It was a wonderful trip and an enlightenment of how the culture is so different than ours in America.

BRITISH ISLE TOUR

On Sept. 16, 1987 our group all met at the Seattle air
port for a 21 day tour of the British Isles via Kennedy air port
in New York to Shannon, Ireland where we checked into the
Limmerick Hotel in Limmerick City. The next day we boarded
a motor coach for Bunratty Folk Park and a live Ceili evening
of traditional Irish hospitality featuring hearty food and drink
to fiddlers jig and reel dancers and story telling.

The next day we enjoyed a jaunting horse drawn cart
ride to Muckross Esate (photo below, Willard in center front
and Louise on the right). The estate was surrounded by 11,500

acres of Emerald Irish countryside. There was time to explore
the folk museum. On our return to our hotel one of the carts
lost a wheel. Our tour guests in that cart got a huge bump

when the cart came to a stop with one wheel on and one wheel off. Lucky no one was hurt; the guide set the wheel back on and reloaded the passengers and off at a fast clip they went.

The following day we went on the Ring of Kerry excursion. It was here that we were presented with a stunning coastal view, dotted with remains of Iron Age forts and in front of us crossed by flocks of sheep as we were driven around the Ring of Kerry.

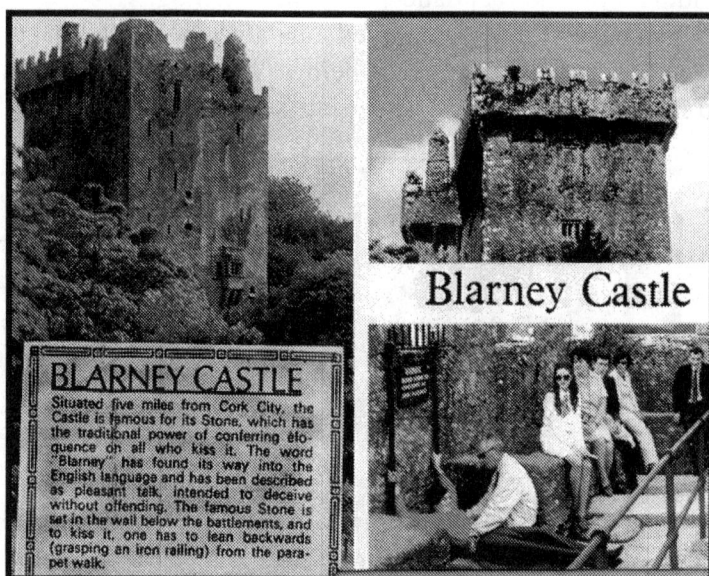

Blarney Castle

BLARNEY CASTLE
Situated five miles from Cork City, the Castle is famous for its Stone, which has the traditional power of conferring eloquence on all who kiss it. The word "Blarney" has found its way into the English language and has been described as pleasant talk, intended to deceive without offending. The famous Stone is set in the wall below the battlements, and to kiss it, one has to lean backwards (grasping an iron railing) from the parapet walk.

On day five we our bus passed the craggy coastlines of Bantry Bay and the gorgeous town of Glengariff along the hills and slate gray lakes leading to Blarney Castle. Of coarse we had to stop to kiss the Blarney Stone and visit the Cork, a bustling seaport. The castle is pictured below and lower right is a tourist kissing the blarney stone for good luck; we were on top of the building and when leaning backward to kiss the stone as you can see it was a very long way down.

Bright and early the next day we boarded a first class train for a ride to Dublin. We saw the Resplendent Book of Kells at Trinity College, St. Patrick's Cathedral and Georgian

Merrion Square. There was time for a little shopping in Dublin and the shops were interesting with a flavor for wool items made of the wool from local sheep.

It was time to leave Ireland the next day as we were taken to the Port of Dun Laoghaire we boarded our ferry and

crossed the Irish Sea to the Isle of Anglessey then over to Chester, England. Our tour took us to Glasgow then along the Scottish border over to Lochlomond and up by Sterling Castle to Edinburgh, Scotland. Our highlights were always to visit the most famous and the majestic castle was one of those. Afterward the bus brought us down the Royal mile to Queen Mary's Holy Road House. That night was a Scottish roast beef banquet featuring bag pipers and dancers.

Our tour kept us on the move; there was much more to see. We did stop long enough for a group photo; I (Willard) and Louise are pictured at the far left.

We visited Castle Howard amidst lakes, fountains and gardens then continued to the city of York. Timelessness gave ground to the vivid man made sights of the ancient minister and Jorvik Viking Centre.

One of our tour guests on visiting one of the churches pointed to the list of names on the ceiling. It was he told us his Scottish ancestors name written on the ceiling and it was the reason he had taken this tour was to get a view and photos of what he believed to be his ancestral connection. It is known that churches kept records of the followers of the early churches by writing their names on the ceilings.

The next day we visited Warwick castle then we were on our way to Shakespear's Stratford beside the peaceful river Avon. We saw the Bard's home and his sweetheart Anne Hathaway's cottage in nearby Shottrey. The next morning we visited Bath and Winsor Castle. We then toured the renowned Stonehenge. It was quite an impressive sight. There are many stories written of this massive column structures. It is said by some that the ancients that build it were from another place in space. It is said by some that the structures gave a view by the residents to see and communicate beyond. Is it truth or lure; you decide. It was a fascinating conjecture.

One of Louise's highlights was a chance to shop at the famous department store in downtown London (pictured below). You could buy almost anything here we were told; even a pink elephant for an American Hollywood party if you had the money to have it shipped! This department store had a food pavilion that took up nearly half of the main floor on the street level. Their fish department had squid and every other kind of fish imaginable.

The English viewed our English American language as colloquial and so we thought nip was a word used to take a drink not to nip under a table as the English used it..

It was also unusual to see milk being delivered from door to door in the morning and especially unusual to see the milk in glass bottles. In spite of our language and cultural differences, we understood each other very well and had a jolly good time of it too.

Our final destination was in London, we visited the British museum, Piccadilly Circus and changing of the guards at the palace gates where the uniformed young men stared straight ahead with guns at side with no smiles nor did they allow themselves any distractions.

We saw many other places too many to mention; even did a little antique shopping in that famous section of the city where shops of antiquity were everywhere.

Oh yes we had to take in a theater play one evening; it was a play that they said to have been running 30 years. We Americans stood out in the crowded theater; when we laughed at the comedy, the English were as sober as church mice! When they laughed at an act, we did not see the funny side!

A standard for all to see though was the Big Ben clock in the middle of Trafalgar Square in downtown near the also famous London Bridge. When that clock struck on the quarter hour one knew it from the sound echoing down the streets. You also knew you were in London when you stopped by a pub to have a beer with the locals; this is when you really got the flavor of what it was like to be an Englishman drinking a mug of beer and eating one of their famous fish and chips.

Another quaint thing is that no one abroad seemed to understand that Louise's name was not pronounced Louis. They keep saying Louis no matter how many times corrected and ask why a man's name. After explaining and explaining, Louise finally gave up and Louis it was.

We said our goodbyes to our guide and bused to the London airport for our flight home to the U.S.A.

PUERTO VALLARTA, MEXICO

April 22, 1988 Orvil and Doris Terril, Louise and I (Willard) Ingraham left Pasco airport to fly to Puerto Vallarta via San Francisco to Los Angeles. Orvil and Doris had been on many of our tours but this time we all decided we needed a slow pace vacation. We picked Puerto Vallarto, Mexico to spend our resting 12 day vacation.

It was refreshing to spend a few days at the same hotel; sleep in then spend the rest of the day touring the local sites at our leisure. There were sunshine days with long walks but time to take an island tour by boat. Swimming in the hotel pools was great. The local scene was colorful and the food was good except one had to be careful of the spices. It was a restful trip taken with two good friends.

Willard took the photo below; Orvil and Doris Terril are at the left and Louise on the right.

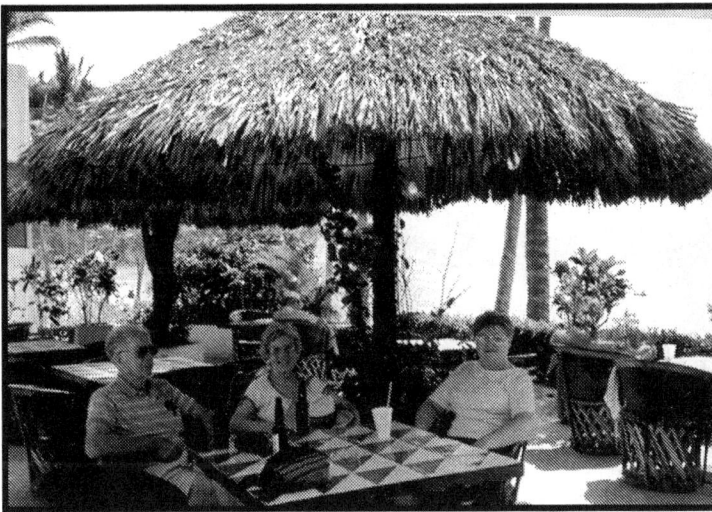

THE FIRST INGRAHAM REUNION

Louise and I (Willard) had a membership at Lake Easton that is located in the mountains near Snoqualmie Pass in Washington State. We decided to start our first Ingraham reunion here in July of 1988. The Ingraham families brought motor home or trailers and others rented cabins.

The main clubhouse is pictured below.

There was plenty of food for our potlucks and we purchased breakfast at the recreation center. The group played horseshoes and some swam in the pool but mostly it was a time to visit and enjoy the other Ingraham's company. There were 20 Ingraham's at this first reunion; not everyone came but it was successful and a good start for the first reunion.

HONG KONG, BANGKOK, THAILAND, TAIPE, TIWAN 1988

On August 18 – August 30th Louise and I (Willard) led a tour for 12 days. We traveled to Bangkok, Thailand and stayed at the Royal Orchid Hotel.

We were lucky to have Chusak Piriyapul invite us to his home in Bangkok. Chusak had been a student in the USA and had lived with our minister Rev. Wooldridge and his wife Dorothy in the US while he attended the university with the Wooldridge boys.

When in Bangkok the friend of the Wooldridges, Chusak, sent a chauffer in a car to pick Louise and I (Willard) up at the hotel. He took us to a seven story building that was both business and home to the Chusaks. The family lived on two flours and his business was on the other floors. It was magnificent; there was a huge swimming pool on the roof of the building. In one area of their home was a Buddhist shrine for prayer and in honor of Chusak's parents.

Chusak was an entrepreneur with his eye on America's super markets. He showed us the blue prints of his planned big super store that was under construction at that time.

Our stay in Bangkok was interesting and informative. We too were looking for ideas to bring back to the US for retail as well as enjoying the culture of the city. During our stay at Bangkok we traveled north by bus with a guide to a park setting. We spent the day being entertained with culture dances, music and trained elephants. Some of the group was even brave enough to ride an elephant around a track.

Try riding a Tu Tu, a rickshaw pulled by a human, through the traffic of Bangkok. We did and I can tell you it was a ride not to be forgotten. Traffic was side by side; no direct lane traffic here and everyone for themselves. The buses loomed everywhere as did automobiles and motor cycles and then there was us in a rickshaw. A ride I would not want to have missed but one I would not want to repeat either.

Our next stop was Taipei, Taiwan. We stayed at the Taipei Fortuna Hotel. The downtown streets were colorful and unique of other street scenes in the world. The Presidential Palace, The National Palace Museum and many others of their national shrines were all very different and interesting to view.

We spent some of our time visiting wholesale companies. We visited a factory that used seed pearls for jewelry and it was amazing what they made from such intricate pearls. We were fortunate to be able to purchase necklaces and other items of pearl that we could take home.

The food served at the hotel was all wonderful and a buffet was filled with numerous kinds of fish prepared in numerous ways. We had eaten so many Chinese dishes by this time it was a treat believe it our not to go down the block from the hotel and have breakfast at an American McDonald's.

One of our tour guests, Michelle Wiggins was celebrating her birthday in Taiwan; her mother, Marty Wiggins had found a restaurant that served American cuisine including ice cream concoctions that we were all thrilled to partake of. It was a birthday party American – Chinese style. A birthday for Michelle to remember!

Our last stop of the tour was at Hong Kong. We had more interesting sites to see. We were intrigued by their building styles; tall and many stories high was faced with bamboo structures for the workers to use while building. We were told that many workers lost their lives during a construction job and one could see why. The bamboo was built like trellises and none looked sturdy enough to hold a worker.

We visited the fishing docks in the bay and saw that people were actually living on small boats in the harbor and making a living fishing. Some of the small boats contained crates that the Chinese kept their chickens in. It was one way to have daily fresh eggs. On the docks there was fish and venders everywhere; the stink from the fish was overwhelming but it was a living for many and the smells to the venders were incidental.

The women on the tour loved to shop and a highlight for some was a visit to a huge outdoor market place that sold name brand clothing, shoes, jewelry that was listed as authentic but actual was black marketed brands. It is the way of the world and while in another country one simply enjoys what they see as remarkable feats of ingenuity to make a living.

We left Hong Kong on our flight home to the USA with many memories; it had been a trip full of surprises and unusual cultural difference that we would treasurer as a unique experience.

CARIBBEAN TOUR

Oct. 16, 1988 we took a group of people on an eight day Caribbean tour through Puerto Rico, Barbados, Trinidad and Tobago. It was a business orientated tour where we had prearranged meetings with the local government officials to preview future trade arrangements.

In Tobago we were wined and dined by the US embassy at one of their homes. It was official but it was relaxing; I think the Americans present were happy just to visit with Americans that had just arrived from the states with news of economic interest.

Besides our business meetings we were invited on a day long boat cruise to an island off Tobago. It was so beautiful there and the day went too fast.

I loved relaxing on the sandy beaches during the day and in the evening we enjoyed the band of steel drum music echoing through out the area. We sat in easy chairs under the umbrellas as the sun was beginning to sink in the western skies. As we sat enjoying sipping our cool drinks waiting for the evening meal to come it was magic in the air with music and friends but when the food was served the laughter and conversations stopped and a quiet fellowship took over.

I was fortune to be able to purchase an authentic steel drum. I packed it away in one of my suitcases for the trip home. It was a memory of the islands and just recently I gave the steel drum to my son-in-law Joe Hicks. I look forward to hearing him play for our own family gatherings.

SMITHSONIAN WASHINGTON DC

Louise took a four day World Banking seminar in Washington D.C. on March 6, 1989 so on Mar. 5th we flew to Washington DC where we had reservations at the Days Inn at Tyson Corner, Virginia. It was about 20 miles out of

Washington D.C. so we made arrangements to go into downtown via commuter train. The Days Inn courtesy bus took us the three miles to catch the commuter train. We bought week long passes for $20.00 each and each morning and night made the trip from and to downtown DC.

Each day I went with Louise to her stop at the World Bank building. After I saw her safely indoors at the guarded door I took the train to the Smithsonian buildings. For three days I kept the same routine. With my commuter train pass I could get on and off the train easily.

The last day of Louise's seminar she got tickets for both of us to tour the White House. It was exciting to walk the corridors that we had only read about. The paintings that were lining the walls alone where so impressive.

On Friday Louise joined me and we purchased all day bus tickets for touring the Kennedy Center, Lincoln Memorial, Arlington National Cemetery, The Library of Congress and The Ford Theater where Lincoln was assassinated. We visited the Congress and the Supreme Court building, they were not in session and the FBI building. We were on and off that bus all day long; it was tiring but it was worth it all. Louise only visited the Smithsonian for a little while but I had gotten to spend 4 days there and will never forget the magnitude of it all.

On Sunday we caught our train for downtown DC but changed trains and traveled southeast to Dulles airport where we caught a tour bus that took us to the George Washington estate along the Potomac River called Mount Vernon. The house and building on the estate were just as they had been when Washington lived there. The tour was well worth the time it took to go out there by bus. The Washington's burial site overlooks the Potomac River; one could see why the family had loved this spot so much.

Louise had a memorable seminar on World Banking but I had my leisure time to view the many displays at the Smithsonian besides time to see the other sites with Louise. It was a trip we have captured in our minds as we watch stories of DC making history and visualizing we were there if only for a short time.

2ND INGRAHAM REUNION

July 28, 29, 30, 1989 was a reunion held with other Ingraham families at SunLakes Resort, Washington. This reunion brought Ingraham out of California and Montana who came to meet their relatives; many met for the first time. In fact we had forty one signed signatures of attendance that all came to enjoy meeting close relatives that they did not know until this time. Everyone had a wonderful time.

Below is Louise, Willard and grandson Paul.

Many people that attended that reunion are no longer with us. Look what we would have missed had a reunion not taken place.

AUSTRALIA, NEW ZEALAND AND FIJI

September 1989 we escorted a group for 21 days through Australia, New Zealand and Fiji. In New Zealand we toured the Bay of Islands, Rotorua, Queenstown, Mt. Cook, and Christ Church. New Zealand is mostly covered with beautiful green fields with flocks and flocks of sheep. In fact our tour group was divided up into small groups and we spent one night at a farm home raising different crops and animals.

Louise and I visited a dairy farm. It was much like at home except the terrain was so different than what we saw at home. Also the dinner meal served by the family was roast leg of lamb with served with their famous green sauce and kiwi pie for dessert.

Some of our group enjoyed a stay at a horse breeding farm of race horses and another at a typical sheep farm. These were personal experiences for each group and ones we would all repeat. Matter of fact we repeated the same kind of culture exchange while in Christ Church when our group again was divided into small groups and we were invited to dine with families that were interested in an exchange program to visit families in the USA.

Below are unusual rocks along the sea shore; they are called Moebaki boulders.

In Australia, we visited the Great Barrier Reef and treated to a day cruise over the reef. The brave ones of the groups had and opportunity to swim on the reef. They stopped the boat about a mile from shore on a coral reef and told us to

get out in about 4 ft deep water. They warned us not to get close to the edge of the reef a few hundred feet from one side of the boat; the drop off into the ocean was thousands of feet.

Have you ever visited a butterfly sanctuary? We did and it was one I will never forget; butterflies of all colors flying in the open around you from all directions.

This also is the land of the kangaroo and we saw many of them along the roads as we were bused north from Sydney and on our return trip.

Sydney was impressive; the famous opera house is near the bay so there was water everywhere that added to the beauty of such a setting for an opera (pictured below).

A stop over on the way to the states was Fiji Islands with 300 separate islands. Now that was a culture experience. They dressed in their native attire which was colorful and different as was the island music and dances. The food was on

the spicy side but delicious. Our stop over was perfect for the last day out and our next destination was USA and home.

3RD INGRAHAM REUNION

We held our third Ingraham northwest family reunion on July 27, 28, 29, 1990. A group area was set aside at the American Heritage Campground near Tumwater, Washington.

It is a short distance from Olympia, Washington, the capital of Washington state.

The campground had heated pools, recreation hall, convenience store, laundry, volley ball court, horse shoe and a huge sheltered picnic pavilion. There were go-cart rentals and nightly horse drawn wagon rides. Everyone again enjoyed meeting all their relatives and many new ones according to our sign in book we had at least 55 people in our group.

A photo of the group is below.

ALLIED SERVICES

In the summer of 1990 Joe and Mary Ann Hicks wanted to sell Allied Services and move back to Arizona. Louise and I did not want to run the business alone so we sold it. Joe went ahead to Arizona and got a teaching job. It was all preplanned that after Joe left the rest of us would stay until the store was sold.

Louise had retired in April, 1989 from branch management at Washington Mutual so as soon as the store the new owners of the store took over we were both retired and free to take the trip to Arizona.. Mary Ann had sold their home in Kennewick and was anxious to get to Arizona to join Joe.

Below is how the store front looked when we sold out.

It was late in September 1990 that we loaded Mary Ann and Joe's household items in our motor home ready for the trip south. Even the Izuzu pickup I would be towing was loaded as well as Mary Ann and Joe's car that she would be driving down. We left in a caravan for Arizona with Mary Ann and Shannon; the plan was for Louise and I to stay until the new house Joe and Mary Ann was having built in Gilbert was completed.

We pulled our motor home into a park at Apache Junction where Joe was already staying in his parent's park model unit. All the household items were put in storage and Shannon was enrolled in school.

The new house was under construction at Val Vista Lake at Gilbert and Joe was teaching everyday. The three of us, Mary Ann, Louise and I (Willard) did what we could in electrical installations and painting as the contractor built the new home. It was a fun time; we would take Shannon to school in the morning and then we had the pleasure of driving all over Phoenix to help Mary Ann find appliances, lighting fixtures and replacing furniture for their new home. By Xmas they moved in and before the New Year came Louise and I headed back home to the Tri-Cites. Mary Ann went to work for an engineer company.

THREE WEEK TRIP THROUGH 8 STATES

At 8:00 A.M, May 6, 1991, Willard and Louise Ingraham and Arnold and Lucille Steffens left Kennewick, Wa. headed for a three week trip that took us through 8 states and Mexico. We took our 1985 Chevrolet Blazer and covered over 5000 miles. Richard and Charlene Williams lived in Boise, Idaho so we met them at Dennys for a coffee break. We enjoyed our visit and were on our way stopping at a Best Western in Mountain Home, Idaho overnight.

May 7th we drove about 50 miles to Buhl, Idaho and had breakfast at a restaurant with Arnold's friend from his service years in World War II. From this stop we drove to Evanston, Utah where we stayed at another Best Western.

May 8th we drove to Ft. Bridger and visited the fort there and had breakfast before continuing through the Flaming Gorge and on to Vernal, Utah to a dinosaur quarry near Dinosaur, Utah. There we observed thousands of dinosaur fossils. Workers were excavating while we were there and we were able to observe how very tedious their work was but also how dedicated they were in searching for new finds.

The photo below is a reconstructed skeleton of a dinosaur that the bones had been found in the rocks near the location of the museum.

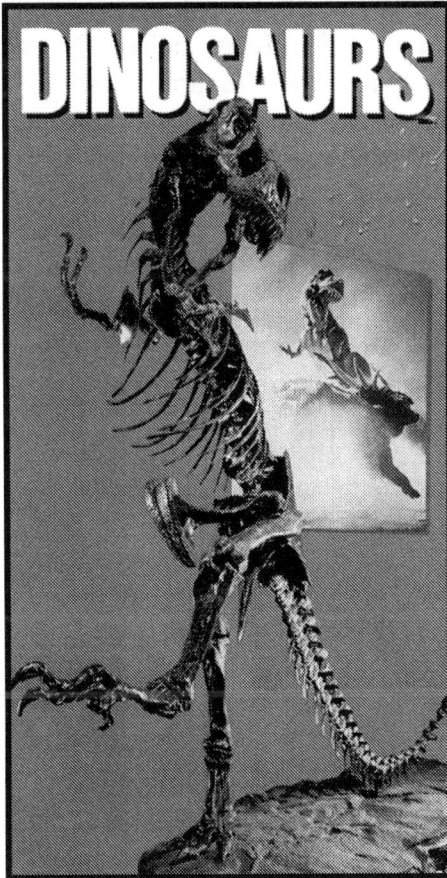

This was back country at its wildest and we saw hundreds of antelopes roaming the green river area; some were close to the road. We were fortunate to have been directed to see the petrogliphics on the walls of the hills in that area. It was Indian country passed that was for sure but they had left their images for us to marvel at their communication skills during their time. The end of the trail that day was the cabin of Josie Bassett Morris. It was much like Josie had left it except the cabin was weathered and the grasses tall as if many seasons had gone by with no human visitors. It was a lonely spot now with only the wild animals as intruders.

We drove back the road we came in to Craig, Colorado. It was a western town where everyone knew each other except we were the strangers and the locals spotted us as such when we went into the restaurant that evening. They were friendly but more curious to why we came their way.

486

May 9th we left Craig, Colorado and traveled hi-way 789 to Rifle where we entered hiway 70 traveling through Eisenhower tunnel (1 mile long) and through Vail, Co. then over Loveland Pass. The roadway sides were lined with trees and the mountains areas reflected a call of the skiers in Colorado's winter season. We could still see patches of snow on the banks even though this was May. We turned north to +Estes Park and it was a strange site to have the trees open up to a lodge and in the center of the huge clearing was a steam engine train. It had been left there as a memorial and reminder of the early days when tracks actually led through this area.

Our trip took us from Estes Park to the main north-south hiway into Denver. There was so much to see in Denver that we stayed two nights at the Inn at the Mart. It was the morning of the 10th that we toured the capital

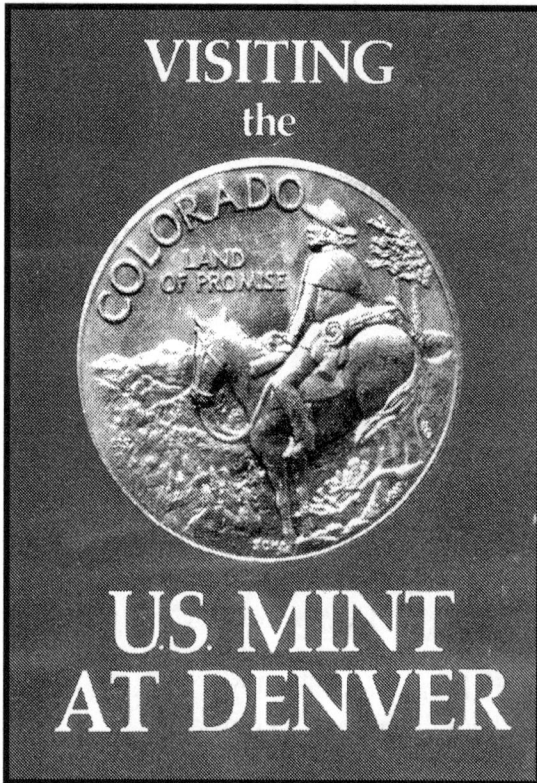

VISITING the COLORADO LAND OF PROMISE U.S. MINT AT DENVER

building and the U.S. mint where all the coins are stamped with a D on them (above is a photo); this is their signature of the Denver minted coin.

487

Then we walked to Larimer Square on the big mall of Denver and back to our motel.

Randle and Linda Shelton lived in Denver at that time so we gave them a call and they came to our hotel where we all enjoyed their company and dinner together at the hotel restaurant.

Our stay at Denver had been fun but we were ready for the next excursion and headed south to Colorado Springs. Just north of the city is the academy for cadets. It is a huge campus and full of young energetic cadets. Some where there from appointments by their senators and others were lucky to be able to attend such a prestigious academy without recommendations. All had to pass the same entrance examine and upon graduation would have officer positions in the service.

We stayed in Colorado Springs at a Holliday Inn. We always looked for good rated hotels with upscale accommodations. The Holliday was no exception; they had a suite that was normally at that time $125 a night and with a little co-horsing and passing out our travel hosting cards we were able to stay for $50.00 a night. Our suite had two bedrooms, with baths, a kitchen and a dining living room area. It was a perfect spot to stay and close enough to all the sites we had on our itinerary to see.

The day we arrived they were having an auction in the public area of the hotel; we had fun looking and bought down pillows!

The sing song story of Cripple Creek was on a round record that Louise and Lucille's parents had on an old megaphone type player that went like this; "Going up Cripple Creek, Going up Cripple Creek without a paddle" and so on. The girls had a Cripple Creek stop on the agenda and so it was we drove out to the old mining town turned tourist attraction the next day. It was in mining country all right; there were vacant mining holes all around that old town. The shopping was fun and I bought Louise a turquoise and coral watchband. A photo of Cripple Creek and area is below.

From Cripple Creek we were told we could take a short cut to Royal Gorge bridge. This area was desolate and looked much like the terrain around Cripple Creek.

Soon we were on a dirt road going into a canyon. We drove 27 miles on a shelf road with a deep canyon below. The roadway was all dirt winding around the canyon walls. We were advised before we took this route to only go if we had a 4-wheel drive. It was not unusual they told us to have washouts on the road, the road would be narrow and there would be no gas stations for miles. I enjoyed the drive but Louise did not. She did not like the narrow road hanging and clinging high up on the side of the cliff. After a very scenic 40 mile drive the canyon road opened up and we came to Canyon City. Louise called this not a city but a heap in the middle of the road; a few buildings and not much else except an old fashioned dilapidated building called a service station.

A short distance from there we drove across some flat land. Just ahead, the road opened up on the brink of a canyon with a towering bridge across it that was 1,055 feet above the rushing Arkansas River. This is the Royal Gorge Bridge (photo below)and is the world's highest suspension bridge and a major attraction in Colorado. It was a spectacular view from the bridge. I stopped the car and got out and looked over the edge in mid span. I couldn't get any one else to get out of the car. Louise was more than a little apprehensive going across that bridge in the car. It did have a slight sway; it was a suspension bridge.

Our return trip back to Colorado Springs was not on the short cut we had taken from Cripple Creek. We were able to connect to a freeway not far from the Royal Gorge by taken a road to the south. It was a little further but far safer.

That night we stayed again at the Holiday Inn in our luxury suite at Colorado Springs. We were enjoying the hotel so much we took it for an additional day. There were more things to see.

The next day we took a cog wheel train ride up Pikes Peak and back. The cog wheel train had been there 100 years and they were celebrating the occasion. The tour took 3 hours and the temperature was 22 degrees on top of Pikes Peak. It was a bird eye view up there and a clear day so we could really see the longer distance into the far away haze.

The Garden of the Gods was our next stop and very picturesque. The stone entrance looked like God must have put it all together for all of us just to be awed when we viewed it. Louise remembered that her mother had a picture postcard of the Garden of the Gods written by her sister Oral in the 1920s when she lived at Colorado Springs.

The Wind Caves were nearby and still had evidence of the Indian fire pits in some of the caves. Carvings were on the walls and stones piled up in places. It was no wonder the Indians used these caves to live in; they were safely embedded in the side of huge steep hills where they could see and keep any invaders out.

The Will Roger shrine is located in Colorado Springs. It has a zoo and a tower built on the side of a mountainous fortress. The road winds around to get up to the zoo and to the tower. The tower steps are spiral and along the walls are pictures of Will Rogers. It was all impressive.

The seven falls in Colorado Springs was beautiful; of coarse it was commercialized with lights in the evening but one did not think of that when we saw the 7 falls flowing out and down the rocks from the side of that mountain. This is considered on of natures beauties; even the locals they say never tire of taking excursions to the falls area and having family picnics in the park near the falls.

That Sunday was Mothers Day and we guys took our girls out to a Mothers Day dinner at the Mason Jar Restaurant. It was old fashioned; we drank our water out of old mason jars but the food was wonderful and the girls loved it.

May 13th, we started this day by attending the Pro
Cowboy Hall of Fame.

We had to have our photo taken in front of the Pro
Cowboy Hall; below left to right Willard and Louise and
Lucille and Arnold.

Our next was to visit the Hall of the Presidents. All the
presidents were done in wax figures. The artistic ability of
these artists was incredible. We made our last stop of the day
at the Van Briggle Art Pottery barn. Louise bought some
pottery that was signed.

May 14th we left Colorado Springs at 7:10 A.M. going
south on 25 toward Pueblo. A stop at Cimmeron, New Mexico
and local cowboy lure was evident here at the hotel; they even
had gun shot holes in the salon tables. They told us that the
ghosts of these cowboys gone on visited every night. They
invited us to view one of the up stair rooms and told us to
watch as we went up and back down on the stairs as we just
might see the shadow of one of those cowboys. The only

shadows I saw were our own but Louise thought she could smell the gun smoke of the cowboy days!

Our road took us around Three Sisters Mountain to Pueblo and the Quant Indian Villiage on the Toas Indian reservation. We visited the village but it was so commercialized it took the fun out of it. The best part was the little Indian children; we watched them play and could imagine their games were not much different than their ancestors.

We left for Chamos and Santa Fe, New Mexico and overnight at Santa Fe. May 15th we were up early and drove down to the Santa Fe Plaza.

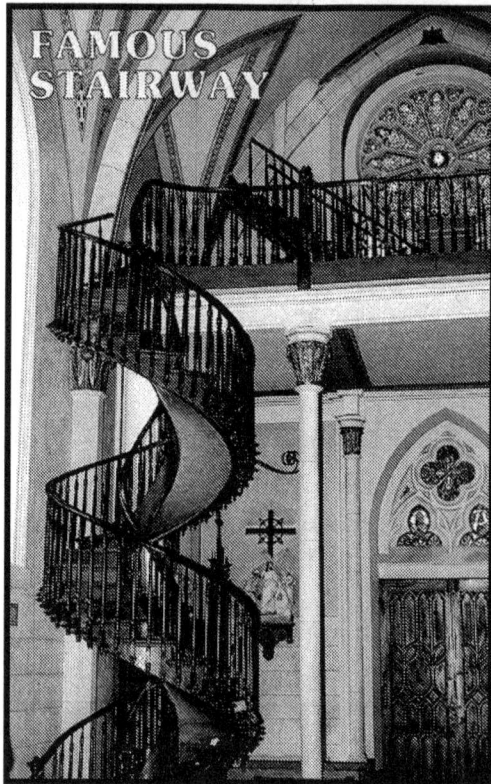

We visited the Loretto Chapel. (photo left) Legend has it that the church needed a stairway to the balcony but no one knew how to build it. An old man appeared about that time who happened to be a carpenter. With hammer, saw and chisel he built this suspended stairway with nothing holding it up. Upon finishing the staircase the old man asked nothing for his wages and disappeared like he came leaving the modern day architects still in amazement at how the suspended stair case was build and still stands. The miracle staircase without support it is called.

493

Our next excursion was down highway 14 to Sandia Crest which is the highest scenic drive in the southwest. It is a winding road up to the top to 10,678 feet overlooking Albuquerque, N. Mexico. That night we stayed at the Comfort Inn in Albuquerque and the next day drove to the continental divide which is 7275 feet in elevation. Rainfall divides at this point; to the west it drains into the Pacific Ocean and to the East into the Atlantic Ocean.

Traveling on the next day we passed into the state of Arizona and visited the Petrified Forrest National Park. We saw beautiful petrified wood in multiple colors. It was amazing that so much petrified wood was still lying around in pieces and clumps after so many years gone by. We stayed that night at Adobe Inn at Holbrook, Arizona.

May 17th we visited the meteor crater in northern Arizona. We had our photo taken on the rim of the crater.

LOUISE, WILLARD INGRAHAM AND FAMILY

About 49,500 years ago, an unbroken level plain stretched across this whole area of the crater. Out of the north a bright pin point of light rose rapidly into a blazing sun as it approached this spot. It was traveling nearly 43,000 miles per hour and with deafening sound and blinding light a huge nickel iron meteorite or cluster of such meteorites weighing millions of tons struck the solid rock of the level plain with forces greater than any recorded nuclear explosion. The main mass was instantly converted to a gaseous state and a huge mushroom shaped cloud arose far into the stratosphere. From this cloud rained meteoritic droplets mixed with rock debris for miles around; every tree was flattened and no living creature survived. Before impact pieces of meteorite weighing up to a ton or more were stripped from the mass by friction of the lower atmosphere. In all about 300 million tons of rock were displaced much of it forming the raise rim around the crater. The floor of the crater is 560 feet deep. The rim is more than 3 miles in circumference. The crater was first reported by white men in 1871.

From the crater area we visited the Grand Canyon at South Rim above the Colorado River that runs deep in the canyon. Louise and I shot the rapids of the Colorado River through these canyons in May of 1973. We could see the mule trail we had taken out of the canyon from phantom ranch and view rubber raft boats way down there on the river. The trail down to Phantom Ranch is called the Bright Angel Trail. We stayed over night at a Travel Lodge at Flagstaff, Arizona.

May 18th we traveled down highway 17 to Sedona; a very colorful and interesting place to visit. They claim they have a vortex where all the energies of the universe meet that those believing can form miracles here. It is a magical spot and the atmosphere is full of energy like electrical currents.

The desert surround these Sedona sights was in bloom with the pincushion cactus, desert poppies, ocotillos, desert primrose and dandelions and thousands of saguaro cacti.

Our next stop was Jerome, Arizona that precariously clings to the side of Cleopatra Hill overlooking the Verde Valley. Jerome was once known as the Billion Dollar Copper Camp. After most of the town's 15,000 residents departed in 1953 it is now called a ghost town. Jerome survived and is now a gold and silver mining community.

We left the Jerome area traveling south to Gilbert, a suburb of Phoenix to our daughter Mary Ann, son-in-law's Joe Hick's and granddaughter Shannon Hicks home to visit on May 19-20, 1991. All of us visited the Phoenix Zoo the next day and in the evening attended a western program and theatre with country music and dinner.

On May 21st we drove to Nogales, Mexico for site seeing returning to Tucson for overnight. It was the next day on the 22nd that we went to the International Wildlife Museum then to Old Tucson. Old Tucson is an old western town that many movies are filmed at. We saw an old western shoot out in the streets; all live actors in a two hour outside live show. It was so real it took us back to the old western days.

We drove back to Joe and Mary Ann's and stayed another day or two; they always make you feel right at home when visiting them. It was most enjoyable to see everyone again and reacquaint with our granddaughter Shannon.

We said our goodbyes on May 25th and headed for Havasu, Arizona. A highlight there is the old London Bridge that the locals had shipped in from England piece by piece and reconstructed on the edge of their town; it is a tourist attraction but because it is authentic it is also history.

Our last major stop was Las Vegas and taking in the sites on the strip. Our highlight here was Circus Circus acts performed nightly and great to watch. At our hotel, they offered wonderful around the clock buffets. Next day we left Las Vegas and a day and half drive home. We reveled in the memories and carried with us photos to go with the memories. We had gone full circle so to speak from Wash. and back.

LOUISE, WILLARD INGRAHAM AND FAMILY

4TH INGRAHAM REUNION

Jim and Fern Goemmer and Louise and I (Willard) agreed to host the 4th Ingraham reunion on July 25, 26, 27, 28, 1991 at Westgate Motor and Trailer Court at Ocean Park, Washington on Long Beach.

Long Beach boasts of being the World's longest sandy beach where there is much to do like clam digging, beach combing, charter boat fishing for various types of fishing including salmon.

The location of the camp grounds that we stayed (pictured above) is right along the ocean beach and over the sand dunes we could hear the mystical roar of the ocean waves all night. We had our pot luck and wiener roasts right out on the sandy ocean beach. Harry and Wildred Ingraham were our professional musicians and singers as was Lisa Ingraham (wife of Rick Ingraham) a professional violinist. During our stay there was lots of music and enjoyment by all. Lisa plays in the symphony at Tacoma where she lives.

We ended the last morning of our stay here at a no host breakfast and short meeting at Grannie Annie's restaurant in their Surf Room at Ocean Park. It was another successful reunion with 45 people attending. The next reunion date was planned for 1992 and to be hosted by Marvin and Mavy Ingraham and Harry and Wildred Ingraham at Laurel, Montana.

5TH INGRAHAM REUNION

July 23, 1992 Louise and I (Willard) left our home in Kennewick, Wa. for Laurel, Montana to attend the 5th Ingraham family reunion at Marvin and Mavy Ingraham's home. We had reservations at the Best Western Locomotive Inn in Laurel.

Our hosts had a lovely program planned and all the Ingraham's and familys joined in. Again Harry and Wildred Ingraham played and sang beautiful songs and dance music.

Photo below is left to right; Harry, Wildred, Willard, Mavy and Marvin Ingraham.

Kenneth Weatherford, son of Bob and Cenra Weatherford, a National Roller Skating Champion gave us a demonstration at his parent's public roller skating rink in Laurel. I must say that Kenneth's exhibition on skates was indeed professional. It was great watching him.

Our hosts planned a no host dinner at the Palm Beach Supper Club and again there was music and entertainment including a dancing exhibition from Claud and Lorreine Ingraham. They were members of the Sons Of Norway Round

Dancing group and their skills on the dance floor were wonderful.

The Ingraham's above posed for a photo and are backrow left to right: Willard, Harold, Harry, Norman, Ray, Roy, Marvin and Leonard Ingraham. The ladies in front are left to right: Lorraine Johnston, Lorna Lindeman, Claud Ingraham, Harriet Drawns and Fern Goemmer.

The last morning we met at a no host breakfast at the Locomotive Inn banquet room. There was a short meeting to see who would host the 1993 Ingraham reunion and Jim and Lorna Lindeman won that honor. This 1992 reunion was another successful reunion with 69 attending.

Louise and I decided to extend our vacation and left Laurel for Jamestown, N.D. on July 27, 1992. We stopped at Bismark, N.D., the state capital of North Dakota to get additional information for my genealogy records. While in the capital building we walked by George A. Sinner's office. He was the governor of N. D. He was not in at that time but his

secretary said go ahead and set in the governor's chair to get a
picture. I did (photo below) and kidding said now I was
governor of North Dakota for one minute.

We drove across the Missouri River Bridge to Ft.
Mandan where Lt. Col. George Custer was stationed before he
went to his death in the Custer massacre in Montana. We
noticed there were oil wells in North Dakota. We stopped at
the Dakota Inn at Jamestown, N. D. that night where they had a
nice restaurant. We called my relatives to join us and my Aunt
Louise Schuff, Aunt Esther Sorenson, Aunt Doris Rosenau and
husband Ray along with cousin, Harriet and husband Vern
Wahl all joined us for dinner. It was a gathering of the clan
and we shared family information way into the night.

The next day we headed south to Sioux Falls, S. Dakota
where we met with my Aunt Gladys Steffen and cousins,

Harold and Luella Steffen and Don and Marie Steffen. It was another evening with dinner and sharing family information.

On the road again we saw the corn palace at Mitchell, S.D. and on to Mt. Rushmore, S.D. where we saw the great stone faces of George Washington, Thomas, Jefferson, Theodore Roosevelt, Abraham Lincoln and the still unfinished carving of Crazy Horse and his horse (photo below).

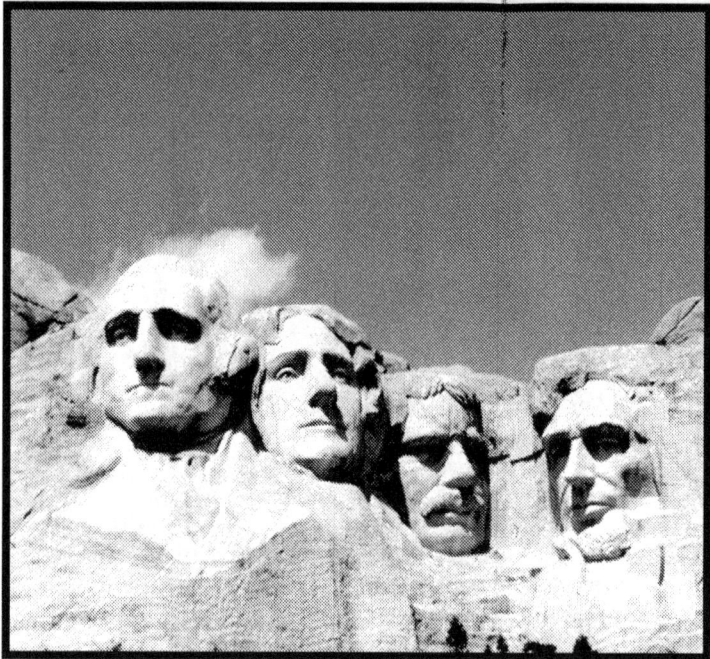

We continued on to Rapid City, S.D. where we visited more cousins, Charles Johnson and wife Delores, Sandra and her husband Juel Dahlke. Charles and Sandra are brothers and sister to Lois Knudson. My cousins took us out to the Elks for dinner and dancing. What a wonderful time we had.

The next day we drove to Yellowstone National Park. It was quite a change from the last time we saw it years ago. We had bears stopping us all along the road in the park then but this time we never saw one bear. In their place we did see many buffalo and the remains after a forest fire had gone through and had destroyed much of the greenery. The terrain was bleak and the scenery was dismal compared to what it had been on our first visit.

After Yellow Stone it was time to go back home to Kennewick, Washington.

6TH INGRAHAM FAMILY REUNION

July 23, 1993 Lorna and Jim Lindeman hosted the Ingraham reunion at Red River Hot Springs near Elk City, Idaho. It is a resort in the mountains with a swimming pool fed by a hot water spring. The lodge here is rustic and primitive compared to most resorts with outlying one room cabins to stay in but the setting was what one would expect in a remote area.

The pool was from a hot springs pictured below with the clubhouse to the right.

At night we were all aware of the bears and wild animals that roamed the compound and were all careful to stay indoors. Oh yes, Louise reminded me it was necessary to have an indoor potty; the bathrooms were located at the swimming pool area in the center of the compound. It could be a dangerous walk at night from cabin to bathroom.

The resort we were told was a favorite place for deer and elk hunters in the fall of the year. The road getting into the lodge was a muddy trail; our grandson Paul Jordan can attest to that. He rode a motorcycle coming in and it had been raining; the roadbed was mucky and slick (photo below).

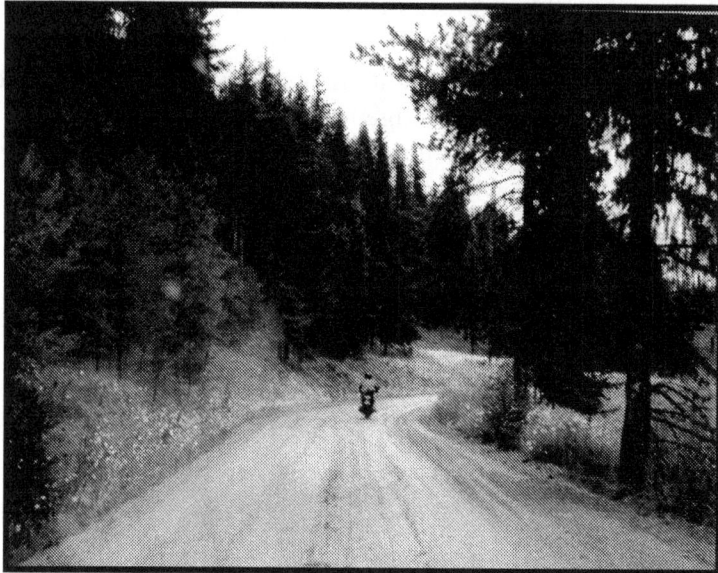

Paul was lucky he only took one spill and was happy that his cousin's Mark and Debbie loaded his cycle onto their pickup for the trip back out at the end of the reunion.

We enjoyed the warm water swimming and pot luck meals the reunion group provided. We also played various games including water volley ball. 20 persons attended this reunion in this mountainous area.

The 1994 reunion was to be hosted by Marijean Ingraham of Salt Lake City, Utah. It was called off at the last moment because of the death of one of her grandchildren.

DISNEY WORLD

October 28, 1993 Arnold and Lucille Steffens and Louise and I (Willard) Ingraham left the Pasco, Wa. Air port headed for Orlando, Fl. Via Salt Lake City, Ut. and Atlanta,

Georga. We signed in at the Holiday Inn at Orlando where Arnold's 2072 army group was having a reunion held at our hotel. A photo of Orlando is above.

We spent the week-end enjoying the reunion group. They had lots of snacks and a program as well as had dinners planned for the group. Everyone was so friendly and cordial; it was a reunion that they made Louise and I feel a part of.

While we were there we visited the Kennedy Space Center and Cape Kennedy where a shuttle was sitting on a pad ready to launch in a few days. The area had on display the first space ship; it was awesome to think what science had accomplished. It seemed to us that space travel would one day in the future be a natural accepted journey rather than a phenomenon.

When the reunion was over one of Arnold's friends drove us to Disney World where we had three day reservations with tickets included to tour Disney World and the Universal Studios. The next days were full; walking through Disney World and using our tickets we had purchased to take advantage of the numerous rides available. One of the rides we liked was a boat ride down the steep slide into a pool. It was awesome.

We also took in some of the shows at the Universal Studios that included an IMAX theatre with Mr. Ed and his talking horse. We saw the famous son of Lassie perform at an open theatre. It was magic and I would recommend Disney World and the Universal Studios to any family. It was a lot of fun and so much to see. I do not know how many times Louise and I wished our grandchildren had been with us, as did Arnold and Lucille.

JIM AND FERN GOEMMER'S 50TH ANNIVERSARY

Left photo: L t R: Vivian and Robert, Fern and Jim and daughter Carolynn and son Billie. Fern and Jim celebrated their 50th anniversary on April 4, 1994 at Gig Harbor, Washington at the community clubhouse where they live. Louise and I (Willard) attended; we were happy to be a part of the celebration with relatives and many friends. It was lovely with memories and photo sharing and later dinner was hosted by Jim and Fern.

505

OUR HOBBIES

It was in 1994 and 1995 that Louise and I (Willard) tried to slow our pace of life a little by beginning our oil painting hobby. Soon we started to fill up our walls and those of our family with paintings. Then we bought a couple of ceramic kilns and fired ceramic figures of birds, animals, flower vases and other articles. These too began to pile up with our painting projects and I got interested in zipper art that my brother Ray Ingraham taught me. He had learned the art while wintering in Arizona as a snow bird. This art was fascinating to me; I outlined figures of birds, animals and objects all in pieces of zippers then I filled in the enclosed areas with colored sand (below is photo of my zipper art).

I have not forgotten my wood shop and the times I made wood tables from black walnut tree slabs that I had cut to size and planned the smaller boards for fine furniture. I made complete sets; one was a Victorian library table and sofa table set for the living room. I turned the legs with a turning lathe; this set was one of a kind that we still have today.

Also like the rock tables I had made for years I designed and used my semi precious stones that I had cut with a rock saw as well as slabs of petrified wood and agates all cut into ¼ inch slabs and set everything into a design on the table tops. These then were all embedded into resin that gave not only a hard surface but a 3d look (photo of tables below).

After working with the finer arts, Louise and I got interested in stain glass projects. There were window and wall hangings that we cut and soldered into designs. At first, we both made small window hangings of flowers and simple art. Then we progressed to larger pieces; Louise made one of an

ocean scene. One of my favorites is the carousel horse that
hangs in one of our windows (photo below).

(photo above); it was going to be a stained glass village and
Louise started the first piece; got to the grocery store roof and
said, "this is too intricate for me." I took over and increased
the size of the village with numerous glass buildings including
a church, a stream of water flowing around the perimeter and a
train to run on the tracks I built. -

All for a purpose and it was quite a day when I finally talked Louise into letting me display the stained glass village onto a bigger table set up in the living room. At first she couldn't believe she had allowed me to take over such a big corner of the room but with lights and wall mirrors I think she has adjusted to having it in place. The problem is always one wants to increase the collection and after our visit to the carousel museum in up state New York we were ready to make a stained glass carousel. (photo below).

It just sort of evolved in more than one carousel, stained glass lamps and other glass art. Louise was interested in hot glass so she turned to making stained glass objects from designing and melting the glass in a kiln to portray her designs.

Willard's oil paintings, a landscape above and a deer painting below are a couple examples of his oil expertise.

Louise was producing oil paints also; one ocean scene is below.

With our carousel and ceramic horse collection and angels on the mantle along with our nativity set, stained glass lamps and other stained glass with our oil paintings displayed, we are told the room looks more like a museum than a living room.

There is so much one can stretch the mind into making art designs of all kind. We have filled the walls of Mary Ann and Joe's home with our art; even our grandson Paul took an oil painting to Seattle. Louise turned to photography on the computer and designs, illustrates and writes her own versus for greeting cards. With the living room full I turned to the back yard with stepping stones of concrete and painted designs on top and other stepping stones with embedded stain glass designs of animals and birds on the top. After the pathways were full the next was a garden table top of stained glass designed with beautiful butterflies. Louise got interested in mosaic glass patterns for our garden benches tops and together we surrounded our yard with our handy-work.

I turned to stained glass jewelry boxes, bathroom tissue sets and napkin holders; soon I had stained glass all over the house and it was time to turn to another kind of productivity.

OUR PETS

March 1993; when our granddaughter Shannon Ann Hicks was a very young girl she raised purebred Maltese dogs. Her Maltese had long lists of recorded show dogs in their pedigrees. Shannon cared for her animals even in the time of birthing for all the puppies that came along. She had a knack for handling these small little animals and they loved her as their care taker and handler.

Shannon was also very generous and she asked me if I was to have a dog what would I name it. I told her that I did not want a dog but Shannon was persistent and finally I told her if I had a dog it would be called invisible because it would be invisible. So it was in 1993 Shannon gave me a Maltese puppy for my birthday. She called me to tell me she had a cute little puppy and said, "Grandpa I have your little dog Invisible." I was taken back for a moment but said no I do not want a dog. Again, Shannon was very persuasive and finally I agreed; she then said, "what are you going to call your dog?" I told her that was easy; it would be Indy which was short for invisible.

So it was that we brought Indy home to Washington. In 1995 Indy was old enough to breed so we took her to Yakima to a breeder of show dogs, all Maltese. The papers on these Maltese were impressive with a line of show dogs in record. So it was Indy had her own litter. I wasn't as good at bringing the puppies through as Shannon. One puppy arrived breach that I lost and another so very small that it died soon after but the third one, Cuddles, we saved. That was a puppy pay back that was for Shannon and her generosity.

LOUISE, WILLARD INGRAHAM AND FAMILY

The Maltese are expensive so this project for Shannon not only loved the animals but it was way for her to make her own money. It was in March of 1995 when Shannon was 14 years old and she had a week of spring vacation from school so she bought an airline ticket with her parent's permission and came to Kennewick, Washington to visit us. She would be taking Cuddles home on the plane.

While Shannon was here Louise and I took Shannon to Surfside Resort near Lincoln City, Oregon located overlooking the beach of the Pacific Ocean. It is a beautiful place to spend a vacation; our resort accommodations were just above the ocean se we could see the sea lions sunning themselves and frolicking in the water.

Shannon wanted to swim in the ocean but I could not let her because there were very dangerous under currents and rip tides in that area and it was too dangerous to take any chances. Shannon was a beautiful swimmer with blue ribbons to her credit but a good swimmer is no match for the rip tides so we convinced her that the resort had a nice big indoor pool and the beach was a good place to wade and play in the sand.

It was a beautiful time we had spending a vacation with our granddaughter and oh yes her puppy, Cuddles. We had brought her Maltese with us so that Shannon could get acquainted with her new puppy before boarding the plane with her to take her home.

We had checked with the airlines and as long as Cuddles was in a dog carrier Shannon could place the bag and puppy on the floor in front of her seat. We were nervous because Shannon was young and was flying alone with a puppy and a plane change in Salt Lake. We need not have worried as we were told that Shannon and Cuddles was the flight attraction with all and the stewardess helped to make sure all went well even at Salt Lake with the plane change. I have to give Shannon credit for handling it all so well; she was a very mature, self confident lady at 14 and her smile could melt anyone.

My dog Indy needed obedience training so I signed her
up with a group class. I was her personnel trainer and took her
through her paces; she learned all the commands to sit, stay,
heel, come and hold a position in a room full of other dogs of
all breeds well within the eight week class. In fact she earned a
blue ribbon along with her certificate. Indy was superb; we
knew she was smart but she excelled with my voice and
understanding. What more can one expect from ones little
friend who only wants to please you. Indy gives back ten fold
for all the love she poured out to us as a family pet.

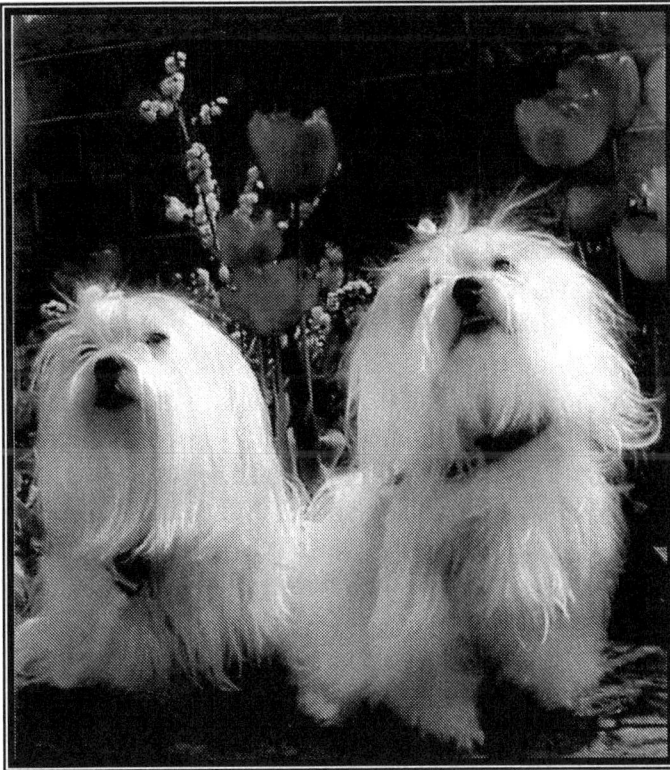

In 1998 Shannon gave Louise a bundle of fur, a Maltese
named Mitzie (photos of Mitzie and Indy above). Mitzie too
had the same obedience training. I took her through her paces

of learning at obedience and Louise handled Indy in the group training classes, as the instructor felt watching Indy perform would encourage the others to follow her lead.

Mitzie also came out of the class receiving a blue ribbon but she has an entirely different personality than Indy and a mind of her own. I left her sitting during the final testing and walked away. She sat there until somehow she knew the time was up even though the instructor had misjudged and not called it; Mitzie had her own way of solving the problem as she just walked off the floor with her head held high.

OUR CALIFORNIA TRIP

We did take time off in October of 1995 to take a trip to California with Arnold and Lucille Steffens. I drove our 1992 blazer and we left on Otober 4, 1995. Our first night was at Winnemucca, Nevada. This overnight gave us a short drive the next day to Reno where we checked out the casinos.

We traveled from Reno across the mountains into Sacramento, California. The mountains were full of abandon gold mines from the 1849 gold rush days. Even the small towns we went through had the look of a forgotten era.

In Sacramento, we joined Arnold's army group for a army reunion. Louise and I enjoyed the friendly group and the program and dinner they had planned. While we were there Louise and I went to Rainbow Glass Works and purchased a small fast flux ceramic kiln with Paragon controls and had it shipped home.

Arnold and I had a cousin, Dorothy Clare that lived near Sacramento and she had invited us to come to her home for dinner. Dorothy is the daughter of our Aunt Gladys Steffen of Sioux Falls, South Dakota. We met Dorothy's husband Kenneth Clare and their daughter Sandra and her husband Bruce Wade. It was a wonderful dinner and our visit was special.

The next day we headed north traveling toward the coast and through the red wood and the tree of Mystery. We drove the blazer through the arched opening in a huge chandelier redwood tree (photo below)..

A stop at the Paul Bunyan stature and gift shop was a must. We saw the world famous tree house, the big tree heights was 304 feet, diameter 21.6 feet and circumference 68 feet. It is estimated to be 1500 years old.

We ended up at the Adobe Resort Hotel at Yachats, Oregon that night. The next day we traveled all the way up the 101 west coast high way of Oregon cutting back to I-5 freeway and ending up at Sherwood Inn, Portland, Oregon.

Our planned stop the next morning was Cline Glass Company in Portland where we picked up 700 lbs of crated stain glass. Our destination that day was home and we arrived in Kennewick as planned on October 12, 1995.

7TH INGRAHAM REUNION AT WILLISTON, N.D.

July 24, 1996 Louise and I (Willard) Ingraham were on our way to the Ingraham reunion with Arnold and Lucille Steffens. We took a route through Montana going west where we saw a big herd of buffalo grazing in the distant meadow. We got to Great Falls, Montana in the late afternoon at the home of Grace Steffens. Grace was the widow of Arnold's brother Gordon Steffens.

We planned to visit the area and on the 25th we visited the Chas. M. Russell museum at Great Falls. Chas Russell was the famous oil painter of western art that his paintings tell a story.

The next day we left for Williston, North Dakota and checked into the International Inn. We stayed there for the

next three nights to attend the reunion (photo above).

The hosts for this reunion were Richard and Kathy Vestal who opened their home in Williston with food and entertainment. They were generous with food set out for everyone anytime of the day.

One of the evenings in Williston was a planned no host dinner at a restaurant and we were fortune to have Rick Ingraham, an excellent singer entertain us. Rick is the son of Roy Ingraham and the grandson of Ralph and Rose Ingraham of Laurel, Montana. Rick had with him a son named Chauncey Ingraham. His son was named after his great great grandfather Chauncey Ingraham. It was another successful family reunion with about 30 attending.

When we left Williston our destination was Minot, North Dakota to visit Angela Hawks and family. She is the daughter of Grace Steffens. Angela was attending college to become a teacher and her husband was a nurse on the army base there. They treated us royally with dinner and we had a chance to get acquainted with their two school age boys.

The next day we were on our way again across the Northern part of the state headed for North Dakota. We visited Rugby where there is a pyramid type structure there that is marked geographically as the center of North America, Rugby, N.D. A very interesting old western town museum is there and we walked through it all viewing all the antiques. We left this area for Michigan, North Dakota where we stopped to see the town where my great grandfather's father Charlie Ingraham raised a second family.

From there we drove to Devils Lake, N.D. and stayed at a motel there. It was on Indian reservation territory and one of our stops on the reservation the next day was at an Indian owned complex of stores; the store owners were pleasant but not overly friendly as we were viewed as the outsiders off the reservation.

We went on to new Rockford, N.D. where we stopped to see Bill Starkey, a school mate of mine, then we went to Joe Andersons farm, another school mate of mine when we lived at

New Rockford in 1937-1941. We also drove by our old farm there that no one was living at that time. Wheat had grown up around the buildings.

We drove on to Carrington, N.D. and stayed at Chiefton Motel. The following day we drove into Pettibone, N.D. where my brother Ray Ingraham was born and where Arnold's grandfather, August Steffens had lived on a farm located about 3 miles north of Pettibone, N.D.

We then drove on to Woodworth where both Arnold and I, (Willard) was born on a farm a few miles out of Woodworth. Arnold was born on the 16th of June and I was born on the 23rd of June in 1924. We were cousins whose families were close and we grew up together then in 1947 we married sisters so now we were cousins and brother-in-law.

We met Magdalena Clark at Woodworth; she was 101 years old and was a good friend of my parents, Lyle and Gena Ingraham. Her two son's Harrison and Bill Clarke were at Magdalena's home. Harrison was especially happy to see us and wanted to show us his collection of old autos under the name of Clark Enterprises. He had more than 150 old cars and parts collectibles and license plates on his property and in this garage.

It was a great visit but we left heading for Duane and Lois Knudson's home in Jamestown. We stayed with them for 3 nights. Lois took us to a unique farm restaurant out of Midina, North Dakota for a tradition farm dinner. Duane is a farm claim adjuster and he was working so could not join us.

Lois and Duane had a family dinner gathering at their home while we were there and it was a time to see and visit with all our Jamestown relatives.

Our stay was over and we were on our way again headed west to the North Dakota state capital at Bismark, N.D. After we crossed the Missouri River to Mandan, N.D. and saw the Fort Lincoln State Park. It was at Mandan that we saw Custer's house. We stayed at the Comfort Inn at Bismark overnight and left early the next morning for Laurel, Mt. and another overnight at the Best Western Locomotive Inn. Our Laurel relatives joined us for breakfast the next morning and after visiting a while we traveled west through Montana stopping at the Silver Inn where we saw the 10,000 silver dollar bar on display.

Home again at Kennewick, Wa. and we arrived with lots of memories and having had an enjoyable trip.

DOUBLE 50TH WEDDING ANNIVERSARIES

In 1997 Willard and Louise Ingraham of Kennewick and Arnold and Lucille Steffens of Grandview, Wa. celebrated their golden wedding anniversaries together as they had their weddings 50 years ago. The two couples were married in a double wedding ceremony September 13, 1947 at the bride's parent's ranch in the Glade area south of Mabton. The couples and their families celebrated the Ingraham and Steffens 50th wedding anniversaries on August 16, 1997 at a family picnic and reunion at Leslie Grove Park in Richland, Washington (photo below).

Their children planned the anniversary celebration and there were 80 family members and friends present.

With great sadness on Dec. 15, 1998 Arnold Steffens passed away. He had been ill with cancer and it was difficult for his family and friends to say goodbye. I lost my friend, my cousin, my brother-in-law and my life long buddy.

It was 1999 and time to do some upgrading and remodeling again; we chose the three bathrooms. The master bath off the bedroom needed replacement of the tile around the tub. It was a big project removing all the tile and wallboard from the walls around the tub down to the studs and then replacing it with new concrete water retention wall board and finishing it with ceramic tile on all the walls in all of the room as well as the floor. A new sink and faucets and shower head was installed and a new toilet along with mirrored shelves for storage and a large medicine cabinet with wall hung mirrors.

This was only one bathroom so my next projects were to redo the flooring on the other two bathrooms with ceramic tile. That was my 1999 project. It was a lot of hard work but worth it once I had completed the jobs.

In the year 2000 it was time to get back to some of my hobbies making more stain glass stepping stones for the yard and adding other features. I upgraded the landscape in the front yard using pink block for the retaining wall across the front of the yard using red edging stripes then I planted many miniature roses and perennial flowers for accents.

It was also the year 2000 that Louise, my wife, began the research on writing her book, "Sapien's Journey Through Time and Space. It is a very interesting book that takes the life of the soul from the beginning of time and follows it through time and space. She finished writing her book in 2002 and found it difficult to find a publisher sooner than two years out to publish her genre. We decided it wasn't acceptable to wait that long and proceeded to do the research for setting up table top bindery for a finished book. Our search took us to Portland and we successfully purchased all the equipment needed to

finish a book including a commercial laser printer to go with
our existing computers. It was an experience in itself but we
worked through it step by step and had a studio workshop set
up ready for printing and binding. We completed our project
with ISBN numbers and registered copyrights and the book
was published and ready to market.

It was during the summer of 2002 that I decided my
project was going to be to make a waterfall, small stream and
pond in one corner of our back yard by using petrified wood,
agate and glacier rock for accents. The scene includes a small
model windmill, a rock house and places for my gnome
collection (photo below). I did complete the project and with it
a very sore back but we have enjoyed the finished project to
date.

In the year 2003 Louise asked to have the patio area in
the back yard enlarged so we could have patio parties and a
place for barbeque parties with a lot of good back yard living.
I already had planned the park area in the back yard with a lot
of various type flowering and shade trees around the perimeter

for beauty and privacy. We discussed the look and I drew up plans to section off the back in the north end of the yard using steps to go to an upper level (photo below).

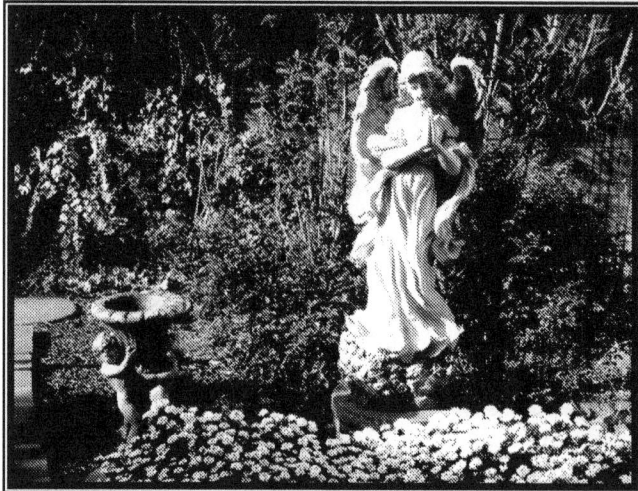

My next project was making an English garden looking finished area with angel, cherubs and many flowers with a walkway around it. I painted the angel and set her in place with all the other things and then added lighting. She stands serene in that garden area and the light bathing down on her makes her look truly angel like in stature.

523

I was able to incorporate a very small garden in that area for a few tomatoes, green peppers, Swiss chard and cucumbers.

Just down the steps to the south is where I constructed my planned outdoor patio. I lined the perimeter with pink block as edging and for the steps installed 2" x 8" x 12" red block for the patio floor. We made stained glass picturesque stepping-stones. Louise worked up the designs on paper and I lay in the stained glass to fit the design; then I cut borders of glass and poured each stepping-stone in concrete. After the stepping-stones curried I then placed them on a bed for my walkway. We also set in park benches around the edges with

stain glass tops as picnic benches for the area.

In January of 2004 lest we forget we do get snow here some winters one night we got about 10 inches. It tied up our street out front blocked with snow; no plows came to the side streets so our 4 wheel drive vehicle came in handy for about two days until the street was plowed out. Even the mail man had to have chains on his mail carrier and still he got stuck out in front of our house.

LOUISE, WILLARD INGRAHAM AND FAMILY

Louise was finishing her second book, "Atlantis A New View," about a mythical place called Atlantis. In her research and conclusions, she wrote that Atlantis had existed. She prepared her manuscript for publishing. She wanted to spend her time writing so this time instead of printing in our studio; we talked our daughter and son-in-law Mary Ann and Joe Hicks into being publishers. They formed their corporation and set up the business with commercial demand printing. This meant one book at a time was then printed commercially instead of offset press where many books were printed at one time and the author had to warehousing a large number of books for sale. It also meant that the books were offered for retail at both Barnes and Noble and Amazon.com and other outlets

Because of the many photos Louise now uses in her books she now does all of her own illustrations. She took advantage of in-house expertise on her first two books and her grandson, Ryan Ingraham did the illustrations for the cover and between chapters. Ryan works professionally as an illustrator for a medical research laboratory.

I served almost three years in World War II in the European theater of operations of that war. I served from March 18, 1943 to December 29, 1945 with two years served in Wales, British Isles waiting for D-Day and from there France, Belgian, Luxemburg and into Germany until the end of the war plus six more months in Wiesbaden, Germany serving as guard in Wiesbaden guarding the town as German soldiers were being filtered back into civilian life after the war.

They wanted our army unit, 526 Armored Infantry Battalion, to do this because we were battle tested soldiers that could do the job.

When I was discharged and back in civilian life I did not want to talk about the past three years but 60 some years later my family including my grandchildren wanted me to write a book on my experiences of that war. I did not want to go there but their persistence won out. On June 23, 2004 my book, "Farm Boy To Soldier" was published and on the market. My wife, Louise, held an 80th birthday party and book signing party for me in our back yard celebrating my June 23rd birthday.

In November, 2004 Shannon Ann Hicks married Ryan Briehl (Peters) Ingraham at Chandler, Arizona. Shannon is the daughter of Joe and Mary Ann Hicks of Mesa, Arizona. Louise and I flew down to attend the wedding. It was a beautiful wedding. They invited me to anoint the couple with holy water that I had brought back from the Holy Land. It was a privilege; Shannon is our granddaughter and Ryan our grandson.

We all had another sad loss; Lucille Steffens passed away November 19, 2004. She had bravely fought cancer for several years and the time to go had come. All of us missed her with her quick smile and stories she liked to tell.

Our first great grandson Torryn Briehl Ingraham was born in 2005. Louise and I flew down to Phoenix in October to get acquainted with our great grandson. We are so proud of him. We kind of spoiled him while we were there but Ryan and Shannon told us it was alright.

Then on January 12, 2007 Ivry Rae Ingraham was born to parent's Ryan and Shannon Ingraham. Ivry was our first great granddaughter. Later this fall Louise and I will fly down to get acquainted and reacquaint with her brother Torryn. We have photos that have been sent us of both the children and we love them both. Joe and Mary Ann Hicks are the proud grandparents and are already spoiling them both. They say that it is their privilege.

My brothers and sister all live within 35 miles from each other. We have felt pretty lucky that Ray and Anna Ingraham, Norman and Verdell Ingraham, Lorraine Johnston and Louise and I get together often to go out and eat then gather to have a good game of cards. All the years of this century Norman and Verdell have invited all of us to their place to celebrate the New Year coming in.

LOUISE, WILLARD INGRAHAM AND FAMILY

Last year was an anniversary year for Ray and Anna and Norman and Verdell. They all celebrated their 60th wedding anniversaries.

Louise and I (Willard) also get together with our friends Marty and Tom Vickerman to eat out and play cards (their photo is below). We enjoy their company during the spring and summer but they are snowbirds who go to Phoenix, Az. During the winter but back each spring to live in their Kennewick home.

As time goes on things change and so it is with our group. It is sad to say but we lost Anna Rose Ingraham; she passed away on April 1, 2007 and was laid to rest at the Prosser, Wa. cemetery. Ray is now living in the extended care home at Prosser, Washington.

The year 2007 has been a busy one for Louise and I. She has just finished writing her third book, "The Pioneer Spirit of Minnie, Charley Williams and Family," and now has it published and on the market. It is a book about her Williams and Bromley heritage back to the early eighteen hundreds and how her family came west to Washington and homesteaded here. She wrote of family life through 1977; the good and hard times of homesteading. The book includes stories from all ten sibling's families.

This year in 2007 I am finishing writing my second book, "Echos Past, Links to the Mayflower." It is about the descendents of the Ingrahams from the ship Mayflower that came to America in 1620 and the relationships to five people who came over on the Mayflower, John Alden and wife Priscilla Mullins and Priscilla's parents, William and Alice Mullins, and Captain Myles Standish. It is written in genealogical style so that anyone that can cut their family into the Ingraham line will have records of their own family back to the Mayflower roots. I have documented the heritage to the Mayflower and I am a member of the Mayflower Society.

This is a milestone year for Louise and me; on September 13, 2007, we celebrated our 60th wedding anniversary.

LOUISE, WILLARD INGRAHAM AND FAMILY

MAHRIA CAROL JORDAN

Our little girl Carol Jean Ingraham was born this morning at 9:07 A.M. April 5, 1948 in the Prosser, Washington hospital. She was born to Willard and Louise Ingraham who had a farm four miles west of Prosser.

Louise and I were so happy and proud to have a little girl come to join us in our lives. We knew our lives would change and only be more interesting and happy. We both loved children and now we had a little girl we could boast about of our own. Her grandparents Lyle and Gena Ingraham and Charley and Minnie Williams were also happy to see her.

Carol was only five months old in Sept, 1948 when we

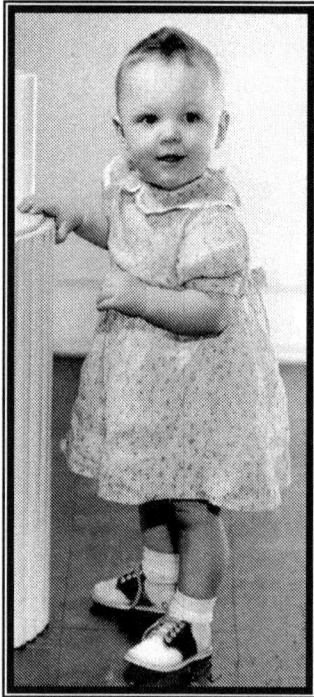

decided to go back to North Dakota via the Yellowstone Park in Montana to show Carol off to the many relatives she had in Montana and North Dakota. In Jamestown, North Dakota, we visited many of our relatives and took pictures of Carol's great grandmother, Laura Johnson holding her.

We then went to see Carol's great grandparents, Chauncey and Myrtle Ingraham. There I got a good picture of Louise and my grandparents Chauncey and Myrtle Ingraham holding our baby Carol. Both sets of grandparents then lived in Jamestown.

We got back home to Prosser in time to pick our concord grape crop. From then on, the years seemed to melt one into another because of our busy lives. At one-year-old (above), Carol was already starting to walk and saying some words. Louise and I wondered what Carol was trying to say after we put her to bed each night. To our amazement, we listened carefully and each night she would go through repeating all the words she already knew and add to her list as the days went on.

In September of 1949, Grandpa and Grandma Chauncey Ingraham came to visit Lyle and Gena Ingraham. While they were visiting, I got a picture of the women in the Ingraham family, Louise, Carol, Myrtle and Gena Ingraham.

Time passed quickly during these years and 1954 was there with Carol catching a bus to go to first grade at school (her photo is below). So that I would have more time I sold the dairy cows and bought some Hereford cattle to feed on the pasture land we had.

It soon became obvious to me that my farm was not big enough to make a good living on any more so it was decision time; to buy a bigger farm and go full time farming or go back to college for additional education and earn more money. A few months later, I bid on an apprentice meterman position what required a three-year apprenticeship-training program and we had to relocate in Kennewick, Wa. This was fine with me because at Kennewick I could take advantage of the college in Pasco.

In March 1957, we sold the farm. We bought a house in Kennewick and we moved there. In the fall of that year, the girls had only to walk down over the hill to a new grade school.

Both Carol Jean and Mary Ann got involved in the Methodist Church. The girls having gone through baptismal services joined the Methodist church. Both of the girls enjoyed their involvement in the youth fellowship programs the church offered. A photo of our Kennewick home is below.

Both girls took music lessons; Carol Jean on the piano accordion and Mary Ann on the piano. They both got good at playing and joined a little band and the group played at Christmas and other functions in the area. The band consisted of clarinet and trumpet players. Their music teacher was a retired Navy Band leader.

The girls were studying diligently in school and with their music so we wanted them to have some playtime also. We hooked up our trailer and off we went camping along the Oregon coast of the Pacific Ocean. It was very relaxing for all of us to bask in the sun and walk the sandy beaches.

In the fall of the year, we took the trailer up to Mt. Adams area to pick huckleberries for sauce and for making pies (photo above). In the evenings after picking, we would clean and can the berries right there in camp. Many times Louise would make a fresh huckleberry pie right there in camp. What a treat – m-m good!

When Carol Jean was age 14, she wrote a 1000 word essay that she received recognition for and another story she wrote, "What I Can Do For My Country."

In 1962, Carol wanted to do a science project involving two white rats. Yes, I said two white rats that she brought into our home in a cage. I protested at first but then relented. She actually made great pets of the rats. She bathed them daily and played with them enough that the rats would do anything for her. She ended up being the grand prizewinner of the junior division at the Mid-Columbia Science Fair at Richland, Wa.

Carol (below) was always quite popular in school and involved in many projects. In 1965, the girl's league voted Carol the October girl of the month, most friendly in school.

Miss Ingraham Selected

By STEPHANIE ONEY
Kennewick High Correspondent

Carl Jean Ingraham, daughter of Mr. and Mrs. Willard S. Ingraham, 2624 S. Everett St., Kennewick, was chosen October's girl of the month by Girl's League for the quality "friendliness."

Carol is a member of Thespians and is the costume chairman this year. She especially enjoyed her part as Sleeping Beauty in last years children's play.

She has served on the hospitality for Girl's League the last two years and is an active member of French Club, Foreign Student Club and National Honor Society.

HER HOBBIES INCLUDE hiking, water skiing, music and reading.

Miss Ingraham, a senior,

CAROL INGRAHAM
... Most Friendly

hopes to attend the University of Hawaii or the University of Washington next year.

Class officers for the following year were elected last Friday. They are:

Sophomores — president, Jim Ady; vice-president, Phyllis Davis; and secretary, Kim Mark.

Juniors — president, Steve Matheson; vice-president, Dave Kukkola; and secretary, Kitty Olson.

Seniors — president, Don Cofer; vice-president, Mauro Baltazar; and secretary, Mary Anne Thuot.

Judging the fourth annual class competition one-act plays were Daniel Sarton, 715 W. Brown St., Pasco, and Mrs. George Crosta, 5805 W. Yellowstone Ave., Kennewick.

Life was sometimes hectic at our house. Once Carol planned a house, party at our home and was only to invite a few kids. She invited her whole class and some others. Party time came and around 100 signed in. To say the least we set up some quick rules; if a guest left they were not allowed to return and we had several trusted students milling the crowd downstairs to make sure nothing got out of hand. That was the last house part Carol had!

Carol Jean Ingraham graduated from Kennewick High School in 1966 at the age of 18 (photo below).

There was a major change in the life of our family in October 1966 when I took a risk by changing jobs. I left a good job with Benton County P.U.D. where I had worked 19 years with the last 6 years as a journeyman meterman at Kennewick, Wa. to accept a job with Cowlitz County P.U.D. at Longview, Wa. as meter technician. In 6 months, they gave me the formanship of the meter department. Carol decided to remain in Kennewick. She married Garry Robert Rosson of Kennewick. They moved to Seattle in 1967.

On August 28, 1967, Jon Garry Rosson was born in Seattle, Wa. at the Virginia Mason Hospital at 8:43 P>M. to parents Garry and Carol Rosson. Jon's photo is below.

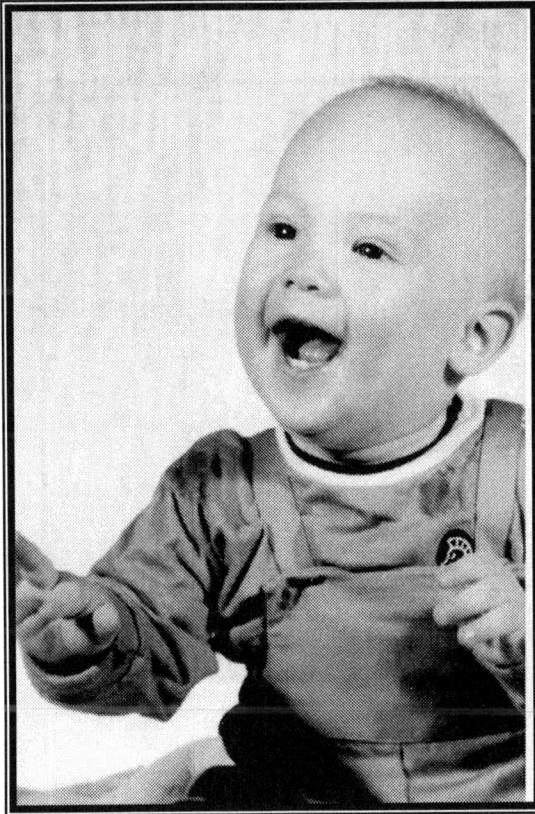

Garry and Carol divorced about 1969. Jon was three years old when he came to live with his grand parents Willard and Louise Ingraham at Longivew. He was with us until about 1972 and he went back to Seattle to live with his father Garry Rosson.

It was in 1972 that Carol Rosson met Clayton John Straight and they were married in Oregon. They moved to Eugene, Oregon to live. James Jacob Straight was born February 28, 1973 at Eugene, Oregon and Paul Joshua Straight was born at Seaside, Oregon February 1, 1975. Carol and Clayton John Straight were divorced about 1976.

Carol then with her two boys James and Paul moved to Longview, Washington. Louise and I helped her set up house keeping in Longview and purchased her a reliable second hand car so she would have good transportation for her and the boys. Carol enrolled in college in Longivew.

LOUISE, WILLARD INGRAHAM AND FAMILY

Louise and I took advantage at this time to be better acquainted with our two grandsons. It was enjoyable to hear their gleeful laughter and note their bundle of energy (photo of Mom Mahria and front left Paul and James below).

Louise and I had moved back to Kennewick in 1978 and September 1981. I had retired but kept busy with my remodeling projects on the home we had purchased.

Louise was still in management at Washington Mutual. Everyone was busy but we were happy to see Carol move to Pasco, Wa. with her two boys James and Paul. She lived in Pasco at a nice apartment complex and enrolled in college. Later she moved to a rental home in Kennewick.

During this time, Carol was gaining skills at college. She majored in art. This was a big change in her educational plans. The art was not a subject she was thinking would give her the work skills she needed but would open doors in the art appreciation.

We soon discovered she was quite a talented artist with oils and watercolors (photo below is of one of her works of art).

Around 1988 Carol decided to move back to Seattle where she felt she could obtain a better paying job in her field. I helped her move to Lynnwood, Washington. Auto Cad was the new software that meeting acceptance in Engineering fields and Carol had the computer skills needed in this area. She found jobs on contract helping set up Auto Cad in engineering departments. For many years, she followed computer needs in engineering departments until about 2006 and she went from contract to regular payroll jobs still in the engineering computer field with auto cad.

For personal reasons in 1991, Carol Jean Straight changed her last name and her boys James Jacob and Paul Joshua to Jordan.

LOUISE, WILLARD INGRAHAM AND FAMILY

JON GARRY ROSSON

Jon Garry Rosson was born August 28, 1967 at 8:43 A.M. to Garry Robert and Carol Jean Rosson in the Virginia Mason Hospital at Seattle, Washington.

In 1969, Gary and Carol divorced and Jon went to Longivew, Wa. where his grandparents Willard and Louise Ingraham were living. Jon was a bundle of joy and we both enjoyed Jon living with us (his photo below). He fit into our family.

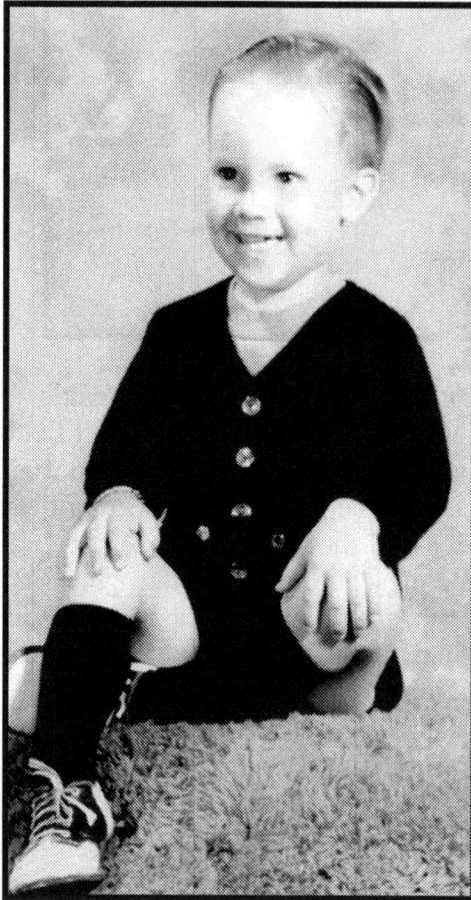

Louise was working away from home so Jon spent the weekdays at a church day care center. He loved playing with all the children; it was like a kindergarten school and besides the fun times he was learning what school would be like to write and read.

On the weekends, many times we went camping at Long Beach where we could see the ocean and were only a couple of blocks from the sandy beaches. These were happy times with Jon but in 1972 Jon's father, Garry wanted him to live with him in Seattle. We reluctantly gave him up hoping we had made the best decision long term for Jon.

Jon grew up in Seattle where he graduated from High School and attended the University of Washington. Left is Jon at age twenty-one.

His interests were in computer programming and he spent several years in that business. He sold his successful company and invested in real estate. He took a long-term lease on some warehouse buildings on Queen Ann Hill in Seattle and remodeled the inside of the buildings into commerce studios plus living quarters. It was a successful enterprise and he purchased some buildings and built others. He had his enterprises near the Seattle Space Needle. It was a good location. He also leased and operated a tavern in the Queen Ann Hill area. Below, 1991, is left Mom, Mahria, Jon, Paul and James.

I asked Jon one day, "don't you ever think about slowing up and settling down and get married?" His answer was, "Grandpa I am too busy to get married." He knows he has our best wishes always.

538

JAMES JACOB JORDAN

James Jacob Jordan was born in Eugene, Oregon on February 28, 1973 to Clayton John and Carol Jean Straight. Clayton was working with a roofing contractor shingling and repairing roofs. Later they moved to Seaside, Oregon.

Left is James age two.

Carol and John were divorced around 1976. Carol then moved with her boys James and Paul to Longview, Washington. Louise and I were living at Longview at the time and we were able to see the boys often.

In 1981 Carol with James and Paul moved to Pasco, Washington. Later they moved to Kennewick. The boys attended the Kennewick schools. James was interested in school football.

Right is a photo of Mom, Mahria and two boys, James left and Paul.

Then in 1988, the little family moved to Lynnwood, Washington where the boys attended school. At the age of 17, James made an application at Marsing Job Corps C.C.C. not far from Homedale, Idaho. He entered high school classes while there and at the same time took up welding and carpenters training. Later James got his certifications for all.

They offered James two years of college at a school in Oregon but he choose to drop out. Since this time, he has picked and chosen his own way in the world.

A photo of James below taken 1991.

PAUL JOSHUA JORDAN

Paul Joshua Jordan was born at Seaside, Oregon on February 1, 1975; parents Clayton John and Carol Jean Straight. Later in 1976, Carol and John were divorced.

Paul's photo below, 1979, at age four;.

Carol and the boys moved to Longview, Washington where Louise and I lived at the time. It was fun to have the boys living near by. In 1981, Carol and the boys moved to Pasco, Wa. Louise and I were living in Kennewick so we again had opportunities to enjoy the boys.

Paul was a little blonde headed boy with a big smile. Many said he looked like his grandfather and of course, that made me proud. His temperament was a lot like mine.

We did spend as much time with the two boys as we could. I had retired and was remodeling the kitchen in our home so Paul came over to help me with the kitchen cabinets and handed me the tools as I named them.

Photo right is Mom, Mahria, Paul on the right and James left.

At the age of 12, (below) Paul was interested in school football and played in the school games.

Paul also was determined to make his own spending money and took on the job of delivering the early morning Tri-City Herald each day. It was a big undertaking and he got himself up while everyone was sleeping and kept his route on a regular basis.

It was in the year of 1988 that they moved to Lynnwood, Washington. I helped them move; I had rented a big u-haul truck for the move and after loading the truck, it was late in the evening before we left Kennewick to go to Lynnwood, Wa. It was over 200 miles away, we had to go over the Snoqualmie Pass in the Cascade Mountains, and it was snowing so hard that the windshield wiper would not take the snow off the windshield.

Paul was riding with me in the truck and Carol was following me in my 4-wheel drive Izuzu pickup with James. We got the truck on the other side of the pass, I found a good place to park the truck, and there Paul and I waited for Carol and James to come. It seemed like an hour before Carol finally showed up; believe me I spent many anxious minutes waiting because I had no knowledge of where we were going except I knew we had to go to Lynnwood. I worried that Carol had a problem getting over the pass; she had been right behind me in all that snow that was falling. I wondered is she also had somehow slipped by me without me seeing her; what a dilemma.

We had waited so long that Paul had fallen asleep. Finally, Carol came and parked behind me. She said she could not see and she had no 4-wheel drive. I told her that before we went up over the pass when we had stopped I had engaged the 4-wheel drive in her rig. I went back to check and there I found that James had unknowingly disengaged the 4-wheel shift gear.

It still did not explain why it took them so long to come across the pass when she had been right behind me but we got to Lynnwood at 11:30 P.M and still had to unload the truck and set up the beds.

Paul and James enrolled in school in the Lynwood school district and continued their formal education. When Paul was older in about 1996, he got a job with an irrigation company. He told me once that it was hard work but he said, "Grandpa you would be proud of me." We are proud of Paul, his accomplishments and how he has made good choices to better himself.

Paul has worked for the railroad in Seattle for the last ten years. He just recently accepted an apprenticeship with the longshoremen in Seattle and is working on the docks.

Paul is a well-informed computer tech. He builds computers from the base up.

Paul has invested with his long time girlfriend Terra Krammer in a commercial studio apartment complex in the old Rainer building. He is presently working on the improvements and will have several floors in his section connected with spiral stairs. The building will house other studio living apartments and a gallery of various types of art displayed for the public viewing and retail.

Paul has a knack for design and finishing; we are looking forward to seeing his last project upon completion.

LOUISE, WILLARD INGRAHAM AND FAMILY

MARY ANN (INGRAHAM) HICKS

It was on December 28, 1949 that Mary Ann Ingraham was born in the hospital at Sunnyside, Wa. I took mother and baby home on December 30, 1949. The next day was the beginning of one of the worst winters we had. The next six weeks we fought cold and snow and the Columbia River froze over near the bridge in Kennewick. Some people walked across the river on the ice.

We had bought a new oil heater that fall and had closed off the bedrooms and lived in the living room and kitchen. The whole house was ice cold except the living room and the kitchen. We put the crib next to the oil heater so baby would not get cold. We were experiencing 28 degree below zero weather. The water pipes were freezing up for us and for others all over the area. We operated the new oil heater so high that winter that it burned out the fire pot.

When Mary Ann was less than one year old, we would see Carol holding her little sister up trying to make her walk. Carol was anxious for Mary Ann to be able to run and play around the yard. At left is a photo of Carol taking Mary Ann for a walk.

It did not take long for our little girls to grow up. They would love to put their red overhauls on and come out to try to help Daddy. One Saturday they insisted they help me. I realized that the pasture was getting some Canadian Thistles starting to grow up in the pasture so I gave Mary Ann a short handled hoe with about a two-foot handle and Carol a little longer handled hoe and we all went to the pasture to clean out those nasty weeds in our pasture. About ten minutes and Carol discovered there was a little work doing hoeing and it ceased to be fun. She was ready to go back to the house. I said that it would be fine for both to go back to the house but Mary Ann asked me, "are you going too Daddy," I told her no but that was all right but Mary Ann insisted she was not going until I quit too. We worked about a half an hour and I noticed Mary Ann's little face was getting red and I took her back to the house. She was not going to give up.

Left is Dad, Mary Ann and Carol ready for work.

Time passed quickly during these years and 1954 was there with Carol catching a bus to go to first grade at school. So that I would have, more time I sold the dairy cows and bought some Hereford cattle to feed on the pastureland we had.

It soon became obvious to me that my farm was not big enough to make a good living on any more so it was decision time; to buy a bigger farm and go full time farming or go back to college for additional education and earn more money. By 1954, the construction on our remodeled home was almost finished to where we now lived very comfortable in our house.

LOUISE, WILLARD INGRAHAM AND FAMILY

In the fall of 1956, it was a big exciting day for Mary Ann when she walked out to catch the school bus with Carol. At this time, I had finished building our house so in early 1957, I bid on a job where I worked to become an apprentice meterman. It was a three year on the job apprenticeship training to become a journeyman meter man and it meant that if I got the job, we would have to sell our farm and move to Kennewick. I did get the job and we did move to Kennewick. This was fine with me because at Kennewick I could take advantage of the college in Pasco.

In March 1957, we sold the farm. We bought a house in Kennewick and we moved there. In the fall that year, the girls had only to walk down over the hill to a new grade school.

We purchased an all brick house in an all-new development. The grade school was just down the hill from our home. The girls were required to walk to school.

Left is Mary Ann and Carol ready for the first day of school.

Everybody was busy; we signed the girls up for music classes with a teacher coming to our home to teach Mary Ann the piano and Carol the piano accordion. Both the girls got good playing their instruments and the teacher formed a band with all the children he was teaching.

547

We became good friends with Howard and Gladys Brightman who had two boys the same age of our girls. One played the trumpet and the other boy played the saxophone. The boy's names were Mike and Dennis. The four played very well together and at Christmas played at special functions even on TV a few times (the bands photo is left; Mary Ann is at the piano, Dennis next, Carol and her accordion and Mike with the saxophone.

Below Mary Ann is practicing on the piano.

Louise and I tried to get ourselves organized also. I signed up for some college courses in the evenings after work and Louise attended college during the day.

We also joined our neighborhood bridge group that met once a month at each others homes for dinner and playing cards.

Louise and I both liked dancing. The only dance classes offered were square dancing so we joined a square dance group. There were classes and even diplomas (photo to the left).

The girls, Mary Ann and Carol were studying hard also and we wanted family recreation together so we purchased a 15-foot travel trailer that we used weekends and on vacations. We went to the west coast and camped along the ocean on the Oregon coast numerous times. Also I was into rock hunting and many of our excursions were in areas to find rocks; especially petrified rock and agates.

Photo below was taken camping on the Oregon coast.

We all studied hard and the years just floated by before we knew it. I made a family decision that affected all of the family members. I felt there was more I had to offer in my selected vocation. I now had my journeyman meterman's card and had worked as a journeyman for six years. I had continued my college studies that left me feeling I had more to offer the electrical field so I bid on a job at the Cowlitz County Public Utility District as a meter technician located at Longview, Wa.

The family assured me before I bid on the job if I got the position they were not happy with a move but would back me. I got the job and we moved. The first change was Mary Ann was in her junior year in high school and wanted to stay in Kennewick to finish her junior year. She would stay at a girl friends house, Joyce Clinger; we knew the family and knew it would be a nice family for her to stay with if the parents approved. It was OK with them so we agreed and Mary Ann stayed in Kennewick the rest of her junior year.

Carol was eighteen years old and had graduated from high school; had a serious boyfriend, they wanted to get married, and they would live in Kennewick. They did get married.

Mary Ann finished the junior year in Kennewick and came to Longview, Wa. to live with us. She signed up for her senior year at the Longview school and graduated there. Mary Ann was a good student and maintained good grades (her graduation photo is above).

LOUISE, WILLARD INGRAHAM AND FAMILY

After graduating, from high school Mary Ann went to work for a bank in Longview. In March of 1978 Louise, my wife had been assistant manager at Washington Mutual Bank for a number of years and they offered her a job at the Kennewick Branch in management. I already had worked 30 years for the Benton and Cowlitz county P.U.Ds and had full retirement at 53 years of age. Louise and I were already taking groups of people on tours as the group leaders; if I retired, I could devote full time to putting tours together and Louise and I could continue to travel with groups around the world so I agreed to retire.

We bought a home(below) in Kennewick, Washington and moved. There was plenty for me to do at our new home. I remodeled the kitchen and upgraded the house throughout.

Louise settled into her new job at the Kennewick

branch of Washington Mutual. She put in long hours; it was boom time in 1978 in Kennewick and many families were buying homes.

Mary Ann was living in Kennewick when we moved there. She was working at the Hanford area in an engineer department for the Hanford Project as a drafts person.

Again everyone was busy; my folks, Lyle and Gena Ingraham lived in Kennewick across town so all of us spent a lot of time together.

Mary Ann met and dated a young man in Kennewick. Her friend was Milton Lewis Hicks (Joe) who was a teacher. It was on November 18, 1978 that Mary Ann Ingraham and

Milton Lewis Hicks were married (photo above). They made their home in Kennewick for the next year

.

It was 1979 and Joe and Mary Ann had a new house built at West Bourne Acres at Burbank, Washington located about ten miles east of Pasco, Washington. The house was completely finished but Joe and Mary Ann never lived in that home because they decided they wanted to move to Arizona to live. Joe had graduated from the Arizona State University in Phoenix and liked the open winters there.

Joe owned a 35 foot trailer that he had lived in while attending Arizona State University while in Phoenix, Az. He had a 68 Ford Mercury, four door sedan that he pulled the trailer with. About the middle of July, 1979 they moved and the trailer, the 68 Ford Mercury, 1978 Cougar and Javelin all had to go to Phoenix, Az.

I decided to help and we left our place in about the middle of July, hot weather time, from Kennewick at 6 A.M; the temperature had been up close to the 100-degree mark. Joe was driving the Mercury pulling the 35-foot trailer; I (Willard) was driving the 1978 Cougar and Mary Ann was driving the Javelin.

Near Twin Falls, Id. we had a flat tire on the trailer; this was our second day on the road. We stopped by a lake at Willard Park, Utah for a break. It was getting hot and Joe and Mary Ann had no air condition in their cars so I did not use the one I had in the car I was driving either. I felt sorry for Joe pulling that 35 foot trailer and leaving the heater on because he discovered that the car ran a little cooler by doing that.

Near Provo, the Mercury was acting up so we had to have the gas line and the gas tank blown out and cleaned. We stayed at Provo, Utah that night and the next morning we drove to Nephi, Utah. We were eating breakfast when the water hose to the radiator blew completely out in the Mercury at Kanab, Utah. We had to have the bushing on the fan of the Mercury repaired.

We had to stop to cool and put more water in the radiator periodically. Then we came to the nine-mile hill and we had to stop and fill the radiator before starting up the hill. I went ahead to pick a turn off space we all had CB communication in our cars. I was on top of the long 9-mile hill and found a good place to park off the road. I could hear Joe coming up with the trailer. When he called and said the car was getting really hot and he may have to stop. I advised him do not stop but bring it on up to the top because by the sound I could tell he was not very far from the top. Joe finally got to the top and opened the hood to let it cool. He got the radiator cap off, poured the water in very slowly, and discovered we were out of water.

Joe said on the way up that hill pulling that big trailer with his car the temperature was bouncing almost on red. He said, "I was thinking of the story of the Little Red Engine that said, it could. I think I can, I think I can. I think I can"

Mary Ann took off with her car to get the water; we could not go many miles before we had to stop to cool the radiator and add more water. We babied the Mercury until we got into Page, Arizona and had a new water pump put in the Mercury. We got a room in a motel at Page for the night. The temperature was well over a hundred degrees, 112, so the first thing we did was get a big cool drink to sit and enjoy then changed into our swimming suits and had a nice swim in the big pool.

We got into Phoenix the next day in the afternoon; I suggested we go to the Elks and get a cold drink like ice tea and stay at the Elks until later that evening when it would get a little cooler because the temperature then was 118 degrees and we were feeling every degree of it.

Later we got to the trailer court, backed the trailer into a spot. I said, "let's get a good resort place with a pool and air conditioning and have a good meal. We can stay a couple of days and set the trailer up during the day then come back to the resort and live it up for a couple of days.

The plan worked out very well because all of us needed a good relaxing place to stay after that hot four-day trip getting there. We got the trailer all set up with the hook ups and air conditioning and afterward they took me to the Phoenix airport to fly back home.

Mary Ann and Joe settled into the trailer court and Mary Ann started to work for an engineering company out of Phoenix, Az. Joe was back teaching and in their spare time, they looked around for a house to buy. They found their home in Tempe, Az.

It was 1980 and Louise and I flew down to visit them. That is when we learned we were going to be grandparents.

Mary Ann spoiled us with coffee in bed the first thing in the morning.

The day we flew home, it was a beautiful sunshine day. We flew near Mt. Hood in Oregon and Mt. St. Helens, Mt. Adams and Mt. Rainier in Washington. I got a good picture of these mountains from the window of the plane; one picture I snapped all five mountains from the window. The picture I took of the five mountains in a row are left to right, Mt. Rainier, Mt. Adams in Washington, Mt. Jefferson and Mt. Hood in Oregon and Mt. St. Helens in Washington as shown on this page. The picture does not show the mountains as clearly as I saw them from the plane window that day.

Louise and I had purchased a new 1980 Omega Oldsmobile for Louise to drive back and forth from our home in Kennewick to Grandview, Wa where Louise was managing the Grandview branch of Washington Mutual Bank. We did not want to move to Grandview; the drive was 100 miles a day. Our daughter Carol had no car to get around in so we decided to give her our 1970 Oldsmobile 88 that was in mint condition.

Then on April 27, 1981 at 11:10 P.M. Shannon Ann Hicks was born at Tempe hospital, Maricopa County in Tempe, Arizona. Before 11:30 P.M. Mary Ann called us to inform us of our new granddaughter. It wasn't long and the proud parents sent us pictures so we would also have some bragging rights and soon with the computers we got we had constant updates of our beautiful little granddaughter.

In December of 1981 Joe and Mary Ann invited us, Louise and I, to be their guests over Christmas. We arranged for airplane tickets and were at Phoenix before Christmas.

Joe and Mary Ann brought Shannon to the Phoenix airport when they picked us up to take us to their home in Tempe, Arizona; what a cute baby. It was not long that Shannon was coming to us all the time and we spoiled her.

Mom, Mary Ann and Shannon below.

By this time Joe and Mary Ann were using their new swimming pool and we were spending our vacation sitting around the pool under an umbrella sipping cold drinks in 90 degree weather while we watched Joe teach baby Shannon how to swim. Joe was a swimming coach and used his expertise to teach baby daughter Shannon to swim. It was so cute watching that little girl swim safely across that pool with her Dad's guidance and supervision. Shannon looked like a little fish swimming with her legs kicking together in unison and her little behind following in and out of the water with the grace of a fish in water.

Mary Ann spoiled Louise and I by serving us coffee in bed every morning and then breakfast at poolside. I felt that I should be doing something while there so I asked Mary Ann and Joe if there was something I could do for them while visiting. Mary Ann said that it would be nice if her microwave was installed in the wall next to her kitchen cupboards. I got the material needed and the next day I had her microwave mounted on the wall in her kitchen.

Joe said that their open patio was so hot that they had to use their big umbrella there instead of by the pool where they would like to use it. We got the material and in a couple of days, we built an open shade cover over their patio that gave them shade any time of the day. We built the shade with 2" x 6" material across the patio by placing them all in a slanted position so that there were no rays from the sun coming down onto the patio area. It made the patio comfortable with open breezes flowing and yet shaded all day.

Mardell Wiggins and daughter's Voni and Michelle were living in the area at that time. Mardell is Joe's sister. She invited all of us over to her home for Christmas Eve including her parent's Gerry and Willie Hicks and Mardell's mother-in-law, Lucille Wiggins.

This was still a very sad time for Mardell as in August, 1979 she had lost her husband Mickael and son Vance in an airplane accident in New York state. Mickael was on an observation flight as a pilot for Washington State University with an observer aboard and his son Vance when the plane had mechanical failure and crashed. All three aboard died in the crash. We admired Mardell on how she held up against her losses and through the years devoted her life to raising her girls.

Having us all over for Christmas Eve was so like her thinking of others. We had a wonderful Christmas Eve with Mardell's hospitality and enjoyed the time of fellowship with all remembering the birth of our Lord Jesus Christ.

After Christmas, we heard of a family in Phoenix that wanted to sell their motor home. Louise and I thought, "what the heck, let's go look at it." We did look, bought and drove away with our twenty-two foot Travel Craft 1979 motor home. We drove it back to Joe and Mary Ann's home then Joe wanted to show us where he worked at Eloy, Arizona teaching. It was about 70 miles distance south from Tempe and we decided traveling there would give us a good test run of how everything was working in the motor home.

It was a fun trip. We saw where Joe had to drive 5 days a week for his Special Ed teaching position. It was a long drive for him to go to work.

When we got back to Tempe we had found that all seemed to be in good shape with the motor home so we decided to all go to Mexico and really try the motor home out. It was fun packing up for the trip and the drive to the border went great. We stopped at the border and walked on into Mexico and shopped for about two hours then went back to our motor home and drove to Tucsan, Arizona for the night. The next day we visited Old Tuscan and the Pima Air Museum before driving back to Tempe, Az.

By this time, vacation was over for Louise and I and it was time to think about going home. Gerry and Willy Hicks lived at their winter home in Superstition Springs Resort at Apache Junction, Arizona each winter. They also said it was time for them to make the trip back to their Kennewick home so both Louise and I (Willard) and Gerry and Willy Hicks decided to travel back to Washington at the same time.

Gerry and Willy pulled a big Airstream trailer with their Mercury station wagon and Louise and I traveled with our

Travel Craft motor home. Three days later, we were back in Kennewick. Gerry and Willy were our neighbors two door away on the same street in Kennewick so we saw each other often and their son Joe was married to our daughter Mary Ann so we had close family ties.

It was in 1983 that Joe and Mary Ann Hicks decided to move back to Kennewick, Wa. to start a business. They sold their home in Tempe, Arizona, rented a u-haul truck, and moved back to Kennewick. They stored their furniture in our garage and lived with us until their business, Allied Services, was ready to open for business.

This gave them time to look around and then to buy their home in Kennewick. Allied Services was a shipping and mailing service that was orientated with other services such as Airborne and Fed. Express and services for notary public, money orders, western union and other like services. Later they added a food bar. This business was one of the first of its kind in Kennewick. Start up took a while with lots of work but the business caught on. I helped Mary Ann and Joe operate the business they called Allied Services.

After the business took off Joe and Mary Ann bought a nice home in Kennewick, (photo above).

Their first home was nice but too big with a huge yard. They sold it and purchased a smaller home with a small yard and a swimming pool. They lived there until moving back to Arizona, (photo below).

The years went by and in 1990, Joe and Mary Ann decided to return to Phoenix, Az. The business was sold and to close in September of that year. Joe went ahead to Arizona that summer to be there for teaching that fall at the start of the year. By this time, Louise had retired from her job as bank manager and we wanted to help them move.

Before we left for Arizona Mary Ann sold all of their furniture leaving only personal things to load. We loaded in the motor home and on top of the motor home. I pulled an Isuzu pickup that had a cover on the back and that was also loaded. Mary Ann and Shannon followed in their car, a 1980 Tornado Oldsmobile that was also loaded.

The morning we took off it was a hot day and all vehicles were loaded. We did not travel without some problems on this trip. We got as far as Cabbage Hill, just past Pendleton, Oregon and the radiator hose blew out on the motor home; then near Salt Lake City, a tire blew. About 20 miles from Needles, Ca. and inside dual tire blew. By driving very slow, we made it to Needles (120 degrees) where I purchased a new set of tires for the motor home. We got into Superstition Springs Resort at Apache Junction in late afternoon.

When our caravan got there, it was in the middle of September. At the resort at Apache Junction, we got a space across the street from Gerry and Willy Hick's park model. Gerry and Willy had not come down from Kennewick for the winter so Joe was living in their unit. I set up our motor home and turned down the awning then set up table and chairs under the awning for our living area. The weather was beautiful; we lived here until Mary Ann and Joe's home was finished in December.

When Joe had arrived in Arizona during the summer ahead of Mary Ann and Shannon he purchased a lot they had agreed on and ordered a home built on it.

The lot was in an area with walled enclosures around all of the subdivisions. Behind the house they built was a community park. It was an attractive complex with lots of amenities and a near by huge community clubhouse and pool area. Even the man-made lake had a beach of sand just like an ocean beach and the waterfalls was beautiful with the lights at night holding a serene and peaceful are to swim, picnic and relax. Best of all Shannon's school was within a few blocks of their home. They had made a great choice to build here; it was property that would increase in value.

Shannon entered grade school near her new home, we drove her to school about 15 miles away, and back to Superstition Springs each school day until their home was finished.

Joe was teaching during the week and Mary Ann, Louise and I became really acquainted with Phoenix with our search for furniture etc for the new home. Mary Ann would purchase what she wanted and we loaded it onto the Isuzu and off to storage with it until the house was finished.

561

We had so much fun in helping Mary Ann select all the furniture for their new home and bringing it back in the Isuzu pickup for storage; some days it was a riot. Sometimes we would travel from Apache Junction through all the cities of Mesa, Gilbert, Tempe, Phoenix and Scottsdale that actually is one city running into the other and is about 75 miles across.

One time we went to Scottsdale where Mary Ann purchased a davenport and two matching stuffed chairs. We stuffed the two chairs in the pickup and tied the davenport on top and over the cab. Believe me we looked like Ma and Pa Kettle on some days moving all those purchases to the storage area that was located near their new home that was under construction.

That winter I put over 3000 miles on the pickup and we really got to know the streets in the whole area.

Later that fall we got into painting and I worked on some electrical hook-ups for the new home. When the house was finished a couple of days before Christmas we had all the furniture in the house and Louise and Mary Ann cooked a delicious Christmas dinner for everyone; besides Mary Ann, Joe, Shannon, Louise and I the guests were Gerry and Willie and Mardell and two girls.

A photo of the finished home is above.

Christmas 1990 was over and Louise and I had an obligation to be back in Kennewick before the end of the year so we had to leave right after Mary Ann's birthday on Dec. 28th.

After the New Year Mary Ann went to work for an engineering organization and Joe continued teaching at Eloy, Az. Later Joe taught special ed at a school in Phoenix and then decided to change jobs and work for the city of Phoenix at the airport screening luggage as the passengers passed into a secure area. He had an interesting job; one time he caught a few passengers trying to sneak a gun through but with the screen he caught the culprits and they were arrested on the spot.

Joe and Mary Ann took time out to celebrate their 25th wedding anniversary on November 18, 2003. It did not seem possible that they had been married that many years and I nearly forgot their special day event.

Joe worked at the airport until he took a job in maintenance with the city of Phoenix where he worked until his retirement in 2006.

Joe lost his father Gerry Hicks on January 14, 2006. Gerry was laid to rest at the Desert Memorial Cemetery at Kennewick, Washington.

For a number of years, Mary Ann has worked for DHR (Diversified Human Resources); they are a PEO (Professional Employees Organization). They do the account for company payroll, unemployment, insurance and all benefits including setting up new hire files that a company offers for their employees. DHR has nation wide services for corporations and their headquarters is located in Scottsdale, Arizona where Mary Ann works.

Since Joe's retirement from the city, he is working with Mary Ann in the filing department. They have the same hours and are able to travel to and from work together.

Joe and Mary Ann also have their own business called, Bizy Enterprises, Inc. They have a binding system set up for small books and offer publishing for short run books as well as providing editing and graphics. They also offer pdf digital setups for demand printing for volume size books in both true and fiction writing. They have book publishing for both soft side printing and hard cover printing. Besides the larger page editions for authors, they specialize for those authors wanting to write their own family books, children books, cookbooks as well as other themes. It is truly a service for printing a few books or many all at affordable prices. They have a web site that one can view their offerings: WWW.Mindseyevision.com.

LOUISE, WILLARD INGRAHAM AND FAMILY

MY FAMILY
By: Mary Ann Hicks

Having been born into the Ingraham family means I am part of a whole that represents caring, sharing and loving all of the parts. I have many good memories of picnics and gatherings that always meant lots of Ingraham laughter. Even as the years have gone by, I have noticed that the Ingraham's have not aged. They just look wiser; and that is what I say when I look in the mirror and I am sticking to it.

Jackie once wrote that her mom and dad have never let her down. I believe that goes for Ray and Anna Rose and their family and Lorraine and her family. I know without a doubt that it goes for my mom and dad too. If I had been allowed to choose our parents before we were born, then I made one smart decision to come into the world with them. They have always been there through thick and thin. They have always supported me in my choices.

One choice was marrying Joe. Some of my friends called it a rebound. I called it heaven sent and mom & dad welcomed Joe and his family into their hearts right along with me. There is not one day that goes by that I don't look into Joe's eyes and know I am one lucky person. Then the blessings kept coming. I have watched Shannon through the years and I hope she knows how proud we are of her and all of the things she does. She chose Ryan, he has been more than a son to us, and it just keeps getting better. Now we have Torryn and Ivry!

With every generation, it all falls back on those Ingraham roots. Grandpa and Grandma's perseverance and determination to keep the family close, brought the laughter and music that held us all together and molded us for our own families. The love in our hearts and eagerness to share our souls and our gifts of giving brought us all close to each other. Thank you family!!

Mary Ann (Ingraham) Hicks

SHANNON ANN (HICKS) INGRAHAM

A new little baby came to live with her parents Milton Lewis (Joe) Hicks and Mary Ann Hicks. Shannon Ann Hicks was born April 27, 1981 at 11:10 P.M. in the Mesa Hospital, Mesa, Arizona in Maricopa County. With in a few minutes after birth her mother Mary Ann called us, (Willard and Louise Ingraham) to inform us that we were now grandparents of a bouncing little baby girl. Shannon is our only granddaughter (her photo is below).

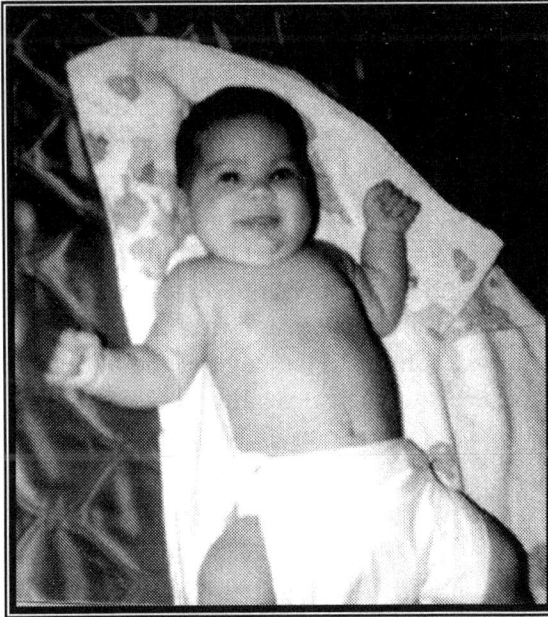

We have three grandsons by our daughter Mahria Jordan.

It was July of 1981 before Louise and I could fly down to see our little granddaughter. It was very hot when Joe and Mary Ann and Shannon picked us up at the Phoenix airport but they had good air conditioning in their car and at their home and besides they had a nice big pool in their backyard. We changed into our swimming suits and sat around the pool under a big umbrella sipping cold drinks and watching Joe teaching Shannon how to swim. Joe was also a swimming coach. Shannon just loved getting into the water.

Yes, it was fun being acquainted with Shannon and I did not forget how to change a diaper. That vacation went too fast and we had to leave for home but in December of 1981, we flew back to Arizona to spend Christmas with the Hicks family.

While we were in Arizona on that trip, we bought a twenty-two foot Travel Craft motor home and decided to try it out. Joe, Mary Ann, Shannon, Louise and I loaded up and headed for Mexico. We parked the motor home on the US side of the border and walked into Mexico. We spent about two hours there then came back to Tucson, Arizona and spent some time looking it over. We visited Old Tucson, a place where many movies have been filmed and are still being filmed.

In addition, we saw the large enclosure of hundreds of stored American airplanes from WWII sitting in the desert sun wasting away. They call this place, The Pima Air Museum,

Later in the summer of 1982, I had to fly to Phoenix, Az. to work with Fellowship Tours Agency to put together the itinerary for another international tour.

When I arrived in Tempe Shannon had a tricycle that she rode around and around the family pool as fast as she could go at the same time cutting the corners and riding closer and closer to the edge of the pool until one wheel would go bump as she cut the corner. One day Joe and Mary Ann said the inevitable did happen and in the pool Shannon went with tricycle and all; being dunked in the water did not phase her because she knew how to swim and Joe and Mary Ann was always watching her so if needed they could pull her out immediately. It was a lesson for Shannon not to get too close so there would be no repeat performances.

In the front of their home was a big maple tree (photo above) spreading out across the yard near the sidewalk.

Shannon had a game she played; when she walked to the side door of the house she would look up at me and say 1-2-3 go and away she would race to the big tree. She loved to do that and of course, she would win most of the time but really, she could run very fast for a little one less than two years old. When Shannon would win, she would screech for joy.

It was in 1983 when Joe and Mary Ann with Shannon moved to Kennewick from Tempe, Az. They stayed with Louise and I in our home at Kennewick, Washington for several months until their business, Allied Services was constructed and open for business. This gave them a chance to survey the area and find a home that would suit their needs.

Having them in our home also gave Louise and I a chance to be better acquainted with Shannon and as grandparents spoil her a little bit. Shannon loved music. She was about two and a half years old at that time, we would turn on the music, and I would pick her up and with her hanging on to my neck and the other arm in my hand we would dance and twirl around the room cheek to cheek. She loved this and never wanted to stop. It was fun times for Louise and I. Shannon was a happy little girl and always had a big smile on her face. It was such a joy having her running around our home; she livened up the days.

Their business, Allied Services opened, got off the ground and up and running in 1984. It was a new business so a lot of promotion was necessary. The services of shipping and mailing, Airborne, Federal Express, UPS, Western Union, Notary and money orders etc. It was services orientated and very much in demand so the doors were always swinging all day long. Later they added a food bar for snacks for customers to enjoy.

Mary Ann was manager and Joe and I (Willard) helped to run the business. Shannon was only three years old then at that time; she had a well-lighted corner in the back room for a space to play for her own. She was always so good while the rest of us were always busy. She worked out a routine every day that kept her busy and happy all day and never came into the front of the store to interrupt any of us. Her routine went like this: first go under the table where there was a cubbyhole and play with school toys, second; listen to records and sing a long. Then lunch and third watch Sesame Street and Mr. Rogers on T.V. Fourth color and draw and fifth watch channel 2 on the T.V. where they would work out and she exercised with them.

When we came to work in the mornings, Shannon would like a short dance with me by standing on my toes while we danced away. Then of course, she would have to have her swing time by sitting on my toes and having me swing around and around with her. This was fun for a while until she was getting to heavy for my legs.

The time was flying and soon Shannon was going to school in the first grade. It was in the Bluebirds that Shannon and others had to sell cookies. Shannon brought her box of cookies to Allied and her parent gave her a stool and counter space across the room from the main counter where she was to sit but was told not to say anything. Customers would come in and see that cute little girl just sitting there with a winning smile and her cookies for sale. They walked right over to her and bought. Shannon sold the most cookies of any one in her Bluebird group.

Halloween time was a fun time when Shannon dressed up in her Halloween costumes and we walked with her around our neighborhood to collect goodies in her small bag. When we got back to the house, there was time to listen to the happy chatter and all have a little hot chocolate.

Shannon went to a private school for several years until Joe and Mary Ann sold their big home with a large yard and purchased a smaller home with a swimming pool in their back yard. Shannon then went to a different school until 1990 when Allied Services was sold and Joe, Mary Ann and Shannon planned a moved to Gilbert, Arizona. Joe went to Apache

Junction, Arizona ahead of his family to take a teaching position at Eloy, Arizona.

Louise had retired as bank manager so when the business sold we went with Mary Ann and Shannon to Arizona to help them move. We all stayed in our motor home at Apache Junction until Joe and Mary Ann's new home was built at Gilbert, Arizona.

On arriving in Arizona immediately, Shannon was enrolled in a grade school just a few blocks from where their new home was being built. We were staying in Apache Junction about 15 miles from the school so every day we took Shannon to school and picked her up in the afternoon. We did this until December when their new house was finished and they moved into their new home by December 24 of 1990.

Joe and Mary Ann in 1993 was driving around looking the area over around Phoenix and found themselves twenty miles northeast of Scottsdale, Az. in a small tourist and retirement town called Fountain Hills. It got the name because of the lake and large fountain that shoots water 560 feet into the air five foot higher than the Washington Monument. The fountain is brilliantly illuminated at night. The lake is almost in the center of the town.

Joe and Mary Ann rented their home in Gilbert and bought a house with a pool in Fountain Hills pending the sale of their home in Gilbert. They had a block fence all around the property. We vacationed with them in and enjoyed our time there. It was nice to get up in the mornings, go out to their grapefruit tree, and select the nicest one on the tree. The pool was wonderful in that hot weather.

One night the police were speeding up and down the streets with sirens and lights blinking that awakened us. We knew something was going on out there but did not find out until the next morning; it seems a black bear was going around and picking the pool he wanted to cool off in.

This is wild country all around Fountain Hills; it is actually in the middle of the desert with many kinds of animals and wild life out there in the open areas. Shannon would go out there by herself with her little dog Peaches. One time she said she encountered a bunch of pigs in the desert and the pigs were really eying her little dog so she picked Peaches up and walked away ignoring the pigs. I asked her if she realized how dangerous those wild pigs were and she said,"they wouldn't hurt me because they are not that big". I explained to her just how dangerous those wild pigs were.

It was then early spring and I cautioned Shannon on the rattlesnakes that would be coming out too. She insisted she had been walking all over and had not seen any yet. Later Joe and Mary Ann wanted to take all of us for a walk on the edge of town. We were walking on a road and Mary Ann and Shannon wanted to leave the road and go up the draw. Birds were flying around and landing on the rocks with small stick like bushes sticking up then we saw something I had never seen before. As the birds were flying around suddenly there were about ten rattle snakes popping up like sticks out of the rocks and swaying in the wind enticing the birds to land on them thinking they were the limb of a bush that were abundant there. If we had walked up that draw, we would have walked by that rock pile and the snake den with 100s of snakes in the den. Believe me that sure made a believer out of Shannon from then on.

Joe and Mary Ann's home in Gilbert did not sell so they moved back to their home in Gilbert. In 1993, Shannon decided to go into business on her own at the age of 12. She always liked small dogs and when she saw some little pedigreed Maltese puppies, she fell in love with them and decided to buy a small female. Later she bought another Maltese male so she would have a male and female to raise pedigree Maltese puppies. Shannon was very successful in her adventure.

She read all about the care and feeding of them plus the breeding and whelping at birth. She handled all of these jobs by herself with very good luck by saving all her little additions.

She loved caringly for all their needs and the little Maltese loved her back to where it was hard for her to sell them when they were ready to go. Of course, they all sold with their documented pedigree records. Many of these puppies' ancestors were prized show dogs but Shannon was too busy to train them and go on tour with them as show dogs. Her puppies sold for around $700 or $800 apiece in the beginning and more later.

Shannon continued to ask me, "Grandpa wouldn't you like one of these cute little puppies"? I would always tell her no that I do not want a dog. Then Shannon would call me on the phone and ask me, "Grandpa if you had a dog what would you call it"? I would answer her that I do not want a dog and then she would say, "no, but Grandpa if you had a dog what would you call it"? I then told her if I had a dog, it would be invisible. No more was said after that so I concluded that the subject was settled. Not so; several months after this discussion Shannon called me and said, "Grandpa I have your little Invisible." I again informed her that I did not want a dog. Her argument was persuasive and Grandpa melted and gave in. Then she said, "Grandpa what will you call your dog"? I said that is easy Shannon, the dog will be called Indy for invisible.

It was in October of 1994 that Louise and I drove down to Gilbert, Arizona, picked up our little Indy, and brought her back to Kennewick. On the way back home, we drove around through California because it was in December and the weather was bad. We drove until noon and decided to stop by a restaurant where we could look out the window and observe Indy in a cage in our blazer. After lunch, I opened the cage to refill her water dish but when I opened the cage door, I noticed Indy was getting sick and she had upchucked up in her water dish without getting anything out of the dish. It was easy to go to a faucet near by and clean it all up. Now I marveled at what a smart dog I had and she was only about six months old. Several months later, I found out just how smart she was when I took her to obedience school. She took the blue ribbon above all the other dogs in the class. Yes, I was quite proud of her and still am.

This is the year 2007, Indy is thirteen years old, and I am still very proud of her. She is the best dog that I have ever had. When Indy was old, enough we took her to Yakima, Washington and had her bred by a registered Maltese show dog that had a pedigree behind him recording many other show dogs.

When Indy had her puppy I helped her in birthing; three little beautiful Maltese puppies came and one was perfect. We named her Cuddles. The second puppy was breach, I lost her, and the third puppy was a runt and would not eat. I tried feeding him by a small bottle but it would not eat. We took him to the vets and they gave him a shot that killed him within five minutes of getting there. I said that they took him and gave a shot to kill him and charged us $100 to do it.

In 1995, Shannon wanted to come and visit us in Washington from Arizona. She took her own money earned from raising her dogs and came on the plane at the age of 14. She had spring school vacation so we gave her Cuddles and packed up the Blazer including Cuddles and all went to the Oregon coast to a resort overlooking the Pacific Ocean at Surf Rider Resort.

Shannon loved this resort and now with little Cuddles with her they she was enjoying bonding with her little pet. When we put Shannon on the plane with Cuddles in a carry on, we were concerned about the flight and plane change in Salt Lake. We need not have worried; we learned later that Shannon and pet were the highlight for the passengers and the flight attendants helped with the plane change in Salt Lake.

In 1997, Shannon convinced Louise to take one of her Maltese puppies. Joe Hicks helped his parents Gerry and Willie Hicks drive back from Apache Junction, Az. where they owned a park model to their home in Kennewick, Washington. They brought Mitzie with them. Louise called her Mitzie and she definitely has a mind of her own and does not mind showing it at times. I took her though obedience classes and did end up with the blue ribbon and best in the class. Mitzie is different from Indy as I could always count on Indy to go through all her paces without question but not Mitzie. I was not sure sometimes if she was going to mind or not.

Mitzie is on the left and Indy, both showing off.

In the year 2000, Shannon signed up for a six-year term with the Air force National Guard. She was able to get her education paid for this way and had only to serve on weekends and several weeks every summer. If she had been ordered to go though she would have had to serve over seas. Her unit was on alert a few times but in all the six years served, she did not have to go over seas.

On June 23, 2004, my birthday, Louise, my wife held an 80th birthday party and a book signing celebration in our backyard. I had just finished writing my book of my war stories in WWII and it was published. I had a box of books, "Farm Boy To Soldier" ready to sell. This was the first time we got to meet Shannon's boy friend Ryan Peters.

Both Louise and I liked him at our first meeting. Later we were informed that they were being married and wondered if it would be all right if they used our name Ingraham for their last name if it was all right with us because they had planned to change their last names. I told them we would be proud to have Ryan in our family and I pointed out some of the problems they would encounter when they changed their name but we would be very proud if they wanted to have the Ingraham name.

574

LOUISE, WILLARD INGRAHAM AND FAMILY

In 2004, they did get married as Ingraham in Chandler, Az. at the home of Ryan's parent' and we were there. It was a beautiful setting in the backyard. What a beautiful and happy couple they were. Ryan got down on one knee and asked Shannon to marry him and it was a very touching part of the ceremony. Ryan and Shannon asked me if I would anoint them as part of the ceremony and I did saying to them, "one time when Louise and I was visiting Jerusalem we obtained this bottle of holy water from the Jordan River. With this Holy water I would like to give God's blessings upon this marriage of Ryan and Shannon and to all those who come after from this union. May you have a long and happy life together." At the same time I related this message I anointed Ryan and Shannon with the Holy water.

Then their minister married them as they stood under the arch of flowers in the backyard. Following was the reception with a lot of food that most of it had been prepared by Ryan and Shannon. We were up to the wee hours of the morning. There was lots of visiting and conversation that followed until the newly weds were sent on their way for their honeymoon.

Shannon Ingraham Meyers Eng 101 Essay 2

24 Sep. 05

I LOVE MY FAMILY

Love, it is the breath of natures proliferating knowledge of one's higher self. Love is the antithesis of both the lowest and the highest degrees of energy, it is found deeper than the paradox itself. The meaning of life is love, and the solely greatest inspiring love I have found, is in my nine month old son Torryn, and husband Ryan, both of whom are apart of my forever loving family. Love truly makes life worth living, and replacing the roll of toilet paper worth doing ... well, most of the time. Much of my egotistical Quirks, and the "world rotates around my navel" attitude, have long since dissolved, and have been replaced with the precedence of love. Both Ryan and Torryn have opened my mind to see flawless beauty and whole hearted compassion in life's rawest creations. Through baby excrement, sputum, and tripping over mountains of laundry, there is not a day that goes by where I don't thank god for my family. Both on our own circuitous paths, had Ryan and I not met, I do not know where I would be in life.

Ryan came into my chaotic and eccentric picture when I was nearly 21. I was full of restless energy, working two jobs, running 15 miles a week, and drawing abstract art when I had the time. On occasion, I would go out on an obligatory date, which would gradually fizzle somewhere between the sociopathic banter and the sexually explicit innuendos. "Is this all there is out there", I thought? Little did I know there lived a sensitive, creative, and still a stud, named Ryan.

Ryan is a fiery, red headed Sagittarius who seems to have an internal magnetic ball of energy that never ceases to slow down. If you were to ask Ryan to come and eat while he's on a 16 hour non-stop creative role, he would reply "Yeah hang on, I'm almost done." Yeah right, Wi+,h an eloquently poised touch and a meticulous eye for detail in all that he aspires to. Ryan has created beautiful ceramic pottery and abstract works of art in various medium. As an artist, Ryan is spiritually defined, introspective, and focused, all of which emanate throughout his masterpieces. My favorite piece is a pottery piece he made, raku style, about 8 inches tall, 10 inches in diameter, crackled turquoise-blue glaze, tri-pedal coal black base, with a single Chinese Kanji symbol on one face meaning "Patience". Both being highly creative like minded only children, along with sharing a nonconformist approach to thinking, and both holding deep yet unconventional spiritual ideas, it's at least obvious to us as to why we were destined to cross paths.

I met Ryan at Michael's arts and crafts store, as a night stocker. Our relationship took shape, somewhere between flirting by the menagerie of floral décor, and on the scented candle isle, where we made jocular remarks about our "Pat, what the hell is that?" shrew of a boss. Our boss looked like a small mutt giving birth to a long horned bull, and smelled like a feminine hygiene receptacle. By that I mean, she liked to bark, had curly hair that reminded us of molding straw colored steel wool, a scowl that defines "scowl", and a smell unique to her species. That woman was pure evil, or at least bitterness embodied, and made for an environment that was not conducive to a fragile fledgling relationship. As Ryan and I decorated the Michael's Christmas tree displays, a shimmering image of the future played before my mind, of us decorating a perfect Martha Stewart tree in the comforts of our own home. As time quickly passed, contiguous interests grew, and life aspirations emerged alike, I knew someone or something was definitely trying to tell me something, "Ryan is the one." When our bitter old rat faced boss was not looking, Ryan and I managed to sneak away to the Michael's storage shed and "restock items" such as, tickle wars and kissing sessions. Time spent outside of work began to grow exponentially. Our favorite hangout was none other than a 24 hour Perkins diner, where we could split an omelet, and drink numerous cups of coffee, conversing until there was nobody left to come home. I

think our record stay at Perkins was six hours give or take. All
I know is that our servers' polite "please tip" welcoming
attitude turned into a "What? You want more coffee. Yeah,
well get the hell out!" demeanor. Despite the sleep deprivation
and the long hours working together, I do not think Ryan and I
had ever grown weary of one another, and just when you ask
yourself, "Can it get better than this?"...it does.

Our relationship flourished into the never-ending
oblivion when, Ryan asked me to marry him. While driving
through Yosemite national park, Ryan nudged me to pull the
car over to view the tantalizing river below the canyon. Ryan
knew I would give into my conditioned response of having to
pee once the car stopped, providing an ideal set-up for his
surprise. As we got out of the car, sure enough, I was looking
for a bush to pee under. Ryan said, "You go pee, and I will
meet you down by the river bank".

Within a few seconds, I ducked out of the bushes and
zipped up my pants, meandering to the riverbed. As I got closer
to the roar of the water, I yelled out, "Ryan where are you?"

Just then, I saw Ryan's hands waving me closer. As I
stumbled across the gargantuous river rocks, a flash of silver
sparked my eye. Before my brain could register what it was
exactly, I bolted for it without hesitation. Here again, another
habit Ryan had exploited in his lovely ruse, I'm always hunting
for treasure. In my hands shining back at me, was this polished
pure silver box with the words engraved on top,

(Ryan voicing the words aloud as I read) "Shannon,
with all my heart and all my love, will you marry me?"

"Yes, Yes, Yes!" I shouted, dropping the silver box on
the ground. Ryan asked, "Are you going to look in the box? I
shook with exhilaration as I picked up the box off the ground
and opened the fitted lid. There before me, gleamed a white
gold, diamond ring surrounded by two blue sapphire stones,
displayed on a handmade ring pillow, inside the cobalt blue
velvet lined casing. I delicately placed the ring on my finger,
admiring how the sun played on the diamond's facets, revealing

its multi colored transparencies. I knew that this would be one of those moments I would always hold dear in my heart.

Above photo taken at the wedding of Ryan and Shannon Ingraham (center). Left is Shannon' parents, Joe and Mary Ann Hicks. To the far right are Shannon and Ryans grandparents, Willard and Louise Ingraham.

As time passed, Ryan and I moved into our first home (left) At first, our home took on a cold sterile foot, but with a little toasted wheat paint here, Parisian taupe there, and a few throw rugs, our home became aesthetically pleasing.

With help from our family, we were able to get a discounted
washer and dryer, and a lumpy but suitable mattress.
Everything was going like clockwork, except for how I was
feeling physically. I had been enduring sharp jabbing cramps
from my lower abdominals for months, but when they
progressed with agony, I went to see a specialist. Later on that
month, I was informed that I had a condition called PCOS or
Polycystic Ovarian Syndrome. PCOS is a buildup of ovulatory
cysts on the ovaries, stemming from hormonal imbalances.
Along with a plethora of difficult side effects, PCOS can cause
infertility; which in my case was apparent. Doctors
recommended a surgical procedure called ovarian drilling;
which would allow me a one-year window in which to become
pregnant. Always wanting children, Ryan and I began to
realize that it was now or never. Both still engaged, Ryan and I
joked that having a baby now would be like having the "cart
before the wagon". We both agreed "To hell with society's
conformities", the important thing is that we love each other.
So with a leap of faith, I plunged into the sea of IVs, gauze and
sedatives. After the surgery, I awoke in a paralysis state,
watching the hospital's walls take on a spectral quality.
Luckily, Ryan was there to revive me, and lead me back to
coherency. All throughout post operation, Ryan tended to my
every need. He bathed me, fed me and made sure I found the
toilet okay. Again, what would I do without Ryan?

   About five months and a wedding later, I experienced a
bout of queasiness that left me strongly embracing porcelain.
Could I be pregnant? Ryan's job at a medical lab, allowed us to
take advantage of free blood testing. After getting my blood
drawn, I began the hard five-day wait for the pregnancy results.
In suspense, Ryan asked the lab a day earlier about the
outcome of my results. Although the results were indeed in,
sadly I was not pregnant, so they thought. The days seemed
like years, as I began to grow sicker and sicker, trying to
withhold urges of projectile vomit. I thought I had a disease,
such as pelvic inflammatory or even ovarian cancer. Things

were not making any sense, the nausea, the bloating, the acid reflux syndrome, until the day Ryan solved the mystery. Apparently the Phlebotomist at the lab was looking at the wrong part of the result. I not only was pregnant, but four weeks shy of starting my second trimester. All that was left was breaking the news to me. That very day, Ryan rushed home from work early, sneaking in the house a congratulating surprise. Ryan said, "Come here, I have something for you."

Still in a pre-barf state, I ran up the stairs fumbling for the lights. I peered slightly behind the bedroom doorway to see Ryan sitting on the bed by a gorgeous decorous arrangement of white roses and a lavish bottle of wine. With a card in his hands, Ryan said, "I think you need to open this."

With much anticipation, I opened the card that revealed a picture of a baby with a stethoscope around his neck; it read, "I have your diagnosis and it doesn't make sense, nice people should not be sick." Down below, written in black pen, read, "Congratulations, we're pregnant". I shouted: "We're going to have a baby, and I'm not dying!"

I was so uplifted and exuberated with joy; I almost went to celebrate with a drink of wine, "Oh yeah, that's probably not a good idea."

After about seven months mild abuse to my body (not to mention the stretch marks), and a quick visit to the hospital, I gave birth to our son, Torryn. Watching him grow is healing, and in some ways feels like it is restoring my lost innocence. Torryn is a soul like many, purely observing life's farcicalities to enhance his own opinion of what is normal. Torryn is a whisper of new beginnings, with the potential of a voice loud enough to manifest good on this dying planet. Torryn is the reminder of how precious life is, and how inevitably fast its grace flourishes then withers. Most importantly, Torryn is the love that shines through Ryan and I., and makes our family whole.

Again I will say, "I don't know what I would do if I hadn't met Ryan.

TORRYN BRIEHL INGRAHAM

On Thursday, February 3, 2005 at 8:37 P.M. Torryn Briehl Ingraham was born at Mesa Hospital, Mesa, Az. It just so happened that his mom Shannon was born at this very hospital also. Father Ryan was right there witnessing the birth of his son and holding Shannon's hand. Ryan took many photos right away of baby Torryn and mother Shannon and shared the pictures with us. One of those photos is below.

It was April of 2005 before Louise and I could get down to see our first great grandson. It did not take long to be acquainted and form a bond with Torryn.

While we were visiting with them at Mesa, Arizona Ryan and Shannon wanted me to anoint their son Torryn Briehl Ingraham so it was on April 17, 2005 your great grandfather, Willard Stanley Ingraham said, "I anoint you with this holy water that came from the Jordan River that was obtained in Jerusalem, Israel. Your great grandmother, Louise Ingraham and I on one of our trips brought this holy water back home from Israel. We had the privilege of visiting in the Holy Lands seven times where our Lord Jesus Christ lived and died for all our sins so that we mortals living beings may have ever lasting life.

LOUISE, WILLARD INGRAHAM AND FAMILY

I will now anoint you with this holy water and ask God's blessings for this most precious boy who will grow up and do many honorable things in God's light and blessings always. AH-Men." The photo below is Shannon holding Torryn and great grandpa anointing little Torryn.

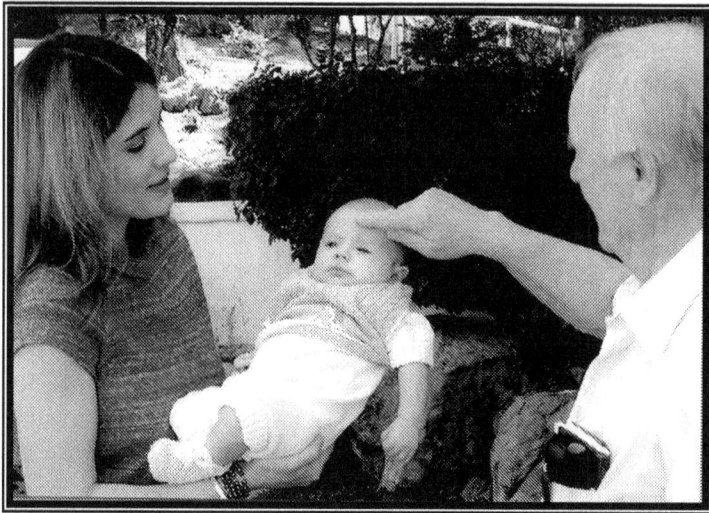

I am told by his parents that Torryn is the best little boy. All he wants is his bottle of milk and his regular change periodically then he rewards them with a big satisfied smile. I can vouch for that because when we visited them and we were together a lot there was very few times that I heard Torryn cry.

On October 25 of 2006, Louise and I flew to Phoenix, Az. to visit Joe and Mary Ann at their home in Mesa, Az. on the 27th of Oct. Mary Ann, Shannon and Louise went shopping. Joe and I baby-sat Torryn as Ryan had to work. In the evening, we had dinner at Joe and Mary Ann's home. When Ryan joined us we all of went in two cars to the IMAX Theater. The movie was a birthday gift for Louise from Joe and Mary Ann. They knew she loved to know more about Atlantis and this was a 3-d movie, "Atlantis at Santorini", one of the Greek Islands that is thought to be the location of the mythical island of Atlantis. The movie was wonderful and thought provoking.

Torryn's eyes were as big as saucers when he watched the screen but he did not become frightened as long as he was sitting on dad Ryan's lap.

The next day Joe, Ryan, Torryn and I went to the air force museum where they had on display WWII fighter planes, army jeeps that Torryn loved to sit in and pretend drive. There was a small plane replica of a Navy plane and they allowed small children like Torryn to sit in it and be pushed by adults. He loved it.

The photo below is special; grandpa Joe Hicks did a little magic with Torryn in the plane and off he flew over the ocean.

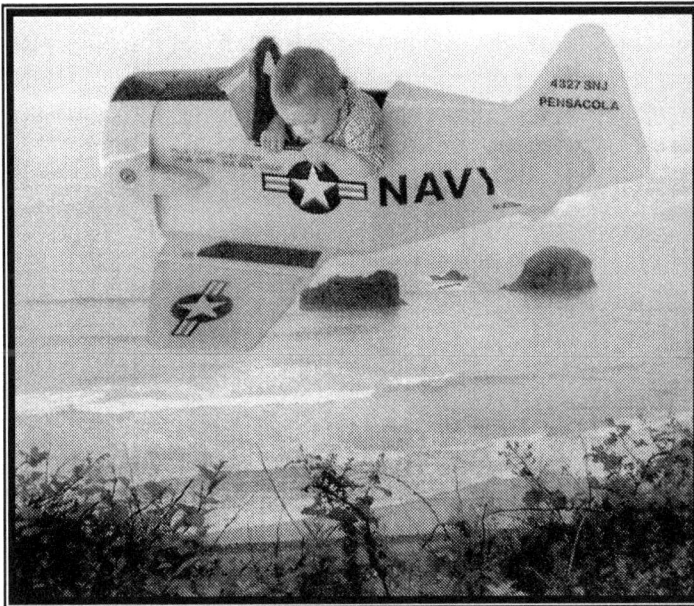

Then we took him to lunch and watched Torryn stack six of those coffee creamers up; one on another like no problem at all. He was only a year and half old and his coordination was exemplatory.

After lunch, Ryan wanted to take us out to an old western tavern and store where many movies have been made. An old tavern had regular horse saddles for sitting as you bellied up to the bar. Can you imagine here was a father, grandfather and great grandfather all taking little Torryn to a bar and drinking sarsaparilla? This place was about 20 miles out of Apache Junction. Later that evening all of us including the women went to a restaurant called, "My Big Fat Greek," It was exciting and fun; we were guests of Mary Ann and Joe and celebrating Louise's birthday.

On Oct. 29, 2006 we all loaded up in two cars, all seven of us, and went to the Phoenix Zoo. To many cars in the close up parking area so we parked in a big parking lot away from the zoo gate. A free charter bus took us to and from the parking lot to the zoo grounds. Torryn loved all the animals, birds and his ride on the merry-go-round on a carousel horse.

As we walked the zoo grounds, we took turns carrying Torryn. He rode on the men's shoulders where he could look above the crowd and see everything. It took five hours to walk the zoo grounds. It was a wonderful day and afterward we went to a pizza place where they had many kinds of pizza that one could choose from while a man played a huge organ on a stage that went around, around, and up and down while he played all the good songs of the 1940s and 1950s. Torryn watched intently and kept time to the music; a very long day for him but he was wide-eyed and still ready to go.

Monday, Oct. 30, 2006 Mary Ann and Joe had the day off. We started the day off by purchasing some scones at coffee house and Mary Ann called Marty and Tom Vickerman who lived nearby to join us. We all met at the pool area of Los Palmos and enjoyed our scones and espressos while playing the Thought Game.

This Thought Game is a sharing of thoughts; the leader asked all the players the same question and each player is to write down their answer. There is no strict rule on the type of question just that each first writes the answer and shares their thoughts or opinions around the circle of players. The fun of it is that everyone has the opportunity to voice his or her own thoughts without the influence of what someone else is thinking. After the game Joe and Mary Ann went swimming then we went back to their house.

October 31, 2006 was a workday for Mary Ann and Joe as well as Ryan. Shannon had to go to a biology class so she dropped Torryn off for us to enjoy all day. In the afternoon, we called Marty and Tom to come over to play cards while Torryn played with his toys in between his bouts on each of our laps as he watched us play cards. Torryn's favorite game was to borrow Tom's shoes and walk around the room in them. He loved the clop clop.

It was also Halloween night and Ryan and Shannon invited Joe, Mary Ann, Louise and I over for dinner. When we arrived at their home, we found Ryan sitting outside on the front porch carving a Jack-o-lantern then putting lighted candles in the lantern. You can see from the photo below that

these are extra ordinary carvings. They were very attractive lanterns all lighted up with the light showing through the carvings.

Ryan also took time to serve trick and treaters a sweet.

Joe, Shannon and I took Torryn around the block for his first trick-n-treat. After going to the first house he knew what to do; he knocked on the door and when he received the treat he would tell them thank you, go to the next house, and do the same. He loved this because along the way he could pop a candy in his mouth. Later Shannon served a delicious dinner and then we enjoyed an evening of conversation.

On Nov. 1, 2006 Joe and Mary Ann took another day off which meant we all slept in until 7:30 A.M., ate breakfast then went out and sat on their screened in porch. We all played the Thought game then off to Costco to get pictures developed. Mary Ann and Joe purchased an all in-one printer that when they got home it did not take long to set up.

The next day everyone was back at work and Shannon in class so we got to keep Torryn again. In the afternoon, we played cards with Tom and Marty and in the evening, everyone gathered to enjoy a special Italian dinner prepared by Mary Ann. Afterward we played the Thought game and another enjoyable day passed by.

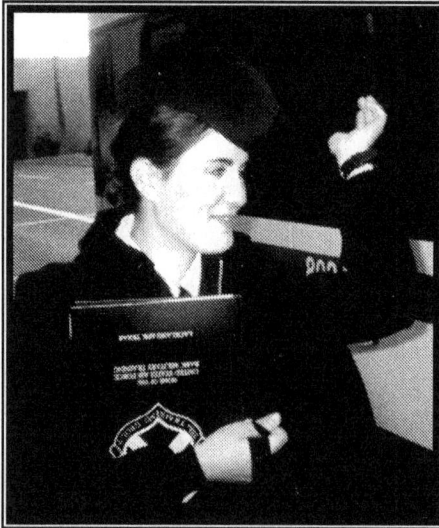

The following day was the Los Palmos community annual yard sale. It was a lot of fun and the prices were very reasonable. Joe and Mary Ann lucked out and purchased two almost alike new bicycles. Shannon by now had almost served six years in the air force National Guard (photo above). She took basics in Texas and Florida for special training but was fortune that she was able to serve at the Phoenix base.

Mary Ann and Joe had purchased massages for all four of us so we drove about thirty miles from their home to a resort for the massages. The massage was wonderful and afterward we drove to a picturesque valley that was called Gold Canyon in a new development in the foothills of the Superstition Mountains.

On one day, the whole family met at the Country Club restaurant; Marty and Tom had picked up Marty and Joe's mother Willie. Shannon had to go to the air force national guard that day but Ryan brought Torryn. .

After our lunch, Marty and Tom took Willie home then joined the rest of us at a new development called Olive Grove Gardens where we took the tour and they showed us how olive oil was processed. That evening we went to a movie called Talking To God.

Above we all posed for a timed photo op: Left to right in back, Shannon, Mary Ann and Louise; in front left to right Ryan and little Torryn, Joe and Willard.

Our outing the next day was to IKEA. Joe and Mary Ann drove us about fifteen miles out of Phoenix to a large international retail outlet owned by Japanese. They sold many different country wares and called themselves IKEA. It was a very interesting place to visit. Our next stop was the Golden Corral Restaurant. It was new, nice buffet and had good food.

Our vacation was over so the next day Joe and Mary Ann took Louise and I to the Phoenix airport for our early flight home.

IVRY RAE INGRAHAM

Ivry Rae Ingraham was born on January 12, 2007 at Mesa hospital in Mesa, Arizona to the proud parents Shannon and Ryan Ingraham. A photo of Ivry is below.

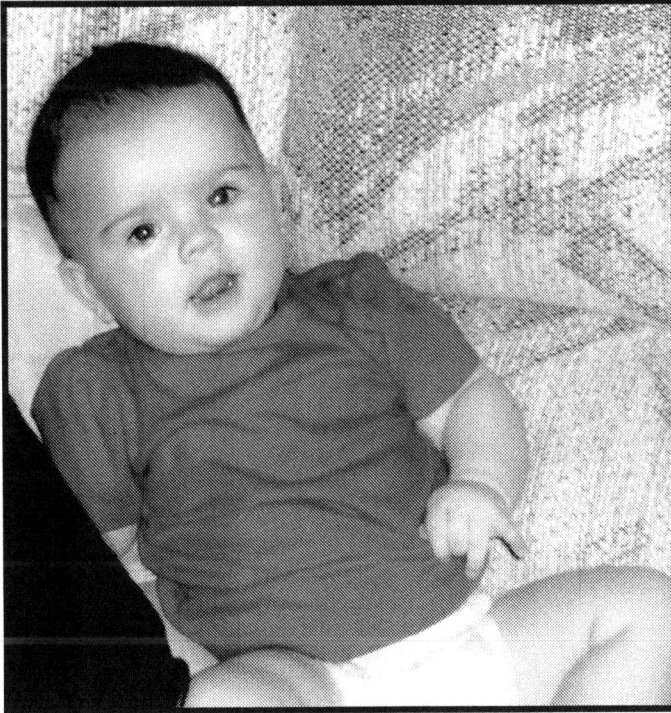

Ivry was born at the same hospital where mother Shannon was born and also Ivry's brother Torryn.

We have not seen our new great granddaughter but we have seen many photos that her parents have sent us. We think she looks very much like her grandmother Mary Ann at that age.

Louise and I have not had the opportunity to hold Ivry yet but we plan to go down to Arizona in the fall and be acquainted with our new little great granddaughter. Ivry has stolen the hearts of her grandparents, Joe and Mary Ann.

Grandmother Mary Ann says Ivry is very much like Torryn at that age and hardly ever cries and has a quick flash of a big smile.

Grandmother Mary Ann tells us that Ivry lays in her crib and her eyes follows her as she walks around the room then when she looks over at her Ivry quickly flashes that big winning smile.

As time goes by there will be much to say about this little happy contended soul as she develops and grows to be a respected wise person.

Above is a photo of this special Ingraham family left to right: Ivry, Ryan, Shannon and Torryn.

GALLERY OF IVRY AND TORRYN 2007

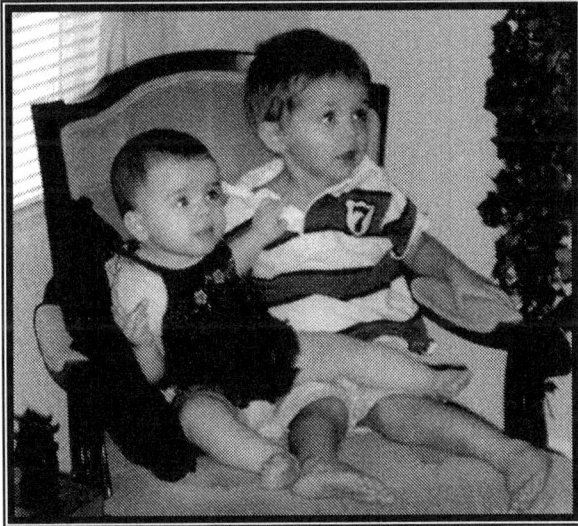

Left,
Brother
Torryn and
sister Ivry

Torryn left and new truck.
Below Ivry all smiles

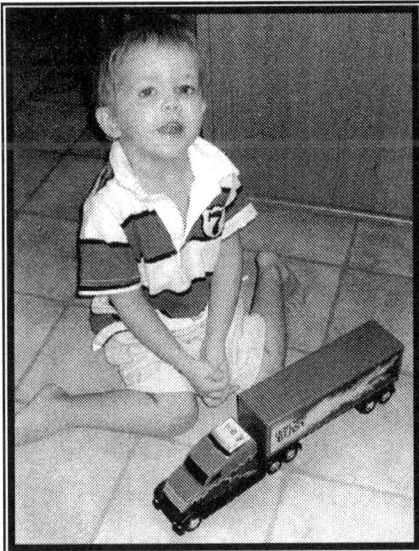

LOUISE, WILLARD INGRAHAM AND FAMILY

CHAPTER XIV:
    LORRAINE INGRAHAM JOHNSTON STORY
By: Lorraine Johnston

My name is Lorraine Jennette Ingraham Mott Johnston. I am eighty years old. I was born in Woodworth, N. D. on August 12, 1926. It doesn't seem that I should be eighty already. (Lorraine celebrating her 80th birthday below)

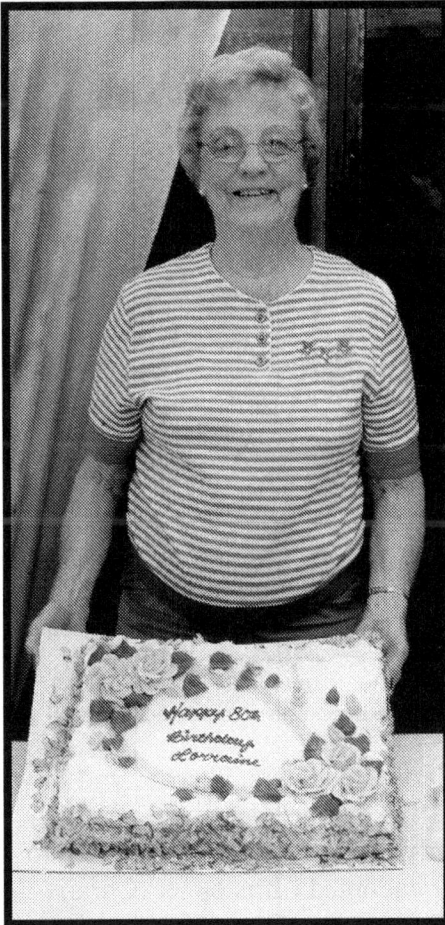

I was born to Lyle and Gena Johnson Ingraham. A better set of parents never existed. They were very hard workers and they taught us responsibility, love and honesty. They had loved one another from the time Mom was nine and Dad was twelve years old. Mom would see this cute little fellow playing the violin for dances with his parents and really adored him.

I was blessed with three wonderful brothers. Today Ray is 87, Norman 84 and Willard is 82. I love my brothers very much. They are wonderful and very supportive.

At seventeen, I married Lester Clayton Mott.
(They were married on Xmas Dec. 25, 1943; photo below.)

We had three wonderful daughters. Sherry Lynn Mott
was adopted when she was five months old. She is a very nice
addition to our family. Sherry is 57 years old and married to
William Fisher Emery. They adopted Christopher (Chris)
Emery when he was a baby. He is now 31 years old and a
wonderful son and grandson. Sherry is very talented. She
worked as a graphic artist for the Tri-City Herald (newspaper)

for 25 years. She recently retired and is doing other work she enjoys.

After 13 years we had a big surprise. Along came Kimberlee (Kim) Ann Mott. Kim is now fifty years old. She was married to Daryl Madtson, but is now divorced.

Our three daughters photo is at left taken 1964

Left to right is Sherry, Kim and Lori Mott.

Kims photo is at left.

She had two girls from a previous marriage and she and Daryl had a son together.

Daryl Madtson's photo is below

The first daughter was Lynn Madtson, now 30 and married to Brian Rudolph. They have two wonderful children, Michael age 13 and Alyssa age three; both are special children. Next was daughter Crystal Sunshine. She is 27 and married to Tim Reed; both very sweet people. Aaron is their son and is 18 years old. He is almost a genius in computer science. Aaron is taking college credits and high school credits together so when he graduates he will have a high school diploma and two years of college already completed.

Above is a photo left to right: Crystal, Aaron and Lynn. The photo was taken when all the children were younger. Unfortunately, I do not have recent photos of Aaron now 18 or the girls, Crystal and Lynn and their families.

Our last daughter, after 17 years, was born 46 years ago. Her name is Lori René Mott.

Lori's photo is at left taken 2006.

Lori has three lovely children. Mellissa, Randall and Nathan.

Mellissa's photo is to the right; Mellissa Mott, now age 27 is married to Eric Richardson. Mellissa is a registered nurse specializing in heart and cardiac problems.

599

Lori's son Randall is 20 years old and is going to college. He also has an impressive job as district manager training 10 young men under him. He wants to be a physical therapist when he is through college.

Randy's photo is left; taken in 2007.

Randy lives with me and is a very good person.

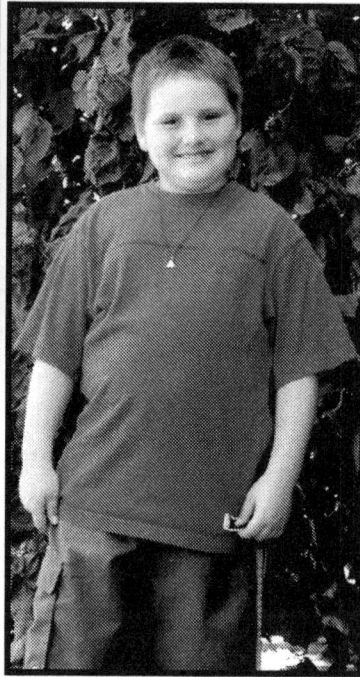

Then there is Nathan age eight. Nathan's photo is at the right; Nathan is a very active young man and a very good student like his sister and brother before him. They all are very studious persons as is their mother Lori. She has a master's degree in city planning. It was a lot of hard work.

LORRAINE INGRAHAM JOHNSTON STORY

Then there is Lorraine. I have achieved several things I have wanted to in my lifetime. I attended college taking criminal law. I counseled adolescents and prepared income tax etc. I was an adolescent counselor for Mental Health for sometime. I didn't care for the way they punished youth by pinning them down on the floor, sitting on their back and crossing their arms behind their back.

I owned a Merle Norman cosmetics business. I took cosmology training in L.A. I studied music for three years and played the piano, accordion and organ; all of which I like to this day. Our family was and is a very musical family. It was our life. We had many "jam" sessions in our home.

I also spent nine years with Employment Security in Centralia, WA, as a computer operator. I really enjoyed the people.

The thing I like best of all is serving as a care provider with Senior Life Resources. I work with seniors who need special care and I specialize in Alzheimer patients. I took care of my dear sweet mother for the last three and one half years of her life in my home and I never regretted it. At the same time I had an Alzheimer's patient and a 95-year old crippled lady that I cared for. I loved them all from the very bottom of my heart. I have had more than 12 years in this occupation.

My best friends are Jesus and God. I could not have made it without them. I divorced from Lester after 30 years of marriage. After several years I married Bud Johnston who died several years ago when his heart gave out after two major heart surgeries.

All of these things taught me one thing. Without God and Jesus in our lives we are nothing but with them helping our lives are beautiful and we can do anything.

SHERRY EMERY'S FAMILY STORY

By: Sherry Emery

I was born an orphan in San Francisco, CA, on Sept. 14, 1949 and spent the next four months of my life in one of the many cribs lining a hallway of the orphanage. But then, a handsome man with a shiny gold watch and a pretty lady with blonde hair and blue eyes picked me up and said they would take me home (that's the short version).
Lester Clayton Mott and his lovely wife, Lorraine Jannette Ingraham Mott adopted me and thus my named changed from Jean Doe to Sherry Lynn Mott.

Most of my preteen life was spent growing up on an 80-acre farm in Clovis, CA., where we raised 250-head of sheep, 20-plus acres of cotton, about 10 acres of Thompson seedless grapes, 10 acres of alfalfa and seven acres of oranges. There were always two or three dogs to play with and more farm cats than we could count. Dad had a huge shop for repairing just about anything, including a blue Ford tractor, a D-2 Cat and a classic green John Deere tractor. A rustic red barn was a favorite play area for all of the kids that would come to visit. Mom was a great cook and nearly every Sunday our home was filled with relatives who loved her spotless house and sumptuous meals and seemed to think we got our food free because we owned a farm.

As with just about every small farm, it was not self-sustaining and Dad had to work a full-time job to keep the farm going and shoes on us kids. In time, mom and dad were blessed with two biological children — daughters Kimberlee Ann and Lori René were born seven and eleven years after I was adopted.

In the summer of 1964 I was 14 years old, the Beatles were gaining popularity, the Beach Boys had released "Fun, Fun, Fun," I had finished my freshman year at Clovis High School, and Mom and Dad sold the farm. They moved us to Washington State, specifically the southeast corner of the state.

LORRAINE INGRAHAM JOHNSTON STORY

I was sure that I had been torn from my
beautiful home at the foot of the Sierra Nevada
Mountains and plopped into the pit of Hell. Often
when people think of Washington, visions of
evergreens, mountains, the lush greenery of
Seattle come to mind. Forget that — Eastern
Washington is arid desert averaging, at most,
seven inches of rain a year. And, for this
California Girl, the winters were cold enough to
send me into an arctic depression. The summers are
hot, but it's a dry heat. I actually love the
summers here.

Luckily, many of the Ingraham clan were
living in the Yakima Valley and Mid-Columbia,
names by which regions in this area of the state
are known. Mom's three brothers and their
families lived within a forty-five minute drive,
or less, from each other. We settled into our new
home in Kennewick where Mom's parents, Lyle and
Gena Ingraham and her brother Willard and his
family lived. As much as I hated being separated
from my lifelong friends in California, it was fun
to get to know my eight cousins, to snuggle up to
grandma, hear grandpa's loud and raspy laugh, and
feel the warmth of love during frequent family
get-togethers.

Of course, the Ingrahams couldn't get
together without food, music and pinochle. Grandma
or Mom played the piano and grandpa and/or the
uncles played the fiddle. Oh, the laughter, joy
and contentment that flowed from those happy
times! Fresh, hot, homemade lefse from grandma's
kitchen was always a special treat and I also was
particularly fond of her filled sugar cookies. On
the other hand, the game of pinochle was taken
much more seriously and could illicit a, "God
dammit" from my grandfather and a loud resounding
thump from the big rock ring on his finger being
slammed on the table.

Some of the other wonderful memories I have:
Grandpa and grandma's garden — the heady smell of
lush tomato plants, huge-leafed ruby red rhubarb
and potatoes freshly dug from the rich, moist

603

soil; Grandma's preserves made from yellow pear
tomatoes; her canned fruit, especially seeing the
sweet pears floating pearly-white in her emerald
green bowl. Discarded office supplies that Grandpa
and grandma would rescue from the trash for us
children when they worked at the P.U.D. — we would
spend hours in the basement writing out "orders"
and other such important business. I loved to
watch grandma crochet and tat and I treasure the
few precious pieces I have of her labors of love.

Left is Sherry
Motts photo taken
1967 for graduation
from Kennewick high
school.

        Uncle Willard took our families on the much-
hated rock hounding trips — certainly not
considered exciting by us kids — Carol, MaryAnn
and I would play card games in a stifling-hot
camper or trailer while the adults "hunted."
However, the tables, clocks and other items he
created with those slices of rock were in high
demand and beautiful to behold. Although I would
not have admitted it then, I found looking at the
rocks quite fascinating.

Riding horses at my Uncle Norman's ranch in Prosser was always anticipated with mixed emotions — I loved riding, but was terrified of those huge animals, too. And, I don't remember the horse's name, but Jerome, Jannette and Jackie had a pet skunk we played with. Auntie Verdell made a dish called "Peter's Pot" made with rice and seafood that I still make to this day for special gatherings — usually New Year's Eve.

Uncle Ray and Auntie Anna Rose's home in Benton City was always so comfy and welcoming and I remember hours and hours spent playing Canasta, Kings in a Corner and Monopoly with cousins Dorothy, Linda and Lloyd. Auntie also was an incredible cook.

I treasure the hugs all of my uncles so freely gave to all of us kids.

We cousins grew apart as we matured, graduated and moved from the area. I was married in 1970 to William Fisher Emery, nearly 15 years my senior, and as of this writing in 2007, we still are happily married, living in Kennewick, and together have raised over 30 foster children, Bill's two beautiful daughters, Cynthia and Dorilynn (René) and our adopted son, Christopher.

Sherry and Bill Emery's photo above was taken in 2003.

Our son, Christopher's photo is below.

       I have worked as a house painter and roofer next to my husband in our own business; as a landscape designer and plant specialist; and for 25 years, a newspaper graphic artist. Now, semi retired, I work as a biofeedback and pain relief therapist.

CHAPTER XV

CONCLUSION

If one could put everything we have learned about our heritage into a capsule and pass it on I would do so. In a sense, this book is that capsule. I retraced the family history of the Ingrahams and Johnstons through genealogy using recorded documents. Those recordings are in the following pages of my Index of generations.

It is my desire that others wishing to trace their own family lines to the past will use a similar outline to this book and connect the dots to their own past. If anyone related to me is searching, the index recordings can be followed.

For the story, I started in England where the Mayflower ship set sail with one hundred and two aboard then landed in New England in North America where they started a colony. From that point, I followed the lives of five people from the Mayflower and their descendents to the homesteads of North Dakota.

I included the hardships they endured and used the depression era of 1929 as real history about the difficult period people lived through. I dedicated many chapters to my own parents Gena and Lyle Ingraham and their move from North Dakota to Washington State. The last chapters were stories of my own brothers and sister and my own family.

My own life and that of my family was my way of tracing the growth of families striving to meet lifes challenges; many challenges are our own goals.

My wife, Louise and I both were interested in writing. After we retired from our professions, we set about writing books about subjects that were of importance to us. Louise wrote and published "Sapien's Journey Through Time And Space", "Atlantis, A New View" and her own family story "The Pioneer Spirit of Minnie, Charley Williams And Family".

I wrote two books; "Farm Boy To Soldier and now this one, "Echos Past with Links To The Mayflower".

Louise and I have just celebrated our 60th wedding anniversary on Sept. 13, 2007. We enjoy life and have many more things to accomplish that interests us. Recently we decided to take a college course, "Understanding The Universe".

With modern technology we found Alex Filippenko's, a professor at the University of California, Berkeley series of 96 lectures on DVD to be our answer.

Choices are each of our God given right as we make our way through life. Louise and I feel that if we make those choices together those are more likely to be right for both of us. If we put prayer also into those choices, we have the spiritual element helping us. We look forward to what may lay ahead knowing it will be interesting.

I hope this book has opened the potential for others interested in reviewing their own heritage. It is an important part of each of our lives and gives one an inkling of who we are or most importantly, who we want to be.

I leave you with, "for tomorrow we can take our minds anywhere".

GENERATIONS FROM

JOHN ALDEN AND
PRISCILLA MULLENS
CAPT. MYLES
STANDISH AND
BARBARA STANDISH

INDEX: GENEALOGY FAMILIES RELATED TO
INGRAHAM FAMILIES

JOHN ALDEN – B-1598-possible in England
D-Sept.12,1687-Duxbury, Mass. Ab. 89 years
M-PRISCILLA MULLINS-before 1623
-1602-England-D-1686-Duxbury, Mass.
Parents-William and Alice Mullins
Children of John Alden and Priscilla Mullins
Elizabeth Alden-B-1624-1625-M-Wm Pabodie
John Alden-B-1626-M-Elizabeth Phillips
JOSEPH ALDEN-B-May 22, 1627-M-Marry Everill
Simmons
Sarah Alden-B-maybe BF 1630-1640M-Alexander Standish
Jonathan Alden-B-1633-M-Abigail Hallett
Ruth Alden-B-1637-M-John Bass
Rebecca Alden-B-Bef 1649-M-Thomas Delano
Mary Alden
Priscilla Alden
David Alden-B-1645-50-M-Mary South Worth

JOSEPH ALDEN-b-May 22,1627-Plymouth, Mass.
D-Feb.8, 1696-Bridgewater, Mass.
M-MARY SIMMONS-B-1641-D-after Mar. 10,1674
Parents Moses and Sarah Simmons
Children of Joseph and Mary Simmons Alden
Sarah Alden-B-1665-M-Joseph Crossman
Isaac Alden-B-1666-M-Mehitable Allen
Joseph Alden-B-1668-M-Hannah Dunham
Mercy Alden-B-1669-M-John Burrill
Hopestill Alden-B-1671-M-Joseph Snow
Elizabeth Alden-B-1673-M-Benjamin Snow
JOHN ALDEN-B-1674-M-Hannah White
All children born at Bridgewater, Mass. Joseph was a surveyor
of highways and laid out all ways in Bridgewater.

JOHN ALDEN-B-1674-D-Sept.1730-Middleborough, Mass.
M-**HANNAH WHITE**-B-May 12,1681-Weymouth, Mass.D-
Oct. 15,1732
Parents-Capt. Ebenezer White and Hannah Phillips
Children of John Alden and Hannah White:
David Alden-B-May 18, 1702-M-Judith Paddleford
Priscilla Alden-B-Mar.2,1703/4-M-Abraham Barden
Thankful Alden-B-May 30,1705-M-Francis Eaton
Hannah Alden-B-Mar.24,1705-M-Thomas Wood
LYDIA ALDEN-B-Dec.18, 1710-M-Samuel Eddy
Mary Alden-B-Nov.18,1712,-M-Noah Thomas
Abigail Alden-B-Sept.28,1714-M-Nathan Thomas
Joseph Alden-B-Sept.11,1716-M-Hannah Hall
John Alden-B-Sept.10,1718-M-Lydia Lazell
Ebenezer Alden-B-Oct.8,1720-M-Ann Whitaker
Nathan Alden-B-June 12,1723- Not in father's will 1730
Noah Alden-B-May 31,1725-M-Joanna Vaughn

LYDIA ALDEN-B-Dec.18,1710-Middleborough
D-Mar.11,1803-Middleborough, Mass. Age 93
M-**SAMUEL EDDY**-B-1710-Middleborough-Eddyville
D-1746-Eddyville-age 36
Parents-Samuel Eddy and Melatiah Pratt
Children of Samuel Eddy and Lydia Alden
NATHAN EDDY-B-Sept.8,1733-M-**EUNICE SAMPSON**
Joshua Eddy-B-Mar. 6, 1734/5-D-bef.2-May,1760
Susanna Eddy-B-Nov.22,1736-D-July 1817-81 yrs. UNM.
Mary Eddy-B-May9,1740-D.Y.
Samuel Eddy-B-Jan.12,1742-Anna Morton
Seth Eddy-B-Feb.11,1744-D-bef. May 2,1760

Below is Captain Myles Standish Heritage

Barbara Standish arrived on the ship Anne in 1623
from England and she was the mother of all Myles children.

2nd Generation

Alexander Standish B. 1626, Plymouth, Mass; d July 6,
1702 at Duxbury, Mass.
His parents, Captain Myles and Barbara Standish
He married Sarah Alden; B about 1630; D before June
13, 1688. Sarah Alden was the daughter of Pilgrims John and
Priscilla Mullins Alden.
Alexander M 1688 Disire Holmes; they had two sons
and one daughter.
Children of **Alexander and Sarah Alden**
Lora Standish M. Abraham Sampson
Lydia Standish M. Isaac Sampson
Elizabeth Standish M. Samuel Delano
Mercey Standish M. 1684 Caleb Sampson
Myles Standish M. 1702 Experience ShermanSarah B
1666 M. 1694 Benjamin Soule
Ebenezer B 1672 M 1697 Hannah Sturtevant
David Standish died before Feb. 14, 1689

The following children of Alexander Standish and
Desire Holmes:
Desire B. May 5, 1689 M 1715 Nathan Weston
Thomas B. Jan 29, 1690 M. 1717 Mary Carver
Ichabod B. June 10, 1693 M. 1719 Phebe Ring

Alexander gave power of attorney to Robert Orchard in
1687 to claim his right to this property per insert. There was a
great deal of intermarriage of cousins in those days and it is
suspected that the first wife of Myles Standish who came on
the Mayflower with Myles may have been a cousin whose

Alexander Standish-B-1626-Plymouth,Ma.-D-July 6,1702-
Duxbury,Ma.
Parents:Capt.Myles Standish and Barbara Standish
M-(1)Sarah Alden_B-abt.1630-D-bef.June 13,1688
Daughter of Pilgrims, John and Priscilla (Mullins)Alden
Alexander-M-(2)1688-Desire Holmes
Children of Alexander and Sarah Alden
Lora Standish-M-Abraham Sampson
Lydia Standish-M-Isaac Sampson
Elizabeth Standish-M-Samuel Delano
Mercey Standish-M-1684-Caleb Sampson
Myles Standish-M-1702-Experience Sherman
Sarah Standish-M-1694-Benjamin Soule
Ebenezer Standish-B-1672-M-1697-Hannah Sturtevant
David Standish-D-bef.Feb.14,1689
Desire Standish-B-May 5,1689-M-1715-Nathan Weston
Thomas Standish-B-Jan.29,1690-M-1717-Mary Carver
Ichabod Standish-B-June 10,1693-M-1719-Phebe Ring
Last three names Mother was Desire Holmes

Lydia Standish-B-April30,1734-Duxbury,Ma.
Parents:Alexander Standish and Sarah Alden
Married:Oct.26,1686-Isaac Sampson-B-1661
D-1726-Son of Abraham and (Nash)Sampson
Children of Isaac Sampson and Lydia Standish
Isaac Sampson-B-April18,1688
Jonathan Sampson-B-Feb.9,1690
Josiah Sampson-B-June5,1692-D-Mar.29,1730
Lydia Sampson-B-April22,1694
Ephraim Sampson-B-May 8,1698-M-Abigail Horrell
Peleg Sampson-B-Nov.12,1700
Priscella Sampson-B-Nov.12,1700
Barnabas Sampson-B-Feb.12,1704

THIRD GENERATION

EPHRAIM SAMPSON
AND
ABIGAIL HORRELL

FOURTH GENERATION
EUNICE SAMPSON
AND
NATHAN EDDY

Plympton, Cordwainer. On the same day abt. 30 April, 1734 Lydia Sampson of Plympton widow also quit claimed her share. No Plymouth Co. Pr for Lydia Sampson or daughter Lydia Sampson.

4th Generation

Ephraim Sampson B. Plymouth May 8, 1698, D. Middleboro April 11, 1787. He m. Plympton, Nov.. 15, 1728 Abigail Horrell B Beverly May II, 1708 D. Middleboro Mar. 29, 1777; parents Humphery Harrel and Elizabeth Smith. Ephraim Sampsons parents were Isaac Sampson and Lydia Standish
    Children of **Ephraim and Abigail Sampson**
    Abigail Sampson b Oct. 25, 1729
    Elizabeth Sampson b Mar. 29, 1732
    Lusanna Sampson b. Nov. 7, 1734
    Eunice Sampson b. May 15, 1737, m. Nathan Eddy
    Sarah Sampson b. Jan. 31, 1742
    Mary Sampson b. April 10, 1745
    Priscilla Sampson b. April 10, 1745
No other personal information on Ephraim

5th Generation
Nathan Eddy B. Sept. 8, 1733, Middleboro, Mass. d. Feb. 28, 1802
Pittsfield, VT Parents — Samuel Eddy –Lydia Alden
He married Eunice Sampson b. May 15, 1737, Plympton, Mass. d Mar. 25, 1802 Pittsfield, Vt. Her parents – Ephraim Sampson and Abigail Horrell
Children of **Nathan and Eunice Sampson** b Middleboro
    Ephraim Eddy b. Dec. 21, 1759
    Lydia Eddy b. Sept. 16, 1762
    Hannah Eddy b. Feb. 1, 1766
    Nathaniel Eddy b. July 6, 1768
    Nathan Eddy b. April 21, 1771

NATHAN EDDY-B-Sept.8,1733-Middleboro,Ma-D-
Feb.28,1804-Pittsfield,Vt.
Parents-Samuel Eddy-Lydia Alden
He married **EUNICE SAMPSON**-B-May15,1737-
Plympton,Ma.-D-Mar.25,1802-Pittsfield,Vt.
Her parents-Ephraim Sampson and Abigail Horrell
Children of Nathan Eddy and Eunice Sampson-B-Middleboro
Ephraim Eddy-B-Dec.21,1759
Lydia Eddy-B-Sept.16,1762
Hannah Eddy-B-Feb.1,1766
Nathaniel Eddy-B-July6,1768
Nathan Eddy-B-April21,1771
ISAAC EDDY-B-June24,1774-M-Betsy McCary-
Aug.12,1796
Zachariah Eddy-B-Nov.18,1778
     As Eunice Sampson was the granddaughter of Isaac and Lydia (Standish) Sampson and and since Lydia Standish was the daughter of Alexander and Sarah (Alden) Standish and granddaughter of Myles and Barbara Standish; all Eddys who can trace their descendents to Nathan and Eunice (Sampson)Eddy are eligible to the Mayflower Society through both Nathan and Eunice.

ISAAC EDDY

Soon after his birth Isaac's parents went to Vermont and finally settle in Woodstock. After his marriage he moved to Pittsfield, Vt. He became a leading citizen of that place. He was a justice of the peace and also served several terms in the Vermont assembly. In 1802 he was in the clothier business, then a merchant, but his position as scribe in the little church in Pittsfield that had been formed in 1803 with sixteen members soon developed. He was forty-four years of age when he was licensed to preach. He then moved to Locke,N.Y. in 1824. He settled in Jamestown, N.Y. He was known as "good father Eddy" in the town. In his church at Jamestown,N.Y. a tablet has been placed to his memory.

Isaac Eddy-B-Middleboro,Mass,June 24,1774-D- June 26,1833-at Jamestown,N.Y. Parents were Nathan Eddy and Eunice Sampson. He married Aug. 12,1796, Woodstock, Vt. To Betsy McCary. She was born Sept. 7, 1772 at Lyme, Conn.-d-Feb.16,1863
Children born Woodstock, Vt.
Children of **ISAAC EDDY** and **BETSY(MCCARY)EDDY**
Elizabeth Eddy-B-June 5,1797
EUNICE EDDY-B-Dec.29,1799-m.Alvah Brown
Isaac Eddy-B-Nov.29,1801
William McCary Eddy-B-Sept.16,1803
Nathaniel Eddy-B-Nov.29,1805
Elmina Eddy-B-Aug.10,1807
Safford Eddy-B-April15,1810
Hiram Eddy-B-Mar.17,1813
Zecheriah Eddy-B-Dec.19,1815(he changed his name to Zachary

BROWN FAMILIES

Parents-Daniel Brown - ? Steadman
Son-**ALVAH BROWN**-B-Dec.25,1792-D-1860-M
EUNICE EDDY-Mar. 8,1821-B-Dec.29,1799
Woodstock,Vt. D-Dec.4,1882-Kiantone, N.Y.

Children:
Ephraim Eddy Brown-B-Jan.20,1822-Groton,N.Y.
Russell McCary Brown-B-June 13, 1823-Locke, N.Y.
Amos King Brown-B-July 9, 1825-Locke, N.Y.
William Eddy Brown-B-Feb.22,1828
Albert Alfonzo Brown-B-Dec.25,1830-Ellicott,N.Y.
Safford Zachary Brown-B-Oct.1,1833-Kiantone,N.Y
MARY ELIZABETH BROWN-B-Aug.14,1836-
Kiantone,N.Y.
Charles Henry Brown-B-June 27,1839-Kiantone,N.Y.

C INDEX

JOHN COWLES-B-Mar.18,1645-Hartford,Ct.
D-Dec.11,1711-Hatfield, Ma.
Parents, John Cowles
DEBORAH BARTLETT-B-Mar.18,1645-Hartford,Ct.
M-Nove.22,1668-Hatfield,Ma.
Children of John Cowles and Deborah Bartlett
Hannah Cowles-B-Nov.24,1668-Hatfield,Ma.
JONATHAN COWLES-B-Jan.26,1670-Hatfield,Ma.
Samuel Cowles-B-May,27,1673-Hatfield,Ma.
John Jr. Cowles-B-June15,1676-Hatfield,Ma.
Abigail Cowles-B-Feb.1,1677-Hatfield,Ma.
Sarah Cowles-B-June 5,1681-Hatfield,Ma.
Mary Cowles-B-Nov.3,1683-Hatfield,Ma.
Esther Cowles-B-April14,1686-Hatfield,Ma.

JONATHAN COWLES-B-Jan.26,1670-Hatfield,Ma.
d-Nov.13,1756-Hatfield,Ma.
Parents, John Cowles and Deborah Bartlett
PRUDENCE FRARY-B-May,1677-Medfield,Ma.
M-Nov.22,1668-Hatfield,Ma.
Children of Jonathan Cowles and Prudence Frary
Abigail Cowles-B-May24,1698-Hatfield,Ma.
JOHN COWLES-B-Dec.27,1700-Hatfield,Ma.
Jonathan Jr. Cowles-B-June30,1703-Hatfield,Ma.
Timothy Cowles-B-April9,1706-Hatfield,Ma.
Kezia Cowles-B-Sept.6,1708-Hatfield,Ma.
Nathaniel Cowles-B-Mar.21,1710-Hatfield,Ma.
Eleazer Cowles-B-Sept.18,1713-Hatfield,Ma.
Elisha Cowles-B-April19,1716-Hatfield,Ma.
Eunice Cowles-B-Aug.18,1719-Hatfield,Ma.
Abia Cowles-B-Oct.27,1722-Hatfield,Ma.

JOHN COWLES-b-Dec.27,1700-Hatfield,Ma.
D-June,1745-Amherst,Ma.
Parents Jonathan Cowles and Deborah Bartlett
MARY JENNINGS-B-1707-Brookfield,Ma.
Children of John Cowles and Mary Jennings
Israel Cowles-B-Sept.28,1726-Hatfield,Ma.
Abia Cowles-B-Dec.22,1729-Hatfield,Ma.
JOHN JR. COWLES-B-July28,1731-Hatfield,Ma.
Martha Cowles-B-Nove.14,1734-Hatfield,Ma.
Mary Cowles-B-Sept.23,1742-Hatfield,Ma.

JOHN JR. COWLES-B-July 28,1731-Amherst,Ma.
D-Sept.19,1811-Belchertown,Ma.
Parents,John Cowles and Mary Jennings
HANNAH BARDWELL-B-Dec.23,1739-Belchertown,Ma.
M-Feb.21,1757-Belchertown,Ma.
Children,
JOHN COWLES-B-Nov.26,1757-Belchertown,Ma.
Hannah Cowles-B-May12,1759-Belchertown,Ma.
Abner Cowles-B-Feb.7,1761-Belchertown,Ma.
Azubah Cowles-B-Jan.28,1763-Belchertown,Ma.
Lewis Cowles-B-Aug.15,1772-Belchertown,Ma.
Joshua Cowles-B-April28,1775-Belchertown,Ma.
Enos Cowles-B-Jan.20,1777-Belchertown,Ma.
Vester Cowles-B-Oct.15,1779-Belchertown,Ma.

JOHN COWLES-B-Nov.26,1757-Belchertown,Ma.
John Jr. Cowles and Hannah Bardwell
D-1830-Belchertown,Ma.-M-Appril23,1777
ELIZABETH SMITH-B-Jan.30,1761-Belchertown,Ma.
Children
Elijah Smith Cowles-B-Oct.21,1780-Belchertown,Ma.
Hannah Cowles-B-Jan.14,1782-Belchertown,Ma.
Deliah Cowles-B-Aug.29,1783-Belchertown,Ma.
Elizabeth Cowles-B-May9,1785-Belchertown,Ma.
Oliver Cowles-B-Jan.10,1787-Belchertown,Ma.
Ethan Smith Cowles-B-Jan.10,1790-Belchertown,Ma.
Joshua Cowles-B-Oct.27,1791-Belchertown,Ma.
REMEMBER JOSHUA COWLES-B-July10,1796-
Belchertown,Ma.
Samantha Cowles-B-Oct.19,1800-Belchertown,Ma.
Sibyl Cowles-B-July19,1802-Belchertown,Ma.

REMEMBER JOSHUA COWLES-B-July10,1796-
Belchertown,Ma.
Parents, John Cowles and Elizabeth Smith
SIBYL WRIGHT-B-May29,1800-Genesse,N.Y.
M-Oct.17,1816 in Genesee, N.Y.-D-Aug.23,1887
Children
Ethan Smith Cowles-B-Aug.4,1817-Farmington,Penn.
Orson Joshua Cowles-B-Sept.15,1818-Farmington,Penn.
Elbridge Dewill Cowles-B-July8,1820-Farmington,Penn.
Sibyl Lodema Cowles-B-June8,1822-Farmington,Penn.
Dimis Aldania Cowles-B-Mar.21,1824-Farmington,Penn.
Jasper Milton Cowles-B-Mar.17,1826-Farmington,Penn.
Betsey Ann Cowles-B-May15,1828-Farmington,Penn.
Remember John Cowles-B-July29,1830-Farmington,Penn.
Almeron Orlando Cowles-B-July10,1832-Farmington,Penn.
DEMARCUS LEROY COWLES-B-Oct.5,1834-
Farmington,Penn.
Oscar Secratus Cowles-B-Nov.9,1836-Farmington,Penn.
Olive Diantha Cowles-B-Mar.18,1839-Farmington,Penn.
Mary Mendania Cowles-B-Mar.18,1839-Farmington,Penn.

DEMARCUS LEROY COWLES-B-Oct.5,1834-Sugar Grove,Pa.
D-Mar.30,1925-Bur. West Concord,Mn.
Parents Remember Joshua Cowles and Sybil Might
M-April6,1857-Dixon,Ill.
MARY ELIZABETH BOWN-B-Aug.14,1837-Kiontone,N.Y.
Parents, Alvah Brown and Eunice Eddy
Children of Demarcus LeRoy Cowles and Mary Elizabeth Brown
Ardille Cowles-B-Aug.29,1860-Mantorville,Mn.
M-William Kellogg
Children-Glen-Eugene and Fannie
Eddy Jerome Cowles-B-Mar.15,1862-M-Cora Vanderkyde-1883
Fred Jay Cowles-B-Nov.18,1867-M-Louisa Orcutt-June2
Willis Eugene Cowles-B-Nov.21,1871-M-Elsie Peck
MYRTLE JUNE COWLES-B-Dec.30,1873-Mantorville,Mn.
M-**CHAUNCEY LEE INGRAHAM**-Jan.9,1893

E- EDDY FAMILIES

      William Eddy was an educator at Trinity College and the University of Cambridge receiving a degree of Master of Arts in 1586. He became a minister (vicar) for the St. Dunstan's Church (Church of England) at Cranbrook and was there from 1591 to his death in 1616. There is a tablet and also three stained glass windows in this church dedicated to him. His son, Samuel, was trained as a tailor and came to America as did the son, John.

      REV. WILLIAM EDDY-B-Bristol, England, D-Cranbrook Co.,Kent, England, Nov.23,1616-

M-(1) Nov. 20,1587

MARY FOSTEN-her parents, John Fosten and Ellen (Munn) Fosten

M(2)Feb. 22,1613 at Cranbrook to Sarah Taylor, a widow.

She died before Feb. 5, 1639

Children: (all) born in England

Nathaniel Eddy –Bapt.,Mar.30,1589, died young

Mary Eddy-Bapt., Sept.1591

Phineas Eddy-Bapt. Sept. 1593

John Eddy-Bapt. 1597

Eleanor Eddy-Bapt. 1599

Abigail Eddy-Bapt. Oct. 1601

Anna Eddy-Bapt. May, 1603

Elizabeth Eddy-Bapt. Dec. 1606

SAMUEL EDDY-Bapt. Sept. 15, 1608

Zacharia Eddy-Bapt. March 1610

Nathaniel Eddy-Bapt. July, 1611

Priscilla Eddy-Bapt. Dec. 10, 1614-mother, Sarah Eddy

SAMUEL EDDY-B-May15,1608-Kent, England-D-
Nov.12,1687 –Swansea, Ma.
His parents-Rev. Wm Eddy and Mary Foster
Wifes parents-John Fosten and Ellen Munn
He married-Elizabeth Savery-B-1607
D-May 24,1689-Swansea, Ma.
Children:
John Eddy-B-Dec.25,1637
Zachariah Eddy-B-1639
Caleb Eddy-B-1643
OBADIAH EDDY-B-1645
Hannah Eddy-B-June 23,1647

OBADIAH EDDY-B-About 1645-Plymouth, Ma.-D-1727
His parents-Samuel Eddy and Elizabeth Savery
He married-Bennett Ellis-B-Feb.27,1649-Died after Feb.
27,1702- Parents-Jon Ellis and Elizabeth Freeman
Children:
John Eddy-B-Mar.22,1669
Hazadiah Eddy-B-Apr.18,1672-M-May29,1695-Samuel
Sampson
SAMUEL EDDY-B-1675
Zachariah Eddy
Jabez Eddy
Benjamin Eddy
Joel Eddy
Mercey Eddy
Elizabeth Eddy
Mary Eddy
Bennett Eddy
Hannah Eddy –M-Dec.28,1696-Israel,Woodward

SAMUEL EDDY –B-1675-D-1752
Parents-Obadiah Eddy and Bennett Elis
He married Melatiah Pratt-B-Dec.11,1676
MiddleBoro,Ma.-D-1768
Her parents-Jonathan Pratt-Abigail Atwood
Children of Samuel Eddy-Melatiah (Pratt)Eddy
SAMUEL EDDY-B-1710-Middleboro,Ma.
Zachariah Eddy-B-1712-Middleboro,Ma.
Melatiah Eddy-M-Mar/23.1730-Samuel Tinkham
Bennett Eddy-M-Wm. Redding-Feb.7,1738
Fear Eddy-M-George Williamson-Nov.7,1738

SAMUEL EDDY-B-1710-Middleboro,Married Lydia Alden-
D-Nov.3,1746-age36-Middleboro,Mass.
Parents-Samuel Eddy-Melatiah Pratt
Lydia Alden-B-Dec.18,1710-D-Mar.1,1803-age 92 years
Parents-John Alden and Hannah White
Children all born-Middleboro,Mass. Of **SAMUEL EDDY** and
LYDIA ALDEN
NATHAN EDDY-B-Sept.8,1733
Joshua EddyB-Mar.6,1734d.y.-
Susannah Eddy-B-Nov.22,1736-D-July29,1817-Not M.
Mary Eddy-B-May 9,1740-D.y-
Samuel Eddy-B-Jan12,1742
Seth Eddy-B-Feb.11,1744 d.y-

  After Samuel's death and 36 years old Lydia married
April 27,1792 to John Fuller-B-Mar.20,1692. He was the son
of John and Mercy (Nelson)Fuller.

  All Eddys that can trace their descendents back to
Samuel and Lydia(Alden)Eddy are eligible for membership to
the Mayflower Society

H

ROBERTS HICKS-B-1570-England
D-Mar.24,1647-Plymouth,Ma.
Parents, James Hicks and Phebe Allyne
Married (1) 1596 in England to Elizabeth Morgan
She died 1607
Children:
Thomas Hicks-B-1603- England
John Hicks-B-1605-England
Sarah Hicks-B-1607-England
Stephen Hicks
(2)married MARGARET WINSLOW-D-Mar.24,1647
Plymouth, Ma.
Children:
Samuel Hicks-B-1612-England
Ephriem Hicks
Lydia Hicks-B-1608
Phebe Hicks-B-1610
Daniel Hicks
Robert Hicks came to Plymouth-Dec.19,1621 on the ship
Fortune from Southwark,England. Margaret came over to
Plymouth two years later on the ship Little James

THOMAS HICKS-B-1677-Dartmouth, Ma.D-Nov.20,1759
Parents-Thomas Hicks and Mary Albro
ANNA CLARK-M-1704-D-1710
Parents; Weston Clarke and Mary Easton
Children:
BENJAMIN HICKS-B-Jan.25,1709-Dartmouth,Ma.
THOMAS HICKS-B-1650-D1698
Parents; Samuel Hicks and Lydia Doane
MARY ALBRO-d-1710
Parents: John Albro and Dorothy Potter
Children of Thomas Hicks and Mary Albro
THOMAS HICKS-B-1677
SAMUEL HICKS-B-1612
Parents-Robert Hicks and Margaret Morgan
LYDIA DOANE-M-1645
Parents: John Doane and Abigail
Children of Samuel Hicks and John Doane

BENJAMIN HICKS-B-Jan.25,1709-Dartmouth,Ma
D-June 9,1798-Pomfret,Ct.
Parents: Thomas Hicks and Anna Clark
ANNA ORNSBEE-B-Feb.13,1713-Rehoboth,Ma.
Parents: Jermiah Ornsbee and Mehitabel Ornsbee
Children of Benjamin Hicks and Anna Ornsbee
ISRAEL HICKS-B-Sept.19,1734-Rehoboth,Ma.
Aaron Hicks-B-Sept.10,1736-Rehoboth,Ma.
JoAnna Hicks-B-Mar.10,1741-Rehoboth,Ma.
Benjamin Hicks-B-July 18,1745
Anna Hicks-B-Jan.25,1747
Bettey Hicks-B-Mar.4,1750-Rhoboth,Ma.
Mehittabell Hicks-B-Mar.4,1750-Triplets-Rhoboth,Ma
Jabez Hicks-B-Mar.,1750

ISRAEL HICKS-B-Sept.19,1734-Rhoboth,Ma.
D-Mar.12,1813-Pomfret,Ct.-B-Abington Cemetery
Parents: Benjamin Hicks and Anna Ornsbee
ELIZABETH BOWEN-B-Mar.6,1740-Rehoboth,Ma.
D-April 7,1833-Pomfret, Ct.-Bur-Abington Cem.-M-
Dec.2,1762
Parents: Tabez Bowen and Johanny Salisburg
Children of Israel Hicks and Elizabeth Bowen
Elizabeth Hicks-B-Oct.20,1773-Rehoboth,Ma.
ISRAEL HICKS JR.-B-Sept.18,1776
Aaron Hicks-B-April 22,1768
Mehitable Hicks-B-Feb.11,1770
Zeriah Hicks-B-Jan.4,1772
Zephaniah Hicks-B-Nov.21,1773
Jemina Hicks-B-Oct.1,1775
Nancy Hicks-B-Nov.27,1779
Darius Hicks-B-Dec.15,1781
Susannah Hicks
Lucinda Hicks

ISRAEL HICKS JR-B-Sept.18,1776-Rehoboth,Ma.
D-Sept.15,1839-Pomfret, Ct.
Parents: Israel Hicks Sr. and Elizabeth Bowen
PHEBE GROW-B-April 2,1772-Pomfret,Ct.
D-Jan.6,1853-Pomfret_M-Dec.3,1795-Pomfret,Ct.
Parents: Thomas Grow and Experience Goodell
Children of Israel Hicks Jr. and Phebe Grow
Loretta Hicks-B-Feb.2,1797-Pomfret,Ct.
Zadoc Hicks-B-Sept.29,1798-Pomfret,Ct.
Arba Hicks-B-Dec.17,1800-Pomfret,Ct.
Chloe Hicks-B-Sept.25,1802-Pomfret,Ct.
Experience Hicks-B-June 14,1804-Pomfret,Ct.
Thomas Hicks-B-Nov.24,1805-Pomfret,Ct.
ZEPHANIAH HICKS-B-Oct.6,1807-Pomfret,Ct.
Eliza Hicks-B-Mar.3,1810-Pomfret,Ct.

Israell Rodolphus-B-April10,1812-Pomfret,Ct.

ZEPHANIAH HICKS-B-Oct.6,1807-Pomfret,Ct.
D-Aug.8,1858-Athens,Pa.
Parents Israel Hicks Jr. and Phoebe Grow
MARY EATON SAMPSON-B-Aug.14,1809-Plymton,Ma.
M-Dec.22,1829-Homer,N.Y.-D-Dec.22,1854-Athens,Pa
Parents: George Washington Sampson and Hannah Crossman
Shaw
Children of Zehaniah Hicks and Mary Eaton Sampson
Children
George Sampson Hicksw-B-Sept.30,1830-Pomfret,Ct.
Israel Lewis Hicks-B-Nov.10,1832-Homer,N.Y.
Polly E. Hicks-B-Feb.16,1835-Homer,N.Y.
Phebe G. Hicks-B-Dec.12,1836-Truxton,N.Y.
Alfred Bennett Hicks-B-Aug.27,1838-Berkshire,NY.
Marshall O. Hicks-B-Jan.27,1850-Virgil,N.Y.
Deborah S. Hicks-B-Dec.3,1842-Caroline,N.Y.
HORATIO GATES HICKS-B-Nov.18,1844-Richfor,N.Y.
Hannah C. Hicks-B-May23,1848-Truxton,N.Y.

HORATIO GATES HICKS-B-Nov.18,1844-Richford,N.Y.
D.-May 2,1922-Farnam,Ne.
Parents: Zephania Hicks and Mary Easton Sampson
CATHERINE RIPKA WHITAKER-m-Sept.17,1879-
D-Nov.19,1917
Parents: Charles Whitaker and Catherin Ripka
Children of Horatio Gates Hicks and Catherine Whitaker
Arthur Oliver Hicks-B-Sept.18,1881-Stratford,Ia.
JOSEPH LEWIS HICKS-B-May 11,1883-Stratford,Ia.
Catherine Ripka Hicks-B-Mar.16,1885-Farnam,Ne.
Helen Amelia Hicks-B-Feb.29,1888-Farnam,Ne.

JOSEPH LEWIS HICKS-B-May 11,1883-Stratford,Ia.
Parents: Horatio Gates Hicks and Catherine Whitaker
CLARA IRWIN-M-Oct.5,1910-D-May29,1957-Farnam,Ne.
Children:
Mildred Evelyn Hicks-B-July 29,1911-Farnam,Ne
HORATIO GERALD HICKS-B-Feb.15,1918-Farnam,Ne

Mildred Evelyn Hicks-B-July29,1911-Farnam,Ne.
Parents-Joseph Lewis Hicks and Catherine Whitaker
Earl Edson-M-Nov.28,1934-D-Sept.25,1960
Children:
Evelyn Frances Edson-B-Dec.30,1935
Lois Marlea Edson-B-April30,1940
Audrey Lou Edson-B-Dec.14,1946

HORATO GERALD HICKS-B-Feb.15,1918-Farnam,Ne.
D-Jan.14,2006-Mesa,Az.
Parents: Joseph Lewis Hicks and Clara Irwin
Married: VERNONA MAY WILHITE-B-May 30,1918-
Gordon-Ne.
Children of Horato Gerald Hicks and Vernona May Wilhite
M-April 11,1941-Pasadena,Ca.
Phyllis Mardell Hicks-B-Aug.20,1942-San Diego,Ca.
MILTON LEWIS HICKS-B-Dec.8,1945

Phyllis Mardell Hicks-B-Aug.20,1942-SanDiego,Ca.
Parents: Horato Gerald Hicks and Vernona May Wilhite
Michael Orwin Wiggines-B-June12,1943-Everett,Wa.
M-Aug.24,1963-D-Aug.1979
Children:
Vance James Wiggins-B-Jan5,1967—Ft. Worth,Tx. D-Aug. 1979
Voni Jane Wiggins-B-Aug.31,1968-Chico,Ca.
Michelle Lee Wiggins-B-Aug.28,1972-K.J.Sawyer,AFB.Mi.

Michelle Lee Wiggins-B-Aug.28,1972-Sawyer,AFB,Mi
Parents:Phyllis Mardel Wiggins and Michael Orwin Wiggins
Wm Dave Evans-M-Dec.23,1993
Children:
Micah Vance Evans-B-May13,1997-Phoenix,Az.
Haley Fae Evans-B-July6, 1999-Seattle,Wa.

MILTON LEWIS HICKS-B-Dec.8,1945-Rushville,Ne.
Parents: Horatio Gerald Hicks and Vernona May Wilhite
MARY ANN INGRAHAM-B-Dec.28,1949-Sunnyside,Wa.
M-Nov.18,1978-Reno,Nv.
Parents: Willard Stanley Ingraham and Louise Ingraham
Children of Milton Lewis Hicks and Mary Ann Ingraham
SHANNON ANN HICKS-B-April 27,1981-Tempe,Az.

Shannon Ann Hicks-B-April27,1981-Tempe,Az.
Parents: Milton Lewis Hicks and Mary Ann Ingraham
Ryan Ingraham-M-Nov.14,2004-Chandler,Az. Ryan Dillon
Peters legally changed his name to Ingraham
Children:
Torryn Briehl Ingraham-B-Feb.3,2005-Mesa,Az.
Ivry Rae Ingraham-B-Jan.12, 2007, Mesa Az.

I

DAVID F. INGRAHAM-B-1824-New York
D-Dec.15,1881-Mantorville-Mn.Bur.-Everbreen Cemetery
M-1845-SOPHIA INGRAHAM-B-1823-Wales,Great Britian
Children:
George D. Ingraham-B-Dec.11,1846-Ohio-Mn-
Ennia CalHoun-Dec.16,1868
CHARLES H. INGRAHAM-B-1848-Ohio-Mn.
Mark Ingraham-B-1860-Mantorville,Mn
Frank E. Ingraham-B-1863-Mantorville,Mn.
Gordon Ingraham-B-1864-Mantorville,Mn.
Chester Ingraham-B-1865-Mantorville,Mn.
David and Sophia Ingraham with their children George D. and
Charles H. Ingraham moved from Ohio to Mantorvill,Mn in
1857

George D. Ingraham-B-Dec.11,1846-Ohio
D-May26,1925-National Soldiers Home,Sawtelle,Ca.
Bur.-National Cemetery-Sawtelle,Ca.
Parents-David D. Ingraham and Sophia Ingraham
Emma Amanda Calhoun-B-May 18,1849-Brasher,N.Y.
D-May16,1906-Concord,Mn.-Bur-Evergreen Cem.-
Mantorville,Mn.
Parents: Caleb Barton Calhoun and Elisa Nelson
M-Dec.16,1868-Mantorville,Mn.
Children of George D. Ingraham and Emma Amanda Calhoun
Bertha Ingraham-B-Oct.4,1873-Concord,Mn.
Grace Ingraham-B-1876-Dodge Center,Mn.
George D. Ingraham moved to Sawtelle,Ca. 1910
George D. Ingraham-B-Dec.11,1846-Ohio
M-Margaret Skinner-after 1910-Sawtell,Ca.

CHARLIE H. INGRAHAM-B-1849-Ohio
Parents David F. Ingraham and Sophia
M-**EDNA L. STRONG**-B-1852-Il.-D-Mantorville,Mn
Bur.-1879-St. Charles,Mn-(Winona)
Children of Charlie H. Ingraham and Edna L. Strong
CHAUNCEY LEE INGRAHAM-B-Oct.28,1868-
Mantorville,Mn.
M-Myrtle June Cowles-B-Dec.30,1878-Mantorville,Mn.

Mary Ingraham-B-Apr.18,1872-Mantorville,Mn.
D-Jan.2,1948-Whittier,Ca.-Rosehill Memorial
She never married-lived to age 76

Charlie H. Ingraham-B-1849-Ohio
Parents-David F. Ingraham and Sophia
Wife #2-M-Lucretia June Shipton-B-April22,1857
Parents-R.G.Shipton and Marietta Bear
Children of Charlie Ingraham and Lucretia Shipton
Charles Eugene Ingraham-B-Oct.20,1878-M-JoHanah Taft
Jessie Evelyn Ingraham-B-Aug.7,1880
Nellie Pearl Ingraham-B-May 30,1885-M-Ernest R. Leeper
Lucy Blanche Ingraham-B-Nov.28,1890
George Robert Ingraham-B-Mar.23,1893-M-Josephine
Svoboda
Ella M. Ingraham-B-Aug.7,1880M-Fred Wright
Ethel Ingraham-B-1889-Bacinville,N.D.
Lucretia June Shipton is Charlie H. Ingraham's second wife.
She later married her second husband-last name Loomis

Fred Wright-B-July 6,1867-D-Oct.15,1955-Auburn,Wa.
M-Ella M. Ingraham-B-Aug.7,1880-M-Oct.12,1896
Michigan,N.D.-D-Mar.16,1956-Auburn,Wa.
Parents-Charlie H. Ingraham and Lucretia June Shipton
Children of Fred Wright and Ella M. Ingraham
George Montman Wright-B-Aug.20,1897-M-Edna
Edith Pearl Wright-B-June 14,1902-M
Clarence Wright—M-Alice
Fred Leon Wright
Lee Wright
Glendon Wright-B-Dec.25,1914-M-Florence
Fred Wright is a cousin of the famous Wright brothers-Wilbur
and Orville, who built the airplane and successfully flew the
first flight on Dec.17,1903 at Kitty Hawk,N.C.

CHAUNCEY LEE INGRAHAM-B-Oct.28,1868-
Mantorville,Mn.D-Aug.2,1954-Laurel,Mt.Bur-
Billings,Mt.Sunset Memorial
Parents-Charlie H. Ingraham and Edna Strong
Jan.9,1893-M-**MYRTLE JUNE COWLES**-B-Dec.30,1873-
Mantorville,Mn.-D-Feb18,1982-Laurel,Mt.-Bur-Billings,Mt-
Sunset Memorial
Parents-Demarcus LeRoy Cowles and Mary Elizabeth Cowles
Children of Chauncey Ingraham and Myrtle June Cowles
Lee George Ingraham-B-June 25,1895-Dodge Center,Mn.
LYLE JAY INGRAHAM-B-Jan.30,1897-Pine Island,Mn.
Ralph Dean Ingraham-B-Aug.21,1898-Pine Island,Mn.
Edna Iowne Ingraham-B-Jan.29,1902-Mantorville,Mn.
Esther Sophia Ingraham-B-Sept.5,1903-Mantorville,Mn.
Floyd Ray Ingraham-B-Nov.24,1907-Woodworth,N.D.
Claude Melvin Ingraham-B-Dec.28,1915-Woodworth,N.D.

LEE GEORGE INGRAHAM-B-June 25,1895-
Mantorville,Mn.
D-Nov.3,1987-Gig Harbor,Wa.-Haven of Rest
Parents-Chauncey Ingraham and Myrtle Cowles
Nov.4,1922-M-Mae Elien Thompson-B-May22,1897-
Ottertail,Mn
D-Jan.10,1985-Gig Harbor,Wa.-Haven of Rest.
Parents-Nels Thompson and Anne Anderson
Children of Lee Ingraham and Mae Elien Thompson
ROBERT LELAND INGRAHAM-B-Aug. 6,1923-
Woodworth,N.D.
D-June 25,1990-Gig Harbor-Haven Of Rest
M-Shirley Johnson-Oct.25,-1947-parents-Otto and Nelda
Johnson
Children of Robert and Shirley Ingraham
Mark David Ingraham-B-Jan.18,1952-Tacoma,Wa.
Rick Olen Ingraham-B-Feb.28,1954-Tacoma,Wa.
Wife #2-Norma Beatrice Hawker Howard-B-Sept.29,1922
Brian Douglas Howard
Bruce Neil Howard
Roy Warren Howard
FERN ELAINE INGRAHAM-B-Dec.8,1924-
Woodworth,N.D.
Parents-Lee Ingraham and Mae Elien Thompson
Mar 30,1944-M-James Harland Goemmer-B-Nov.21,1919
Parents-Rinehart Goemmer and Katheyn Godfrey
Children
Robert James Goemmer-B-Sept.15,1947-Seattle,Wa.
Carolynn Elien Goemmer-B-Jan.7,1951-Tacoma,Wa.
Carolynn's son- Bill Meszaros-B-April24,1970-Tampa,Fl.

LYLE JAY INGRAHAM-B-Jan.30,1897-Mannorville,Mn.
D-July 21,1982-Kennewick,Wa.-Bur-Desert Lawn Memoria
Parents-Chauncey Ingraham and Myrtle Cowles
1-7-1919,Jamestown,N.D.-M-**GENA ALFEA JOHNSON**-B-
12-1-1900-Elbow Lake,Mn.
D-Aug.19,1986-Kennewick, Wa.-Bur-Desert Lawn Memorial
Parents-Gunder Johnson and Laura Bah
Children of Lyle Ingraham and Gena Johnson
RAYMOND LLOYD INGRAHAM-B-8-21-1919-
Pittibone,N.D.
Charles LeRoy Ingraham-B-1920Woodworth,N.D.-Died as
baby
LeRoy Norman Ingraham-B-Sept.9,1921-Woodworth,N.D.
Died as baby
NORMAN JEROME INGRAHAM-B-Sept.11,1922-
Woodworth,N.D.
WILLARD STANLEY INGRAHAM-B-June 23,1924-
Woodworth,N.D.
LORRAINE JAINETTE INGRAHAM-B-Aug.12,1926-
Woodworth,N.D.
Gerada Agnes Ingraham-B-Dec.22,1930-Woodworth,N.D.-
died as a baby

RAYMOND LLOYD INGRAHAM-B-Aug.21,1919-
Pettibone,N.D.
Parents-Lyle Jay Ingraham and Gena Alfea Johnson
ANNA ROSE CROSBY-B-July 25,1926-Prosser,Wn.
M-July 12,1946-Lewiston,Id.-D-April 1, 2007, Prosser
Hospital- buried Prosser Cemetery
Parents-James Edward Crosby and F. Della Linthicum
Children of Raymond Ingraham and Anna Rose Crosby
Dorothy Jean Ingraham-B-Aug.18,1946-Sunnyside,Wa.
Linda Rae Ingraham-B-July 11,1947-Sunnyside,Wa.
Lloyd Raymond Ingraham-B-Oct.28,1948-Sunnyside,Wa.
DOROTHY JEAN INGRAHAM-B-Aug.18,1946-
Sunnyside,Wa.
Parents-Raymond Lloyd Ingraham and Anna Rose Crosby
Ronald Chapin Rideout-B-June 5,1941-Brewer,Maine
M-June 27,1965-Benton City,Wa.-D-Oct.20,1987-Twin
Falls,Id.
Parents-Chapin Merril Rideout and Phllis Irene Breede
Children of Dorothy Jean Ingraham and Ronald C. Rideout
Deborah Ann Rideout-B-July 4,1966-Richland,Wa.
Phyllis Jean Rideout-B-June 1,1967-Richland,Wa.
Michael Dean Rideout-B-June 10,1969-Richland,Wa.
Kevin Chapin Rideout-B-Sept.20,1971-Richland,Wa.
DOROTHY JEAN RIDEOUT-M-John Wolters-B-10-13-40
Married-Nov.5,1989-Twin Falls,Id.

Deborah Ann Rideout-B-July 4,1966-Richland,Wa
Parents-Ronald Chapin Rideout and Dorothy Jean Ingraham
Mark Thomas McCllum-B-Sept.27,1963-Tyronza,Ak.
M-Nov.23,1984-Benton City,Wa.
Parents-Issac McCollum and Rosetto Delk
Children of Mark Thomas McCollum and Deborah Ann
Rideout
Amanda Lynn McCullum-B-Nov.17,1985-Richland,Wa.
Scott Thomas McCollum-B-Sept.8,1991-Richland,Wa.

Michael Dean Rideout-B-June 10,1969-Richland,Wa.
Parents-Ronald Chapin Rideout and Dorothy Jean Ingraham
M-Marya Soto
Children of Michael Dean Rideout and Marya
Mathew Dean Rideout-B-Aug.8,1992-Burley,Id.
Brandon Rideout-B-Nov.16,1994-Burley,Id.
(#2) Amy Chambers
Children
Nicholas Rideout-B-Dec.10,2001
Tashenna J. Rideout-B-Jan.9,2003

LINDA RAE INGRAHAM-B-July 11,1947-Sunnyside,Wa.
Parents-Raymond Lloyd Ingraham and Anna Rose Crosby
Danny L. Giles-B-Aug.3,1946-Webster,S.D.
M-Aug.5,1967-Benton City,Wa.
Parents-Herbert W. Giles and Hazel Almira Egeburg
Children of Danny L. Giles and Linda Rae Ingraham
Michelle Lynn Giles-B-Sept.11,1969-Yakima,Wa.
Michael Lee Giles-B-April27,1971-Yakima,Wa.

Michelle Lynn Giles-B-Sept.11,1969-Yakima,Wa.
Parents-Danny L. Giles and Linda Rae Ingraham
M-Wm LeRoy Pleake III-B-June 3,1967-Prosser,Wa.
Parents-Wm.L. Pleake II and Deanne Brown
Children of Wm LeRoy Pleake III and Michelle Lynn Giles
Josephine Morgan Pleake-B-June 9,1994-Prosser,Wa.
Benjamin Pleake-B-Prosser,Wa.

Michael Lee Giles-B-April 27,1971-Yakima,Wa.
Parents-Danny L. Giles and Linda Rae Ingraham
M-Jody Elizabeth Pleake-B-Sept.21,1973-Prosser,Wa.
M-July 31,1993-Prosser,Wa.
Parents-Wm. L. Pleake II and Deanne Brown
Children of Michael Lee Giles and Judy Elizabeth Pleake
Emilee Alexis Giles-B-Feb.26,1995-Prosser,Wa.
Baillee Giles-B-Prosser,Wa.-B-Nov. 18, 1977, Richland, Wa.
Nattlee Giles-B-Prosser,Wa.-B-Dec. 23, 2002, Yakima, Wa.

LLOYD RAYMOND INGRAHAM-B-Oct.28,1948-
Sunnyside,Wa.
Parents-Raymond Lloyd Ingraham and Anna Rose Crosby
Tamara Lynn Dickson-B-June 11,1958-M-June 14,1981
Parents-Don Dickson and Barbara Hightower
Children
Bryan Raymond Ingraham-B-May 12,1983-Richland,Wa.

Lloyd Raymond Ingraham-B-Oct.28,1948-Sunnyside,Wa.
Parents-Raymond Lloyd Ingraham and Anna Rose Crosby
Kennewick,Wa.-M-May 14,1988-Lorraine Patrica Dewall-B-
Jan.15,1947-Tacoma,Wa.
#1 George Watkins
Lorraine Patrica Dewall
Parents-John Dewall and Norma Hanson

NORMAN JEROME INGRAHAM-B-Sept.11,1922-
Woodworth,N.D.
Parents-Lyle Jay Ingraham and Gena Alfea Johnson
VERDELL NOBLE-B-Dec.4,1927-Van Buren,Ak.
M-July 1946-Prosser,Wa.
Parents-Chester Lee Noble and Ethel Cox
Children of Norman Jerome Ingraham and Verdell Noble
Jerome Jay Ingraham-B-May26,1951-Prosser,Wa.
Janette Marie Ingrham-B-Nov.18,1953-Prosser,Wa.
Jacquelyn Ingraham-B-Aug.28,1955-Prosser,Wa.

JEROME JAY INGRAHAM-B-May26,1951-Prosser,Wa.
Parents:Norman Jerome Ingraham and Verdell Noble
Sharen Lea Miller-B-Feb.29-M-Feb.20,1971-Kennewick,Wa.
Parents-Richard Miller and Sharol
Children of Jerome Jay Ingraham and Sharon Miller
Robert Jerome Ingraham-B-Dec.30,1972-Walla Walla,Wa.
Kelly Ray Ingraham-B-Jan.10,1977-Kennewick,Wa.

JEROME JAY INGRAHAM-b-May,26,1951-Prosser,Wa.
Parents Norman Jerome Ingraham and Verdell Noble
Elizabeth Anne Cook-M-Sept.14.1990-Portland, Oregon
Children:
J.W. Ingraham-B-June 30,1999-Clarkston,Wa.
Robert Jerome Ingraham-B-Dec.30,1972-Walla Walla,Wa.
Parents-Jerome Jay Ingraham and Sharon Lea Miller
Roberta (Bobbie) Wagner-B-Aug.29,1973, Portland, Oregon-
M-Nov.26,1993, Coer-D-Alene, Id.
Children of Robert Jerome Ingraham and Roberta Wagner
Casey Marie Ingraham-B-4,26,1997, Prosser,Wa.
Kori Ann Ingraham-B-2,15,1999-Proser,Wa.
Cody Ingraham-B-5,12,00-Prosser,Wa.

Parents – Jerome Jay Ingraham and Sharon Miller:
Kelly Rae Ingraham-B-Jan.10,1977-Kennewick,Wa.
M-Donald Allen Brown –b-April 15, 1976, Sunnyside, Was.
Children:
Ashlynn Lea Brown-B-Oct. 5, 1999-Richland, Wa.
Deegan Andrewer-B-May 4, 2001,Prosser, Wa.

JANETTE MARIE INGRAHAM-B-Nov.18,1953-
Prosser,Wa.
Parents:Norman Jerome Ingraham and Verdell Noble
Edward Allen Hall-B- M-June 17,1972-Prosser,Wa.
Parents-Thad Hall and Mrs. Hall
Children of Edward Allen Hall and Janette Marie Ingraham
Shannon Marie Hall-B-April21,1974-KilleenTx.

Shannon Marie Hall-B-April 21,1974-Killeen,Tx.
Parents Edward Allen Hall and Janette Marie Ingraham
Johnny Santoy-B-   -M-Sept.26,1996-Prosser,Wa.
Children of Johnny Santoy and Shannon Marie Hall
Andre Santoy-B-April30,1998-Prosser,Wa.
Mercedes Santoy-B-April1,2002-Prosser,Wa.

JANETTE MARIE HALL-B-Nov.18,1953-Prosser,Wa.
Parents:Norman Jerome Ingraham and Verdell Noble
Yancey Wesley K. Burgess-B-Apr.28,1947-Tellico Plains,Tx.
M-June 2,1979-Benton City,Wa.-D-Mar.11,2003
Parents Heardrick Burgess and Vivian Lei
Children
McKenzie Lesley Burgess-B-Oct.17,1985-Richland,Wa.
A.Scott Garberg-M-Nov.19,2005-Prosser,Wa.

JACQUELYN INGRAHAM-B-Aug.28,1955-Prosser,Wa.
Parent:Norman Jerome Ingraham and Verdell Noble
Robert Wayne Haley-M-Sept.15,1973-Prosser,Wa.
Parents:Ernest Haley and Kate Haley-Sunnyside,Wa.
Children of Robert Wayne Haley and Jacquelyn Ingraham
Tamara Waynette Haley-B-Sept.23,1974-Pasco,Wa.
Steffani Ann Haley-B-Mar.26,1978-Richland,Wa.

JACQUELYN HALEY-B-Aug.28,1955-Prosser,Wa.
Parents:Norman Jerome Ingraham and Verdell Noble
Robert Turner-M-2000

Tammie Waynette Haley-B-Sept.23,1974-Pasco,Wa.
Parents:Jacquelyn Ingraham and Robert Wayne Halley
Daryl Brown-B-Oct.26,1964-M-11,5,1997-Reno,Nv.
Children
Nate Lucas Brown-B-Dec.10,1998-Yakima,Wa.

Tammie Waynette Brown-B-Sept.23,1974-Pasco,Wa.
Parents: Jacquelyn Ingraham and Robert Wayne Haley
Randall George Peters-B-Feb.26,1967-Monroe,Wa.
M-Sept.3,2004-Richland,Wa.
Parents:George Peters and Clara Wikelhorn
Children of Tammie Waynette Brown and Randall G. Peters
Jaden Skyler Peters-B-Nov.15,2005-Yakima,Wa.

Steffani Ann Haley-B-Mar.26,1978-Richland,Wa.
Parents: Jacquelyn Ingraham and Robert Wayne Haley
Doug Lee Cooper-B-Mar.28,1962-Prosser,Wa.
Parents: Everett Cooper and Lenora Higgins
Children of Steffani Ann Haley and Doug Lee Cooper
Jazmin Wikcole Cooper-B-Oct.1,2003-Richland,Wa.
Conner Cooper-B-Aug.4,2005-Richland,Wa.

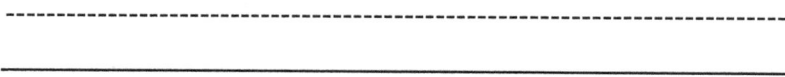

WILLARD STANLEY INGRAHAM-B-June 23,1924-
Woodworth,N.D.
Parents:Lyle Jay Ingraham and Gena Alfea Johnson
LOUISE WILLIAMS-B-Oct. 6,1930-Mabton,Wa.
M-Sept.13,1947-Mabton(Glade)Wa.
Parents:Charley Allen Williams and Minnie Bromley
Children of Willard Stanley Ingraham and Louise Williasm
Carol Jean Ingraham-B-April5,1948-Prosser,Wa.
Mary Ann Ingraham-B-Dec.28,1949-Sunnyside,Wa.

CAROL JEAN INGRAHAM-B-April 5,1948-Prosser,Wa.
Parents:Willard Stanley Ingraham and Louise Williams
Garry Rosson-M-Dec.19,1966-Kennewick, Wa.
Parents:Robert Rosson and Margarite Block
Children of Gary Rosson and Carol Jean Ingraham
Jon Garry Rosson-B-Aug.28,1967-Seattle,Wa.

CAROL JEAN ROSSON-B-April5,1948-Prosser,Wa.
Parents:Willard Stanley Ingraham and Louise Williams
Clayton John Straight-B-1946-N.Y.-M-1972-Oregon
Children:
James Jacob Straight-B-Feb.28,1973-Eugene,Or.
Paul Joshua Straight-B-Feb.1,1975-Seaside,Or.
Court records changing names-Kennewick,Wa.-Mar.1,1991
Carol Jean Straight to Mahria Carol Jordan-No.84-2-01060-3
James Jacob Straight to James Jacob Jordan-No.136-73-31770
Paul Joshua Straight to Paul Joshua Jordan-136-75-05401

MARY ANN INGRAHAM-B-Dec.28,1949-Sunnyside,Wa.
Parents:Willard Stanley Ingraham and Louise Williams
Milton Lewis Hicks-B-Dec.8,1945-Rushville,Ne.
M-Nov.18,1978-Reno,Nev.
Parents: Haratio Gerald Hicks and Vernona May Wilhite
Children of Mary Ann Ingraham and Milton Lewis Hicks
Shannon Ann Hicks-B-April 27,1981-Mesa,Az.

Shannon Ann Hicks-B-April27,1981-Mesa,Az.
Parents Milton Lewis Hicks and Mary Ann Ingraham
Ryan Briehl (Peters) Ingraham-B-Nov. 23, 1977-Phoenix, Az.
M-Nov.14,2004
Children
Torryn Briehl Ingraham-B-Feb.3,2005-Mesa,Az.
Ivry Rae Ingraham-B-Jan. 12, 2007- Mesa, Az.

LORRAINE JENETTE MOTT-B-Aug.12,1926-
Woodworth,N.D.
Parents:Lyle Jay Ingraham and Gena Alfea Johnson
Lester Mott-B-Sept.12,1919-New York
M-Dec.25,1943-Prosser,Wa.
Parents:Heraold Mott and Bernice Brown
Children of Lorrain Jennette Ingraham and Lester Mott
Sherry Mott-B-Sept.14,1949-San Francisco,Ca.
Kimberly Mott-B-May 15,1956-Fresno,Ca.
Lori Mott-B-June 2,1960-Fresno,Cal
LORRAINE JENETTE MOTT-B-Aug.12,1926-
Woodworth,N.D.
Parents:Lyle Jay Ingraham and Gena Alfea Johnson
Cyril Glenn Johnston-M-Jan.1st-1943
Sherry Mott-B-Sept.14,1949-San Francisco,Ca.
Parents:Lester Mott and Lorraine Jenette Ingraham
William Emery Jr.-B-1935-M-Jan.30,1970-Kennewick,Wa.
Parents:William Emery Sr. and Betty Emery
Children of Sherry Mott and Wm. Emery Jr.
Christopher Emery-B-Jan21,1975-Kennewick,Wa.

Kimberlee Ann Mott-B-May5,1956-Fresno,Ca.
Parents:Lester Mott and Lorraine Jenette Ingraham
Pat Young
Children:
Lynn Jennete Young-B-Feb.21,1977-San Jose,Ca.
Kimberlee Ann Mott-B-May5,1956-Fresno,Ca.
Parents:Lester Mott and Lorraine Jenette Ingraham
Silas Goodille
Children
Crystal Sunshine Goodille-B-Sept.21,1979
Kimberlee Ann Goodill-B-May5,1956-Fresno,Ca.
Parents:Lester Mott and Lorraine Jennette Ingraham
Daryl Madtson
Children:Aaron M.Madtson-B-June 9,1989-Centralia,Wa.

Lori Rene Mott-B-June2,1960-Fresno,Ca.
Parents:Lester Mott and Lorraine Jenette Ingraham
Kevin Matheson-B-May28,1957-Seattle,Wa.
Parents:Ray Matheson and Esther Matheson
Children of Lori Rene Mott and Kevin Matheson
Meilissa Colleen Matheson-B-Jan.20,1979-Richland,Wa.

Lori Rene Mott-B-June 2,1960-Fresno,Ca.
Parents:Lester Mott and Lorraine Jenette Ingraham
Joseph C. Holt
Children:
Randy Stewert Holt(Mott)-B-Oct.6,1986-Richland,Wa.

Lori Rene Mott-B-June2,1960-Fresno,Ca.
Parents Lester Mott and Lorraine Jenette Ingraham
Children: of Lori Rene Mott
Nathaniel Mott-B-Sept.8,1998

RALPH DEAN INGRAHAM-B-Aug.21,1898-Pine
Island,Mn.
D-July 5,1989-Billings,Mt.-Sunset Memorial-Billings,Mt.
Parents:Chauncey Lee Ingraham and Myrtle June Cowles
Rose Wutzke-B-1899-D-May6,1993-Laurel,Mt.Bur.Sunset
Memorial,Billings,Mt.
Parents:Daniel S. Wutzke-D-1876-1960-Wilhelmuna1875-
1969
Children of Ralph Dean Ingraham and Rose Wutzke
Harold Ingraham-B-June4,1921-Woodworth,N.D.
Harry Ingraham-B-Nov.9,1923-Woodworth,N.D.
Leonard Roy Ingraham-B-Dec.28,1925-Woodworth,N.D.
Walter Ray Ingraham-B-Aug.4,1928-Woodworth,N.D.
Roy Ingraham-B-Sept.22,1931-Woodworth,N.D.
Curtis Norman Ingraham-B-July19,1934-Woodworth,N.D.
Marvin Ingraham-B-May25,1939-Edgar,Mt.

HAROLD INGRAHAM-B-June 4,1921-Woodworth,N.D.
D-June 14,1998-Laurel,Mt.
Parents:Ralph Dean Ingraham and Rose Wilhelmuna
Wilma Blohm-B-May9,1925-Beulah,N.D.
Parents:Fred A Blohm and Mamie Miller
Children of Harold Ingraham and Wilma Blohm
Dean Ingraham-B-Dec.26,1945-Billings,Mt.
Diana Ingraham-B-May29,1948-Billings,Mt.
Donna Ingraham-B-June27,1950-Billings,Mt.

Dean Ingraham-B-Dec.26,1945-Billings,Mt.
Parents:Harold Ingraham and Wilma Blohm
Sharon Quarnburg-M
Parents:Arthur Quarburg and Margaret
Children of Dean Ingraham and Sharen Quarnburg
John Dean Ingraham-B-
Sherilyn Ingraham
Chad Harold Ingraham

Diane Ingraham-B-May29,1948-Billings,Mt.
Parents:Harold Ingraham and Wilma Blohm
Bruce C. Watson-M-Jan.13,1968-Laurel,Mt.
Children
Jason C. Watson
Heather Wilma Watson

Donna Rose Ingraham-B-June27,1950-Billings,Mt.
Parents Harold Ingraham and Wilma Blohm
Ronald Dean Hanni-B-Aug.19,1943-Nov.13,1971
Children:
Ranee Leann Hanni-B-June30,1973-M-Stephen S. Carmean Jr.
Hyla Lynn Hanni-B-June 10,1974
Joylene Kay Hanni-B-July 20,1975
Angela Ann Hanni-B-April29,1978-M-Clifton Gene Greuter-
July 20,2002-Billings,Mt.

HARRY INGRAHAM-B-Nov.9,1923-Woodworth,N.D.
Parents Ralph Dean Ingraham and Rose Wutzke
Mary Fox-M-Dec.31,1946
Parents: John Fox and Elizabeth Knaub
Parents of Harry Ingraham and Mary Fox
Children:
Sandra Fay Ingraham-B-Aug.6,1947-Laurel,Mt.
Harry Wayne Ingraham-B-Feb.20,1948-Laurel,Mt.
Sarah Ingraham-B-Feb.19,1955-Laurel,Mt.
Farren Allen Ingraham-B-Feb.20,1957-Laurel,Mt.

HARRY INGRAHAM-B-Nov.9,1923-Woodworth,N.D.
Parents Ralph Dean Ingraham and Rose Wutzke
M-Wildred Miller-B-Nov.18,1926-Conrad Miller-d-2006
Parents: Joseph Miller and Irene
Wildred Miller's son; Larry John Empereur

Harry Wayne Ingraham-B-Feb.20,1949-Laurel,Mt.
Parents:Harry Ingraham and Mary Fox
Gail Singleton-B-Jan.5,1953-M-May 7,1980

Sandra Fay Ingraham-B-Aug.6,1947-Laurel,Mt.
Parents:Harry Ingraham and Mary Fox
Bill Franklyn

LEONARD ROY INGRAHAM-B-Dec.28,1925-
Woodworth,N.D.
Parents:Ralph Roy Ingraham and Rose Wutzke
Carol Keller-M-1947-Laurel,Mt.
Children
Leonard Warren Ingraham-B-Oct.24,1948-Laurel,Mt.
LEONARD ROY INGRAHAM-B-Dec.28,1925-
Woodworth,N.D
Parents:Ralph Roy Ingraham and Rose Wutzke
Sharon Allen-B-Sept.25,1939
Parents:Jack Allen and Mrs. Allen
Children of Leonard Roy Ingraham and Sharen Allen
Miles John Ingraham-B-April 9,1963-Palo Alto,Ca.
Meagan Rose Ingraham-B-July 16,1964-Palo Alto,Ca.

Leonard Warren Ingraham-B-Oct.24,1948-Laurel,Mt.
Leonard Roy Ingraham and Carol Keller
Lori
Children
Joshua Ingraham-B-1976-Sacramento,Ca.
Meagan Rose Ingraham-B-July16,1964-Palo Alto,Ca.
Parents:Leonard Roy Ingraham and Sharen Allen
Scott Kindred
Children
Kelly Ann Kindred-B-Oct.5,1986
Courtney Rose Kindred-B-Sept.27,1988
Cassidy Kindred-B-July 5,1990

WALTER RAY INGRAHAM-B-Aug.4,1928-
Woodworth,N.D.-D-1958
Parents:Ralph Dean Ingraham and Rose Wutzke
Marijean McKinney-M-Sept.21,1947-Laurel,Mt.
Children
Larry Ray Ingraham-B
Garry Lee Ingraham-B
Stevan Hal Ingraham-B-May 17,1951

Walter Ray Ingraham-D-1928-1958-Mountview
Cemetery,Billings,Mt.

Larry Ray Ingraham-B-Laurel,Mt.-D-June 11, 2006
Parents Walter Ray Ingraham and Marijean McKinney
Mary Jordan-M-Salt Lake City, Ut.
April Ingraham-Salt Lake City,Ut.
Chase Ingraham-Salt Lake City,Ut.

Gary Lee Ingraham-B-Laurel,Mt.
Parents:Walter Ray Ingraham and Marijean McKinney
M-Ann Neilsen-Salt Lake City,Ut.
Children
Scott Ingraham
Tara Ingraham

Stevan Hal Ingraham-B-May17,1951-M-Teresa Cummings
Children:
Jennifer Gayle Ingraham-B-May28,1975
Brian Scott Ingraham-B-Dec.20,1978

ROY INGRAHAM-B-Sept.22,1931-Woodworth,N.D.
D-2005
Parents: Ralph Dean Ingraham and Rose Wutzke
M-Pat Bender
Parents:Ed Bender and Dorothy Bender
Children
Kathy Ingraham
Rick Ingraham
Tammy Ingraham
Tim Ingraham

Kathy Ingraham-B-April17,1955-Laurel,Mt.
Parents:Roy Ingraham and Pat Bender
M-Richard Vestal-B-Feb.1948-M-Aug.29,1980
Children
Christian J. Lund-B-July 1,1976-
Richard Ian Vestal-B-Aug.14,1977
Amber Dawn Vestal-B-Oct.2,1981
Trevor Elton Vestal-B-Oct.6,1982
Travis Roy Vestal-B-Oct.6,1982
Torrey Jean Vestal-B-April17,1984

Rick Allen Ingraham-B-Nov.1956
Parents:Roy Ingraham Pat Bender
Terry Foster
Children
Chauncey Wilbur Ingraham-B-Aug.12,1984

CURTIS NORMAN INGRAHAM-B-July19,1934-
Woodworth,N.D.
Parents: Ralph Dean Ingraham and Rose Wutzke
Paulette Cook-B-Jan.18,1939-Joliet,Mt.-M-June 7,1958
Children of Curtis Norman Ingraham and Paulette Cook
Bridget Ann Ingraham-B-Jan.3,1959-Missoula,Mt.
Mark Curtis Ingraham-B-June18,1961-Missoula,Mt.
Scott Walter Ingraham-B-April,1964-Missoula,Mt.
Mathew Ingraham-B-May,1968
Paul Joshua Ingraham-B-Sept.24,1972

MARVIN INGRAHAM-B-May 25,1939-Edgar,Mt.
Parents-Ralph Dean Ingraham and Rose Wutzke
Jo-Anne Kreger
Children
Paula Jane Ingraham-M-Randy Adams
Lisa Rosanne Ingraham-M-Marvin Stickia
Jacqlin Ingraham
Nickoa Ann Ingraham
MARVIN INGRAHAM-B-May 25,1939-Edgar,Mt.
Parents: Ralph Dean Ingraham and Rose Wutzke
M-Mavy(Frances)Odom-B-Jan.20,1942-Plenty,Mt.
Mavy's children
Tom Odom
Tammy Odom
John Jr. Odom

EDNA IONE INGRAHAM-Jan.29,1902-Mantorville,Mn
D-Nov.3,1982-Bur.Homewood,Il.-Oak Hill Cemetery
Parents:Chauncey Ingraham and Myrtle Cowles
M-Henry Anklam-Dec.19,1921-D-Jan.27,1923-
Woodworth,N.D.
Children
Henry Albert Anklam-B-Jan.29,1923-Woodworth,N.D.
D-Mar.1932-Chicago,Il.-11 yrs. Old.
EDNA IONE ANKLAM-B-Jan29,1902-Mantorville,Mn
D-Nov.3,1982-Bur.Merrionette Park,Il.
M-Theodore Ernst Anklam-B-Sept.18,1891-M-Nov.25,1924-
Woodworth,N.D.-D-Aug.7,1951-Chicago,Il
Children
HARRIET BERNIECE ANKLAM-B-Sept.17,1926-
Milwaukee,Wi.
M-Glen John Drawns-June 21,1947-D-July30,1983

HAROLD THEODORE ANKLAM-B-Aug.10,1935-
Chicago,Il.
M-Ann Louise Albrecht-Sept.5,1954

EDNA ANKLAM-B-Jan.29, 1902-Mantorville,Mn
D-Nov.3,1982-Bur-Merrionette Park,Il
M-Clarence Theodore Patno-B-1907-June 5,1970
D-Sept.25,1977-Chicago,Il.

ESTHER SOPHIA INGRAHAM-B-Sept.5,1903-
Mantorville,Mn.
D-Chicago,Il-July23,1968-Bethanim Cemetery,Justice,Il.
Parents: Chauncey Lee Ingraham and Myrtle Cowles
D-June 16,1969-Otto George Warnke-B-Sept.22,1901-M.-
Nov.6,1922
Children of Esther Sophia Ingraham and Otto G. Warnke
Gustave Otto Warnke-B-April 16,1923-Eauclair,Wi.
Marvin Melvin Warnke-B-May16,1925-Eauclair,Wi.
Lois Augusta Myrtle Warnke-B-July 22,1926-Eauclair,Wi.
Deloris Jean Ann Warnke-B-June 10,1935-Eauclair,Wi.
Arlene Phillis Warnke-B-Oct.10,1937-Eauclair,Wi.
Donna Joan Warnke-B-Feb.8,1939-Chicago,Il
Carol Mar Warnke-B-Mar.24,1947-Chicago,Il.

GUSTAVE OTTO WARNKE-B-April 16,1923-Eauclair,Wi.
D-Oct.19,1963-Chicago,Il.-Bur.Bethesda Cemetery-Justice,Il.
Parents:Otto George Warnke and Esther Sophia Ingraham
Genivieve Marie Warnke-B-Dec.12,1923-Chicago,Il.M-
Dec.25,1941
Children of Gustave Otto Warnke and Genivieve Maria
Charles John Warnke-B-Dec.20,1942-Chicago,Il.
Sharon Lynn Warnke-B-Feb.29,1948-Chicago,Il.
Lloyd George Warnke-B-Jan.20,1952-Chicago,Il.
Genivieve Marie Warnke-M-Ron Ray-B-June 26,1929-M-
Sept.4,1965

MARVIN MELVIN WARNKE-B-May16,1925,Eauclair,Wi.
D-Feb.1945-Killed in Germany-WWII
Bur.Bethesda Cemetery,Justice,Il.
Married-Dorothy Forester

657

LOIS AUGUSTA MYRTLE WARNKE-BJuly22,1926-
Eauclair,Wi
Parents:Otto George Warnke and Esther Sophia Ingraham
M-Clarence Kunstman-B-Feb.13,1917-D-Mar.14,1988
Children
Marvin Melvin Kunstman-B-Oct.30,1945-Chicago,Il
Terrina Lee Kunstman-B-Oct.15,1951-Chicago,Il.
Dennis Lee Kunstman-B-Oct.15,1969
DELORIS JEAN WARNKE-B-June 10,Eauclair,Wi.
Parents:Otto George Warnki-B-Sept.22,1901-Wi.
Robert LeRoy Stamp-B-Mar.18,1934-M-Jan.16,1954-
Chicago,Il.
Children
Micheal LeRoy Stamp-B-June 14,1955-M-Debra Schlaffir
Barbara Jean Stamp-B-June17,1960-M-Donal Rathman
Donna Gail Stamp-B-Aug.8,1967-M-Thomas F. Hartman
DONNA JOAN WARNKE-B-Feb.8,1939-Eauclair,Wi
Parents:Otto George Warnke and Esther Sophia Ingraham
Fred Schuster-B-May14,1943-M-Nov.18,1972
ARLENE PHILLIS WARNKE-B-Oct.10,1937-Chicago,Il.
Parents:Otto George Warnke and Esther Sophia Ingrham
Albert Alex Sawicki-B-May28,1932-Chicago,Il.
Married-July23,1955-Chicago,Il.
Children
Bruce Albert Sawicki-B-Sept.23,1959-Chicago,Il.
Cherilene Esther Sawicki-B-Mar.6,1964-Chicago,Il.
CAROL MAR WARNKE-B-Mar.24,1947-Chicago,Il.
Parents:Otto George Warnke and Esther Sophia Ingraham
Garry Robert Hine-B-May18,1947-Chicago,Il.
M-May21,1966-Chicago,Il.
Children
Garry Robert Hine Jr.-B-Feb.20,1967-Chicago,Il.
Allan Stevan Hine-B-June20,1970-Chicago,Il.

FLOYD RAY INGRAHAM-B-Nov.24,1907-
Woodworth,N.D.
D-Feb.10,1991-Alleene,Ak-Bur.-Ashdown,Ak.
Parents:Chauncey Lee Ingraham and Myrtle Sophia Ingraham
Inez Milspaugh-B-June 16,1905-M-1927-D-Feb.1990
Children of Floyd Ray Ingraham and Inez Milspaugh
Orland Floyd Ingraham-B-Jan.4,1929-Chicago,Il.
Delmer Dean Ingraham-B-Sept.11,1934-Mt. Pelier,N.D.
Gordan Ray Ingraham-B-May24,1940-California
Lorna Gayle Ingraham-B-Nov.21,1942-California

FLOYD RAY INGRAHAM-B-Nov.24,1907-
Woodworth,N.D.
D-Feb.10,1991-Alleene,Ak.-Bur.Ashdown,Ak.
Parents: Chauncey Lee Ingraham and Myrtle Sophia Ingraham
Married Oma Ingraham

ORLAN FLOYD INGRAHAM-B-Jan.4,1929-Chicago,Il.
Parents:Floyd Ray Ingraham and Inez Milspaugh
Geraldine Davis
Children
Gloria Ann Ingraham

Orland Floyd Ingraham-B-Jan.4,1929-Chicago,Il.
Parents:Floyd Ray Ingraham and Inez Milspaugh
Evelyn Zanders
Children
Orland L. Ingraham

DELMER DEAN INGRAHAM-B-Sept.11,1934-Mt.
Pelier,N.D.
Parents Floyd Ray Ingraham and Inez Milspaugh
Ruth Olive Moorehouse-B-Feb.2,1935-Corvalles,Or.
M-June15,1952-Yuma,Az.
Children
Deana Rae Ingraham-B-July25,1953-Cottage Grove,Or.
Michael Dean Ingraham-B-Sept.1,1955-Arcadia,Ca.
Kathryn Jean Ingraham-B-Aug.17,1957-Arcadia,Ca.
Bruce Allen Ingraham-B-Feb.13,1959-Eureka,Ca.
Melanie Ann Ingraham-B-Mar.26,1960-Fortuna,Ca.

Deana Rae Ingraham-B-July25,1953-Cottage Grove,Or.
Parents:Delmer Dean Ingraham and Ruth Olive Moorehouse
Leslie Cox-M-Sept.7,1970-Longbeach,Ca.
Children
Corinna Marie Cox-B-Mar.31,1973-Cresent City,Ca.
Jason Allen Cox-B-Nov.24,1975

Deana Rae Ingraham-B-July25,1953-Cottage Grove,Or.
Parents:Delmer Dean Ingraham and Ruth Olive Moorehouse
Daniel Rogers-M-Oct.11,1980-Bremerton,Wa.

Michael Dean Ingraham-B-Sept.1,1955-Arcada,Ca.
Parents:Delmer Dean Ingraham and Ruth Olive Moorehouse
Sandee Demaree-M-Oct.18,1980-Vegas,Nv.
Children
Tyson Kimball Fiacco-B-June 18,1980
Ryan Dean Ingraham-B-Feb.15,1982
Kevin Michael Ingraham-B-May21,1989-Everett,Wa.

Kathryn Jean Ingraham-B-Aug.17,1957-Arcada,Ca.
Parents:Delmer Dean Ingraham and Ruth Olive Moorehouse
Terry Lee Dick Gamble-M-June 7,1974
Children:Terry Lee Ingraham (toGamble Jr)-B-Oct.30,1979

Kathryn Jean Ingraham-B-Aug.17,1957-Arcada,Ca.
Parents:Delmer Dean Ingraham and Ruth Olive Moorehouse
Brian Scott Frakes-M-Jan.9,1983-Long Beach,Wa.
Children
Scott Brian Frakes-B-Jan.3,1985

Bruce Allen Ingraham-B-Feb.13,1959-Eureka,Ca.
Parents:Delmer Dean Ingraham and Ruth Olive Moorehouse
Terry Lynn Coburn-B-Jan.12,1956-Kirkland,Wa.
M-May15,1976-Long Beach,Wa.
Children
Carrie Lynn Ingraham-B-Nov.23,1979-Bremerton,Wa.
Laura Ann Ingraham-B-July24,1981-Bremerton,Wa.
Grace Marie Ingraham-B-May18,1988-Bremerton,Wa.
Mary Louise Ingraham-B-May23,1990-Bremerton,Wa.

Melanie Ann Ingraham-B-Mar.26,1960-Fortune,Ca.
Parents:Delmer Dean Ingraham and Ruth Olive Moorehouse
Kenneth Powell-M-Nov.18,1975-Arcada,Ca.
Children
Marlynne Luran Powell-B-Feb.5,1976-Tacoma,Wa.
Tanya Lee Powell-B-June 3,1978-Tacoma,Wa.
Kennita Rose Powell-B-Feb.7,1980-Tacoma,Wa.

Delmer Dean Ingraham-B-Sept.11,1934-Mt.Pelier,N.D.
Parents:Floyd Ray Ingraham and Inez Milspaugh
Roberta Kenower-M-1964
Children
Joyce Inez Ingraham-B-Dec.21,1965

Delmer Dean Ingraham-M-Jeanette Severance
Cliff Severance-Jeanettes children
Kathy Severance from prev. marriage

GORDON RAY INGRAHAM-B-May24,1940-Garden
Grove,Ca.
Parents: Floyd Ray Ingraham and Inez Milspaugh
Sandy Noyes-M-1957
Children
Ricky Ray Ingraham

GORDON RAY INGRAHAM-B-May24,1940-Garden
Grove,Ca.
Parents:Floyd Ray Ingraham and Inez Milspaugh
Sharon Kemper
Children
Donny Ingraham

GORDON RAY INGRAHAM-B-May24,1940-Garden
Grove,Ca.
Parents: Floyd Ray Ingraham and Inez Milspaugh
Beverly

LORNA GAYLE INGRAHAM-B-Nov.21,1942-Artesia,Ca.
Parents:Floyd Ray Ingraham and Inez Milspaugh
Wyatt Eugene Chambers-M-June2,1960-California
Children
Rhonda Maria Chambers-B-Nov.11,1962-Ca.
LORNA GAYLE INGRAHAM-B-Nov.21,1942-Artesia,Ca.
Parents: Floyd Ray Ingraham and Inez Milspaugh
Harry Hart Miller-M-Nov.21,1973
Children
Chuck Miller and Leo Miller: from Millers Prev. Marriage
LORNA GAYLE INGRAHAM-B-Nov.21,1942-Artesia,Ca.
Parents:Floyd Ray Ingraham and Inez Milspaugh
James Donald Lindeman-M-Dec.31,1978
Children
Jeff Lindeman

CLAUD MELVIN INGRAHAM-B-Dec.28,1915-
Woodworth,N.D.
Parents:Chauncey Lee Ingraham and Myrtle Sophia Cowles
Lorreine Gennett Nelson,-B-Aug.21,1918-Woodworth,N.D.
M-June 10,1937-Jamestown,N.D.
Parents:Juluis Arthur Nelson and Cassie Jannette French
Children
Delton Dean Ingraham-B-Sept.22,1938-Woodworth,N.D.-D-
Feb.3,1939
Cenra Jean Ingraham-B-June 2,1940-Woodworth,N.D.
Denel Owen Ingraham-B-April 9,1942-Woodworth,N.D.

CENRA JEAN INGRAHAM-B-June 2,1940-
Woodworth,N.D.
Parents:Claud Melvin Ingraham and Lorreine Gnnette Nelson
Robert Weatherford-M-June 2,1960-Laurel,Mt.
Children
Kimberly Ann Weatherford-B-June 11,1961-Laurel,Mt.
Keith Robert Weatherford-B-Sept.11,1964-Laurel,Mt.
Kenneth Todd Weatherford-B-Mar.29,1975-Laurel,Mt.

Kimberly Ann Weatherford-B-June 11,1961-Laurel,Mt.
Parents: Robert Weatherford and Cennra Jean Ingraham
Paul Edward Jeroma-B-Nov.19,1960-Laurel,Mt.
M-June 19,1982-Laurel,Mt.
Children of Paul Edward Jeroma and Kimberly Ann
Weatherford
Kristen Elizabeth Jeroma-B-Dec.10,1985-Kent,Wa.
Mathew Paul Jeroma-B-May 11,1993-Kent,Wa.

Keith Robert Weatherford-B-Sept.11,1964-Laurel,Mt.
Parents Robert Weatherford and Cenra Jean Ingraham
M-Kirstan Lee-Sept.15,1990-Laurel,Mt.
Children
Keenan Robert Weatherford-B-Mar.9,1991

Keith Robert Weatherford-B-Sept.11,1964-Laurel,Mt.
Parents:Robert Weatherford and Cenra Jean Ingraham
M-Kirstan Lee-Sept.15,1990-Laurel,Mt.
Children
Keenan Robert Weatherford-B-Mar.9,1991

Kenneth Todd Weatherford-April 29,1975
Parents: Robert Weatherford and Cennra Jean Ingraham
Meghen Louise Demarco-M-Aug.11,2001-Billings,Mt.
Parents-Michael DeMarco and Jan DeMarco

DENEL OWEN INGRAHAM-B-April9,1942-
Woodworth,N.D.
Parents:Claud Melvin Ingraham and Lorreine Gennette Nelson
Judy Shay-M-June 22,1962
Children
Randy Allen Ingraham-B-June7,1963-Bozeman,Mt.
Kerri Rae Ingraham-B-Sept.5,1965-Bozeman,Mt.

Randy Allen Ingraham-June 7,1963-Bozeman,Mt.
Parents:Denel Owen Ingraham and Judy Shay
Julie Bold
Children
Nathan Ingraham-B-Dec.27,1992
Jesse Ingraham-B-Dec.27,1992

Kerri Rae Ingraham-B-Sept.5,1965-Bozeman,Mt.
Parents:Denel Owen Ingraham and Judy Shay
M-Lee McGuire-B-Aug.21,1963-Married 1988

J

THE JOHNSONS
Thosten and Gunulf were brothers: they both changed their
names to Johnson when they came to America
Gunulf Soiem Johnson –B-July 14, 1840-Telmark, Norway d-
Jan 20, 1893-Norway-M-1874-Evanshville, M.
GUNHILD TANGEN SOIEM JOHNSON-b-Oct.1840-
Sygdale,Norway
D-Aug.1899-Evansville,Mn.
Thosten and Gunulf were brothers when Thosten died in the
great blizzard in 1873. Gunulf married Gunhild Tangent
Johnson
Children were:
Bertina Johnson –B- July, 1875-Evansville, Mn.-d-July 1937
Theodore Johnson-B-1877, Evansville, Mn.-d-June 16, 1888
GUNDER JOHNSON –B-Oct. 11, 1879, Evansville, Mn.-d-
Nov. 11, 1943, Jamestown, N.D.
Married **Laura Bah** Nov. 10, 1899 –Erdahl, Mn.

GUNULF (SOIEM)JOHNSON-B-July14,1840-Telmark
(Tin)Norway.
M-Before 1875-Evansville,Mn.-changed name abt.1868
Brother-Thosten Soiem-who also changed name
Children
Bertina Johnson-B-July 20,1875-Evansville,Mn.
M-Oct.16,1897 to Ole Elvested-D-July16,1937
Theodore Olaves JohnsonB-6-23-1876-6-16-1888
Gunder Johnson –b-Oct. 11, 1879 Evansville, -D-Nov. 11,
1943 Jamestown,N.D.–M-Laura Bah-Nov.10,1899-Erdahl, Mn.
Martin Gunerius Olson Bah-B-Nov.9, 1849, Rodnes,Norway-
D-Dec. 10, 1915-Erdahl,Mn.
M-Nov.10, 1880-Erdahl, Mn.--Anna Marie (Thompson)
Aasjer-B-May 18, 1857-Norway-D-July 30,1926-Erdahl,Mn.
Children:

Laura Bah-B-April 12, 1883-Erdahl,Mn
Olga Bertina Bah-B-Mar. 10, 1886-Erdahl,Mn
Gilbert Theadore Bah-B-Nov. 25,1892-Erdahl,Mn.
Thora Alfia Bah-B-Nov.25, 1893-Erdahl, Mn.
Minnie Sophia Bah-B-June 3,1896 Erdahl, Mn.
There are notes in my mother Gena Ingraham's records that
Anna Marie Aasjer is a sister to Thosten Thompson

LAURA BAH-B-April 12, 1883-Eradahl, Mn.-D-Mar. 3, 1965
buried at Lunde Cemetery, Woodworth, N. D. with husband
Gunders Johnson

GUNDER AND LAURA JOHNSON FAMILIES

GUNERIOS (GUNDER) JOHNSON-B-10-11-1879-
M-Laura Bah
D-Nov.11,1943-Jamestown,N.D.
Laura Bah relatives are:
Alga Bertina Bah.-B-March 10, 1886-d-Mar. 10, 1908-M-
Jacob Soller
Gilbert Thedore Bah-B-Nov. 25, 1893-m-Andrew Thomson_b-
Jan. 31, 1896-Erdahl, Mn.-d-Jan. 30, 1983-M-Nov.19, 1934
Elbow Lake Mn.
Minnie Soph A. Bah-B-June 3, 1896-Erdeahl, Mn.-d-Sept. 3,
1961-m-Nov. 24, 1914-Elbow Lake George Martin Hammer –
B-Oct. 9, 1891-Eradahl, Mn. –d-Mar. 22, 1978-Fergus Falls,
Mn.
Thosten Thompson-B-1864-Norway –d-1943, Jamestown, N.d.
–m-Nekolenae Johnson-b-1851-Norway-d-May 2, 1934-
Woodworth, N.D.
Thosten and Nekolenae are both buried at Woodworth, N.D.,
Lunde Cemetery. Thosten is the brother to **ANNA MARIE
THOMSPSON AASJER-LAURA BAH JOHNSONS
MOTHER**

Nekolenea had two sons, Martin and Ole Johnson from a previous marriage. Thosten and Nekolenae had one child. Melvin Thompson-b-Jan. 23, 1898-Woodworth, N.D.-M-Lora Rose-B-Now. 19, 1900. In the 1940s they lived at Hoodriver, Oregon. They moved to Lancaster, Ca. where Melvin died April 18, 1980 and Lora died Nov. 19, June 20, 1983. Both are buried in Lancaster, CA.

GUNDER JOHNSON-B-Oct.11,1879-Evansville,Mn. D-Nov. 11, 1943 -Jamestown,N.D.-Bur-Woodworth,N.D.-Lunde Cemetery
\Parents:Gunulf Johnson and Gunhild Tangen Soiem
LAURA BAH-B-April,1883-Erdahl,Mn.M-Nov.10,1899 D-Mar.3,1965-Jamestown,N.D.-Bur-Woodworth,N.D.Lunde Cemetery
Children of Gunder Johnson and Laura Bah
GENA ALFEA JOHNSON-B-Dec.1,1900-Evansville,Mn.-Married-Lyle Ingraham
Louise Clara Johnson-B-July 19,1903-Evansville,Mn.-M-Phil Schuff
Elenora Bessie Johnson-B-Oct.24,1905-Woodworth,N.D.-Married-Art Steffens
Gladys Hilma Johnson-B-Feb.16,1908-Woodworth,N.D.-Married-Claus Steffens
Theodore Orville Johnson-B-Aug.21,1911-Woodworth,N.D. Married-Irene Holtz
Lovida Masie Johnson-B-Jan.7,1914-Woodworth,N.D. Married-M-Harold Holtz
Hilda Amanda Johnson-B-Jan.2,1916-Woodworth,N.D. Married-Harry Schuff
Esther Grace Johnson-B-April16,1918-Woodworth,N.D. Married-Lloyd Sorenson
Olga Johnson-B-April 16,1918-Twin-Bur.April16,1918-Launde Cemetery

Avis Lillian Johnson-B-Oct.27,1920-Woodworth,N.D.-
Married Danny Glowac
Doris Evelyn Johnson-B-May27,1923-Woodworth,N.D.
Married-Ray Roseneau
Gordon Laurance-B-Sept.15,1925-Woodworth,N.D.
D-Aug.30,1926
Laura Bah's parents; Martin Gunerius(Olson)Bah and Anna
Marie Johnson
Both Olga and Gordon-Bur-Woodworth,N.D.Lunde Cemetery

GENA ALFEA JOHNSON-B-Dec.1,1900-Evansville,Mn.
D-Sept19,1986-Kennewick,Wa-DesertLawn,Kenn.,Wa
Parents Gunder Johnson and Laura Bah
M-Jan.7,1919-LYLE JAY INGRAHAM-B-Jan.30,1897-
Mantorville,Mn.
D-July21,1982-Kennewick,Wa.-B-Desert Lawn,Kenn.,Wa.
Parents Chauncey Ingraham and Myrtle Cowles
Children
Raymond Lloyd Ingraham-B-Aug.21,1919-Pettibone,N.D.
Charles LeRoy Ingraham-B-1920-Woodworth,N.D.-D-as baby-
Lunde Cemetery
LeRoy Norman Ingraham-B-1921-Woodworth,N.D.-D-as
baby-Lunde Cemetery
Norman Jerome Ingraham-B-Sept.11,1922-Woodworth,N.D.
Willard Stanley Ingraham-B-June 23,1924-Woodworth,N.D.
Lorraine Jainette Ingraham-B-Aug.12,1926-Woodworth,N.D.
Gerada Agnes Ingraham-B-Dec.22,1930-Died as baby

RAYMOND LLOYD INGRAHAM-B-Aug.21,1919-
Petibonne,N.D.
Anna Rose Crosby-B-July 25,1926-Prosser,A.
M-July 12,1946-Lewiston,Id.-d-April 1, 2007
Children
Dorothy Jean Ingraham-B-Aug.18,1946-Sunnyside,Wa.
Linda Rae Ingraham-B-July11,1947-Sunnyside,Wa.
Lloyd Raymond Ingraham-B-Oct.28,1948-Sunnyside,Wa

NORMAN JEROME INGRAHAM-B-Sept.11,1922-
Woodworth,N.D.
Verdell Noble-B-Dec.4,1927-Van Buren,Ark.
M-July 27,1946-Prosser,Wa.
Children
Jerome Jay Ingraham-B-May26,1951-Prosser,Wa.
Janette Marie Ingraham-B-Nov.18,1953
Jacquelyn Ingraham-B-Aug.28,1955-Prosser,Wa.
WILLARD STANLEY INGRAHAM-B-June 23,1924-
Woodworth,N.D.
Louise Williams-B-Oct. 6,1930-Mabton(Glade)Wa.
M-Sept.13,1947-Mabton(Glade)Wa.
Children
Carol Jean Ingraham-B-April5,1948-Prosser,Wa.
Mary Ann Ingraham-B-Dec.28,1949-Sunnyside,Wa.

LORRAINE JAINETTE INGRAHAM-B-Aug.12,1926-
Woodworth,N.D.
Lester Mott-B-Sept.12,1919-New York
M-Dec.25,1943-Prosser,Wa.
Children
Sherry Mott-B-Sept.14,1949-San Francisco,Ca.
Kimberlee Ann Mott-B-May 5,1956-Fresno,Ca.
Lori Rene Mott-B-June 2,1960-Fresno,Ca.

LOUISE CLARA JOHNSON-B-July 19,1903-
Evansville,Mn.
D-April1,1994-Jamestown,N.D.-M-Nov.22,1921-
Jamestown,N.D.
Parents:Gunder Johnson and Laura Bah
M-Philip Clifford Schuff-B-Feb.5,1889-D-Dec.29,1966-
Jamestown,N.D.
Parents-Emil Schuff and Laura Schmidt
Children of Phil Schuff and Louise Johnson
Harriet Phyllis Schuff-B-July 6,1926-Woodworth,N.D.

Orville Chester Schuff-B-Nov.11,1929-Woodworth,N.D.
Donald Schuff-B-Dec.11,1934-Woodworth,N.D.

Harriet Phyllis Schuff-B-July 6,1926-Woodworth,N.D.
Vernon Arthur Wahl-B-July3,1923-M-Jan.11,1945
Children
Wayne Arthur Scuff-B-Oct.19,1946-Jamestown,N.D.
Gene Orville Schuff-B-Jan.27,1948-Jamestown,N.D.
Brad Roland Schuff-B-Sept.14,1953-Jamestown,N.D.

Orville Chester Schuff-B-Nov.11,1929-Woodworth,N.D.
Beverly Guenther-B-Sept.16,1931-M-Sept.18,1949-d-Sept.7,
2001
Children
Gregory Schuff-B-May 9,1951-Jamestown,N.D.
Marcus Schuff-B-May3,1953-Jamestown,N.D.
Karen Schuff-B-Feb.22,1955-Jamestown,N.D.
Roger Allen Schuff-B-Oct.13,1959-Janestown,N.D.

Donald Schuff-B-Dec.11,1934-Woodworth,N.D.-D-Dec. 22,
2003
Marlys Klose-B-Aug.30,1934-M-Feb.14,1951
Children
Debra Schuff-B-Jan.27,1952
Brenda Schuff
Danny Schuff
Brent Schuff
Marlys and Donald divorced
Marlys died June 3,1992

Donald Schuff-B-Dec.11,1934-Woodworth,N.D.-D-Dec. 22,
2003
Married Nelda
Children
Dee Etta Schuff
John Philip Schuff

ELENOR BESSIE JOHNSON-B-Nov.24,1905-
Evansville,Mn.
D-Feb.9,2001-Yakima,Wa.-Bur.Mabton,Wa. Cemetery
Parents:Gunder Johnson and Laura Bah
Arthur Henry Steffens-B-May31,1901-M-Nov.5,1923
D-Feb.7,1968-Mabton,Wa.-Bur.Mabton Cemetery
Children of Elenora Johnson and Arthur Steffens
Arnold Burnell Steffens-B-June 16,1924-Woodworth,N.D.
Helen Marie Steffens-B-May 25,1927-Jamestown,N.D.
Gordon Henry Steffens-B-Feb.16,1929-Woodworth,N.D.
Rosella Loretta Steffens-B-April 8,1931-Woodworth,N.D.
Harry Raymond Steffens-B-Mar.12,1934-Jamestown,N.D.
Jerome Arthur Steffens-B-Jan.30,1937-Jamestown,N.D.
Gene Curtis Steffens-B-Jan.10,1938-Jamestown,N.D.
Shirley Susan Steffens-B-Mar.27,1942-Jamestown,N.D.
Margaret Elaine Steffens-B-Nov.21,1945-Mabton,Wa.

Arnold Burnell Steffens-B-June 16,1924-Woodworth,N.D.
Lucille Williams-B-April 9,1928-M-Sept.13,1947-d-Nov. 19,
2004
Children
James Jay Steffens-B-Sept.28,1949-Richland,Wa.
Jeffrey Allen Steffens-B-Nov.18,1951-Richland,Wa.
Loretta Ann Steffens-B-May23,1954-Richland,Wa.
Janis Marie Steffens-B-Dec.14,1955-Richland,Wa.

Helen Marie Steffens-B-May25,1927-Jamestown,N.D.
Bernard Smolen-B-Nov.13,1921-M-July 17,1949-
D-Jan.29, 1983
Children
Gary Smolen-B-May 4, 1954-Richland,Wa.
Earl Smolen-B-July 26,1956-Richland,Wa.

Gordon Henry Steffens-B-Feb.16,1929-Woodworth,N.D.
D-June 26,1984-Great Falls,Mt.
Grace Mauran Tonio-B-Sept.13,1931-M-Oct.1955

Children
Angela Kay Steffens-B-April 28,1957-Great Falls,Mt.
Shirley May Steffens-B-July 19,1958-Great Falls,Mt.
Thomas Arthur Steffens-B-April 9, 1960-Great Falls,Mt.
Joseph Edward Steffens-B-Feb.11,1965-Great Falls,Mt.

Rosella Loretta Steffens-B-April 8,1931-Woodworth,N.D.
Carl Kirkwood-B-Dec.26,1913-M-Dec.22,1950-D-Jan.28,2000

Harry Raymond Steffens-B-Mar.12,1934-Jamestown,N.D.-D-
March 14, 2007 –buried March 19, 2007 Lower Valley
Memorial Gardens, Sunnyside, Wa.
Edna Elizabeth Tipman-B-Feb.20,1933-M-May 4,1956
Children
Michael Eric Steffens-B-May 5,1962-Seattle,Wa.

Jerome Arthur Steffens-B-Jan.30,1937-Jamestown,N.D.
Reba Fisher-B-June 6,1932-M-1958
Children
Vickie Lynn Steffens-B-Jan.30,1957-Elkins,W. Virginia
Hazel Kathleen Steffens-B-May22,1961-W. Virginia

Jerome Arthur Steffens-B-Jan.30,1937-Woodworth,N.D.
D-Dec.28,1988-Mt. Vernon,Wa.
Maiba Irene Callaway-B-Sept.5,1933-Nov.9,1963
Children
Angela Fern Steffens-B-April15,1958-Toppenish,Wa.
Michael Theodore Steffens-B-Aug.27,1961-Toppenish,Wa.
Carrie Marlene Steffens-B-April 19,1957-Renton,Wa.
Eric Jerome Steffens-B-Mar.7,1964-Lynwood,Wa.
Jerome Adopted Irene's children
Eric Jerome belongs Jerome and Irene

Gene Curtis Steffens-B-Jan.10,1939-Jamestown,N.D.
1st M-Phyllis LaBarge-div.
2ndM-Loretta Ellison-B-Oct.26,1946-M-Oct.13,1968

Shirley Susan Steffens-B-Mar.27,1942
Roger Barajas-B-Jan.31,1938-M-April 10,1960
Children
Randy Curtis Barajas-B-Feb.13,1961-Sunnyside,Wa.
Sandra Ellison Barajas-B-Sept.7,1963-Sunnyside,Wa.

GLADYS HILMA JOHNSON-B-Feb.16,1908-
Woodworth,N.D.
D-Feb.4,2000-Sioux Falls,S.D.-M-Feb.4,1928-Fargo,N.D.
Parents-Gunder Johnson and Laura Bah
Claus Henry Steffen-B-Sept.5,1900-Esensee,Germany
D-July 1,1980-Sioux Falls,S.D.
Parents:Jurgen Heinrich Steffens and Rebecca Ann Stuven
Children of Gladys Hilma Johnson and Claus Henry Steffen
Harold James Steffen-B-June 30,1928-Fargo,N.D.
Dorothy Rebecca Steffen-B-June 19,1931-Sioux Falls,S.D.
Donald Eugene Steffen-B-Aug. 29,1932-Sioux Falls,S.D.
Robert Clayton Steffen-B-April 3, 1935-Died in Germany

Harold James Steffen-B-June 30,1928-Fargo,N.D.
Louella Louise Petratz-B-April25,1930-Canova,S.D.
Children
Cindy Lou Steffen-B-July 7,1952-Sioux Falls,S.D.
Peggy Louise Steffen-B-Jan.17,1954-Sioux Falls,S.D.
Richard Harold Steffen-B-Sept.26,1955-Sioux Falls,S.D.
Nancy JoAnne Steffen-B-Oct.20,1956-Sioux Falls,S.D.
Lynda Lee Steffen-B-Dec.20,1957-Sioux Falls,S.D.
Carol Jean Steffen-B-July 7,1961-Sioux Falls,S.D.
Kenneth Harold Steffen-B-Mar.26,1963-Sioux Falls,S.D

Dorothy Rebecca Steffen-B-June 19,1931-Sioux Falls,S.D.
William Raski-M-Aug.21,1953-Carson City,Nv-D-1975
Children
Robert William Raski-B-Aug.12,1954-Stockton,Ca.
Sandra Lee Raski-B-Aug.29,1959-Stockton,Ca.

Dorothy Rebecca Raski-B-June 19,1931-Sioux Falls,S.D.
Kenneth Clare-B-Nov.21,1922-M-Mar.9,1985-Stockton,Ca.

Donald Eugene Steffen-B-Aug.29,1932-Sioux Falls,S.D.
Marie Chistine Swanson-B-Mar.7,1934-Montrose,S.D.
M-April 10,1959-Sioux Falls,S.D.
Children
Lori Ann Steffen-B-May 26,1961-Sioux Falls,S.D.
Darin Mack Steffen-B-Oct.1,1965-Sioux Falls,S.D.

THEODORE ORVILLE JOHNSON-B-Aug.21,1911-
Woodworth,N.D.
D-Feb.22,1974-Jamestown,N.D.-M-Mar.15,1933- New
Rockford,N.D.
Parents:Gunder Johnson and Laura Bah
Irene Eziabeth Holtz-B-Mar.1,1914-New Rockford,N.D.
D-May26,1979-Jamestown,N.D.-M-Mar.15,1933-New
Rockford,N.D.
Parents: Henry Holtz and Elizabeth Forman
Children of Theodore Johnson and Irene Holtz
Lois May Johnson-B-Dec.12,1933-Woodworth,N.D.
Duane Orville Johnson-B-Sept.2,1935-Jamestown,N.D.
Charles Burnell Johnson-B-Sept.4,1937-Woodworth,N.D.
Quentine Darle Johnson-B-Sept.30,1939-Woodworth,N.D.
Jerald Dean Johnson-B-Oct.22,1941-Woodworth,N.D.
Glen Alan Johnson-B-Feb.12,1944-Jamestown,N.D.
Sandra Lee Johnson-B-Sept.13,1946-Jamestown,N.D.

Lois Mae Johnson-B-Dec.12,1933-Woodworth,N.D.
Curtis Gordon Burkhardt-B-Nov.12,1931-Jamestown,N.D.
D-Oct.1,1960-Jamestown,N.D.M-Dec.20,1952
Children
Dennis Rae Burkhardt-B-July8,1954-Jamestown,N.D.
Corrine Elizabeth Burkhardt-B-April3,1958-Jamestown,N.D.
Cheryll Renee Burkhardt-B-Sept.18,1959-Jamestown,N.D.

Lois Mae Burkhardt-B-Dec.12,1933-Woodworth,N.D.
Duane Allen Knudson-B-Oct.22,1934-Kensal,N.D.
M-Sept.22,1962-Jamestown,N.D.
Children
Craig Allen Knudson-B-July 23,1963-Jamestown,N.D.

Duane Orville Johnson-B-Sept.2,1935-Jamestown,N.D.
Adeline Marie Schielke-B-Oct.13,1936-M-McClusky,N.D.
M-July 10,1955-Jamestown,N.D.-D-Sept.17, 2004
Children
Timothy Lee Johnson-B-Mar.7,1953-Jamestown,N.D.
Thomas Lynn Johnson-B-June 15,1960-Jamestown,N.D.
Toran Lane Johnson-B-July 29,1969-Jamestown,N.D.

Charles Burnell Johnson-B-Sept.4,1937-Woodworth,N.D.
Delores Meyers-B-Sept.26,1937-Medina,N.D.
M-Aug.25,1957-Medina,N.D.
Children
Karen Lee Johnson-B-Oct. 10,1958-Jamestown,N.D.
Keven Lynn Johnson-B-Oct.22,1960-Rapid City,N.D.
Keith Loren Johnson-B-April,1962-Rapid City,N.D.

Quentine Darle Johnson-B-Sept.30,1939-Woodworth,N.D.
D-Mar.23,1980-Grafton,N.D.-Bur.Jamestown,N.D.

Jerald Dean Johnson-B-Oct.22,1941-Woodworth,N.D.
Lu Anne Orner-B-May 25,1933-Robinson,N.D.
M-Dec.5,1963-Valley City,N.D.-D-April 12, 2006

Glen Allen Johnson-B-Feb.12,1944-Jamestown,N.D.
Leona Murchie-B-Nov.13,1946-M-April 17,1962
Children
Tammy Marie Jonson-B-Feb.12,1963-Medina,N.D.
Patricia Lee Johnson-B-bJan.3,1966-Medina,N.D.
Cathy Ann Johnson-B-Feb.10,1967-Medina,N.D.
Heidi Faye Johnson-B-July 1,1976-Pipstone,Mn.
Gretchen Elizabeth Johnson-B-Mar.27,1978-Pipstone,Mn.
Glenn Allen Johnson-B-Mar.27,1978-Pipstone,Mn.

Sandra Lee Johnson-B-Sept.13,1946-Jamestown,N.D.
Juel George Dahlke-B-Nov.23,1946-Rapid City,S.D.
M-May 21,1966-Rapid City,S.D.
Children
Dawn Renee Dahlke-B-Aug.23,1973-Jamestown,N.D.
Kimberly Marie Dahlke-B-Dec.29,1976-Rapid City,S.D.
Lana Marie Dahlke-B-Aug.7,1975-Rapid City,S.D.

LOVIDA MASSIE JOHNSON-B-Jan.7,1914-
Woodworth,N.D.
D-Jan.15,1989-Great Falls,Mt.-M-Aug.25,1935-New
Rockford,N.D.
Parents:Gunder Johnson and Laura Bah
Harold Henry Holtz-B-Aug.5,1915-New Rockford,N.D.
D-May28,1979-Portland,Or.
Parents Henry Holtz and Elizabeth Forman

Lovida Massie Johnson-B-Jan.7,1914-Woodworth,N.D.
Mike A. Snow-B-April28,1912-D-Mar.3,1973-Great Falls,Mt.
M-Nov.21,1947-Great Falls,Mt.
Children-adopted
Dean Alan Snow-B-July 29,1950-Jamestown,N.D.

Dean Alan Snow-B-July 29,1950-Jamestown,N.D.
Janet Marie Meek-B-Dec.27,1952-Great Falls,Mt.
M-Jan.20,1973-Great Falls,Mt.
Children
Shannon Lee Snow-B-Nov.20,1986-Great Falls,Mt.
Stacey Lynn Snow-B-May6,1994-Great Falls,Mt.

HILDA AMANDA JOHNSON-B-Jan.2,1916-
Woodworth,N.D.
D-May20,1994-Great Falls,Mt.M-June 21,1933-
Jamestown,N.D.
Parents Gunder Johnson and Laura Bah
Harry Victor Schuff-B-Sept.15,1903-Eau Clare,Wi
D-July 4,1965-Great Falls,Mt.
Parents Emil Schuff and Laura Schmitt
Children
Deloris Lovan Schuff-B-Jan.29,1934-Woodworth,N.D.
Opel Maye Schuff-B-May30,1937-Great Falls,Mt.
Donald LeRoy Schuff-B-Nov.28,1943-Great Falls,Mt.
Eugene Allen Schuff-B-Feb.7,1949-Great Falls,Mt.
Leonard Dean Schuff-B-Aug.9,1951-Great Falls,Mt.
Larry Keith Schuff-B-June 21,1955-Great Falls,Mt.

Deloris Lovan Schuff-B-Jan.29,1934-Woodworth,N.D.
Donald Coleman Brown-Nov.12,1929-Great Falls,Mt.
M-Aug.17,1952-Great Falls,Mt.
Children
Alan Gene Brown-B-Nov.26,1953-Great Falls,Mt.
Carrie Lee Brown-B-Jan.22,1958-Great Falls,Mt.

Opel Maye Schuff-B-May31,1937-Great Falls,Mt.
Wayne Fair Baus-B-Mar.28,1933-Baltimore,Md
M-Jan.29,1950-Great Falls,Mt.
Children
Laura Baus-B-July5,1955-Great Falls,Mt.
Opel Maye Baus-D-May27,2003-Bur.Fort Harrison,Mt.

Donald LeRoy Schuff-B-Nov.28,1943-Great Falls,Mt.
Tana Thompson-B-Mar.12,1949-Forsyth,Mt.
M-Mar.12,1966-Coeur-d-Alene,Id.
Children
David William Schuff-B-Aug.31,1971-Great Falls,Mt.
Donald and Tana Schuff Divorced 1973

ESTHER GRACE JOHNSON-B-April16,1918-
Woodworth,N.D.
Parents:Gunder Johnson and Laura Bah
Lloyd Sorenson-B-Dec.8,1912-Buchanan,N.D.
D-Oct.13,1983-Jamestown,N.D.-Bur.Buchanan,N.D.
Parents:John Sorenson and Margaret Lee
M-Aug.15,1937-Buchanan,N.D.
Children
Linda Sorenson-B-April12,1948-Grand Forks,N.D.

Linda Sorenson-B-April12,1948-Grand Forks,N.D.
Rodney Jordan-M-Nov.11,1972-Fargo,N.D.
Children
Jennifer Jordan-B-April12,1948-B-Grand Forks,N.D.
Lori Jordan-B-April24,1975-Fargo,N.D.
James Townsend-Nov.7 ?   Kelso,Wa.
M-June 21-1978-Kelso,Wa.

AVIS LILLIAN JOHNSON-B-Oct.27,1920-
Woodworth,N.D.
D-Aug.5,1983-Bur.Woodworth,N.D.-Lunde Cemetery
Parents:Gunder Johnson and Laura Bah
Daniel V. Glowac-B-Sept.30,1918-Spiritwood,N.D.
D-Dec.14,1983-Mason City,Iowa
M-Nov.16,1939-Jamestown,N.D.
Children
Robert D. Glowac-B-Nov.13,1940-Jamestown,N.D.
Phyllis Glowac-B-June 7,1943-Jamestown,N.D.
Diane Glowac-B-April4,1946-Jamestown,N.D.
William Glowac-B-Aug.27,1948-Jamestown,N.D.

Robert D. Glowac Sr.-B-Nov.13,1940-Jamestown,N.D.
Marilyn J. Topp-Feb.13,1939-Carrington,N.D.
M-July 1,1962-Grace City,N.D.
Children
Robert D. Glowac Jr.-B-Nov.15,1963-Grand Forks,N.D.

Joseph P. Glowac-B-Dec.24,1965-Huron,S.D.
Rebecca A. Glowac-B-Nov.29,1968-Springfield,Il.

Phyllis Jeanne Glowac-B-June 7,1943-Jamestown,N.D.
Charles W. Christ-B-Mar.30,1940-Jamestown,N.D.
D-Oct.1985-Jamestown,N.D.-M-Feb.15,1960-Jamestown,N.D
Children
Teresa R. Christ-B-Aug.31,-1960-Fargo,N.D.
Kevin R Christ-Feb.11,1963-San Diego,Ca.
Charles R. Christ-B-Jan.6,1965-Jamestown,N.D.
Scott R. Christ-B-Nov.11,1967-Jamestown,N.D.
Steven R. Christ-B-Mar.18,1970-Jamestown,N.D.

Phyllis Jeanne Christ-B-June 7,1943-Jamestown,N.D.
Dennis L. Dallman-B-May 5,1943-Edgely,N.D.
M-May 10,1975-Jamestown,N.D.
Children
Lamra R.Dallman-B-Dec.14,1976-Aberdeen,S.D.

Phyllis Jeane Dallman-B-June 7,1943-Jamestown,N.D.
Warren Rex Hukana-B-May8,1947-Aberdeen,S.D.
M-May 22,1987

Dianne Glowac-B-April 4,1946-Jamestown,N.D.
Ronald Hobgoss Sr.-B-May31,1943-Fargo,N.D.
Children
Ronald Hobgoss Jr.-B-Nov.2,1963-Fargo,N.D.
Michael Hobgoss-B-May 26,1965-Fargo,N.D.
April Hobgoss-B-Oct.29,1970-Albert Lea,Mn

William Glowac-B-Aug.27,1948-Jamestown,N.D.
Kathy Hahan
Children
Chanda Lee Glowac-B-Dec.17,1970-Albert Lea,Mn.
Brana Glowac-B-Sept.21,1972-Albert Lea,Mn.

DORIS EVELYN JOHNSON-B-May 27,1923-
Woodworth,N.D.
D-Oct.1,1999-Jamestown,N.D.
Parents:Gunder Johnson and Laura Bah
Raymond Ervin Rosenau-B-July 5,1921-Redwood County,Mn.
M-Jan.10,1942-Eldridge,N.D.,-D-June 10, 2006
Children
Gary Lee Rosenau-B-Aug.16,1943-Jamestown,N.D.
Rodney Gene Rosenau-B-Sept.15,1947-Jamestown,N.D.
Susan Kay Tosenau-B-Feb.27,1956-Jamestown,N.D.

Gary Lee Rosenau-B-Aug.16,1943-Jamestown,N.D.
Lois Henretta Krabben Ft.-B-Apr.7,1943-Moorehead,Mn
M-Dec.3,1966-Sabin,Mn.
Children
Steven Gary Rosenau-B-June 14,1967-Jamestown,N.D.
Marc Allen Rosenau-B-Sept. 3,1970-Fargo,N.D.
Randall Jon Rosenau-B-Aug.10,1972-Fargo,N.D.
Christopher Lee Rosenau-B-July 14,1977-Neenah,Wi.

Rodney Gene Rosenau-B-Sept.15,1947-Jamestown,N.D.
Vicky Ann Voldahl-B-May27,1949-M-Jamestown,N.D.
Child-Signe Rosenau-B-Nov.24,1987-Fargo,N.D.

Susan Kay Rosenau-B-Feb.27,1956-Jamestown,N.D.
Kerry Howard Peuser-B-Aug.16,1956-M-June 28,1980
Casey Bryan Peuser-B-Mar.27,1991-Fargo,N.D.

M

John Mullins-England
JoAne Bridger-England
Children
William Mullins-B-1572-Surrey,England
John Mullins-B-1577-Surrey,England
Edward Mullins   Surrey,England

William Mullins-B-1572-Surrey,England
D-1621-Plymouth,Ma.
Alice Mullins-D-1621-Plymouth,Ma,M-England
Children
William Mullins-Surrey,England
Sara Mullins-Surrey,England
Priscilla Mullins-Surrey,England
Joseph Mullins-D-1621-Plymouth,Ma.

William Mullins B-Surrey,England
Married Mrs. Mullins-England
Children
Elizabeth Mullins-B-Mar.26,1618-England
Ruth Mullins-B-Oct.31,1619-England
Sara/Sarah Mullins-B-May 5,1622-England

Priscilla Mullins-B-1600/1605-D-Duxbury,Ma.
John Alden-B-1598-England-D-Duxbury,Ma.
Married-1622-Plymouth,Ma.

S

ABRAHAM SAMPSON-B-1602-England-D-after 1686
Parents-Unknown
ESTHER NASH-B-1602-England-M-Duxbury
Parents:Samuel Nash and Elizabeth Seymour
Children of Abraham Sampson and Esther Nash
Samuel Sampson-B-about 1646-killed by Indians
George Sampson-B-1655
ISAAC SAMPSON-B-1660-M-Lydia Standish
Sarah Sampson-B-
And probably other children

Abraham Sampson came to Duxbury from England about 1629
and was probably a brother of Henry Sampson who came on
the Mayflower.
Abraham Sampson was of Duxbury in 1640

ISAAC SAMPSON-B-1660-Duxbury,Ma.
D-Sept.3,1726-Plympton,Ma.
Parents Abraham Sampson and Esther Nash
LYDIA STANDISH-B-1672-Duxbury,Ma.D-1748
M-Oct.26,1686-Duxbury,Ma.
Parents:Alexander Standish and Sara Alden
Children of Isaac Sampson and Lydia Standish
Isaac Sampson-B-April18,1688-Plympton,Ma.
Jonathan Sampson-B-Feb.9,1689-Plympton,Ma.
Josiah Sampson-B-June 5,1692-Plympton,Ma.
Lidiah Sampson-B-April22,1694-Plympton,Ma.
Ephriam Sampson-B-May8,1698-Plympton,Ma.
PELEG SAMPSON-B-Nov.12,1700-Plympton,Ma.
Priscilla Sampson-B-Nov.12,1700-Plympton,Ma.
Barnabas Sampson-B-Feb.12,1705-Plympton,Ma.

PELEG SAMPSON-B-Nov.12,1700-Plymton,Ma.
D-April27,1741-Spanish West Indies
Parents:Isaal Sampson and Lydia Standish
MARY RING-B-Dec.9,1700-Plymouth,Ma.M-Nov.7,1722
Parents:Eleazer Ring and Mary Shaw
Children of Peleg Sampson and Mary Ring
Mary Sampson-1724
Peleg Sampson-B-1726
Mercy Sampson-B-May 15,1731-Kingston,Ma.
SIMEON SAMPSON-B-1736
Priscilla Sampson-B-1739
Jonathan Sampson-B-1733
Ephriam Sampson ?

SIMEON SAMPSON-B-Aug.1736-Kingston,Ma.
D-June 22,1789-Plympton,Ma.
Parents:Peleg Sampson and Mary Ring
DEBORAH CUSHING-B-Nov.1,1759-Hingham,Ma.
D-May19,1830-Homer,NY-M-Nov.1,2759-Plympton
Parents:Seth Cushing and Lydia Fearing
Children of Simeon Sampson and Deborah Cusing
Lydia Sampson-B-Mar.8,1760-Plympton,Ma.
Lydia Sampson-B-Oct.21,1762-Plympton,Ma.
Simeon Sampson-B-May6,1765-Plympton,Ma.
Simeon Sampson-B-Dec.8,1766-Plympton,Ma.
Deborah Sampson-B-1768-Plympton,Ma.
Isaac Sampson-B-Oct.16,1771-Plympton,Ma.
Mary Sampson-B-June 3,1775-Plympton,Ma.
GEORGE WASHINGTON-B-Dec.27,1781-Plympton,Ma.
Maria Sampson-B-June 27,1744-Plympton,Ma.

GEORGE WASHINGTON SAMPSON-B-Dec.27,1781-
Plympton,Ma.-D-Feb.4,1868
Parents:Simeon Sampson and Deborah Cushing
HANNAH C SHAW-B-Sept.17,1782-Kingston,Ma.
M-July28,1805-Plympton,Ma.-D-Oct.22,1865-Homer,NY
Parents:John Shaw and Mary(Polly)Eaton
Children of George Washington Sampson and Hannah C. Shaw
Simeon Sampson-B-Nov.15,1805-Plympton,Ma.
John Shaw Sampson-B-Dec.21,1806-Plympton,Ma.
George Whitfield Sampson-B-Feb.28,1808-Plympton,Ma.
Deborah Cushing Sampson-B-Aug.14,1809-Plympton,Ma.
MARY EATON SAMPSON-B-Aug.14,1809-
M- ZEPPHANIAH HICKS
Lorenzo Sampson-B-Nov.27,1810-Plympton,Ma.
Horatio Gates Sampson-B-July7,1812-Kingston,Ma.
Isaac Marshall Sampson-B-1814-New York

ZEPHANIAH HICKS-B-Oct.6,1807-Pomfret,Ct.
D-Aug.18,1858-Athens,Pa.
Parents Israel Hicks Jr. and Phoebe Grow
MARY EATON SAMPSON-B-Aug.14,1809-Plympton,Ma.
M-Sept.22,1829-Homer,N.Y.
Parents:**GEORGE WASHINGTON SAMPSON AND
HANNAH C. SHAW**
Children of Zehaniah Hicks and Mary Eaton Sampson
George Sampson Hicks-B-Sept.30,1830-Pomfret,Ct.
Israel Lews Hicks-B-Nov.10,1832-Homer,N.Y.
Polley E. Hicks-B-Feb.16,1835-Homer,N.Y.
Phebe G. Hicks-B-Dec.12,1836-Truxton,N.Y.
Alfred Bennett Hicks-B-Aug.27,1838-Berkshire,N.Y.
Deborah S. Hicks-B-Dec.3,1842-Caroline,N.Y.
HORATIO GATES HICKS-B-Nov.18,1844-Richford,N.Y.
Hannah C. Hicks-B-May23,1848-Truxton,N.Y.
Marshall O. Hicks-B-Jan.27,1850-Virgil,N.Y.

GENEALOGY FROM CAPT. MYLES STANDISH
FAMILY TO THE INGRAHAM FAMILIES

Myles Standish family all lived on the Isle Of Man

Thurston De Standish-Great Great Grandfather-
Ralph Standish-Great Grandfather
Hugh Standish-Grandfather

John Standish-Father
Catharina Lace-Mother
Children
Myles Standish-B-abt.1584
William Standish

Capt.Myles Standish
Married Rose Standish-D-1621-Plymouth,Ma.
Capt. Myles Standish-B-1584-Isle Of Man,British Isles
D-Oct.3,1656-Duxbury,Ma.-M-1623-Plymouth,Ma.
Barbara Standish-England-D-Duxbury,Ma
Children
Charles Standish-B-1624-Plymouth,Ma.
Alexander Standish-B-1626-Plymouth,Ma.
John Jr. Standish-B-1627-Plymouth,Ma.
Lora Standish-B-1627-Plymouth,Ma.
Miles Standish-B-1629-Plymouth,Ma.
Josiah Standish-B-1633-Plymouth,Ma.
Charles Standish-B-1634-Plymouth,Ma.
Barbara Standish arrived on the ship Anne in 1623 from
England and she was the mother of all of Myles children

```
ANCESTRY OF 13 GENERATIONS FROM 1620 TO 2007

1.  John Alden : married Priscilla Mullins              1621
2.  Joseph Alden: married Mary Simmons                  1657
3.  John Alden: married Hanna White                     1701
4.  Samuel Eddy: married Lydia Alden                    1705?
5.  Nathan Eddy: married Eunice Sampson                 1757
6.  Isaac Eddy: married Betsey McCary                   1796
7.  Alva Brown: married Eunice Eddy                     1821
8.  Demarcus Cowles: married Mary Brown                 1857
9.  Chauncey Ingraham: married Myrtie Cowles            1893
10. Lyle Ingraham: married Gena Johnson                 1919
11. Willard Ingraham: married Louise Williams           1947
12. Milton Hicks: married Mary Ann Ingraham             1978
13. Ryan Ingraham: marrried Shannon Ann Hicks           2004
14. Children: Shannon and Ryan: Torryn Briehl Ingraham  2005
                                Ivry Rae Ingraham        2007
```

```
ANCESTRY OF 13 GENERATIONS FROM 1620 TO 2007

1.  Capt. Myles Standish: married Barbara Standish       1623
2.  Alexander Standish: married Sarah Alden
3.  Isaac Sampson: married Lydia Standish                1686
4.  Ephraim Sampson: married Abigail Horrel
5.  Nathan Eddy:  married Eunice Sampson                 1757
6.  Isaac Eddy: married Betsey McCary                    1796
7.  Alva Brown: married Ennice Eddy                      1821
8.  Demarcus Cowles: married Mary Brown                  1857
9.  Chauncey Ingraham: married Myrtie Cowles             1893
10. Lyle Ingraham: married Gena Johnson                  1919
11. Willard Ingraham: married Louise Williams            1947
12. Milton Hicks: married Mary Ann Ingraham              1978
13. Ryan Ingraham married:  Shannon Ann Hicks            2004
14. Children of Ryan and Shannon Ingraham:  Torryn Breihl Ingraham  2005
                                            Ivry Rae Ingraham        2007
```

COWLES ANCESTRY OF MYRTLE JUNE COWLES INGRAHAM

Rev. Remember Joshua Cowles (July 10, 1796 - March 29, 1874)
was born in Elmira, New York. His wife Sybil Night (May 29, 1800
-- August 23, 1887) was born in chester County, Mass. At
the age of 12 she moved to Byron Genessee County, N.Y. where
she married R.J. Cowles at the age of 16. Their first home
was in Nightville, later Sugar Grove, Warren, Chataugua or
Ashville. He was a Baptist Minister, school teacher and singer
She was a mother of 13 children and raised Rachel Cowan, a
grand-daughter, when her mother died of Typhoid Fever.
(Rachel's daughter Florence Norton lives in Minn., Minn.)

This is the lineage as far back as 1615 in England:

1. John Cowles 1615-1662 (came to Mass. in 1635)

2. John Cowles 1645 1711

3. Jonathan Cowles 1670-1756

4. John Cowles 1700-1745

5. Capt. John Cowles 1737-1811

6. Corp. John Cowles 1757-1830

7. Remember John Cowles 1796-1874

8. Almeron Orlando Cowles 1932-1908

9. Orson Cowles

10. Oscar Cowles

Demarcus Leroy Cowles (one of Rev. R.J. Cowles 13 children)
was born in the Parsonage in Sugar Grove, Penn. on Oct. 5, 1834
He worked three years a apprintice to the carpenter trade and
two years of the big woods a Shingle Maker. In the spring of
1857 he married Miss Mary Elizabeth Brown at Dixon, Ill. He
learned of the opportunities of Minn. and went to Dodge County
Minn. and they settled on a farm about the middle of April of
the same year. They had 5 children (3 boys and 2 girls).
Ardilla Cowles married Wm. Kellogg
Eddy Jerom Cowles married Cora Vandrhyde
Fred Jay Cowles married Louesa Orcutt
Willis Eugene married Elsie Peck
Myrtle June married Chauncey Ingraham
In the year of 1900 he retired from his farm and moved to West
Concord Minn. His wife Mary passed away June 29, 1909. On
July 1920 he moved to Sowtell Calif. and died there March 30, 1925.
He was buried in the West Concord Cemetery.

<u>EDDY ANCESTRY OF MYRTLE COWLES INGRAHAM</u>

1. REV. WM. EDDY: Vicar of the church of St. Dunetan of the town of Crambrook of the County of Kent, England. He was educated at the Trinity College in Cambridge where he was graduated Bacheler of Arts in 1583. He made Master of Arts in 1586. He is buried in the church yard where he served for 26 years. Two of his sons came to America on the ship "Handmaid" and landed in Plymouth in 1630

2. Samuel Eddy

3. Obadiah Eddy

4. Samuel Eddy

5. Samuel Eddy: Married Lydia Alden

6. Nathan Eddy: Married Eunice Sampson (descendent of Miles Standish)

7. Rev. Isaac Eddy

8. Eunice Eddy: Married Alvah Brown

9. Mary Elizabeth Brown: Married Demarcus LeRoy Cowles

10. Myrtle Cowles: Married Chauncey Ingraham

11. Lyle Jay Ingraham: married Gena Alpha Johnson

12. Willard Stanley Ingraham: married Louise Williams

13. Mary Ann Ingraham: married Milton Lewis Hicks

14. Shannon Ann Hicks:

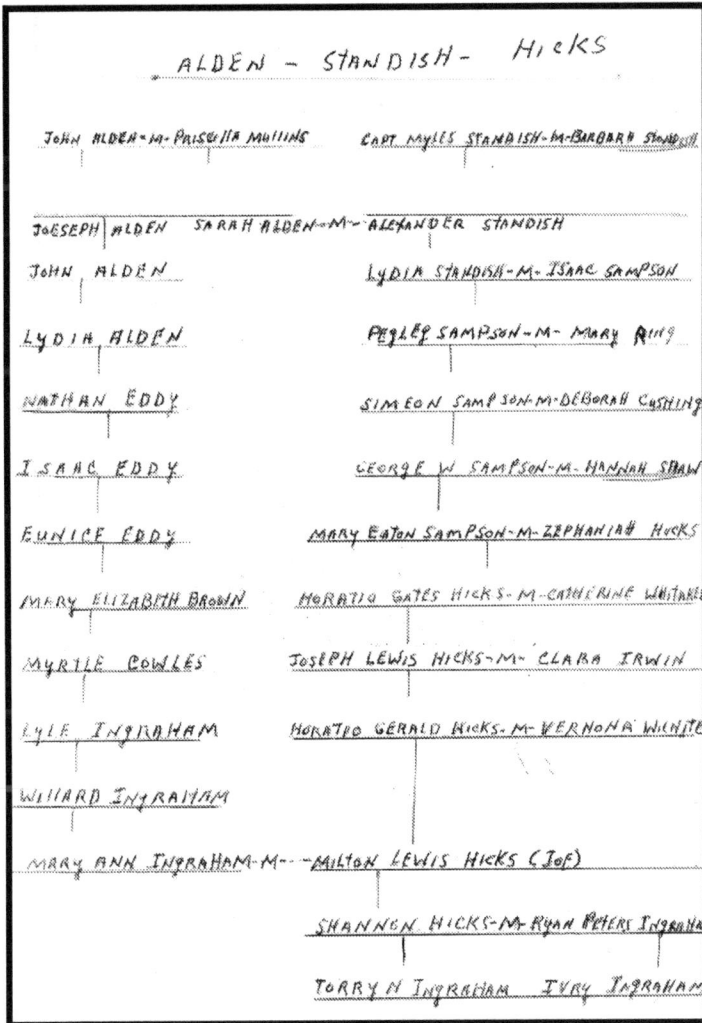

ALDEN — STANDISH — HICKS

JOHN ALDEN~M~PRISCILLA MULLINS   CAPT MYLES STANDISH~M~BARBARA STANDISH

JOESEPH ALDEN   SARAH ALDEN~M~ALEXANDER STANDISH

JOHN ALDEN   LYDIA STANDISH~M~ISAAC SAMPSON

LYDIA ALDEN   PEGLEG SAMPSON~M~MARY RING

NATHAN EDDY   SIMEON SAMPSON~M~DEBORAH CUSHING

ISAAC EDDY   GEORGE W SAMPSON~M~HANNAH SHAW

EUNICE EDDY   MARY EATON SAMPSON~M~ZEPHANIAH HICKS

MARY ELIZABETH BROWN   HORATIO GATES HICKS~M~CATHERINE WHITAKER

MYRTLE COWLES   JOSEPH LEWIS HICKS~M~CLARA IRWIN

LYLE INGRAHAM   HORATIO GERALD HICKS~M~VERNONA WILHITE

WILLARD INGRAHAM

MARY ANN INGRAHAM~M~~MILTON LEWIS HICKS (JOE)

                    SHANNON HICKS~M~RYAN PETERS INGRAHAM

                    TORRYN INGRAHAM   IVRY INGRAHAM

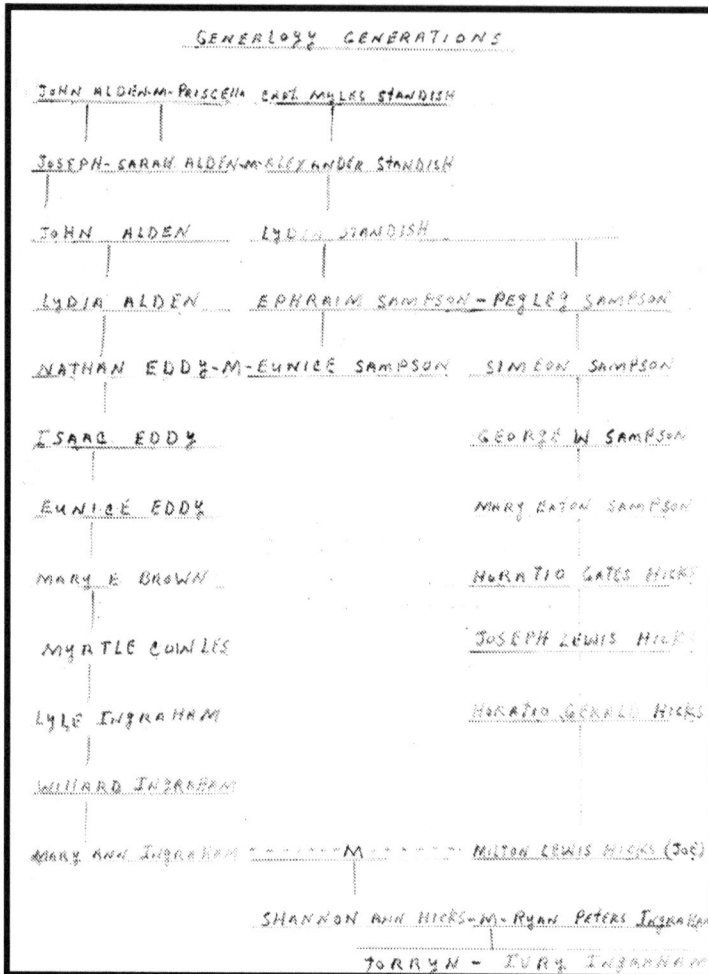

GENERLOGY GENERATIONS

JOHN ALDEN-M-PRISCELLA capt. MYLES STANDISH

JOSEPH-SARAH ALDEN-M-ALEXANDER STANDISH

JOHN ALDEN   LYDIA STANDISH

LYDIA ALDEN   EPHRAIM SAMPSON-PEGLEG SAMPSON

NATHAN EDDY-M-EUNICE SAMPSON   SIMEON SAMPSON

ISAAC EDDY   GEORGE W SAMPSON

EUNICE EDDY   MARY EATON SAMPSON

MARY E BROWN   HORATIO GATES HICKS

MYRTLE COWLES   JOSEPH LEWIS HICKS

LYLE INGRAHAM   HORATIO GERALD HICKS

WILLARD INGRAHAM

MARY ANN INGRAHAM - - - - - - M - - - - - - MILTON LEWIS HICKS (Joe)

SHANNON ANN HICKS-M-RYAN PETERS INGRAHAM

TORRYN - IVRY INGRAHAM

INDEX

ECHOS PAST
